Herbert Francis Hore

The Social State of the Southern and Eastern Counties of Ireland in

the 16th Century

Herbert Francis Hore

The Social State of the Southern and Eastern Counties of Ireland in the 16th Century

ISBN/EAN: 9783337324469

Printed in Europe, USA, Canada, Australia, Japan

Cover: Foto ©Suzi / pixelio.de

More available books at **www.hansebooks.com**

THE SOCIAL STATE

OF THE

SOUTHERN AND EASTERN COUNTIES

OF IRELAND

In the Sixteenth Century:

BEING

THE PRESENTMENTS OF THE GENTLEMEN, COMMONALTY,
AND CITIZENS

OF

CARLOW, CORK, KILKENNY, TIPPERARY, WATERFORD, AND WEXFORD,

MADE IN THE

REIGNS OF HENRY VIII. AND ELIZABETH.

PRINTED FROM THE ORIGINALS IN THE PUBLIC RECORD OFFICE, LONDON.

EDITED BY

THE LATE HERBERT J. HORE, ESQ.,

AND

THE REV. JAMES GRAVES,

A.B., M.R.I.A.

DUBLIN:
PRINTED AT THE UNIVERSITY PRESS,
FOR THE ASSOCIATION.

1870.

INTRODUCTION.

The lamented death of one of the Editors of this Volume having suspended its progress for some years, it is now at length placed in the hands of the Members of the Association in as complete a state as the surviving Editor's care could accomplish.

Unable to gain access to Mr. Hore's MS. collections, he must claim the indulgence of the reader, if the latter portion of the Work is not so fully annotated as doubtless it would have been had Mr. Hore lived to see it through the Press. No pains have been spared, however, to secure the correct rendering of the original documents—documents that, in the very words of the people themselves, give a melancholy but graphic picture of the social state of those counties of Ireland to which they relate, and which, although outside the Pale, were yet more fully colonized by England than other parts of the Island.

JAMES GRAVES.

Inisnag, Stoneyford,
  December 31, 1869.

THE ANNUARY

OF

THE KILKENNY AND SOUTH-EAST OF IRELAND ARCHÆOLOGICAL SOCIETY.

THE PRESENTMENTS OF THE JURIES OF THE COUNTIES OF KILKENNY AND WEXFORD, THE CITY OF KILKENNY, AND THE TOWNS OF WEXFORD AND ROSS, TO THE COMMISSIONERS FOR ORDERING OR REFORMING THE STATE OF IRELAND, ANNO 1537.

A GENERAL view of the state of Ireland during the eventful and memorable reign of Henry the Eighth has recently been presented to historians and archæologists by the publication of two quarto volumes of State Papers. Beside the ordinary political correspondence which passed between the governments in Dublin and London, these volumes include several treatises on the social condition of Ireland. A peculiar class of documents, of the same period and character, the originals of which are also preserved in the State Paper Office, were, however, not published in full, being somewhat prolix, so that their contents appear only in summary. They contain many very curious details respecting the Anglo-Irish inhabitants of certain districts outside the Pale, where Gaelic usages had superseded English laws, and where the authority of Government was scarcely acknowledged. As these public records, in which so remarkable a state of society is described, are obviously of much interest in local as well as historical points of view, it is proposed to print them *in extenso* and *seriatim*; and the following sketch of their origin may serve as an introduction to those now selected for publication.

Soon after the dangerous revolt of the Leinster Geraldines was suppressed, four gentlemen of high quality, Anthony St. Leger, George Paulet, Thomas Moyle (afterwards Knights), and William Berners, Esquires, were sent over from England by Henry VIII. as Commissioners "for the ordre and establishment to be taken and made touching the whole state of our Land of Ireland,. for the reduction of the said land to a due civilitie and obedience, and the advancement of the publique weal of the same." The High Commissioners arrived in September, 1537, and proceeded through the counties of Kildare, Carlow, Kilkenny, Tipperary, Waterford, and Wexford, pursuing their object throughout this journey by holding inquiries or inquests relative to the offences committed, the non-observance of the law, and the general grievances of the counties and towns they visited. These investigations mark the extent of the district which was then but partially under the dominion of, or in an intermediate degree of subjection to, the Crown. Thus, while inquiries were unnecessary in the Pale—that narrow territory where, owing to the vicinity of the seat of government and courts of justice, the laws were tolerably obeyed, the reforming Commissioners never ventured into regions so rude as Thomond and Desmond, and far less into the still wilder tracts of Ulster and Connaught. Juries composed of the principal gentry of the shires and of the most respectable merchants in the cities and boroughs represented upon oath the various grievances which both town and country had to complain of. Accordingly, their "verdicts" contain full evidence of the disorganization of the district which was deemed the Anglo-Irish borders of the Pale; the inhabitants of which—being either surrounded by or intermingled with the denizens of the unsubjugated mountain countries under the rule of Irish chieftains—had become a mixed people, and had long and largely partaken of customs and usages such as the Statute of Kilkenny had forbidden the Englishry to adopt. These presentments therefore portray a state of society similar to that which existed contemporaneously upon the Scottish border, where a fusion of Scotic and Teutonic races had produced a mixed system of clanship and feudalism; and, as these documents are elucidatory of the manners of the time and country, they will assuredly be considered interesting by all who concur in Dr. Johnson's opinion, that the most instructive and valuable portions of history are those which describe the manners of mankind.

In perusing these representations of the social condition of the border counties of Ireland in the middle of the sixteenth century, the reader will, indeed, be frequently reminded of the contemporary state of Scotland, as depicted in the delightful writings of the author of "Waverley," and especially in his admirable Essay on the Antiquities of the Border. It must always be borne in mind that the geographical features of Ireland exercised an influence on her history almost equal to that of her national customs. In Great Britain the frontier line between the hostile nations was well defined; but in Ireland the countries of the Gael were intermingled with the domains of the Anglo-Norman; so that those contested territories, known in Britain by the significant name of "debateable," were interspersed throughout the entire island. Owing to this circumstance, an evil moral state, such as in Scotland was confined to the Highland frontier and the Border, extended throughout Ireland. On comparing the Border laws with the Statute of Kilkenny, many points of close resemblance will be observed. Thus, it was treason and felony to supply Scottishmen with weapons of war; to sell bread or corn to them without license; to pay black-mail or protection money; to let any Scotch offender, taken red-hand, escape; to harbour outlaws and rebels from Scotland; to intermarry with Scottish women; and to hold parleys with the enemy without license from the Lord Warden.

The object of the Commission of 1537 was to restore English law among the Anglo-Irish colonists. Their government and interests had been neglected for many centuries by the great absentee nobility and by the Crown. The tenure by which the colonists held their estates, either under the sovereign or his barons, entitled them, while they on their part performed their feudal services, to protection, and to the due administration of laws which were their birth-right. But as their lands were intermingled with those of the native race, marriages and alliances naturally took place; and the customs and manners of the country began gradually to prevail.

Chief Baron Finglas, who wrote his "Decaie of Ireland" anno 1529, states that the colonies of the south had continued to observe their national laws for a considerable period after their settlement; but he adds:—

"In Kyng Edward III. his dayes, Lionell, duke of Clarence, being the kyng's lieutenant of Irlaund, perceaving not oonly the lordes and gentilmen of Mounster, but alsoo in outher countries, begyning to incline to Irish rule and order, at a parliament holdyn at Kilkenny made certen statuts for the comon-wealth, for the preservation of English order; whych, if they had bene kept, this land had bene obedient to the kyng's lawes hitherto."

He subsequently contrasts the way in which laws were respected by the Anglo-Irish and by the Gaelic people, making an allusion highly honourable to the latter:—

"It is a great abusion and reproach," he writes, "that the laws and statuts made in this lond are not observed ne kept after the making of them eight days; which matter is oone of the distructions of Englishmen of this lond; and divers Irishmen doth observe and kepe suche laws and statuts which they make upon hills in their country firm and stable, without breaking them for any favour or reward."

Attorney-General Sir John Davys, after having remarked that the practice of the Brehon law was made treason by the Statute of Kilkenny, observes:—

"But this law (or act) extended to the English only, and not to the Irish;—for the law is penned in this forme: Item, Forasmuch as the diversitie of government by divers lawes in one land doth make diversity of ligeance, and debates between the people; It is accorded and established, that hereafter no Englishman have debate with another Englishman but according to the course of the common law: and that no Englishmen be ruled in the definition of their debates by the March law, or the Brehon law, which by reason ought not to be named a law, but an evill custom: but that they be ruled, as right is, by the common law of the land, as the lieges of our sovereign lord the king."

The celebrated laws enacted in the city of St. Canice, and therefore known as the Statute of Kilkenny, deserve more lengthened remarks as to their nature and intention than our limits permit. But they bear so thoroughly on the present subject, that they cannot be passed over. Sir John Davys, in his luminous and witty "Discoverie of the true causes why Ireland was never entirely subdued, nor brought under obedience of the Crown of England until the beginning of the reign of James I.," observes that the Duke of

Clarence, during whose viceroyalty the enactment in question was passed, was entitled not only to lands in the north and west of Ireland, in right of his wife, the heiress of De Burgh, Earl of Ulster and Lord of Connaught, but also to a large portion of the shire of Kilkenny. It is probable that the feudal tenants of this latter district had thrown off their vassalage—just as those in the north and west had revolted from their allegiance under the Earldom of Ulster and Lordship of Connaught. Sir John Davys, who was Attorney-General to James I., and the theme of whose clever work is to prove that the Irish did not generally attorn to the Crown until the reign of that monarch, declares that the principal service intended by Clarence was "to reforme the degenerate English colonies, and reduce them to obedience of the English law and magistrate," and that such was the object of the "famous parliament at Kilkenny, wherein many notable lawes wer enacted, which doo shew and lay open (*for the law doth best discover enormities*) how much the English colonies were corrupted at that time; and doe infallibly prove that which is laide downe before, that they were wholy degenerate, and faln away from their obedience." Among the evils arising from the assumption of independence by the heads of families that had once been feudatory and subordinate, but were now become clans, not the least was their adoption of the custom of quartering mercenary soldiers, horsemen, galloglasses, and kerne, upon their tenantry, who were thus compelled to maintain a little standing army for defensive and offensive war. As the power of the noble who exercised this custom depended on the number of military his country could maintain, the right of demanding food and forage for man and horse, known as *coigne* and *livery*, was often ruinously exacted. Chief Baron Finglas ascribes the sudden and enormous increase of the sway of James, ninth Earl of Desmond, to his adoption of this system of supporting a regular force; and observes that his example was imitated in the regions under our notice, commenting in the following words, which were written a few years prior to the Commission of Reform:—

"The countys of Kilkenny and Tipperary wore English habit, and kept the English order and rule, and the king's laws were obeyed there within this fifty one yeres, and there dwelled divers knights, esquires, and gentilmen, who wore the English habit, and kept good order; and the Butlers dwelling in the said two shires; and they seeing the late demeanors of the aforesaid Erle of Desmond's, and of his conquest, they began the said *Coyne* and *Livery*, and used it sithence; soo as by the same they have put these two shires clearly undir their rule, and the king's laws not obeyed, and all the king's subjects be in no better case than the wild Irish."

It must, however, be recollected that, owing to the ungoverned state of the kingdom, each nobleman was obliged to defend his possessions; and that by the custom of Gaelic countries the inhabitants were liable to maintain troops necessary for their defence. To the unrepressed violence of those times the Baron makes the following reference:—

"The grete Lordes, as well of Mounster as of Leinster, then being in grete wealth, and growing into grete name and authoritie, as John fitz-Thomas, then created Erle of Kildare, James Butler, then created Erle of Ormonde, and Maurice fitz-Thomas, then created Erle of Desmond, having division among themselves, began to make alterage with Irishmen for ther strength to resist othir; and disdainid to take punishment of knights being the kyng's justices or deputyes for the tyme; by reason of which division the Erles of Ormonde and Desmond, by strengthes of Irishmen on both sides, fought togither in battayle in Kyng Henry the VIth's days; in whyche battayle all the good men of the towne of Kilkenny, with many othirs, wer slaine."

In the time of Sir Anthony St. Leger, writes Davys, "the three great earles before named did govern their tenants and followers by the Irish or Brehon law; so as no treason, murther, rape, or theft, committed in those countries, was inquired of or punisht by the law of England." The execution of the King's laws had no greater latitude than the Pale, as is manifest by the Statute of 1522, in which it is recited that they are obeyed in four shires only. And Davys quotes a State Paper dated three years subsequently, in which the Master of the Rolls advertises the King that his land of Ireland is so much decayed as that his laws are not obeyed within a compass of twenty miles round the metropolis. So notorious was the misrule in the province of Munster as to give rise to a proverbial saying that "they dwelt by-west the law who dwelt beyond the river Barrow."[a]

Among the many salutary measures which originated in the labours of the Commission was the appointment of provincial arbitrators, who were authorized to hear and determine controversies.[b] This was one step towards superseding the necessity of resorting to the country judges, the Brehons. But it was not for many years afterwards that regular itinerant justices went upon circuit.

It has been well said that a complete history of any family of distinction would be an epitome of the history of their country. In so far as the social condition of the family during the different ages in which the house flourished was described, the progress of civilization would be illustrated, and such a history would thus contain far more than is comprehended in ordinary annals. In this view, the ensuing records and remarks respecting the clan Mac Gilla-

---

[a] Davis's "Discoverie," 12mo, 1747, p. 237.   [b] Ibid, p. 243.

patrick will serve to throw light on the state of the Gaelic people of Leinster at the period under consideration.

Of all human institutions those laws and customs by which the possession and transmission of property and power are regulated exercise the greatest influence in producing the peculiar state of a country. The primitive customs of the Gaelic race in these respects are such as once prevailed throughout the habitable globe, and are as simple as they were universal. Originally, all the men of a tribe descended from a common patriarch owned their country in common, as a *clann*, or kindred children; and their chieftain, or representative of their principal ancestor, was elective. Their chosen HEAD (and such is the literal interpretation of the Gaelic *Ceann* and the Gaulic *Chef*) was their governor in peace and leader in war. But he possessed no territorial rights, beyond a life interest in certain tributes and demesnes provided for his support. Nor had his sons any especial right to inherit either chieftaincy or land; for, by the law of gavelkind, succession to land was an equal and commonable right to all the kinsmen of the deceased; and, by the law of tanistry, a successor-elect, or tanist, was nominated by popular election during the life of the reigning chief, to be ready to succeed on his death; and the choice of the clansmen generally fell on one of their body who was older and more fit to govern than any son of their present head. These customs are directly contrary to feudal tenure, under which a knight's fee or a barony was held as a retaining fee from the monarch by the lord to whom it was granted, with right of hereditary descent to his primogenitural heirs. The distinction between the respective rights of property of baron and chief is marked in the appellations by which their residences are designated. While the principal castle of the former, who owned in subjection to the Crown, is termed *caput baroniæ*, or head of the fief held by *homage, barun*, or *man-service*,—we find the mansion of the elected governor of a clan called " the common house"—a name implying that it was deemed to be public property, and as such it was repaired and supported at the common charge.

After the establishment of feudal colonists in Ireland, their juxtaposition with the native race naturally led to intermarriages, and these alliances engendered a commixture of language and usages. During the fourteenth and fifteenth centuries the power of the Crown was so faintly exerted, that its vassals in general threw off their subjective tenure, and, adopting the native independence, erected themselves into insubordinate chiefs. Strange as it may at first appear, an opposite tendency manifested itself in the next century among the Milesian chieftains themselves. The causes and motives of these changes are obvious. Previous to the times depicted to the Commissioners of 1537, the great Anglo-Irish Earls palatine, Ormond, Kildare, and Desmond, the Lords De Burgh, Le Poer, and the rest, had strengthened themselves by exercising the authority of patriarchal heads over all of their blood of Butlers, Geraldines, Burkes, Powers, &c., and by governing all the Gaelic inhabitants of districts under their sway by customary usages. In order to rule with effect they employed the combined force of chieftainship and feudalism, just as did their compeers, Douglas and Buccleuch, upon the border lands of Scotland. But subsequently to this period, after the ruin of the Leinster Geraldines had proved how unable the proudest earl was to withstand the vigour of the Crown, the *imperia in imperio* of palatine and chief succumbed to the growing authority of law and government, and many heads of clans, a class that had frequently endeavoured to assimilate their rights to those of the feudal nobility, longed hopefully for the total abolition of customs which left them but a precarious interest, and eagerly embraced a system which made them actual owners of territory, with vested rights of inheritance in their posterity. A similar change had gradually been brought about in the Highlands of Scotland, and in Wales; but was more strenuously resisted in Ireland, and for a longer period, by the men of each clan; for they were obviously unwilling to relinquish those rights and prospects, either of property or of succession to power, which accrued to them under their ancient Brehon laws of gavelkind and tanistry. The nature of these laws and their historical effects are so well explained in Moore's History of Ireland, that it is unnecessary to do more than briefly advert to the results which are exhibited in the ensuing interesting representations of the state of the south-east of Ireland in the middle of the sixteenth century. Under the custom of tanistry, a successor-elect, or *tanist*, to the chieftainship was chosen on the accession of the reigning dynast, and at the same time invested with certain martial and governing powers. The tanist was therefore a rival to the ruling chieftain, at whose death he was to succeed; and he found rivals in each of the sons of that chieftain as they grew to manhood and became eligible to be elected to his station in case of his death, when the claim of one of them would be supported by their father, who would be anxious to be succeeded by his son. Under the custom of gavelkind no one had a permanent and hereditary interest in the soil, because the possession of the land assigned to each sept or subordinate branch of the clan was liable to be disturbed by new claims on the increase of the clans-men, as the junior members arrived at man's estate, when the entire country was subject to repartition at the discretion of the chief. Owing to this custom, and perhaps in some measure to the intestine feuds it engendered, the buildings of the country were of an unstable and insufficient description; for no one would build on an uncertain possession, or where his children might not inherit. The power of the leader of a clan depended on the number of men he could bring into the field. He naturally relied upon the attachment and prowess of his immediate relatives, and especially on the number, affection, and valour of his sons; he was therefore tempted to make frequent re-allotments of the clan-country, and to award the more valuable portions to members of his own family. Accordingly, Lord Chancellor Cusack, writing at this time, observes that any lord of a country who had numerous sons was apt to "extort" from the inferior owners, and "pluck their lands from them by cavillations, to the intent that every of his children shall have lands and possessions; whereas," as the Chancellor remarks, "if their lands descended to none but one, ther should be no such abuse used."[a] After the death of their father, the sons of the late ruler were often subjected to a complete reverse of fortune; more especially if they were inimical to his successor. In the words of another State Paper of the time, "the children never enherited the landes, but after the deceas of their faders, their children remaynid in mysery, and a tanyst succeeded."[b] If they proved obnoxious to the new chief they fell into a sort of outlawry, in which they had no means of sustaining life but depredation. The predatory conduct of the times may therefore be ascribed to those laws which left the sons even of great and haughty chieftains in uncertain dependence. And when the young houseless

---

[a] State Papers, vol. iii., p. 326, anno 1541. [b] State Papers, vol. iii., p. 348, anno 1541.

band of swordsmen, proud of their descent, and warlike in their habits, found they were precluded from living industriously and peacefully on lands which might remain to them and their descendants, they saw—

"The world was not their friend, nor the world's law,"

and it is no marvel if they turned freebooters, or sought to exist by desperate incursions into countries cultivated by the Anglo-Norman under securer laws. But whatever may have been the cause of incessant raids and plunderings during mediaeval ages, the effect was to keep up interminable hostility between the dwellers in the plains and the inhabitants of the hills. The marauders found shelter in the various fastnesses of their clansmen's territory; in mountain glens, thick woods, impassable morasses, and lake-surrounded islands; and it was hardly possible even for the chief of their name to do more than drive them for a time from such retreats.

The Crown of England, instead of undertaking the subjugation of Ireland with the full force of its power and authority, as had been done in North Wales by Edward the First, and, indeed, was, on two occasions, magnificently begun, but weakly carried forward, by Richard the Second, sometimes encouraged private enterprises for the conquest of particular districts, and thus gave royal license to private war. Without attempting to discuss the question whether the Crown, in treating the Gaelic race as inveterate and aggressive enemies to its Irish colonies, and considering all acts of retaliation as allowable, acted mistakenly, we may introduce a noticeable case in point. There was an ancient feud between the Mac Gillapatricks of Upper Ossory and the Butlers. When Sir Piers Butler, known as "Red Piers," was Lord Deputy in the year 1522, the hostile and independent chief of the clan Mac Gillapatrick sent an express messenger to London to complain of the Viceroy to Henry the Eighth; which messenger, taking an opportunity of meeting the King in going to chapel, is said to have delivered his embassy in these words:—"Sta pedibus, Domine Rex! Dominus meus Gillapatricius me misit ad te, et jussit dicere, quod si non vis castigare Petrum Rufum, ipse faciet bellum contra te"! This laconic *ultimatum* and minatory declaration of war, delivered—

"With wild, majestic port and tone,
Like envoy of some barbarous throne"—

may have led to the remarkable grant made five years subsequently to Sir Piers, three days after he was created Earl of Ossory. Sir Piers laid claim to the title of Earl of Ormond, which was afterwards granted to him; and he was at the time in rightful possession of the Irish estates of the earldom. His selection for the present of the title of Earl of Ossory seems to have been for the purposes of confirming to him the districts both of Lower Ossory, already under his rule, and Upper Ossory, inhabited by the Mac Gillapatricks, and of creating the entire into a county. He was granted "all and all manner of lands, castles, tenements, meadows, pastures, woods, and domains, with all their appurtenances, which he or his heirs male can conquer, acquire, or recover in the whole lordship or county of Ossorie, and in every parcel thereof, now being in the possession of Irishmen, in which the King or any of his faithful subjects has not possession or interest."[a] By the same grant he also received authority to make war as well against a feudal peer of his own rank, one of "the King's rebels," as against one of "the King's enemies;" for, having " promised to endeavour to

[a] Calendar of Pat. Rolls, Henry VIII., p. 2.

recover the King's castle and lordship of Dungarvan," then held usurped by the Earl of Desmond, he was appointed to be governor thereof whenever he should succeed in recovering them. The projected conquest of the land belonging to the clan Mac Gillapatrick did not succeed. But the apprehensions it awakened may have led, with other sufficient reasons, to the remarkable and permanent change which followed. The Four Masters record at the year 1532, that—"Thomas, the son of Pierce Roe, Earl of Ormond, was slain in Ossory by Dermot Mac Gillapatrick, *who was heir* to the lordship of Ossory." The annalists continue to say that—"Not long after this, Dermot was delivered up by his own brother (the Mac Gillapatrick) to the Earl, by whom he was fettered in revenge of his son and of every other misdeed which he, Dermot, had committed against him up to that time." Further on we read, anno 1546:—"Mac Gillapatrick (Brian) took prisoner his own son, Teige, a distinguished captain, and sent him to Dublin with a statement of his crimes written along with him; and the English of Dublin put him to death at the request of his father." This Brian, a chief who braved the resentment of his clans-men by delivering up to their powerful enemy the very man they had chosen as tanist to succeed himself—and who subsequently sent even one of his own sons to be put to death by the law—was son of that haughty Mac Gillapatrick by whom the majesty of England had once been threatened! But, in showing this alteration of conduct we have anticipated events. Such a difference of disposition between son and father could only have been produced by a change of condition; and this was that the young ruler had determined to adopt the firm and hereditary rights of a feudal baron instead of the precarious state of an elected chieftain, and that his wish had been gladly seconded by the Crown. Sir Anthony St. Leger, one of the Commissioners anno 1537, and subsequently Viceroy, was inimical to the Earl of Ossory—laying claim, indeed, to the Butler estates in right of a late Earl of Ormond's coheiress, who married Sir James St. Leger. He appears to have brought the chieftain of Upper Ossory forward, as a means of lessening the potency of Lord Ossory. He writes to the King, in 1541, before the assembling of Parliament, to which, with wise and salutary policy, it was intended to summon as peers some great chiefs of Irish as well as of Anglo-Irish race :—

"Ther is also one M'Gillapatrike, who is lorde of a faire contrey called Upper Ossrie, that, *at my firste being here your Highnes Commissioner*, becam your Highnes subjecte, and to take his lande of your Highnes, *to him and his heyers*, and to be made lorde of your Parliament; and ever sythe his said submission hathe contynewed your trew and faythfull subjecte, as far as I can hear. Howbeit, he hath not yet your gratius letters patentes for the same. He hathe most instantly desyred me to move eftsones your Majestie therein, so that he moughte be at your next parliament here. *His sonne* hathe bene, this year and more, in your Inglisshe pale, and is well brought up, and speaketh good Inglisshe. If it may please your Majestie also to geve parliamente robes to the said M'Gillapatricke, I thinke your Highnes shall well bestow them. Thus I alwaise move your Majestie to geve. I moste humbly be- seche you of pardon, for I verely truste that your Highnes shall winne more obedience with these small giftes, then perchance hathe been wonne before this tyme with £10,000 spente."[a]

---

[a] This recommendation of making slight presents was in accordance with the usage of the ancient Mile- sian kings of making gifts of horses, raiment, &c., called *biengs*, to their subordinate chiefs or urriaghs; con- sequently, the observance of this ho- nouring custom would be especially intelligible and grateful. Agreeably to another national usage, the liege and submissive chieftain, Mac Gilla- patrick, soon afterwards placed his son in his sovereign's hands as a hos- tage. The young Irishman was sent over as a pledge of peace, not as an envoy of defiance, to the Court in

Following after Sir Anthony's letter are printed "Certen articles and conditions which Mac Gilpatrike did promesse duely to observe and performe at suche tyme as he made his submyssion to the kinge's Majestie."[a] These curious covenants accurately demonstrate the changes necessary to metamorphose a chief and his sept into a feudal lord and tenants. By the first, it will be observed, he renounces the use of his native title of dignity as "the Mac Gillapatrick;" and, by the last, undertakes to hold such land as the King gives him (under the second article) as a regular tenant of the crown, by knight's service. He engages by the third that he and his heirs will take care that such of the estate as may be fit for cultivation shall be tilled, and that houses shall be built for husbandmen. By the fourth his tenants are not to be liable to the extraordinary taxes and exactions ordinarily levied by chieftains; and more than a certain standing force of armed men is not to be maintained. Fifthly, the King's laws and writs are to be obeyed. The covenant runs as follows:—

"I. Firste, the said Mac Gilpatrike doth utterly forsake and refuse the name of Mac Gilpatrike, and all claymes which he might pretende by the same; and promyseth to name himself, for ever

London, where, as Barnaby Fitzpatrick, he became the playmate and bosom friend of the young student King, Edward the Sixth. He distinguished himself on several occasions by his valour, and, on the death of his royal patron, having himself succeeded to his father's title of Lord Upper-Ossory, returned to his native country, where he performed many loyal and important services. In the words of the memoir of him written by Horace Walpole :— "These are a few notices of a man who made so great a figure by his merit, after he had missed making a more showy one by favor."

[a] Lodge states that he made his submission to the King's Commissioners for the Settlement of the Kingdom, 8th October, 1537; and that they indentured with him that he should be Baron of Cowchil or Castleton.

hereafter, by suche name as it shall please the Kinge's Majestie to gyve unto him.

"II. Item, the said Mac Gilpatrike, his heires and assignes, and everie other the inhabiters of suche landes as it shall please the Kinge's Majestie to gyve unto him, shall use the Englishe habites and maner, and to their knowledge, the Inglish language; and they, and every of them, shall, to their power, bring uppe their children after the Englishe maner, and the use of the Englishe tonge.

"III. Item, the said Mac Gilpatrike, his heiers and assignes, shall kepe and put such of the said lands as shall be meet for tillage, in manurance and tillage of howsbandry, and cawse howses to be made and buylt for such persons, as shall be necessary for the manurance thereof, within such time as he conveniently may.

"IV. Item, the said Mac Gilpatrike, his heirs and assigns, nor any of them, shall take, put, or cesse, or cause to be taken, put, or cessed, any maner imposicion or charge upon the King's subjects, inhabitars of the said lauds, other than their yearly rent or custom, but such as the [Lord] Deputie shall be content withall; and that they, ne none of them, shall have any galloglas or kerne, but such, so many, and after such manner, sort, and tyme, as shall stand with the contentation of the said Deputie and Counsaill.

"V. Item, that the said MacGilpatrike, his heirs and assigns, and every of them shall be obedient to the King's Majesty's laws, and answer to His Highness writtes, precepts, and commandments, in His Majestie's castell of Dublin, or in any other place where his Courtes shall be kept, and His Grace's laws ministered; and do what in them is, to cause all the inhabitants of the same to do the semblable, or els they shall bring them, if they may, to justice.

"VI. Item, the said Mac Gilpatrike, his heirs and assigns, and every of them, for the tyme being, shall answer and go with the Kinges Lieutenant or Deputie to all such hostings, roodes, and jorneys, whereunto they shall be warned and assigned; and that, after suche maner, and with such number of company as the marchers of the Countie of Dublin do.

"VII. Item, that the said Mac Gilpatrike, his heirs and assigns, ne any of them, shall maintain or succour, receive or take to sojourn, any of the King's enemies, rebells, or traytors.

"VIII. Item, the said Mac Gilpatrike shall hold his landes by one whole knight's fee."

The original document is signed by the chief himself, who, being unable to write, affixed his mark. He was the first of Gaelic race elevated to the peerage of Ireland; for, in four months after the date of the viceroy's recommendatory letter, he was created a baron by patent, and he sat in the Parliament of 1541 as Lord Upper-Ossory.

To revert to the presentments. Our space will not permit more than a brief notice of the Brehon law, by which a large portion of the presented districts was governed.

Edward Spenser, as Irenæus, in his "View of the State of Ireland," describes the Brehon Law as—

"A rule of right unwritten, but delivered by tradition from one to another, in which oftentimes there appeareth great shew of equity, in determining the right betweene party and party, but in many things repugning quite both to God's Law and man's: as for example in the case of murder, the Brehon, that is their judge, will compound betweene the murderer, and the friends of the party murdered which prosecute the action, that the malefactor shall give unto them, or to the child, or wife of him that is slain, a recompence, which they call an *Eriuch*. By which vilde law of theirs, many murders amongst them are made up and smothered. And this Iudge being as he is called the Lord's Brehon, adjudgeth for the most part a better share unto his Lord, that is the Lord of the soyle, or the head of that Sept, and also unto himselfe for his judgment a greater portion than unto the plaintiffes or parties grieved.

"*Eudox*. This is a most wicked law indeed: but I trust it is not now used in Ireland, since the kings of England have had the absolute dominion thereof, and established their own Lawes there.

"*Iren*. Yes truly, for there be many wide countries in Ireland which the lawes of England were never established in, nor any acknowledgment of subjection made, and also even in those which are subdued, and seem to acknowledge subjection, yet the same Brehon law is practised among themselues, by reason, that dwelling as they doe, whole nations and septs of the Irish together, without any Englishman amongst them, they may doe what they list, and compound or altogether conceale amongst themselves their owne crimes, of which no notice can be had, by them which and might amend the same, by the rule of the Lawes of England" (Dublin, 1633, p. 4).

It is evident from the presentments that extreme confusion was occasioned by the uncertainty how questions as to succession to property and power were to be decided: —whether by the feudal law of descent and regular courts of judicature, or by the rules of the native judges. In the towns "the king's laws" usually prevailed; but, out of them, "the country laws" were almost exclusively observed. It would seem that the crown judges had ceased to hold assizes in some bordering districts for many years prior to these disorganized times. The palatinate jurisdictions of the Earls of Ormond in Tipperary, the Earls of Kildare in Kildare, and the Earls of Shrewsbury in Wexford, gave arbitrary and enormous authority to those noblemen; superadded to which, as has been already noticed, the heads of the houses of Butler and Geraldine governed their vast estates by combining the powers of feudality and clanship, the systems by which respectively the Norman and Gaelic races were ruled. Many inferior Anglo-Irish lords were in a hybrid state—half chiefs, half barons. They exercised the option of enforcing either Statute or Brehon law, according as either was most beneficial to themselves.[a] By the latter an amerceement or mulct was due for every offence; and, in certain cases, was payable to the chief. Such penalties were called *cain*[b] in cases of theft and other

[a] Summary of the Presentments. —State Papers, vol. ii., p. 512.

[b] A *cain* was a fine payable under penal laws, directed to repress particular injuries: thus, the *cuin* of Daire, or penal law of Daire, was intended to secure the repression of the offence of killing cows. The Brehon Laws afford many similar examples.

light injuries, and *eric* in case of manslaughter. They were high in proportion to the substance of the offender, and quality of the sufferer. According to the Waterford presentment, the Brehon, who was appointed by the lord, took payment for his judgment from both plaintiff and defendant. The well-known comments of our philosophic and impartial historian, Dr. Leland, on the Brehon Code, point out the leniency and refined justice of that law. It may be believed that the national law was administered without change or abuse in regions where patriarchal heads of ancient clans exercised undisputed sway over a people who were of their own name and kindred. But the authority of a Brehon jurisconsult under a feudal nobleman must have been confused in character; especially wherever there was an admixture of races and usages. To live under the protection of some neighbouring potentate was, nevertheless, so desirable, that the inferior Milesian septs sometimes voluntarily bound themselves to homage and service; thus the O'Brenans of Idough ranged themselves in the preceding century under the banner of the Earls of Ormond; and, in so doing, agreed to certain payments which are illustrative of this portion of our theme, consenting to pay double penalties, called "*ard-keyn*," i. e. high fines, in case any of them committed transgressions on the Earl's tenants.[a]

Gaelic customs were in full force in Wexfordshire, in those parts of the county which lie nearest the mountains. It was in Shelburne that "paines and canes" were levied by Lord Ormond, and in the *Fasagh*, or wold, of Bantry that his son "occupied brehon law." The State Papers of this period have several recriminative complaints between the noble Earl and the Seneschal of Wexford:—the former

---

[a] Carte's Life of the Duke of Ormond, vol. i., p. lxxiii.; and Transactions of the Kilkenny Archæological Society, vol. i., p. 238.

writes, 16th July, 1538,[a] that the servants, and kerne of William St. Loo, the seneschal, did spend his tenants and farmers in the barony of Dunbrothy, and elsewhere in the county of Wexford, and took of them beeves, and divers other exactions; which was a mean to make all that quarter waste, whereof Irishmen would be right glad. The seneschal, on his side, describes, in a letter to Lord Cromwell, the state of the barony of Bantry,—a district lately in the possession of the rebellious Geraldines,—as adjacent to Lord Kildare's castle of Old Ross, but now leased to a younger son of the loyal Ormond:—

"Also, right honourable good lord, it is unknowen to your lordship how the countie of Wexford is cituated, bordering on the Kavenaghs, wiche dayle burne, spoyle, and distroy the said countrey, so that within this thre days they have wastyd a manor or lordship of the King's, named the Karyck [Ferry-Carrig] coming thorough Master Richard Butler is lands, lett to farm by the kings highnes commissioners, as Mr. St. Leger and others—called the Fasagh of Bantre, parsell of the coyntee of Wexford, where enhabiteth Kavenaghes Irish judges, otherwise Brewys, Rymers, wiche are suffred be the pretense they manure the king's lands under Mr. Rychard; dayle victuayling such enimyes as burne and robbe the saide countrey, the king's servants and subjects. Yea allso in the sayd Fassagh they divide the pore men's goods; and I dare not folow the search onless I have sufficient power to matche the pretensyd tenants as well as the manifest Irish enemyes. Yea allso, my good lord, by colour of tenantshipp and pensions to my Lady of Ormond and others, unneth one obedient to the king's lawes from Arclo to Kylklogan,[b] in distans xxx myles or thereabowtes."[c]

We cannot wonder that, while and wherever the laws were thus conflicting and abnormal, the social state of the

[a] State Papers, vol. iii., part iii., p. 48.

[b] Kilclogan, a preceptory of Knight's Hospitallers near Hook. A "pyle," or tall square castle, of the fifteenth century still exists here.

[c] Letter to the Secretary of State, dated Roscarlon, 21st April, 1538.

country was disordered. This evil was aggravated by contests between the leaders of the Gaelic and Teutonic races on all the frontiers. Each chieftain of a clan saw in the rich lands of neighbouring knights and barons those fertile plains which bard and brehon assured him were the heritage of the Gael. It must be remembered that these were times when, in the words of a Scottish poet,—

> " Tooming faulds, or sweeping of a glen,
> Had still been held the deed of gallant men:"—

and when it might have been asked, in the fierce rejoinder of Roderick the Black :—

> " Where live the mountain chiefs who hold
> That plundering Lowland field and fold
> Is ought but retribution due ? "

If such malcontent neighbours of the *Sassenach* did not lead forays themselves, they were, like Fergus M'Ivor, not ill-pleased when any Donald Bean Lean of their woods lifted a few kine.

Cattle stealing, however, was not the monopoly of any one race, for it appears by the surnames of several robbers named in the verdicts that some of Teutonic blood had turned plunderers. Again, whatever jealousy of the usurpation of broad champaigns in Leinster may have been felt by clansmen under Mac Murrogh and Mac Gillapatrick, it is evident that the passion was shared by the Englishry, in their declarations that the territory round Enniscorthy had at one time been " freeholders' land," and that the remoter regions around Arklow and Carnew formerly belonged to the Crown, to which the colonists plainly looked with eagerness for aid to recover possession of these coveted lands from the descendants of men from whom their own forefathers had once wrested them.

The marked distinction between regions within the county of Wexford which continued under Irish rule, and the district designated "the English Pale" of the shire, the incessant plundering warfare carried on between those hostile territories, and the gradual ousting of the descendants of the Strongbonian invaders from remoter possessions, are remarkably evidenced in the following instance. In the year 1552 a petition was presented to the Lord Deputy by Robert Roche, of Artramont, Lord of Rochesland, setting forth that his ancestors had been possessed of a house and three ploughlands in the parish of Rathalvey,[a] in Farrengynellagh,[b] or barony of Sue, and complaining that Moriertagh *leigh* O'Morrowe,[c] and others, had entered thereon with force, and kept those lands "contrary to right and conscience." The determination of the matter was referred by the Viceroy and Council to Mr. Isham, then seneschal of the county, Mr. Barnewall, resident justiciary of the shire, and Captain Gabriel Blike. This tribunal summoned the defendants to appear, but they made default. Robert Roche then exhibited several ancient deeds, some in French

---

[a] Sir Henry Wallop held in right of Selsker Priory the churches and rectories of Castlesue, Rathaile, and Killusk.—Rot. Pat. No. 7, Jac. I. Rahale is a townland three miles north of Artramont.

[b] The Gaelic name of the barony of Sue (the *caput baroniæ* of which was Castle-Soo), now the barony of Shelmalier West.

[c] Probably the chief of the clan O'Morchoe, now Murphy, which inhabited the country north of, and bordering on, Roche's and Synott's lands, and still called "the Murrows." Murtogh O'Morghowe had a charter, 1 Edw. IV., to entitle him and his issue to use English law in all things. His clan, however, kept their ancient customs, and we find their chiefs retaining armed soldiers down to sixteenth century. Donnell More, of Tubberlumnagh, was "the O'Morchua" in the middle of that century.—[Funeral Entries, Ulster's Office, 1634.] The other principal residences of the clan were Oulartleigh, Jamestown, Ballinroan, and Ballindarragh, all in the county of Wexford.

and some in Latin, bearing date in Edward the Third's days, by which it was proved that the two ploughlands and a half in Rathalvey had been "the rightful inheritance of William Fitz-Eustace and Gydoo Roche, whose heir the said Robert did affirm himself to be." It was also "manifestly proved by honest witnesses that his father, John Roche, retained during his life the yearly rents of money, sheep, butter, and other things of the tenants and dwellers in Rathalvey; and that *whenever any goods were taken* from the tenants of the said town *by the Inglishe Pale* of the county of Wexford, *being in wars with the Morrowes*, the said John Roche *caused the same to be restored*. And that the said lands had been always *free from O'Morrowe's galloglasses*, and other charges.[a] And that the said John died seized of the same." It was decreed, thereupon, that Robert Roche, his heirs and assigns, should hold the premises as fully as the said ancient deeds did limit and bind the same, free from any disturbance from the defendants until they recovered the same by law.[b]

The river, which rises in the valley on the west side of the Forth mountain, passes by the town of Taghmon, and enters the sea near Bannow, hence taking its name from that ancient town, was at one time considered the boundary between the English and Irish baronies of the county. By patent, dated Waterford, 22nd November, 10 Henry IV., the office of custodier and bailiff of the water between the towns of Ross and Wexford was granted

---

[a] That is, free from having the galloglasses, or armed soldiers hired by O'Morchoe as police, and for the defence of his country, quartered upon its tenants; and free also from other charges which were due by tenantry under a chieftaincy.

[b] From a copy of the enrolment entered in MS. No. 75, p. 194, Bibliotheca Egerton., British Museum.

to John [   ], to be held during his life.[a] In
the reign of Henry the Sixth an Act of Parliament was
passed "for building towers uppon ye water or river of
Tamon;"[b] and another enactment was made in the thirty-
second year of the same reign (1453): "That none shall
breake the fortifications or strength of the water of Thamon
in the county of Wexford; nor shall make no waies on the
same water from the wood of Bannow to the pille adjoining
to the river of Slane; saving soe much waies as shall be
made by the commandment and view of the Bishop and
Deane of Ferns, the Seneschall of the Libertie, and Sherrif
of the Crosse in the same countye, or anye three of them."
In 1463 (3 Edward IV.), an order was made by Parliament "for building a castle at Coule upon ye frontiers of
Shirebyrne." Owing to the circumstance that the tide flows
up the Bannow river for some miles, the lower portion was
formerly termed a *pill;* a term derived from the opposite
shores of the Bristol Channel, where it designates numerous
tidal inlets. Under this name it is alluded to by Stanihurst
as marking the boundary of the district in which the Gaelic
language was not spoken. After writing of the district called
Fingal, in the metropolitan county, he continues :—" But
of all other places, Weisford, with the territorie baied and
perclosed within the river called the Pill was so quite es-
tranged from Irishrie, as if a traveller of the Irish (which was
rare in those daies) had pitcht his foot within the Pill and
spoken Irish, the Weisfordians would command him forth-
with to turne the other end of his toong and speake English,
or els bring his trouchman with him." This river boundary
is also noticed in Dymmok's "Treatice of Ireland," recently

---

[a] Calendar. Rotulor. Pat., et Claus., page 189.

[b] Ratified by Act, 7 Edw. IV.— Addit. MSS. 4801 B...... M...eum.

printed by the Irish Archæological Society. As the writer of that Treatise condensed it from a "Description of the Provinces of Ireland," in the Carew MS., No. 635, it will be preferable to give an extract from the original, which appears to have been written soon after the year 1578, when a commission was appointed to form into two shires, Ferns and Wicklow, the extensive and for the most part wooded and mountainous territories surrounding the towns bearing these names :—

"The countie of Wexford was the first countrey where the English set footinge and conquered; as hath bene sene before. This shyre is the largest of any one in that contrie; and one part thereof still inhabited by the auncyent Irishe; which was the cause that sir Henrie Sidney and sir William Drury would have made two other newe shires within yt; the north part should have been called Fernes, and that to the south nere to Dublin, Wicklow. But finding that there were no sufficient and sure gentlemen to be sherifes, nor freholders to make a jury for her Majestie, yt hath bene let fall. Notwithstanding, yt hath a kind of devise within ytself, for the south part, as the most civil part, is contayned within a river called Pill, where the auncyentest gentlemen, descended of the first conquerors, do inhabite; the other also, without the river, is inhabited by the originall Irishe and the Cavanaghes, Moroghes, and Kinselighes, who possesse the wooddy part of the country, and yet are daylie more and more scattered by our Englishe gentlemen, who incroche upon them and plant castles and piles within them."

Among all the evidence these presentments contain of discord in the south-east of Ireland, the details and particulars are the fullest which tell—

"Of rugged deeds and moonlight foray,
Of feuds obscure, and border ravaging,"

between the townsmen of Ross and their neighbours, whether mountain clansmen or country gentlemen. The feud between the burgesses and the mountaineers was of early date; and was such as subsisted elsewhere under similar circumstances. The walls of the city of Newcastle in Northumberland are stated to have been erected because a wealthy burgher of that town was, in the reign of King Edward the First, captured in his own house by a party of Scottish moss-troopers, and carried away to the hills.[a] And the walls of New Ross are said by the chronicler Stanihurst to have been built in order to guard against any repetition of a surprise of this sort. In the legendary account of the matter given by that quaint narrator of the traditions of the Anglo-Irish, he observes that before the town was fortified it was open to "the enemy;" and that the inhabitants were stirred up to enclose it with walls and gates to prevent the recurrence of a slippery trick played on a shopkeeper by an Irish horseman, who, under pretence of cheapening a piece of cloth, had it handed to him on his horse, and then, clapping spurs to his steed, galloped away with the goods.

Stanihurst gives the honour of defraying the charge of the costly undertaking of surrounding New Ross with a wall to a lady described by him as "a chast widow, a politike dame, a bountifull gentlewoman,"—named Rose. If the legend may be credited that one excellent personage, whether female or male, bore the cost of building the town walls of Ross, and if the benefactress was, as it may be believed, no other than that Rose,[b] who is thrice mentioned in the Close

---

[a] Scott's Essay on Border Antiquities.

[b] This lady was probably the widow of Robert Meyler of Duncormuck, whose family owned a large portion of New Ross, and were on more than one occasion active in benefiting the town. Clyn records, under the year 1340, that free passage of all vessels was granted by the King to the port of Ross, at the instance and by the diligence of Ralph Meyler. Rose Meyler is mentioned three times in the printed Calendar of

Rolls of Edward the Third's reign, as the widow of Robert, son and heir of Sir Ralph Meyler, who obtained from that monarch a grant of freedom for the port, then the erection of those fortifications did not take place until the fourteenth century. The first fortifying of the town is ascribed in the well-known Norman-French ballad[a] to a different cause. According to this ancient and highly interesting poem, the original entrenchment was made as early as the year 1265, having been thrown up to guard against the effect of those "deadly wars" noticed by Sir James Ware, as having broken out in the preceding year between the Burghs and Geraldines, and which "wrought bloodsheds and troubles throughout the realm of Ireland." The ancient Annals of Monte-Fernandi notice this war, and those also of New Ross,[b] contained in the "Book of Ross," have an entry, at 1266, that Walter De Burgh was conquered in that year, and that

Patent and Close Rolls. The King's escheator was directed, upon taking an oath of Roesia, wife of Robert Meiler, now deceased, who held lands of the King in fee, that she would not marry without license, to assign her a reasonable dowry out of the lands of her deceased husband.—[Rot. Claus. 29 & 30 Edw. III.] The same rolls contain an entry of the dowry assigned to her by a jury of thirty-six men, at Ross, on the 8th September, 29 Edw. III., out of lands and tenements in English-street in that town, in Montgarret, Clonmines, and Taghmon, in the Forest near Taghmon, and in Duncormuck. The original of this curious record gives the names and services of the various tenants of these lands. Rose is again mentioned in the Rolls, for she unfortunately broke her oath, and re-married without having obtained license from the King, the feudal lord of her lands. On the 12th July, 33 Edw. III., the escheator was directed to release the third part of the manors of Duncormuck, Fynnor, and Lacan; for that Richard Duk of Waterford, who had espoused Rose, widow of Robert Meiler, without the royal license, had paid a fine to obtain pardon for the transgression.

[a] Printed in the Archæologia, vol. xxviii., and republished by Mr. Crofton Croker, with curious elucidatory remarks, and an admirable translation by L. E. L., in "The Popular Songs of Ireland."

[b] Printed with Clyn and Dowling's Annals.

his knights, with many others, were slain." The entrenchment made at this time was long and deep—it is declared in the ballad that the fosse was a league in length and twenty feet in depth. So extensive a rampart must have been intended to include some land adjoining the town in the general security. The poet declares that now this work of safeguard is finished all within may sleep securely. He then enlarges on the great store of warlike weapons possessed by the townsmen—many a shining hauberk and ringing coat of mail, with plenty of strong arblasts for cross-bow-men, and of bows which were handled by many a good archer. If the statistics of this antique ballad are to be relied on, the martial force of the town was considerable. Three hundred and sixty-three men bearing cross-bows, twelve hundred archers, and three thousand spearmen, led by one hundred and four *gens à cheval*, is a large armed array for a town which had not completed its first century. However, as the poem is of unquestionable authenticity, and as the remainder of the author's statistics respecting the number of persons employed in the various trades of the borough has every appearance of veracity, and also as he appeals to a muster-roll in confirmation of the numbers he gives, this remarkable and elegant specimen of ancient poetry may stand in evidence of the extent of the colonization effected during the first century of the conquest of Ireland. As the poet declares, the leaders of the townsmen were well armed for battle, but they were, he at the same time assures his hearers, far from desirous of war, and merely wished to guard themselves from *marcis gens*. No man, he observes, can blame them for enclosing their town—which, he vaticinally boasts, when it shall be completely surrounded by "the wall" (implying it was already so partially) there are no Irish in Ireland so bold as to dare to assail.

Much of the disorder of the times was occasioned by the existence of separate jurisdictions:—thus, while offences committed within guild towns and their lands, and throughout estates owned by the clergy, were cognizable by the King's officers—those which occurred within the franchise or "liberty" of a lord palatine were under his sole jurisdiction. Offenders could not be legally pursued by the officers of one district into another. This difficulty was sought to be remedied by the Statute of Kilkenny, in which it is recited that "divers people commit robberies and felonies in franchises, and fly with their goods into guildable lands, so that the officers of the franchises are unable to execute their office there; and in like manner divers who commit robberies in guildable lands fly with their goods into franchises, so that the officers of our lord the King cannot take the felons with their goods, but they are there with their goods received." A dispute arising from this cause was probably the origin of that foray mentioned in the verdict, when the seneschal of the Liberty of Wexford carried off a mighty prey of cattle from the burgesses of Ross. Edmund Spenser, in his "View of the State of Ireland," notices a common custom under which a creditor, having first demanded his debt, on failing to be paid, "would straight go and take a distress of the debtor's goods and cattle, wherever he could find them, to the value, which he would keep till he were satisfied." He also observes that the charters of most corporate towns contained a clause empowering any townsman "by himself, without an officer (for that were more tolerable) for any debt, to distrain the goods of any Irish, being found within their liberty, or but passing through their towns. And the first permission of this was, for that in those times, when that grant was made, the Irish were not amenable to the law; so as it was not safety for the townsman to go to him forth to demand his debt, nor possible to draw him into law; so that he had leave to be his own bailiff to arrest his said debtor's goods within his own franchise. The which the Irish seeing, thought it as lawful for them to distrain the townsman's goods in the country where they found it. And so, by ensample of that grant to townsmen, they thought it lawful, and made it a use to distrain one another's goods for small debts."

As observed by Friar Michael Bernard of Kildare, the author of the graceful ballad on the entrenchment of New Ross,[a] war truly was not the wish of the burgesses; for their wealth depended upon carrying on as full a trade as the products and the wants of the country enabled them. All trading corporations endeavoured to hold themselves neutral in any conflicts which disturbed and desolated the country around them. A strong and high wall was the best guarantee for the preservation of this neutrality. So long, however, as a borough remained insufficiently fortified and guarded, it was liable to be plundered by any band of marauders who were strong and bold enough to adventure a raid into its streets. Sometimes the brave townsmen donned their armour, and sallied out to repel or avenge such ingressions. The Annals of Ross record that some twenty-seven men of the town were slain by the Irish in the year 1333. At an earlier time [b] the burgesses seized and slew in the town itself a famous robber of their own race, Gilbert Roche, " a killer of just men, and a depredator of the lieges." The same Annals also take brief notice of a considerable battle which occured in 1336, when the Englishry of the county of Wexford were defeated by Mac Murrough, chief of the

---

[a] Archæologia, vol. xxviii. The original MS. is in the British Museum.

[b] Latin Annals (No. 1318), Bibl. Harl. 258.

clan Kavanagh, with the loss of two hundred men, and their leader, Sir Mathew Fitz-Henry, Baron of Kilkevan.

It would appear by the charter of Edward the Third to the sovereign and bailiffs of Rosponte, dated 1374, that the town was not murally fortified even at this date. The charter granted them the usual tolls and customs, " in aid of inclosing the said town, which is situated in the marches (or borders) near the Irish, and is often attacked by their hostile aggressions." It concluded, that the King, compassionating the extreme decay (*grandi ruine*) of the town, exonerated the Corporation from accounting for its tolls before the Exchequer; but desired that an account should be rendered to the Bishop of Ferns and the Abbot of Dunbrody showing that the money levied had been duly expended in enclosing and paving the town. The charter dated the first year of Richard the Third, " for the repair of the town, walls, and port," recites that many merchants of the town had been killed both by sea and land, that the town was one-third depopulated, and that neither law, justice, nor good government, existed in any district around it.

Ross is mentioned but twice by the northern annalists, styled the Four Masters. They record that in the year 1394, soon after the first landing of Richard the Second:—" An army was led by Art Mac Murrough, King of Leinster, against the English; and he burned Ros-mic-Triuin, with its houses and castles, and carried away from it silver, gold, and hostages." Their second notice is that in this town a woman gave a poisonous drink to Mac Murrough, which caused the death of this brave and famous defender of his country, A. D. 1417.

By letters patent, dated 4 Hen. IV., the King, upon petition, granted to the sovereign and commons of the town of Ross, that, as the town was situated in the marches or borders, and surrounded on every side by Irish enemies, so that it had not wherewith to live unless only by sale, &c., of victuals and other small matters, which it behoved to sell to the aforesaid enemies, to avoid their malicious acts, the said sovereign, &c., might treat with the said enemies, and sell them all manner of victuals, &c., as well in time of peace as of war; and also pay yearly to Arthur Mac Murrough, chief of his clan, the ten marks which the townsmen had been compelled to pay him for defending them.

The townsmen thus obtained the King's permission to pay black-mail, the payment of which was forbidden in the laws of the Scottish border. Indeed, the King's Exchequer in Dublin had for many years past paid a black rent of eighty marks to the successive chieftains of the clan Kavanagh. The County of Wexford also paid them a similar stipend. These tributes continued to be discharged with tolerable regularity down to almost the period of the Commission of Inquiry. Whether the annual sum of ten marks from the town of Ross was also continuously paid does not appear. It would seem it was not, as the consideration for which it was payable, namely, that the chief of the clan would exert his power to defend the townsmen from being plundered, was evidently unfulfilled at the time an Act of Parliament was passed, anno 1483 [1 Rich. III. cap. 26], authorizing "the sovereign, port-reeves, &c., of Ross to pursue and present those that robbe them."[a] An earlier statute [16 Edw. IV.] had enacted that "if any Englishman be damaged by an Irishman not amenable to law, he shall be reprised out of the whole sept or nation of the party doing the injury, according to the discretion of the chief governor of the land, and the King's council." By

---

[a] Calendar of Statutes, Add. MS. Brit. Mus., 4801.

certain other acts "every chiefteyn of English lineage" was held answerable "for his son and waged man," and "every man" was to answer "for the defence of his sons." As the learned editor of the Statute of Kilkenny remarks:—

"However extraordinary the above law, 16 Edw. IV., may appear at the present day, it was considered just and necessary at the time of its enactment. It may be observed that this and the other Acts just alluded to bear a strong affinity to the laws of the Irish Brehons, making the whole sept or territory liable for the offences of the individual."—*Hardman's Statute of Kilkenny, p.* 41, *note.*

At the period of the Ross verdict, the inaugurated chieftain of the clan Kavanagh, who is mentioned by the jurors as "the Mac Murrough that now is," was Cahir Mac Ennecross, who had made submission to the viceroy in the preceding year. The warlike leader of the clansmen who is mentioned most frequently, Cahir Mac Art, was, probably, his *tanist*, or lieutenant, and successor elect. After the latter succeeded to the chieftaincy, he became a feudal subject, and was created Baron of Ballyan.

In a letter,[a] dated 16th July, 1538, the Earl of Ormond gives the following curious account of a murderous and unprovoked assault on the Irish, which disgraced Ross at this time :—

" This Sainte Petiris Evin laste paste, at Rosse, when the folke of the towne toke ther station aboute the fyrys,[b] and beinge toward the abbay of the freres in their said station, Watkyne Apoell, oon Baker, and three or foure Englishmen, prepensidly retornede from the Suffrayne and his brethren, and came towarde the condyt of the towne, affermynge that it was to wayshe a hatt of cheries, whiche he hade then in his hande; and the streth being voyde of folke, the said Watkyne and his fellawes dud meth with Cahir McArtes

---

[a] Printed State Papers.
[b] This early allusion to a custom, still kept up, of lighting bonfires on St. Peter's eve, 28th of June, is curious.

standarthe berrer, and 3 more of the said Cahir's men, beinge at peace, and beholdynge the fyrys, and station of the towne, under a pentice besides the said condite of water, and unawisidly did drawe ther daggers, and stickide the said Cahirs men with the same, wherby the said standartberer was oute of hande slayne, and the residue beinge wondide to deathe, flede away, and parte of them constraynide to take the river; and when the Suffrain herde herof, he soghte for the said Watkyne and mete him at his dore, eatinge of the said cherryes, who denyede that it was not his dede, and bade the Suffrayne take the offenders: and aftre the Suffrain fonde oute thEnglishmen, he pute them to warde, and certificde Mr. Thesaurer and others of the Consaile of the same, who willide the Suffrain to kepe them styll, tyll my Lorde Deputie were retornede; by meanes wherof the said Cahir is at werre with theym, and have lately prayede Old Rosse."

The retrospect of the Wexford juries, as may be seen by referring to their presentments, extends over some dozen years. With the exception of a few instances of heinous crime, the offences enumerated are of a character that may be considered as having formed a light calendar for such ungoverned days. As the calm and intelligent historian before quoted remarks, the virtues of private life are not in general the subject of history, which usually is an exposition of actions resulting from the evil passions and contests of mankind. Our remark is especially true of all records of a public and legal nature. The general state of the country is therefore not to be altogether deduced from these presentments, which, like the bills still found by grand juries, only take cognizance of such grievances and enormities as require redress and punishment. It is noticeable enough that the accusations as to the commission of the various offences and injuries described were brought by a jury of fifteen of the principal gentlemen of the county against their own neighbours, who were their equals and kinsmen; and that the accusations were as impartially made against powerful earls and territorial lords as against any loose wood-kerne. However, it must be understood that many of the misdemeanours for which the rural lords were arraigned were owing to those native customs of the country which made each lord, like a Gaelic chieftain, his own avenger of law. When we read of "Alexander Roche, Lord of the Rocheland," having taken to the value of forty shillings from five different individuals, we understand that he levied some special fine, in the manner his neighbour, O'Morchua (Murphy) enforced *cain* due to himself as Tighearna.

It is natural to expect that English law was either unknown or defied in the mountains and countries of Gaelic chiefs, who were as "irregular and wild" as the haughty Welsh insurgent, Glendower;—but its frequent violation by peers of the realm and sheriffs of the Crown proves the absence of strong legal authority. This deficiency is remarkably shown in an instance in which the head of the house of Butler, Piers, the first Earl of Ossory, and eighth Earl of Ormond, supplied the means of recovering a private claim where the arm of law was inadequate. When this potent nobleman marched with his sons, at the head of some six hundred men, as far as Mulrankan Castle, on the southern coast of Wexfordshire, and carried away the goods of its lord, he was induced to lead his "great host" thither by a merchant of Waterford; evidently as the solely possible process of recovering a debt in a case in which the sheriff of the county may have declined to act. Whilst marching back, his son, Lord Butler, levied a fine on the townsmen of Fethard, instead of exacting food and forage for his men and horses. Some years afterwards, the very sheriff of the county, whose duty it was to observe the statute against taking coyne and livery strictly, was less scrupulous as, appears by the following curious letter from the portreeve and men of that town to the viceroy, dated 1549:[a]—

"Oure bounden duty unto your honourabyll Lordshipp, which considered. This ys to advirtise yow howe Mr. Shiref of the countye of Wexford came to Fydyrth of the sayd county this laste Satterday paste with a nombyr of Gharne (Kerne) and Horsemen, in cumpled harnes, whell apuntthid, to fygth agens the Kynges pore subgekes, and then and ther rigourosly and extortly the forsayd Shiref with his nakyd swerde drawen in his hande, in present of many did strike and bett he your pore oratour the Portre of the forsayd towne of Fydyrth, offiser, abowte the hedd, that he hys not abyll as yet to repayre unto your Lordshipe to complayne, and in like manner ran att one of the Burgess ther and cott him in the hand. If he had not borne of the stroke with a staff his hand had been cutte of quite. One of his fyngyrys his in danger never to recover; and a nodyr pore man his fyngyr his cutte of and never had sinys, be cawse he cryed, seyng the Portre so bettyng for refusing the Shireffe of a Nyrisse custome namit Quin and Lewery, that never was paid to no Shiref afore (whiche unconveniens shall be proved bi many honest personys if hit be your Lordshipp his whill).

"In consideratione whereof youre pore compleynanttes besagys your Lordshipp for the love of God of a treu remedy bi this berir in the premisses and thei whill prai to God daly for your honerabill estate in prosperiti long to contenu."

"By your pore compleynanttes and faithefull subjeckts, to ther power, the Portre, and Burgesis of the towne of Fydyrtthe in the County of Wexford."

Superscribed:—

"To our ryght honerabyll goode Lorde, the Lorde Debite of this Reallme of Irlande, delywer this."

[a] MS. State Paper Office.

THE VERDICT OF Y^E COMMONS FOR Y^E BODY OF Y^E COUNTY
OF WEXFORD.

[*October*, 1537.—*MS. State Paper Office.*]

JOHN DEVEREUX.	WALTER BRIAN.	WILL. HAY.
NICHOLAS DEVEREUX.	JOHN KETYNG.	RO. SYNNOT.
JASPER CODDE.	HUGH ROCHFORD.	WATT. FRENCH.
RICHARD WHITTEY.	PAT. LAMPORT.	MYLO ROCHE.
WILLIAM NEVILLE.	THO. SIGON.	PAT. WHITTEY.

First ye said Jury present that the Lord of Ossory entered into the castle of Durbard's Island,[a] with the appurtenances, with force, upon John Devereux, the King's constable there, and the same with force hath withholden since the 22nd yeare of our Sovereign Lord ye King's reign.

Item, they present that one Walter Meyler[b] of Doncormok and

---

[a] Durbard's Island is one of the many names by which the insular piece of land on the Barrow, now known as the Great Island, was designated. In a rental of the lands of the Lords Marshall, anno 1246, it is called Insula Herny.—[Carew MS., 611, fol. 14.] It acquired this name from Hernicus, or Herny Bretoun, of Ross, who is mentioned in a record of 1266.—[Chartæ Privilegiæ, &c., fol. p. 31.] Edward the Second granted it to Luke de Barry, with the manor of Old Ross.—[Cal. Rot. Pat. Hib., p. 19.] By an entry in the same rolls, 10 Rich. II., it had changed its name to that of a new owner, "John Durbaro de Iland," who then obtained license to transport two lasts of salted fish into England. These, probably, contained salmon caught in a famous weir, called Corkery in the above record of 1246. Subsequently, the heirs of the Lord Marshal, namely, the Duke of Norfolk and Sir Maurice Berkeley, were found possessed of "the castle, island, and manor of Durbarr."—[Carew MS.. 611.] By an Act of 3 Edw. IV., the castle and town of Carlow, the town of Ross, and the castle and lordship of Durbare's Island, being in ruin and decay, were seised into the King's hands for sixty years; and their keeping committed to Thomas, eighth Earl of Desmond.--[Statutes of Ireland, Cotton MS., Titus, b. ix.] By a record in the Exchequer, dated 6 James I., it appears there were at that time "a house of lepers, four fishing weirs, and forty messuages" in the island.

[b] In 1570, Walter Meyler, of Downcormock, gent., addressed the Government, stating that he was possessed of the manor of Pryststown (Priestshaggard) in the confines of the county, "adjoining to the salvage nacion of the Cavanaghes," upon the very frontiers of the Irishry, and therefore wasted by their continual incursions. He adds

his ancestors have been in possession of Montgarrett,[a] beside Ross, with the appurtenances, as their inheritance of right, until Piers, Earl of Ossory, into the premises entered with force on the said Walter, the 1st of March the 10th year of yᵉ King's reign, [1518], and it keepeth with force contra statutum Dom. Rex [sic].

Item, they present that William Keting, Commander of Kylklogan,[b] entered with force into a carne of land called Hurbyskayn,[c] with yᵉ appurtenances, in yᵉ Barony of Dunbrody, the 1st of August, yᵉ 20th year of yᵉ King's reign, and keepeth it with force.

Item, they present that the Barony of Karnoo [Carnew?] in the manor of Ferns perteineth to our Sovereign Lord yᵉ King.

Item, that yᵉ Barony of Torkill,[d] with the towne of Arkelowe, in like maner perteineth to the King.

that Priestown was "the key to the county," and proposes to exchange it for the reversion of the rectory of Duncormock. He pleads his services against the Cavanaghs, who, he declares, "have ofttimes shed his blood." —[MS. State Paper Office.]

[a] Edward the Second, in the fourth year of his reign, granted to Robert Russel, of Ros, that he might acquire to himself and his heirs for ever, of Agnes, daughter of John Kempe, two carucates, or ploughlands, and fifty-two acres of land in Mongaret, which were within the manor of Old Ros, and belonged to Roger le Bygod, late Earl of Norfolk.—[Cal. Rot. Pat., p. 18.]

10 Henry IV. (1408), May 9—a royal permission was granted to Patrick Barrett, Bishop of Ferns, which, reciting that he intended to construct a castle of stone, crenellated, in a place called Mountgaret, in the marches of the county of Weysford, empowered him to take *latomos, et cementarios competentes*, i. e. competent quarry-men and masons, within the shires of Kilkenny, Weysford, and Waterford, to work in the construction of the same,

for the tithes of the said bishop.—[Rot. Pat., page 193.]

The Earl of Ormond, above named, conferred Mountgarrett upon his second son, Sir Richard Butler, who was created a viscount, taking his title from this place, anno 1550.

[b] Kilelogan was a commandery or preceptory of the Knights Templars, and, subsequently, of the Knights Hospitallers, or of St. John of Jerusalem, whose grand priory was at Kilmainham. A tall and peculiarly constructed peel-tower still stands at this place. An inquisition taken at Ross, 30th August, 1544, finds that Sir John Rawson, late Prior of Kilmainham, was seized of the manor of Kilelogan, and of the rectories of Hook and Templeton. The house was usually called the Preceptory of Kilelogan. It was granted by Queen Elizabeth to Sir Dudley Loftus; and the Loftus family resided there before they acquired Redmond's, now Loftus, Hall.

[c] Hubbardstown, now called Hobart.

[d] This may be Tor-hill, from the Hill of Tara, near Gorey: or else the land called elsewhere Le Quarkill.

Item, that Douns-corttye,[a] being freeholders' land of this county, that Muryertayth Kevanagh keepeth the said lands by force and arms;—the nation of the freeholders been Rochfords[b] and Prendergasts.

Item, that Thomas Power, with the servants of John Power,

[a] Enniscorthy belonged originally to the see of Ferns. By an indenture in the 11th year of Henry the Third (1227), it was agreed between John, Bishop of Ferns, and Gerald, son and heir of Philip de Prendergast and Maud de Quency, that the said Philip and his wife give and assign to the said bishop and chapter six ploughlands for ever, in exchange for the town of Inscordy, viz., in Ballyregan, five ploughlands, and near Clone, one ploughland, which Fitz-Hernicus held; so as that the said Philip and wife might hold the said town of Inscordy as a lay fee for ever to them and their heirs; and the bishop and chapter hold the said six ploughlands freed from them and their heirs. This indenture was enrolled 4th November, 1595, at the request of Sir Henry Wallop, Knt.—[Egerton MS., Brit. Mus., No. 75, p. 270.] Maud de Quency was heiress of Robert de Quency, Strongbow's standard-bearer. Sir Maurice of Prendergast, near Haverfordwest, in Pembrokeshire, landed at Bannow in 1169, with ten knights and two hundred archers, the day after Fitz-Stephen landed. His chivalrous behaviour towards the King of Ossory during the Conquest is related by Maurice Regan. The territories of Fernegenall (Ferns) and Kinsellagh were granted to him.—[Harris' Hib.] See Archdall's Monasticon for the foundation of the Augustinian Abbey at Enniscorthy by Sir Gerald Prendergast. Philip de Prendergast was one of the Barons of Leinster, 8th of John. Gerald de Prendergast was one of the magnates summoned to the war in Brittany, 13 Henry III.—[Lynch, 293, 298.] By an inquisition taken in that reign, Lord William de Valence had custody of Gerald's great possessions, and his sister and coheir was married to John, Lord Cogan. By another of 6 Edw. I. (No. 41), Geoffrey, son of William Prendergast, was brother and heir to John Prendergast, who owned lands in Ardnesallagh and Fernan.—[Inquis. Tur. Lond.] The Wexfordshire family was afterwards driven southward, and lived in a tower called Gurteen, near the mountain of Forth, at the time of the Heraldic Visitation of the county, in which a brief descent of their line is given.

[b] Rochfords.—The Rochford family were barons from the thirteenth century. —[Lynch's Feudal Dignities, p. 223.] Sir Maurice witnessed Aymer de Valence's charter to Wexford in 1317, and held four and a half knight's fees of that nobleman in Kaldidy and Iuischorty, 17 Edw. II., which were waste by reason of the warring of the Irish. In 1411, the heirs of John Rochford held four knight's fees as the barony of Duffyr, from the late Thomas Mowbray, Earl of Norfolk.—[Carew MS, 611. Inquis. Tur. Lond.] Like their fellow-colonists, the Prendergasts, the Wexfordshire family of Rochford was driven southward as the Irish regained power, and lived at Taghnunan (Mountpleasant) under the mountain of Forth, in 1618.

that tyme Abbot of Tintern, came, robbed, and brent the town of Cullen feloniously, to ye damage of an £100, ye 2nd day of March, ye 25th year of ye raigne of our said sovereign lord.

Item, that Thomas Cusack of Cosingston, gent.[a] being here one of ye King's Commissioners, did compell the tenants holding by custom and use,[b] every tenant to pay ye value of a year's rent, for a fine and an income, to the sum of 100 marks and more, contrary to their laudable use and custom used this C years and more.

Item, they present that Richard Butler,[c] with all ye inhabitants of ye Fassath of Bantre,[d] doth occupie Bryon's Law,[e] and receaveth fynes and canes, being disobedient to the lawes of our sovereign lord.

Item, that Edm. Gangath, Richard Butler's servant, came to Culleyne ye 2° day of August ye 26th year of our sov. Lord's raigne, and then and there robbed from Lawrence Cullen and his tenants feloniously sixty kye and plough horses.

Item, that Thomas Cogge Neville robbed two plough horses feloniously of James Lewis, on St James day last past, price every horse 13s. 4d.

Item, they present that John Sutton, ye son of William, and Edmund Prendergast, ye son of William, came to Templetown on our Lady Day next before Crystymas ye 27th year of ye Kings raigne, then and there stole feloniously linnen cloth of Philip Cotyner[f] to the value of 6 marks.

Item, they find that William McShane, son to Shane McPhilip, and Edm. McDowle of Ramsgrange came to Duncannon ye 10th day of September ye 28th yeare of ye raign of our soveraine lord, and then and there did robb feloniously from Nicholas Ogeyre and James Hore 18 kine and six plough horses.

Item, they present that Laurence Neville came to S^t. Imocks[g] ye last day of November this present year, and brake a house, and

---

[a] Afterwards Sir Thomas Cusack, Lord Chancellor.
[b] That is, not holding by lease.
[c] Sir Richard Butler, son of the Earl of Ossory, afterwards created Viscount Mountgarrett.
[d] The wilderness, or weald, now the barony of Bantry.
[e] Brehon's, or Gaelic law.
[f] Query, Philip the cottoner, or maker of clothing?
[g] Near Bannow.

[took] 10s. of fyne of Margaret Perle in escueing of ye breaking of ye said house.

Item, they present that Gerald Boye Prendergast[a] and Kayer More McForish,[a] constable of Karlough, Edm: Duffe, Seneschall of Kensle,[a] came with McMurroo[b] to Balmager ye third day of August in the 26th year of our soveraine lord [1534], with the number of 1000 men, and then and there brent the towne of Balmagyr,[c] with a banner displayed, and murdered and wounded dyvers servants of John Devereux, and feloniously in goods and chattells did take away to the value of £300 or more.

[a] The revolt of Silken Thomas commenced on the 30th July, 1534. Gerald *buoy* Prendergast was probably a retainer of the Earl of Kildare; and McFioris (Mac Piers Birmingham) constable of his castle of Carlow. They were doubtless sent down to attack Devereux, of Balmagir, the head of whose line usually led the Englishry of Wexford. Mac-Edmond-Duff was the title of the chief of the clan Kinsellagh, that owned the Kinsellagh's country in the north-east of the county of Wexford. This clan descended from Ennagh, a natural son of Dermot-*na-gall*, upon whom the country was conferred by Henry the Second, with the hereditary office of seneschal.—[Carew MS. 635.] The same MS. mentions "three septs of Brian McMorogh, lord of Kinselagh, of whom McEdmond Duffe is chief."

[b] The Mac Murrough, the then chief of the clan Kavanagh.

[c] Balmagir, the residence of the family of Devereux, who were the wealthiest and most powerful of all of Strongbonian race in Wexford. They sprang from the Devereuxs of Herefordshire, ancestors of the famous Earls of Essex. Sir John Devereux founded the convent for friars minors at Ross, in the time of Edward the First. John Devereux, on whom the above-mentioned onslaught was made, had been Justiciary of the county under the Earls of Shrewsbury in the beginning of this reign.—[Inquisition taken in the Castle of Wexford, 2 Hen. VIII., enrolled in the Exchequer, 31 Eliz., m. 113.] He was succeeded in his estate in the year 1540 by his grandson, Sir Nicholas Devereux, Knt. A curious letter from this worthy knight has recently been printed in Mr. Evelyn Shirley's "Original Letters." It is addressed to Sir William Cecil, Lord Burleigh, and is dated 1566. The writer, in recommending his nephew to be Bishop of Ferns, makes "bold to refresh his acquaintance" with the potent Secretary of State, reminding him of having been his schoolfellow in England, when a ward of the Earl of Shrewsbury. An entry in the Carew MS. 621, dated 1574, notes that Devereux "was spoiled of a great part of his inheritance by the Kavanaghs." When Robert Devereux, Earl of Essex, the favourite, was Viceroy of Ireland, he passed a day at Balmagir (23rd June, 1599), while on his march from Waterford to Dublin, and knighted Sir James Devereux, who, according to tradition, sold three townlands to pay for three days' open house on the occasion.

Item, the said Jury present that Edlee Roche came on St Mathew's day, the 28th year of the raigne of our soveraign lord, and feloniously did take from Thomas Keating of Graigscor a horse price seven marks, and seven kyne and plough horses to the valew of four nobles, and other goods.

Item, they present that Oliver Gangath, ye son of William, feloniously did take two plough horses from Stephen Devereux of Baytaillestown ye last day of June ye 29th year of our soveraine lord.

Item, they present that Gilbert Sutton feloniously did take from Stephen Devereux of Battailstowne a cow the price 13s. 4d., at ye feast of S^t. Martin ye 20th year of our sov: lord.

Item, they present that the said William Etle Roche, with divers others wild Irish came to Kolkot[a] ye last day of March ye 28th year of our said soveraine, and there did feloniously take away from Walter McThomas of Kolkot, husbandman, 12 plough horses & 18 kyne, & to ye value of five markes in other goods, and wilfully did murther ye wife of ye said Walter.

Item, they present that the Erle of Ossory taketh paines and kanes[b] in the shire of Shilborn; and for a kane entereth into ye town of Ramsgrange with force, and so keepeth it from John Devereux.

Item, they present that ye inhabitants of the town of Ross do retaile with Irishmen, and selleth them their tillery[c] as well in warre as in peace, and did keep out English men to be murdered of ye enemies.

Item, they present that Katherin Hore and Margaret Hore be general heyres to Harpestone Edmund Hore of all his lands.[d]

---

[a] Coolcotts is a townland close to Wexford.

[b] *Cains*, the Gaelic word for fines payable to the chieftain or lord.

[c] Artillery, viz.: warlike weapons.

[d] There is a very ancient monumental stone in Taghmon Church to William Hore, of this family. It appears by the fourth item in the ensuing verdict, and by the Heraldic Visitation of the county, taken in 1618 [see also Burke's Commoners, 8vo, Lond., 1834, vol. iv.], that David Hore was uncle of the above-named Edmund, who had transgressed the Statute of Kilkenny by taking a wife of Gaelic race, a daughter of Gerald Kavanagh.

The tragedy recounted at p. 46 arose from an endeavour to make the succession pass according to Brehon law, under which a nephew or infant son might be excluded, and which absolutely excluded

Item, they present that John Sherlock, merchant of Waterford,[a] did cause and procure Perse, Earle of Ossory, and Lord James Butler, to come with their great oste violently, with force and arms unto the parish of Mulrankan in ye county of Wexford ye 2nd day of February ye 24th year of ye raigne of our soveraine lord; and then and there did feloniously take away from Walter Browne of Mulrankan, and John Devereux, and certain goods from James Keating, to ye valew of £100 and more; and then the said Lord James Butler with part of the said oste did menace ye commonalty of Federt to have coyne and livery of them; and in eschewing of ye same were compelled to pay unto ye said James 20 marks.

THE VERDICT OF THE JURY FOR THE BODY OF THE SHIRE.

[*October*, 1537.—*MS. State Paper Office.*]

WALTER BROWNE.	WILL. BROWNE.	JASPER CODD.
PHILIP KEATING.	DION. HAY.	JAMES BUTLER.
THO. ROWCETTOR.	JOHN ROCHE.	JOHN FITZJOHN.
JAMES ESMOND.	HAMOND CHEEVER.	ROB. PRENDERGAST.
JASPER BOSHER.	NICH. CODDE.	LAUR. COLEYN.

First, the said Jury present that wherein one Philip Ketyng, gent. with other gentlemen of the said county, ye 25th day of September in ye 15th year (1524) of our Soveraine Lord ye King's raigne that now is, in pursuing the King's Irish rebells had taken them at ye gates of Ross, ne had they been rescued by them of

---

female heirs. The verdict of the jury, however, is in favour of the legal claims of the daughters as "heirs general." It is well known that internecine disputes among the Earls of Desmond, and in other great Anglo-Irish families, arose from similar controversies, whether the succession should pass by Brehon or by Feudal law.

[a] *Merchant of Waterford.*—John Wadeyn (Wadding), merchant of Waterford, complained before the Parliament, held in Wexford, the 3rd year of Edw. IV., on Friday before the feast of St. Martin the Bishop, that Hugh Rochford, Nicholas Stafford, John, son of William Hore, Thomas Neville, Baron of Rosgarland, William, son of Davy Sutton, and other gentlemen of the county, owed him seven score and ten marks for certain contracts, and refused to pay the remaining forty-three. The matter was referred for arbitration to Nicholas Devereux and Robert Browne, Esqrs.—[MS. Abstract of unprinted Statutes.]

Ross; so that in the said pursute, by reason of the said rescue, divers of ye company of ye said Philip were hurt.

Item, they present that wherein ye 17th year of ye King's reigne, Nicholas FitzHarry,[a] with divers other gentlemen of the countey, were pursued by ye Irishmen, and fled to ye towne of Ross, wening there to be sauf;—but the said inhabitants did close the gates of the towne against them, and in no wise wold suffer them to entre the towne for their sauf guard; so that they were there at ye said gates slaine.

Item, they present that in the 17th year divers Irish rebells were pursued by Thomas FitzHarry and others; and had been taken or slaine, ne had they bin rescued by ye inhabitants of ye said town of Ross.

Item, they present that in the 18th year of our soveraigne lord (1526) David Hore feloniously entered and broke ye house of Edmond Hore,[b] and there feloniously did kill and sley ye said Edmond and his wife; she then being great with child of 2 children.

Item, they present that in February in ye 25th year of our soveraign's reigne ye Earl of Ossory with James and Richard his sonnes, with 100 horsemen, 200 galloglasse, and 300 kerne, robbed Walter Browne, and feloniously did take as well from him and his tenants as from other dwelling thereabouts all manner of corne and other goods that they found, to the value of £100 and above.

Item, they present that the Deane of Fernes pursued a bull from ye Court of Rome.

Item, Alexander Keting hath pursued a like bull from Rome.

Item, Gerald Bossher hath pursued a like bull.

---

[a] Sir John Fitz Henry, Knt., held one knight's fee in Kilkevan, from Aymer De Valence, Earl of Pembroke, and also a knight's fee in Mackmine.—[Inquis. Tur. London, 24, E. I., No. 56.] He is one of the witnesses to that nobleman's charter to the town of Wexford. His son, Sir Mathew, was summoned as a Baron to Parliament by Edward the Third, and by Richard the Second. Hence his successors were styled Barons of Kilkevan. Among some curious tales of Ireland contained in a very rare black-letter book, called "Beware the Cat," printed in 1584, a story is told of "Fitzharris and the Prior and Convent of Tintern."

[b] Of Harperstown. David Hore obtained possession of the estate, and transmitted the inheritance to his son, notwithstanding the seventh presentment, at page 44.

Item, that Sir Richard Browne, parson of ye Iland, hath pursued a bull from Rome called sua nob.

Item, they present that ye Abbey of Fernes is ye King's.

Item, they present that the great Iland called Durbard's Island is likewise the King's.

Item, they present that the vicar of Kylcowan died about June last past, whereby the King is entitled to have the first fruits, and is by the yere 5 markes Irish.

Item, they present that Thomas Poyer at the feast of All Saints which was in the 23rd year of ye Kings raigne, with a great company of galowglasses and kernes [came] to ye house of Lawrence Coleyn and there feloniously did robbe ye said Lawrence and all ye towne, and carried away ye goods to ye value of £200, and brent ye houses.

Item, they present that ye said Poyer robbed and brent ye same tyme divers townes and houses in ye county of Wexford; viz. ye Moorctown was robbed and brent, and Ambrosetown robbed.

Item, they present that the Earl of Ossory in ye 13th yeare of ye Kings reigne (1521) did take and wrongfully imprison Walter Browne, the said Walter Browne then being Seneschall of ye country; and kept him in prison by ye space of one quarter of a yeare, to his loss and hindrance of £40, and took of him for a fyne at his delivery £20.^{a}

Item, they present that on St. Mathew's even about two years past Edm. Ganke, then being servant to Richard Butler, with divers others, to ye nombre of 40 persons, feloniously did robbe and steale from Lawr. Coleyn and his tenants 51 kine and horses and 2 hobbyes to ye value of 100 marks.

Item, they present that Richard Baron, servant and horseman to ye said Richard Butler, about two years past came in to the towne of Banoo,^{b} and there feloniously did robbe and steale 6 plough horses out of ye said towne, and more they know not.

---

^{a} This is evidently the same affair as that noticed in the last item in the preceding Presentment; but in which the date assigned is a year earlier.

^{b} Whether "towne" here is to be taken in the usual sense, or for "townland or villa," is doubtful: if the former, it would serve to show that Bannow, long obliterated, was at this period in existence.

WEXFORD TOWN AND CORPORATION.

[*October*, 1537.—*MS. State Paper Office. The Names of the Jurors are not given in the original.*]

The sayde Jury doo present for our Soveraigne Lord ye King that the 26th day of May in the 24th yere of the rayne of our Soveraigne Lord ye King that now is, John Purcell, now Bishop of Fernes in ye county of Wexford, did confederate himself with one Care McArte,[a] enemy to our soveraigne Lord the King, and asyete [?] of ye wylde Irish dwelling in ye little island called McMorough island beside Rosse, and divers other malefactors adherents to ye said Care McArte, to ye said Jury unknowne. And the said day and yere the said Bishop received ye said Care McArte and others ye said malefactors into his dwelling house in the town of Fedred within ye said county, and to them did give meat and drink ye said day, and lodging ye night next ensuing. And ye 27th day of May in ye said 24th yeare ye said Bisshop, of his trayterous and felonious pretence, and contrary to ye statutes in such case provided, conspired and accompanied himselfe with ye said Care McArte and ye said malefactors in ye said 27th day of May, about 3 of ye clock in ye morning, in ye yeare above written, at Fedred aforesaid, procured and abetted ye said malefactors to breake and enter into ye dwelling-house of John Baron, Richard Cole, John Laffan,[b] David Longan, and of others, to ye nombre of 20 persons and above, subjects to our soveraigne Lord, burgesses and inhabitants within ye said towne. Which said malefactors, by the abettment and pro-

---

[a] A redoubted leader of the clan Kavanagh, subsequently created Baron of Ballyan, and personally known as Lord St. Molins.

[b] By letters patent, dated 25th June, 49 Edw. III., the King, in consideration of ten shillings paid unto the treasury, granted to Thomas Lavan, of Ross, that he and his heirs should be free from all Irish servitude, that they may use English laws, and acquire lands, goods, and cattle.—[Patent Rolls.] The grand panel of the county Wexford, in the year 1608, includes "Mac-Laffan of the Sladd" among the gentlemen of Shelburne.—[Carew MS., 600.] Henry Laffan died in 1638, seised of Slade castle and lands; with Porter's-gate and Gallgestown, held of the late Commandery of Kilclogan, by "castle-guard," and 8s. 6d. yearly.—[Printed Inquisition, No. 129, Car. I.]

curement and assistance of the said Bisshop his servants, to the said Jury unknowne in theyr proper persons, did robb and spoyle and take from the inhabitants then and there of theyr money and household stuff to the value of 50s. And further the said Jury present that ye said Bisshop then and there, being on his horse back, oftentimes with open claimor called for fire to have burned ye said houses.

Item, ye said Jury do present that ye said Bisshop, ye 23rd day of November in ye 26 yeare of ye raigne of our soveraigne Lord, procured and abetted ye said Care McArte and other malefactors to the said Jury unknowne, as well to spoyle, take, and dryve away cxv kine, oxen, and garrons, and also a great number of sheep and swyne of ye said inhabitants, as also of ye said Bisshop, to colour his false demeanour and doings. And after ye said day and yeare, Robert Cullen and other servants of the said Bisshop did come peaceably by assent between ye said Bisshop and ye said Care McArte, and did elect and chuse out ye cattell of ye said Bishop; but ye said Care McArte would by no intreaty or meanes whatever redeliver unto ye said inhabitants none of theyr cattell.

Item, ye said Jury do present that ye xi yeare of our soveraigne Lord, Walter Roche, ye son of Nicholas Roche, with his followers, went to the suburbs of Wexford by night, for ye most part feloniously.

Item, ye said Jury present that ye said Walter Roche burned a boat of Robert Canton,[a] ye said yeare feloniously, at ye Rawyne;[b] and the said Walter burnt a towne of William Meyler and Thomas Synnott in ye parish of Kilkeyvan feloniously; and so ye said William and Thomas must give unto the said Walter 20s. to have license to build ye same towne.

Item, ye same Jury present that ye said Walter came with a banner displayed of Irishmen, and tooke with them ye prey, that is to say of kine and cattle of ye towne of Wexford; and also as yet holdeth a Irish woman to his wife.

Item, ye said Jury present that ye 26th yeare of our soveraigne

---

[a] Glascarrig Abbey, on the south-east coast of Wexford, was founded in the thirteenth century by Griffith Caunton, whose ancestors founded St. Dogmael's in Pembrokeshire, from whence the Caunton family came over with Strongbow, and where the name Canton is still common. This family held the barony in the county of Cork, still called Condon's.

[b] Probably the Raven Point at the mouth of the Slaney.

Lord, Philip Roweeter did take a market man going from the market homeward, and also did take of Thomas Dennis by the water in money and ware to the value of 50s.

Item, ye said Jury do present that ye said yeare one Walter Browne, gent., did take John Furlong, merchant, feloniously out of his house that was in ye suburbs of Wexford, till such time as he was rescoused by ye suffering and his comings.[a]

Item, ye said Jury present that ye 19th yeare of our said soveraigne, Edmund Synnott and David Ketteing, the elder, sonne to Phillip Keiting, brought Caire Carrathe[b] with banner displayed, and tooke the prey of Rahaspok;[c] and that ye said Edmund with his followers did take violently Margarett Kinay against her will contrary to the King's laws, out of the towne of Wexford.

---

[a] The sovereign, or chief magistrate, and commonalty of the town of Wexford.

[b] Caher Carragh Kavanagh.

[c] A townland in the parish of the same name, two miles south of Wexford. It was found by Inquisition 20 Ric. II. that Rathaspeck and Ballyhur (Ballyhire) were anciently one parcel of land, as held of the Earl of Pembroke, and of his castle of the manor of Wexford, by military service, viz., 40s. royal service when scutage runs, and suit of court:—that the said parcel was divided; of which Rathaspeck belonged to Richard Codde, to be held for ever of the said manor; and that Ballyhure belonged to Hamyn Lamport, and was parcel of the same manor, to be held for ever of the said Earl:—that Richard C. died so seised, 14 Ric. II., and Nicholas, his son and heir, was then aged seven years; wherefore his ward and marriage belonged to the King, and was worth yearly 26s. 8d.; and also that Martin C. occupied the said lands and tenements from that time. He, being distrained, pleaded that Rathaspuck was held of the castle of Wexford by the service of rendering a rose yearly, and not by military service: but this was denied by the King's attorney-general. The Court of Exchequer not being advised, the barons postponed the case. —[Mem. Rolls, 20 Ric. II.] In the proceedings of Parliament, 16 Edw. IV., cap. 31, it was ordered that "Nicholas and Martin Codd appear or lose their tytle in three plowe lands in Rathaspicke for ever, and the tytle of Robert Browne, of Wexford, merchant, to the same, ratified." Another act is recited, that David Codd of the Carne, and Nicholas and John Codd, should appear before the Barons of the Exchequer on a certain day, or forfeit their title, and that they had made default. —[Acta Regia, Addit. MS. Brit. Mus., 4801, p. 7.] Nicholas Codd, Esq., of Carne, died in 1564, seized of the castle and lands of Rathaspeck.—[Inquis. Exchequer.] Rathaspue signifies the bishop's rath or fort, and may have been the ancient residence of the Bishops of Wexford. The church is still considered the mother church of Wexford, the incumbent of which is consequently first inducted there.

Item, ye said Jury present that ye said Edmund did take certaine corne of Thomas St. John,[a] ye elder, in ye highway. And also ye said Edmund did take Patrick Stafford, ye son of Richard Stafford, in ye highway. And as yett ye said Edmund holdeth an Irish woman to his wife.

Item, ye said Jury present that Walter Browne, gent. did take Stephen Saint John in ye highway, and him did lead to his castell, and there him did imprison after his owne use, contrary to the Kinge's lawes, till he had his fyne.

Item, ye said Jury present that Gerald Hay did take Patrick Furlong within ye towne of Wexford, and so retained him unto such time that ye saffraine and comyns did rescouse him. And also ye said Gerald did take of Dan. Busher, butcher, a beefe that was worth 12s.

Item, ye said Jury present that Patrick Haye, son to Gerald Hay,[b] did take feloniously of William St. John his wife and of his servant in ye highway to ye valew of a noble.

Item, ye Jury present that ye 20th yeare of ye raigne of our said Sovereigne Lord, that Alexander Roche, Lord of ye Roche land,[c] did take from Walter Stafford feloniously in ye King's highway to

---

[a] David St. John brought a plea before the notice of the Parliament, held in Wexford, 11 Edw. IV. (1472), of his having been ousted in a case of title from a house and 100A. in Taghmohagyr (Tomhaggard), and a house and three ploughlands in Monsyn, by John Rowcestre, Nicholas Devereux, and John, son of William Hore, Esqrs., Patrick and Eustace Rouceter, John and Nicholas Synnot, James Browne, Hugh Rochfort, and John Kerr Synnot, gentlemen, Thomas, son of said John, and Marion Mareshall, to whom St. John was cousin. The parties were ordered to appear in the Court of Common Pleas, or lose their title.—[Abstract of Unpublished Statutes.]

[b] Henry the Sixth, in the fifth year of his reign, at the request of Nicholas Hay, son of William Hay, of Slade, and on account of the grateful and laudable services he and his progenitors had performed to the King and his predecessors in many times resisting enemies, and which he would perform in future, *accipit eum in intimum amicum*, constituted him prefect of the Castle of Wexford, and granted him £50 in the name of reward.—[Rot. Claus.]

[c] The family of Roche derive their name from a rock in the western part of Pembrokeshire, on which an ancient castle still stands in picturesque ruin. Several early deeds of the Lords of Roche have been recently published in the "Archæologia Cambrensis." Among the muniments of the Welsh stem is one of the Irish branch, dated 31st Edw. III., by which David de Rupe,

the valew of 40s. in money and other goods of ye said Walter Stafford. And also that ye said Alexander Roche did take feloniously

Dominus de Fermoi, constituted William de R. of Wales, David de R., merchant of Weyseford (Wexford), and Richard de R., his bailiffs to take seisin of his manor of Manor Bir (the birth-place of Giraldus Cambrensis), and Pennaly, to hold courts, levy rents, &c. Adam de Rupe was one of the earliest invaders of Ireland; he is one of the witnesses. with *Dominus* Eustace de R., to Walter of Ridlesford's charter to Donnybrook.—[Regist. All Hallows, 67, 68.] By a deed, not dated, enrolled in 1617. at the request of Piers Sinnott, gent. [Printed Rolls, 15 Jac. I., p. 327] Gerald de Rupe granted to David Fitz-Adam Sinad, "his kinsman, for his homage and service, all the land lying between the divided lands of John de Rupe on the one side, and the port of Wexford, as the water runs from the bridge of Pohregan" (the river Sow or Sue, passing through Poulregan townland) "into the said port, on the other side, to hold to him and his heirs at the rent of one bisancam [bezant] of gold. Witnesses, G. de Mariscis, Lord Justice of Ireland" (anno 1210); Thomas Fitz Anthony de Senleger, Philip de Prendergast, and Gerald, his son; William Grasse, William, Baron of Naas; Walter de Revelsford, Richard de Cogan, *Adam, Lord de Rupe;* Eustace de Rupe, David Fitz Henry de R., Henry de R., his brother; Gilbert, John, and William de R., Adam Fitz Richard de R., William and Henry de R., his brothers; Robert de St. James, parson; Eustace, William, Albic, and William de St. James, Adam de Rupe, brother of Gerald; William, John, Redmond, Henry, and Nicholas, sons of Adam Sinad; Geoffrey,

the clerk, and others." This deed shows that Gerald was then lord of the districts on the northern bank of the Slaney, which are still known as Roche's-land and Sinnot's-land. Sir Thomas Fitz Anthony de St. Leger was Seneschal of Leinster; King John gave him the custody of Waterford and Desmond, with Waterford and Dungarvan Castles. His five coheiresses are named in a roll of 16 Henry III.—[Report Irish Record Com., vol. i., pp. 334-5.] The eldest, Helen, was married to the above-named Gerald; Dionisia to William of Cantilupe; Isabel to Geoffrey Calf (or le Vale) of Norragh; Margaret to John Fitz Thomas (ancestor of the Earls of Desmond); and Dissere, the youngest, to Stephen Archdiacon.

Gerald is stated in the Gormanstown Register [Lansdowne MS.] to have married Rose, fourth coheiress of John le Botiller, by Matilda, daughter of David, Baron of Naas; and to have had a son, George, whose son's name was John. This George obtained a certain writ from the crown, 2 Edw. II.; was summoned as a peer of Parliament (with William de R.) in the following year; and his services against the Scottish and other enemies, during Bruce's invasion, are acknowledged in a royal order of the thirteenth of the same reign.—[Rot. Pat.] He held *five* knight's fees in *Ferugynan* by suit and payment of £10 royal service when scutage ran; and also nine and a half knight's fees in *Schryrmal* and *Kynalo*, by suit and payment of £9 royal service. These large possessions were held in the county of Wexford from Aymer. Earl of Pembroke.—[Inquis

of William Morroghe to ye value of 40s., and did imprison him contrary to ye King's lawes. And ye same Jury do also present

Tur. Lond., 17 Edw. II., No. 75.] He was one of the great magnates to whom Edward I. wrote in 1299, commanding him to prepare himself with horses and arms to serve in Scotland [Holinshed]; and is named in Rymer as again summoned to Scotland in 1302 and 1315. His share of a third of the barony of Naas was divided, about the time of Edward IV., between Margaret and Anastace Flattesbury, as his coheirs.—[Carew MS., 611.]

Henry the Second assigned the service, *inter alia*, of Fernegenal [Conq. of Ireland, c. 3081; Fernegenelan, Harris's Ware, p. 191] and Ferns, with their appurtenances, to the Lordship of Wexford.—[Note in Arch. Misc., vol. i., p. 28.] Probably it was the latter and not the former that was granted to Prendergast—(see p. 41, *supra*.)

The annalist Clyn notices, in his too scant allusions to the events which followed the slaughter of the Earl of Louth, that Sir William Birmingham and his family remained in the summer of 1331 in the woods of the monks of Dowske (Graignamanagh); that *there* Sir Eustace Power married the daughter of the slain nobleman; that, on the following sabbath, nine of the Roches were slain, among whom was one of the family of Fermoy; and that a son of George Roche, a relative of Sir William Birmingham, was taken captive when returning towards Fernegylan from these sylvan nuptials.

Sir John Fitz George de Rupe, Knt., is named second in a list of 120 knights, gentlemen, and freeholders of the county, who were summoned in 1345 to attend the Lord Justice with their horses and arms.—[Extract from Rolls, MS., *penes nuper* Sir William Betham.] He had also been summoned to the war in Scotland, in the year 1335, among others of the same county, viz.:—Sirs George Power and Mathew Fitz Henry; and Richard Whittey, Hamund de Stafford, John de St. John, Reginald Neville, Ralph Meyler, and Stephen Devereux, Esqrs.—[Rymer, Appendix to Grace, p. 175.] Clyn states that he was killed in 1346 by the Ketyngs and Hodnets.—[See also Cal. Rot. Pat., 26 Edw. III., p. 55.]

Sir William (Fitz-Eustace) Roche, Knt., appears to have succeeded to Roche's-land in the time of Edward the Third; in the twenty-ninth year of whose reign he was one of those who elected a sheriff for the county.—[Rot. Pat.] He was appointed Constable of Ferns Castle 23rd November, 1346.—[O'Reilly's MS., R. I. Acad.] In the third year of Richard the Second he forfeited his lands, under the name of Sir William de la Roche, Knt.—[MS. Excerpt. Rot. Excheq., 4 R. II., m. 89.] By inquisition taken at Carlow, 13 Henry IV., it was found that among the knight's fees due in the county of Wexford to the late Thomas Mowbray, Duke of Norfolk, were, from the barony of *Shyrmull* and Kynallyone, coming to £10 yearly, and five from the barony of *Fernegeuagh*, paying the same.—[Carew MS., 611.] On comparing these tenures with those above mentioned, which were held of Valence, it is evident that the fee of the lands in Wexford, belonging to the Lords Marshal, had been divided between Bigod, Earl of Norfolk, and Valence.

John Roche and Thomas Synnot were commissioners in the cantred of

that ye same Alexander Roche did take Ellen Forlong feloniously, and kept her person unto such time he made her fyne. Also they present that ye said Alexander with his company did burne feloniously a bote of John Lyng that was worth 46s. 8d. And that ye said Alexander did take feloniously of William St. John a plough horse. And did take of Walter Talbot feloniously xl^s in money, and a sword that was worth 13s. 4d. And the same Jury present also that ye said Alexander with his followers, William Synnet and others moo, did take of Thomas Synett's wife feloniously a horse that was worth 40s.

Item, ye same Jury present that Bryan McTeage, Moynorth Roch, his servant, killed feloniously Robert Roch, James Dennis his servant, in ye Kings river, and the said Roch and his company did take Thomas Lynse feloniously, and certaine goods to ye valew of 40s.

Item, ye said Jury present that Walter Roch, ye son of Nicholas, did take James Howre feloniously, and tooke of him for his ransom 5 marks. And the said Walter did also take Robert Bolan feloniously, and took of him a ransom to ye valew of 40s. And ye said Walter tooke feloniously Philip Montaine, Eustace O'Morro, Walter Saint John, and divers others amongs the Irishmen, and they present them.

Item, ye said Jury present that Edmund Roch, son of ye said Walter Roch, did take feloniously from William Taylor a swyne that was worth 8^s. And that he did also take feloniously from Thomas Forlong 1^{lb} of silk to ye valew of 2 markes.

Item, ye said Jury present that John Roche and Garrett Roche,

---

Faryngevale (now the Barony of Shelmalier West), for levying 300 marks, granted, 13 Henry IV., to the valiant Thomas Butler, brother of the Earl of Ormond, Prior of Kilmainham, and commander of the Irish force at the siege of Rouen. The grant was a present from the county of Wexford to the Prior for warlike services.—[Rot. Pat., p. 201.] By inquisition taken in 1582, Walter Roche, late of Roche's-land, was found to have died 20th August, 1516, seised in fee of the manors of Ballytorrin, alias Ballytorchan, Horsetown, and Ardtroman, held of the Earl of Shrewsbury, by military service; that his son, Alexander, was then aged 18, and under the Earl's guardianship, which had been committed to John Bretchet, the Earl's seneschal; and that the said Alexander married Alison Devereux.—[Excheq. Records.]

Counties of Kilkenny and Wexford, &c.

sonne unto Walter Roche, did take feloniously from William Taylor in ye King's highway ye valew of 3s.

Item, ye said Jury present that Edmund Roche, son unto Walter Roche, feloniously did take in ye King's highway from a priest much linnen cloth and a booke to ye valew of 13s.

Item, ye same Jury present that William Roche, son to ye said Walter Roche, and his followers, tooke of William Taylor feloniously in the highway the valew of 3s. 4d.

Item, ye said Jury present that ye 26th yeare of ye raigne of our soveraigne Lord, Philip Furlong,[a] and William, his brother, with

[a] *Philip Furlong*, of Carrigmenan, on the Slaney, a place celebrated for the beauty of its scenery. The following is a copy of the original, among the title deeds of the family of Devereux, late of Carrigmenan:—

" Sciant presentes et futuri quod ego Nicholaus Keting, rector de Tamon, dedi, concessi, et hac presentibus confirmavi Johan' fil' Philip' Furlong de Cargemanan, generoso, unum messuagium et unam carucatum terræ cum suis pertinentibus in C.—un' mess' et sexaginta acr' ter' cum suis pert' in Monchean; un' mess' et octaginta acr' ter' in Ballyethyn; un' mess' et sexaginta acr' ter' in Anleghesland; un' mess' et sexaginta acr' ter' in Follegheston, quæ jacent inter Cargemanan predict' et Homeston. Unum mess' et un' car' ter' cum &c. in Bregertin in paroch' de Kylbride; un' mess' et octaginta acr' ter' &c. in Gorgynmore, in par' pred'; un' mess' et sexag' acr' ter' in Keyvaneston juxta Roweston; un' mess' et octag' acr' ter' in Roweston; un' mess' et vigint' ac' ter' in Ballyhit juxta R.; un' mess' et un' caruc' in Yongeston; un' mess' et un' car' in Waddynston; un' mess' et octag' ac' ter' in le Heghton; un' mess' et sexag' acr' in le Moreton; un' mess' et un' car' et vigint' acr' in le Moreton juxta Tyllakenay; un' mess' et duo car' in Cowlmakelan; un' mess' et un' car' in Woolkeenesbagard; un' mess' et sexag' acr', in le Skevyr quæ jacent inter le Vyre Roke et Kylmanan; et duos solidos capitali redditi ex Augean." Dated 1st December, 16 Henry VIII. (1524) " His testibus tunc presentibus, Thomas Furlong, Nicholas Bryan, et Nicholas Hore, cum multis aliis."

By deed of feoffment, dated at Kairgmanan, 4th August, 1539, Philip Furlong, of C., gent., granted to Thomas Rosseter, of Rathmanee, gent., and Sir Walter R., rector of Taghmon, his town and manor of C., with a plowland and a half, containing 180 acres, and gave seisin to them; and the next day, in presence of Patrick Stafford, sovereign of Wexford; Sir Thomas Browne, prebendary of Clone; Nicholas Rochford, recorder of Wexford; and divers others, declared that they should stand seised to the use of Patrick Alen, of Wexford, merchant, and his heirs, for 61 years, from the 30th September, at the yearly rent of two marks and a half; with all casualties, as traces, heriots, wrecks, strays and waifs, with a *prize fish every Wednesday, if it should be taken.*—[Bibl. Egerton, No.

their followers, did take of William St John feloniously 18 salmon, of Powell Turner 7 salmon, in the King's river[a]. And they present that ye said Philip did take feloniously from Ro. Canton a cow with her calfe.

Item, ye said Jury present that ye 6th yeare of said soveraigne lord, Walter Roche, ye sonne of Nicholas, burned feloniously the church of Killpatrick[b] in Rochesland, wherein [were] certain Christian people with much goods.

Item, ye said Jury present that in ye 29th yeare of ye raigne of our soveraigne lord, Sir William Keting, Master of Kilklogan, with his folowers, kept fire in ye steeple doore of St Johns,[c] untill such time as he had out the warde that was within.

Item, ye said Jury present that Hammond Stafford[d] of Balleconnor, gent. tooke William St John feloniously in the King's high-

---

75, p. 220, Brit. Museum.] In 1638, 6th May, James Furlong, Esq., of C., sold his large estate for £2500, to Robert Devereux, Esq.

[a] The right of fishing for salmon in the tideway of the Slaney was and is a public right. Some of the owners of land along the banks of the river owned wicker weirs in the stream. By inquisition, No. 130, Car. I., Thomas Furlong, of Carrigmenan, was found seised of two fish weirs. Sir Henry Wallop, of Enniscorthy, was seised, in right of Selsker Priory, of half the tithe of all fish brought in cots from the country to the parish of St. Peter's, Wexford.—[Inquis. Lageniæ, 1610.]

[b] *Kilpatrick.*—The church of this parish is situated on the north side of the Slaney, over Ferry-Carrig bridge. This church is lately disused. It stands in the fine demesne of Saunders-court, the seat of —— Giles, Esq.

[c] St. John's Hospital stood outside the walls of the town, near St. John's Gate. It was founded in the twelfth century by William Marshall, Earl of Pembroke, for Knights Hospitallers, or of St. John of Jerusalem. Antecedent to the abolition of the Templars, this house, according to Archdall, was the grand commandery of the former Order; but, subsequently, the consequence of this priory gradually diminished, and the preceptory of Kilmainham being granted to the Hospitallers, the latter immediately became the grand commandery of their Order. The Master of Kilclogan Hospital (near the promontory of Hook) may have had some authority with respect to this establishment.

[d] Hamond de Stafford is named among the gentlemen of the county who were summoned in the year 1335 to attend the wars in Scotland.—[Appendix to Grace's Annals.]

This family were formerly distinguished and numerous. Their principal castle was Ballymacarne, in the barony of Forth, which was held by knight's service, in the year 1323, from the Earls of Pembroke.—[Inquis. Tur. London.] The Heraldic Visitation of the county, made in 1618, by Sir Daniel Molyneux, Ulster King-at-Arms, contains a pedigree of the branch of the

way, and imprisoned him in his owne house; and the said Hammond tooke feloniously in ye King's highway from Walter Cooke 3 markes of money, of ye which he made restitution of ye whole summe to ye said Walter Cooke.

Item, they present ye said Hammond did follow Matthias St John, the son of Thomas St John, and did drive him into ye sea; but he was not drowned.

Item, ye said Jury present that Tuesday after Michaelmas day ye 26th yeare of ye raigne of our soveraigne lord, Walter Browne, gent. Tho. Rouseter,[a] gent., Sir Tho. Browne, parson, Rob. Roche, ye son of John oge Roche, with theyr followers, did set fire to ye doore of ye hall of St Patricks feloniously, and brought out ye Master, Keting, and sent him to ward, and ye same day ye said clyents made a varyaunce and so killed one man or two.

Item, ye said Jury present that one John Keting, ye son of

---

[a] The heirs of John and Gregory de Rowcestre held three carucates or ploughlands in Rathmacneeh, anno 1339.—[Inquis. Tur. Lond.] Robert Rowcestre claimed to be patron of Rathmacnee Church, anno 1357.—[Register of All Hallows, p. 67.] John Rowcestre, Esq., was constituted seneschal of the liberty of Wexford by John Talbot Earl of Shrewsbury, 21st Nov., 29 Henry VI., by order dated at Wexford by this celebrated general.—[Cal. Rot. Pat., p. 265.] Thomas Roosetyr was seneschal of the county, 9 Henry VII.—[Mem. Roll. in the Exchequer.] He married Constance Stafford. His son, John Rossiter, Esq., married a daughter of Sir Nicholas Devereux, Knt., and died in 1586. Colonel Thomas R., of Rathmackne, is said to have married a sister of the famous Sarsfield, and to have been drowned in going to France, in the year 1690. In Clarke's life of James the Second, " Colonel Rossiter in Lincolnshire," is mentioned as one of the principal royalists after the death of Cromwell. Rathmacnee Castle is one of the most perfect of the castellated dwellings remaining in the county.

family that resided at Ballyconnor, in the same barony. The first named is Hamond, whose descendant in the fourth generation, Dionysius, married Anastace Berkeley; their son, Hamond, married a daughter of Fitz-Henry, baron of Kilkevan. His son built the tower which still stands, as shown by a stone in the wall above the door of the hall or principal apartment, bearing this inscription:—

Dionisius Stafford de Baliconor et Katerina Sinot uxor eius 1510 [query 1570?] struxerint hanc dom.

His wife was daughter of Simon Sinot of Ballygeary. He died in 1579.—[Inquis. Excheq.] His son, Hamond Stafford, Esq., died in 1630. "The homage, fealty, and escuage of the inheritor of Moche and Little Ballyconnor, &c., were due to the manor of Ballymackarne."—[Printed Inquisitions.]

Philip Keeting, did put hand violently to bring sir Richard Kinay out of our Lady church; and then he was rescoused, and so upon that he was restored.

Item, yᵉ said Jury present that one John, Bishop of Fernes, sir William Keting, Master of Kilklogan, and theyr followers, tooke in yᵉ King's highway feloniously Thomas Turner, John Forthlaw, John Stafford, John Sᵗ John, and imprisoned them in yᵉ Bishop's prison.

Item, yᵉ same Jury present that Rob. Hoore of Harperston[a] took Patrick Lyng and Patrick Mok feloniously, and so imprisoned them in irons, to theyr costs and damages of 40ˢ and more. And yᵉ said Ro. Hoore tooke feloniously of Tho. Sennett, husbandman, of yᵉ parish of Thomhagger, in kye and plough horses to yᵉ value of 12 marks.

Item, yᵉ said Jury present that yᵉ suffreyn and comyns of yᵉ Towne of Wexford kept fire to the doore of yᵉ steeple of Sᵗ Johns for to fett out a thyef that made escape out of yᵉ towne gaole.

Item, they present that yᵉ most part of yᵉ Towne of Wexford doe buy and sell with Irishmen in peace time, as all other citties and townes of Ireland doth.

Item, they present that they know no provision but what bules[b] been put into yᵉ chancellor's hands.

Item, they present that yᵉ curates of yᵉ countrey out townes do accustom to receave 6d. at weddings time, and 2d. at purification; and also find that yᵉ curates doth take 5s. of men's wives when they die.

Item, they present that Wadding[c] of Ballycogly and his son Richard forceably entered on Nicholas Wadding's lands of Waterford, that is to say Boryasses towne and yᵉ Fassath.

---

[a] Robert Hore, of Harperstown, was eldest son of David (see p. 46). There was an inquisition taken, 1 Edward VI., on the extent of his lands.—[Index to Inq. in Chief Rem. Off., MS., T.C.D., E. 3, 4.] William, his second brother, succeeded him in 1547, and was knight of the shire in the Parliament of 1559.—[Lynch's Feudal Dignities, p. 345.]

By inquisition taken 12 Eliz., he was seised of the castle and lands of Harperstown, held of Roche of Drinagh; of the castle and lands of Taghmon, held of the Queen; and of other lands.—[Inquis. Exchequer.]

[b] i. e. Papal provisions and bulls.

[c] David Wadding was sheriff of the county. temp. Hen. V.—[Rot. Pat.

Item, ye said Jury present that ye hole Burgage is 12d. by the yere, which burgage mounteth to ye sum of xvii score 5 and a ¼ of a burgage. Some of this burgage holdeth by patients, some by ostlacheis,^{a} some by hospitall, more 3s. 3d. for bredwyk and alewyk, 40s. for killing of flesh, and 3s. 4d. for the nerreley; and one quarter of beef to ye constable^b every week once for 9^d betweene Martinmas and Christmas, a quarter of mutton every weeke ones between May and the feast of St Michaell for 1d. And this beefe and mutton to be received of strange bouchers that come to the markett.^{c}

p. 233.] The pedigree of Wadding of Ballycogly is entered in the Visitation, anno 1618. Thomas Wadding, then of Ballycogly, was one of the knights of the shire in 1613: he married Margaret, daughter of John Eustace, Esq., of Castlemartin. The branch of this family that resided in Waterford were frequently mayors of this city. On the restoration, the estate of Mr. Thomas Wadding, of Waterford, at Kilbarry, which is styled by Bishop French in the "Unkinde Deserter" "a delicious place," and then worth £1000 a year, was bestowed on Sir George Lane.

^{a} By "Ostlachies," here, is perhaps meant "Owelty," a tenure by which the tenant is bound to pay the same services to the "mesn," or middle-man, as the latter owes to the lord-paramount.

^{b} Probably the constable of Wexford Castle.

^{c} This verdict exhibits the remarkable distinctness that existed, at the time it was drawn up, between the English of the south of Wexfordshire (the district they called "the King's land"), and the Celtic inhabitants of the northern parts of the county. This distinctness had been judiciously fostered by the famous Statute of Kilkenny, which was framed to prevent any such intercourse between the colonists and the invaded clans as had proved destructive to the interests of the former people. It was still penal to hold an Irishwoman to wife, because, obviously, a Una ny Kavanagh, or a Sheela ny Byrne, retained, with her mother tongue, the same affection for her kinsfolk as Delilah (the "heifer" with whom the Philistines "ploughed") to the ensnarers of her husband, Samson. By the laws of the Scottish border, the townsmen of Berwick, Newcastle, &c., were inhibited from furnishing the enemy with armour and weapons, and all articles that would serve the foe during war. And similar provisions were providently introduced into the statute restricting the trade with the Irish borderers. Our Wexford merchants of the time in question, however, acted, either clandestinely or openly, in the spirit of the Dutch admiral, who freely sold gunpowder to the opposing squadron.

The violent attack made by the Bishop of Ferns on some of the townspeople of Fethard is capable of explanation as probably a lawless endeavour to coerce some refractory servants to acknowledge him as their rent-lord. It seems that, during those anarchal times, any aggrieved squire, and even this prelate, brought in the aid of some mountain leader of savage kernes to further his designs, as unscrupulously

COMPLAINTES.

To ye right worshipfull the King's high Commissioners.

Grievously complaining sheweth unto your discreet wisdomes your daylie orator Walt. Devereux of ye parish of Kylkevan in the King's land, husbandman, how Thomas Roche, ye sonne of —— Roche, servant unto Rob. Roche son of John oge Roche, came the 12th day of June this present yeare, and did stele from your said complainant 3 plough horses and a hobby, which cannot be denied; for it is proved upon ye said Thomas by ye arbitrement of Hammond Stafford and of Walter Devereux, gentlemen; but this notwithstanding your said complainant cannot have restitution of his said goods of ye said Robert, nor of his said servant. Wherefore your complainant beseecheth your discreet wisdomes of remedy in ye premises; and this for the love of God and in ye way of charity.

This said Bill is found to be true by the Verdict aforesaid.

To ye right worshipful the King's high Commissioners.

Greeviously complaining sheweth unto your discreet wisdomes your daylie orator John Furlong, ye son of Michaell Furlong, how that Sir Fowke Furlong, brother unto ye said complainant's fader, was seized as well in his demesne as of fee of 20 plough land in the Barony of Camross in the Fassath of Bantre, and so died seised

as Fergus M'Ivor employed a clan underling, a captain of thieves, to seize the Baron of Bradwardine's cows. The feudal towers of the rural lords were used (to compare small things with great), like the castles of the robber chiefs on the Rhine, for the incarceration of wealthy wayfarers, insubmissive peasants, and dunning townsmen. Even churches were not always sanctuaries, although it was boasted that they had been so, legally and practically, prior to the invasion, and though fear and hope long caused them to be made use of as asylums, to which the country people conveyed themselves and their goods during hostile incursions.

We believe that much of the extreme disorder in the English portion of Wexford can be accounted for by the fact that their country was a palatinate. Again, its lords, the Earls of Shrewsbury, were absentees, so that the administration of law in all its forms was delegated to functionaries who either could or did not fulfil their duties with sufficient rigour to overawe the rude squirearchy and aristocracy of warlike ages. The English interest and power had sunk to its lowest ebb at the period under review, and many causes combined to make the work of social reformation a truly herculean task for the politician.

this present yeare; after whose death your said complaynant, as heyre unto y͏ᵉ said Sir Fowke in y͏ᵉ premises, would have entered, but that notwithstanding, John Furlong, the sonne of William Furlong of y͏ᵉ Hortowne, violently with force and armes, without any title of right do interrupt trouble and vex daily your said complaynant that he cannot brouke nor injoy his said inheritance according to right and conscience. Wherefore your said orator beseecheth your discreet wisdomes of a remedy in y͏ᵉ premises; and this for y͏ᵉ love of God and for charitie.

This bill is found to be true by y͏ᵉ Verdict aforesaid.

To y͏ᵉ right worshipful the King's high Commissioners.

Complaining sheweth unto your discreet wisdomes your true and faithful servant and daily orator James Turner, Burges of y͏ᵉ Towne of Wexford, how that his father Patrick Turner was seised as well in his demeane as of fee of 26 acres of land with their appurtenances in and about y͏ᵉ towne of Gracormock in y͏ᵉ manor of Ballymore, by deed of coppyhold conserning y͏ᵉ same, and thereof died seised; after whose descase your orator in y͏ᵉ premises did enter and peacably did broke and enjoy the same lands, till such time as one Philip Keteing of Baldynstone, gent. violently with force and armes the 20th day of August in y͏ᵉ 22^{d} yeare of y͏ᵉ raigne of our soveraigne lord King Henry y͏ᵉ 8th in y͏ᵉ premises did enter, and so kept y͏ᵉ said lands by force during y͏ᵉ space of 2 yeares, to your said complainant's costs and damages of £40 and more; whereof your complainant beseech your discreet wisdomes of remedy in y͏ᵉ premises, and this for y͏ᵉ love of God and for charity.

THE VERDICT OF Y^e INHABITANTS OF Y^B TOWNE OF ROSS.

[*October*, 1537.—*MS. State Paper Office.*]

WALTER HYDE.	JAMES WHITE.	NICH. GREGORY.
THO. BUTLER.	JOHN BENNETT.	WILL. BENNETT.
JAMES TRAVES.	WILL. FRANCON.	LAUR. COLLE.
JOHN CONWAY.	ROB. ARCHER.	ROB. SARY.
PIERSE FITZHARRIS.	ROB. CONSCIENCE.	LAW. NEVILLE.
PIERS M^{c}FYN.	THO. ROCHE.	JOHN FITZ GEOFFREY.
JOHN LEYNAR.	PYERS YOUNG.	

First, ye said Jury present that Thomas Byrton, which was attainted for treason, had at ye time of his death of his owne proper purchase within the franchises of Rosse, 12 acres of arable land which perteineth to our Soveraine Lord ye King that now is, by reason of ye said attainder. And one Walter Archer hath eight of ye said acres in morgage. And ye said Jury present that Nicholas Byrton had in his possession at his death within ye Towne of Rosse 16 messuages of Growne and Culverhouse, one conygre^a lying on ye east part of ye water of ye King's Mill, and of 6 acres parkes of Growne, 1 parke containing 4 acres within the franchises aforesaid; and of 13 acres errable land lying within ye franchises aforesaid; and of one acre of land called Palmeris cerrean; and of one acre of land and a windmill, now being wast, upon ye same, lying within ye said franchises adjoining to ye said conygre, conteyning by estimation 7 acres of errable land, lying to ye ground of Mongarratt, within ye liberty aforesaid, conteyning 6 acres of land errable; and of one messuage in Fydart^b in ye county of Wexford; and of one acre of land lying be south of ye Mole Castle;^{c} and 2 acres land lying to Byrton's great oke, conteyning 4 acres.

---

^{a} A rabbit-warren.

^{b} *Fethard.*—One of the earliest built towns of the Anglo-Norman colony in Wexford. Its castle belonged to the See of Ferns.

^{c} The "Mole Castle" may either have been a tower built on a mole or pier in the river, or may be that which gave the name to "Castle Moyle," a small townland in the neighbourhood.

Item, they present that there is 2 mills with y{e} appurtenances, now being waste, lying within y{e} lyberty aforesaid, and adjoining upon y{e} water of y{e} Castle[a] perteineth to y{e} King, and another mill also, which M{c}Arte[b] made waste.

Item, y{e} said Jury present that the Ferry[c] and y{e} meadowes of Rosse perteineth to y{e} King, the Commons of y{e} said Towne paying to the King 10s. yearly for y{e} Ferry and 5s. for y{e} meadowes.

Item, y{e} said Jury present that one Walter Oke Walsh[d] of y{e} county of Kilkenny do usurp upon y{e} King's possessions of a place called y{e} Stone-house, with the appurtenances, which was found to be the King's by inquisition in times past.

Item, y{e} said Jury present that y{e} lands of John Keiting be escheated to y{e} King, as by inquisition made before this time appeareth.

Item, they present that 3 acres of land lying within y{e} Lyberty aforesaid by Fosterford being escheated to y{e} King.

Item, they present that Scarcynicoll, containing 40 acres, lying within y{e} franchises aforesaid, is escheated to the King, as appeareth by inquisition made before this time.

Item, they present that one Robert Roche, y{e} son of John Roche of y{e} county of Wexford, did this present yeare, contrary to y{e} King's peace, cut off y{e} hand of one David Duffe, mariner of Rosse aforesaid.

Item, they present that Nicholas Roche, then being Seneschall of the county of Wexford, with divers nations of the said county,

---

[a] The charter to Dunbrody Abbey, dated April 1, 1233, given by Richard Marshall Earl of Pembroke, is dated at the castle of Ross.—[Add. MS. 4787, Brit. Mus.] This fortress, which was situated at the place now called Old Ross, must have been a considerable one, has shared the fate of Wexford Castle, and also of that built at Ferry-Carrig on the site of the entrenchment so well contested by the first invader, Fitz-Stephen. Two very curious gourgoyles, or water-spouts, of the Norman period were some time since dug up on the site of the castle of Old Ross, and are now in the Museum of the Kilkenny Archæological Society.

[b] Mac-Art; i.e. the son of Art; one of the clan Kavanagh.

[c] This would seem to show that the old bridge erected by William Marshall Earl of Pembroke, and which gave to the town the ancient name of Ross-pont, or "Nova villa pontis Willielmi Marescalli," had long while disappeared.

[d] Probably one of the Walshes of the Walsh Mountains, who had also possessions in Wexfordshire.

that is to say yᵉ Keitings,ᵃ Suttons,ᵇ Furlongs,ᶜ Hores,ᵈ Hays,ᵉ Fitz-Henrys, Devereux', Synnotts,ᶠ and Nevilles,ᵍ have feloniously taken away with force and armes from yᵉ commons and burgesses of yᵉ towne of Rosse aforesaid a 100 kine 1000 sheep, 40 plough-horses and 2 hackneys, and tooke 6 men of yᵉ Towne aforesaid prisoners with them, for pledge of ransom to be made, of yᵉ which as yet they have had no recompence.

Item, they present that Nicholas Horeʰ of Harperston, with

ᵃ The Keatings were one of the principal Strongbonian families of the county of Wexford. Baldwin and Robert Keting are witnesses to the charter of William Marshall, Earl of Pembroke, to Tintern Abbey. The eldest house had the title of Barons Keating of Kilcowan. Their descent is given in the Heraldic Visitation of the county, anno 1618.

ᵇ Sir Roger de Sutton is one of the witnesses to the charter of William Marshall, Earl of Pembroke, to Dunbrody Abbey.—[Cal. Rot. Pat. Hib., p. 175.]

Ballykeroge, a castle of unusual dimensions, in "Sutton's Parish," near Ross, was their chief house. Junior branches lived at Old Court, Ballysop, and Priestshaggard. We were told by Mr. Sutton, late of Clonmines, then (1849) an aged man, that it was traditionally handed down in his family, that Ballykeroge Castle, having withstood the Parliamentary forces, was fired, and twenty-three of the name of Sutton therein consumed,—two only escaping.

ᶜ The Furlong family were numerous. They first came to Ireland from a place of that name in Devonshire. Eleven gentlemen bearing it were summoned in 1345 to attend the military expedition of that year against O'Brien. Their chief house was Horetown, near Taghmon. John Furlong was knight of the shire in 1613, and owned the manors of Camross and Bridgestown, &c.— [Printed Inquis. Lageniæ.] Another branch owned the manor of Carrigmenan, which they sold in 1635 to the Devereux family. The pedigree of the line that resided at Davidstown, in the Glynn, is given in the Visitation, anno 1618.

ᵈ The principal families of this name were of Pole-Hore and Harperstown. The descent of each of these two lines is given for eleven generations in the Heraldic Visit. of the county, anno 1618.

ᵉ The Hays were a barony of Forth family, and owned the Towers of Hill, Slade, Tacumshene, &c.,—and Castlehaystown, in Bantry.

ᶠ The Sinnotts grew to be the most numerous race of gentry in the county. Their chief house was Ballybrennan, in Forth. They also owned "Sinnottsland," a large tract from Castlebridge to the sea, which had been granted them in the thirteenth century.— [Printed Calendar of Patent Rolls, 15 James I.]

ᵍ Sir Geoffry Neville is one of the witnesses to the Charter to Waterford, dated 1205.—[Chartæ Privileg. Hib., p. 14.] The Nevilles were Barons of Roscarlan, now called Rosegarland.

ʰ He was elder brother of David (see page 46), and married first a Kavanagh, secondly, Joan, daughter of

certeine others with him of y̆ᵉ said countrye of Rosse, and Furlongs, robbed certain men of yᵉ towne of Rosse in a place called Beallugh, being in a boote[a] of the said countrey, yᵉ yeare aforesaid.

Item, they present that about 12 yeares past one Hamond Stafford and his company, then being with him, of yᵉ said country of Rosse, drowned three men with yᵉ boat and yᵉ goods of the Towne aforesaid, by a creek called Ballythick in yᵉ same county, whose names here ensueth; that is to say Thomas Somry, John Britton, and John Morsoo.

Item, they present that one Fitz-Harry that now is, of Kilkevan, robbed yᵉ Towne of Rosse, and killed a man within the Lyberties of the said towne.

Item, the said Jury present that yᵉ said Fitz-Harry that now is, the 13ᵗʰ yeare of yᵉ raigne of our Soveraigne Lord, did take a pray[b] to the some and valew of £100.

Item, the said Jury present that Lamport[c] of Ballyhire in yᵉ county of Wesford, did take James Kent prisoner, and tooke from him feloniously £8.

Item, they present that James Keiting of the county of Wesford feloniously did take one plough horse from Richard Walsh of the said town with certain plough irons and other goods.

Item, yᵉ said Jury present that about 3 years past John Sutton's son of Prysteshagard feloniously did take from Joane Brent and Patrick Cully 7s. 8d. in ready money.

Item, they present that Gilbert Sutton of yᵉ county of Wexford feloniously did take from Piers Harry of yᵉ said towne of Rosse 60 sheep of yᵉ goods and chattalls of yᵉ said Piers contrary to yᵉ King's peace.

Item, they present that yᵉ said Gilbert feloniously did take from

---

Thomas Hay, of Killiane; and thirdly, a daughter of Edmond Walsh, by whom he had a son, Edmond, who was slain by his uncle.—[Visitation of Wexford.]

[a] "Boote" probably signifies a pass, or booter.

[b] "Prey" signifies the booty taken in creagh, or foray; the term, as well as the practice, is obsolete.

[c] Lamport, now Lambert, a Pembrokeshire family that came over with Strongbow. Hugh de Lamport was bishop of Ferns in 1258. Their pedigree is entered in the Heraldic Visitation of Wexford, taken in 1618, by the Ulster King of Arms. Their principal residence was at Ballyhire, near Greenore.

divers other persons of the said county unknowen 100 sheep contrary to the Kinge's peace.

Item, ye said Jury present that John Sutton and William Sutton of Ballykeroke did aid and securre ye said Gilbert in taking of ye said sheep from ye said persons unknown.

Item, they present that Patrick, John Roche and his sonnes wounding of Richard Walsh and John Boy of ye said towne contrary to the King's peace.

Item, they present that Patrick, John Roche his sonne, feloniously did take from Piers Morelowe of ye said towne of Rosse 3 kye, and from Piers Harrys 40 sheep contrary to ye King's lawes; and they present that John Sutton was receivor and maintainer of ye said Patrick and John in ye said doings.

Item, they find that Care McArte^a and his company did kill a man of ye said towne of Rosse within ye gates, and also wounded the porter.

Item, they present that Care McArte, Edmond Kevenagh, Dowling Kevanagh, and Edmond McOone, with other of theyre company, did kill Nicholas Fitz-Harris and Patrick Chevyr^b within the franchises and without the gates of ye said towne.

Item, ye said Jury present that Geffrey McSavage, Cahre McArte's servant, feloniously contrary to ye King's peace did sley one William Coskyer upon ye King's river.

Item, they present that ye said Cahyr McArte and Edm. McOone feloniously contrary to ye King's peace did kill Richard Sutton of Ballekerok and Richard Prendergast^c within the said franchises.

Item, they present that ye said Cahyr McArte and Cahyr Car-

---

^{a} Caher, son of Art, chief of the Kavanaghs of Poulononty.

^{b} Chievers is the name of a Flemish family which settled at an early time in the country. William Chevre is one of the witnesses to the charter to Tintern Abbey.—[Chartæ, &c., IIib.] Patrick Chievre held a knight's fee of the Earl of Pembroke, and witnessed this nobleman's charter to Wexford in 1317. Edward Cheevers was created Viscount Mount-Leinster by James II.

^{c} A branch of this family owned Ballyfernoch, near Ross; and mortgaged Stokestown in 1582 to George Dormer, Justice of the Liberties of the county, and author of the "ballad-royal" called "The Decay of Ross."—[Cal. Rot. Pat. James I., p. 62.] In 1482 Margaret Prendergast, widow, demised her estate in Ross, except three houses, and in Kilkenny, to St. Mary's church, in the former town.—[Bibl. Egerton, Brit. Mus. MS. No. 75, p. 175.]

rogh, Bryan McDonough and Edmond Kevenagh, with theyr followers, feloniously and contrary to ye King's peace, did kill one of ye King's souldiers named Clerke, and one Thomas Roche, yeoman of the said town of Rosse; and also did take Walter Archer and Will. Bennett, Henry Coulen, Robert Lorkenane, John Lenaghe, and John Welsh, prisoners for fyne and ransom to be made.

Item, they present that ye said Cahyr McArte, Care Carraghe[a], and Bryan McDonogh did take in pray from ye commons of ye said towne of Rosse to ye number of 7 score kye and plough horses, and 1000 sheep, with other small beastes.

Item, they present that Cahyr McArte, Cahyr Carraghe, and Bryan McDonogh feloniously did take from certain persons of ye said commons of ye said town of Ross, certain corn, clothis, and other things out of ye King's mill, to ye value of £10.

Item, they present that ye said persons feloniously did take from Walter Archer his plough, and from John Leynagh his boat, and 8s. in ready money, and ye said John sore wounded, the healing whereof cost 16s. The said persons took from John Walsh 10s. in money.

Item, they present that Edmond Kevanagh, and Geralt McArte, James McMorrough, and Donyll Reagh, the said Geralt's son, and Maloghlin O'Ryan, do take excessive customes of all such boates as goeth to Carlow and Athy with wares and merchandizes of ye men of ye town of Rosse aforesaid, to ye value of £20 yearly above ye old customes[b].

Item, they present that ye said Geralt McArte did take from Thomas Caffye a pipe of Spanish wyne and certain iron, figgs, raisons, and other goods, to the sum of 20 marks.

Item, they present that ye said Edmund Kevanagh and Gerralt McArte did take from one Lawr. Clole with force and armes certaine goods upon ye river of ye King's to ye value of £10.

Item, ye said Jury present that Cayre McMorroughe with force and armes did take from Nich. Archer of y^e towne aforesaid 12 swyne.

Item, they present that Dowling Kavanagh about y^e 18th yeare of y^e raigne of our said soveraine Lord did take from the inhabitants

---

[a] *Carragh* is a Gaelic nickname, signifying *the scald*.

[b] These must have been customs exacted by the clan Kavanagh.

of y\ :sup:`e` said towne of Rosse a pray of kye and caplles to y\ :sup:`e` valew of 20 marks.

Item, y\ :sup:`e` said Jury present that about y\ :sup:`e` 23\ :sup:`d` yeare of y\ :sup:`e` raigne of our Sovereign Lord that Geralt Carrogh M\ :sup:`c`\ Dowling Kavanagh hath taken 14 kye and 2 caplles.

Item, y\ :sup:`e` said Jury present that Arte Boye, Geralt Kavanagh's son, contrary to y\ :sup:`e` King's lawes, in y\ :sup:`e` 22\ :sup:`nd` yeare of the reigne of our soveraigne Lord did take 12 kye.

Item, y\ :sup:`e` said Jury present that Donogh Kavanagh, M\ :sup:`c`\ Morogh Kavenagh, Cahyr M\ :sup:`c`\ Arte and Edmond Kavanagh's followers, did take forceably contrary to y\ :sup:`e` King's peace 23 kye and 100 sheep, with certaine clothes, purses, and ready money, to y\ :sup:`e` sum and value of 100s. in y\ :sup:`e` 22\ :sup:`nd` yeare of y\ :sup:`e` raigne of our Soveraine Lord.

Item, they present that M\ :sup:`c`\ Juyne Owkaye Kavenagh, M\ :sup:`c`\ Donogh Kavanagh M\ :sup:`c`\ Guyre Arte boy is sonne's brethren to Morrertagh M\ :sup:`c`\ Arte boy Kavanagh, forceably did take contrary to y\ :sup:`e` King's lawes 26 kye and caplles in y\ :sup:`e` said year and raigne of our soveraigne Lord.

Item, they present that Cahyr M\ :sup:`c`\ Garylt Kavanagh of y\ :sup:`e` Rowre his servant did forceably take, contrary to y\ :sup:`e` King's lawes in the 29\ :sup:`th` year of his raigne, the number of 50 head of cattle, that is to say in sheep, goates, swyne and other beasts.

Item, they present that Gerylt M\ :sup:`c`\ Donogh Kavanagh of y\ :sup:`e` Rowre forceably and contrary to y\ :sup:`e` King's lawes did spoyle and take from Thomas Roche and Robert Archer, John Leynagh, and divers other inhabitants of y\ :sup:`e` said towne of Rosse, certaine goods and ready money to y\ :sup:`e` valew and sum of £40.

Item, y\ :sup:`e` said Jury present that Edmond M\ :sup:`c`\ Donyll Kavanagh of y\ :sup:`e` Rowre forceably and contrary to the King's peace and lawes did in y\ :sup:`e` 26\ :sup:`th` year of our soveraine Lord take from Thomas Carpenter of y\ :sup:`e` said towne of Rosse 3 bushells of mault 1 bushell of wheat and certain lynen cloth to y\ :sup:`e` value of 26s. 8d.

Item, y\ :sup:`e` said Jury present that Morrertagh Mackdermeth Kavanagh of y\ :sup:`e` Earle's wood did take contrary to y\ :sup:`e` King's lawes from Robert Consyence of y\ :sup:`e` towne of Rosse one hackney price £4, and certaine corne to y\ :sup:`e` value of 20s. in y\ :sup:`e` 23 yeare of y\ :sup:`e` raine of our soverayne Lord.

Item, y\ :sup:`e` said Jury present that Geralt Kavanagh's two sons, with theyr servants Morrogh bagkaghe M{c}Geralt M{c}Arte in 29{th} year of our soveraigne Lord, did take from James White's servante, of the said towne of Rosse, y{e} value of 4 marks, and wounded 2 of y{e} said James White's servants.

Item, y{e} same Jury present that M{c}Morrough that now is, contrary to y{e} King's peace & his lawes, did take from one Thomas Roche of y{e} said towne, silk, saffron, and ready money to y{e} valew of 40s. and deteyned y{e} said Thomas in prison with irons, to his great costs and charges for y{e} Termon,[a] the w{ch} was made frustrate and void in y{e} 28{th} yeare of our soveraine Lord.

Item, they present that y{e} 11{th} yeare of the raigne of our said soveraine Lord, Edmond fitz John Butler of y{e} county of Kilkenny, and Morrogh M{c}Arte, with divers others of their adherents take prey of kye to y{e} numbre of 27 and 100 small beasts, from y{e} inhabitants of y{e} said towne of Rosse.

Item, they present that Thomas Richards M{c}Edmund of y{e} said county of certaine persons of y{e} towne of Waterford, that is to say Peirse Dobyn and others, did take Thomas Butler of y{e} towne of Rosse, burgesse, prisoner.

Item, they present that Edmond Bagath[b] Pursell, Edm. Duffe M{c}Awley, Shane Roche, Mares Dermort O'Bryan, and Shane Begg, of y{e} county of Kilkenny, contrary to the King's peace, and in the king's highway, tooke from W{m} Bennett of y{e} towne of Rosse aforesaid his horse, 8s. in money, a mantle and sword, and kept him prisoner the space of 12 months in [   ] Richard Tobyn, and then ransomed him to y{e} sum of £10.

Item, y{e} said Jury present that Teage O'Douan, with divers others of my Lord of Ossory's servants, at y{e} said Lord Ossory's instance, he then being present, did take one Piers Bray of the said towne of Rosse, burgesse, out of his house, in y{e} 23{d} yeare of y{e} raigne of our soveraigne Lord King H. 8.

Item, y{e} same Jury present that on Easter-day in y{e} morning, y{e} 24{th} year of y{e} raigne of our soveraigne Lord, Edm. M{c}Shygh, Edm. Tangath, Donogh O'Dowle, and knowhowre,[c] my Lord of

---

[a] Termon is a Gaelic term, apparently meaning *free land*.
[b] Bacach, i. e. lame.
[c] Cnochor, or Connor.

Ossory's servants, with divers others, did contrary to ye King's peace and lawes, take Thomas Bennett, and drew him from Thomas Roche's house within ye said towne, with hue and cry.

Item, they present that in ye 21st year of ye raigne of our soveraigne Lord, W^m McShane McPhillip, of ye Great Iland, and Edmond McDowle, did take from ye inhabitants of ye said towne of Rosse 18 kine.

Item, they present that in ye 17th yeare of ye raigne of our soveraigne Lord, Edm: McShane Reagh Butler did take from James Travys, burgesse of ye towne of Rosse, 2 kye, at Baily duff in ye county of Kilkenny.

Item, ye said Jury present that Donyll Kavenagh, McMorrogh's brother, did take from Lawr. Clolle, of Rosse, a pipe of Spaynes wyne, 2 quarters of salt, 200 iron, and dicker of leather, at ye bridge of Lethelyn;^{a} and one Monygay, ye warder of ye said Lethelyn,

---

^{a} *Leighlin Castle.*—The dates when this castle and the bridge were erected, and the object in re-edifying the fortress, are stated in the following records. The Memorandum Roll of the Exchequer, 13 & 14 Eliz., contains the enrolment of an inquisition taken at Leighlin, which sets forth that King John, when in Ireland, built the "Black Castle" within the precincts of Leighlin, and also the Bridge: that one Murgh Ballagh Kavanagh, [King of the Leinster clans, who died in 1511] seeing the said castle to be ruinous, repaired it, endowed it with two ploughlands, and appointed constables to keep it: that the fortress then remained eighty years in the possession of the Kavanaghs and their constables: that its precinct is twenty-three yards eastward, and twenty-six yards southward: that Piers Butler, grandfather of the Earl of Ormond, expulsed Donald Doyling Kavanagh out of all the same; and that James Butler, Piers' son and heir, entered into possession of it, and so continued thirty years; when the Lord Deputy, Sir Edward Bellingham, took possession of it for her majesty. There is an order in the Council-book for the reimbursal of Thomas, Earl of Ormond, for the land on which the castle was built; it being his estate, and taken by the Earl of Sussex during his minority, at the time Leix and Offaly were being colonized, in order to protect the colonists. It is also stated in the Memorandum Roll of 10, 11, & 12 Eliz., that Sir Peter Carew was about settling English colonists upon his lately recovered barony of Idrone; and he prayed to have a grant in fee of the Queen's castle of Leighlin, which he had left for a year and three quarters without any wages; but his request was refused, "it being a place specially chosen and fortified heretofore upon the first eviction of Leix and Offally, and always thought meet to remain at our command. Given at Oatlands, 1st June, 1570."—[Communicated by the late lamented J. F. Ferguson, Esq., from records in his custody in the Court of Exchequer.]

heth taken for custome contrary to ye King's lawes, 20s. in ye 26th yeare of ye raigne of our soveraigne Lord King H. 8.

Item, they present that ye 24th yeare of ye raigne of our soveraigne Lord, my Lord of Ossory was convicted in a riott by verdict of 12 men for forceable entry into a house of one Joanne Dobbyn, widow, within ye said towne of Rosse.

Item, ye said Jury present that ye 16th yeare of ye raigne of our soveraigne Lord, James Brenagh with his company, contrary to ye King's lawes and against his peace, wilfully did slay one John Caffry of ye said towne, and at that time wounded Patrick Branan and others of ye said towne, in the King's river.

Item, they present that Will Brenagh, Shane Brenaghe's sonne, and James Brenaghe for ye space of 2 or 3 yeares continually, they robbed and spoyled every man, contrary to ye King's lawes, in ye King's highway, and upon ye river, to their hindrances and costs of £40.

Item, they present that Gilbert Dobbyn of [   ] doth wrongfully withhold from Robert Conscience of ye towne of Rosse 1 parke of land, the wch in ye burgage of Thomstowne.

Item, ye said Jury present that Walter Moore Blodaze, Walter Brenagh's servant and horsegroom, feloniously and contrary to ye King's peace did take in ye King's highway from Will Serman and John Taylor of Rosse 24s. in ready money, besides other things.

Item, they present that Shane Brenagh, Walter Brenagh's^a son, did take from Nich Gregorie's maid of ye said towne 2s. 1d. and a sack price 2s., in ye King's highway at Barcon, within the county of Kilkenny, in ye 25th yeare of our soveraigne Lord.

Item, they present that Phill. Coyne, Walter Brenagh's groom, contrary to ye King's lawes, did take from Rob. Archer of ye towne of Rosse in the King's highway [at] hodds grove^b a sword price 3s. 4d., a mantle, and 22d. in money.

Item, they present that ye soveraigne, burgesses, and portriffes of Rosse for the time being holdeth their burgages of growne and and of ye towne of Rosse of ye Erldom of March,^c ye which now

---

[a] Brenagh *alias* Walsh. Walter Walsh, the head of the Kilkenny sept of that name, signs a document of this period as one of the "gentlemen" of the county.—[MSS., Kilkenny Castle.]

[b] A townland in the county of Kilkenny, not far from Rosbercon.

[c] It is not known how the Seigniory of Ross could have come to the Earl of March. Mortimer, Earl of March and

is in the King's hands, and so it is now holden of our soveraine Lord, paying ye chiefe rents thereof due and accustomed; ye which chief rent our said soveraigne Lord hath granted unto ye said soveraigne and portgrieves and burgesses, and confirmed ye same to them and to theyr successors for ever, without any account rendring to any of ye King's ministers of ye same.

Item, they present that coyne and livery is used in ye county of Kilkenny, Shirebryn, Fassagh-Bentre, and in ye villages without this towne, by ye lords, freeholders, and gentlemen of ye said shire and followers.

Item, they present that Curates take money for theyr reseavor of purification, that is to say 6d. to ye priest and clerke for every

Ulster, inherited a third part of the Liberty of Kilkenny, by right of descent, from Elizabeth, third daughter and coheiress of Gilbert de Clare, Earl of Gloucester and Hereford, Lord of the Liberty of Kilkenny, whose ancestor, Gilbert de Clare, had married one of the daughters of William Earl Mareschal, and so inherited Kilkenny, as the Earls of Norfolk had acquired the Liberty of Wexford through another daughter, and so were lords of Ross. It may be that the townsmen, having felt the evil results arising from their municipality not being recognised as a royal town, thought by this finding to establish their right to the King's protection, as the Earldom of March was, by the extinction of the Mortimer line, at this time in the crown.

The decay of Ross as a port-town had in a great measure arisen from the greater Royal favour shown to Waterford. Henry the Third, in the 14th year of his reign, reciting that his lieges of Waterford had showed to him that merchant vessels frequented the port of Ross, which belonged to William Earl of Mareschal, to the great loss and detriment of the King's city of Waterford, orders the Archbishop of Dublin, then Justiciary of Ireland, to prevent all vessels from putting into the former port, except such as were accustomed to frequent the same before the Baron's Wars.—[Chartæ Privilegiæ, &c., p. 21.] Ross, which was then, as appears by the Customs Returns in the Irish Pipe Rolls, the most flourishing port in Ireland, did not submit to this mandate; for we find the citizens of Waterford, in the 51st year of the same king, complaining that their rivals had, *vi et armis*, compelled to discharge at Ross vessels that intended to put into Waterford. An inquisition was made the same year, and the jurors found that the charge was true; and further declared on their oaths that, since the conquest of Ireland, all ships except those which belonged to the Liberty of the Earl Mareschal, Lord of Leinster, or his heirs, were accustomed to put into the port of Waterford, and not into that of Ross.—[Id., p. 31.] Whereon the King's son, Edward, then Lord of Ireland, issued, in the 52nd year of his father's reign, a mandate ordering proclamation to be made throughout the entire of Leinster, to the effect that no ships, except those that were of the land belonging to the heirs of Walter de Maday of purification. And that ye Curates taken for every wedding 8d. for them and ye clerke.

Item, they present that Edm. Kavanagh of ye Rowre did take from Patrick Dolene of ye said towne, 10s. in money and certaine wares to ye valew of 15s.

Item, they present that my Lord of Ossory wrongfully doth withhold a village called Voocchey in ye county of Kilkenny with the appurtenances, which is one Walter Archer's of Ross.

Item, they present that the citizens of Waterford retayneth of one James Traves, burges of Ross, a ton of wyne called Robbedavy for a weder boote, and from Thomas Tally xiv pipes of Spayne's wyne, and one of Ratfey; from Robert Lorkevan two tons, from Will. Keteyng six tons Spayne's wyne; from Nicholas Gregory one ton Robbedavy; from Walter Hide one pype Robbedavy; from Robert Nevill one ton Robbedavy.[a]

Item, they present that a ballinger called y^e "Trinity of Rosse" was taken with certain persons in her, and brought to ye kaye at reschal, late Earl of Pembroke, in Leinster, should put into the port of Ross, or discharge cargo there; but that on the contrary they should put into Waterford, and there unload.—[Id., p. 32.] In 1377, we find Richard the Second granting to the burgesses of Ross a chief rent of four pounds, then, for certain causes, seised into the King's hands, so long as the said chief rent should so remain in his hands, without any account to be rendered of the same, in consideration of the murder, as well by land as by water, of several merchants of his (the King's) said town of Ross, and to its great impoverishing; so that there is neither law, justice, nor good government in any part about the said town; but that on the contrary rebellion, extortion, murder, slaughter, robbery, and open war, are made on the same by the Irish enemy; so that the burgesses are unable to guard the said town, or repair and maintain their walls and gates without the King's assistance; the said chief rent to be employed in the said repairs.—[Id., p. 73.] In the same year the town obtained by royal charter the important concession, that merchants might take in and discharge cargo at the town of Ross, as well as at the city of Waterford; but this privilege was rescinded by subsequent royal charters; and although that granted by James the Second restored to Ross her ancient privileges, yet her rival and neighbour has contrived to appropriate to herself the entire of the Waterford Harbour, leaving to Ross the jurisdiction alone over her own rivers from Cheek Point to Innistiogue and St. Mullins.—[Id., p. 74.]

[a] Bale, Bishop of Ossory, speaks of "*Rob. Dauye* and *Aqua Vite*," as being "speciall drinks" at the close of the reign of Henry the Eighth, in the taverns of Kilkenny.—[Vocacyon of Johann. Bale, &c. Harleian Miscel., vol. vi., p. 414.]

Waterford, wch said vessell perteineth to ye soveraigne of Rosse. Walter Archer, and ye said towne as yet retaineth sureties for her in ye sum of £7, and one Piers FitzHarry of Rosse aforesaid is put to ye hindrance and damages, and his pledges to ye sum of 20 marks; and they further say that ye said towne of Waterford holdeth from Piers Young of Rosse aforesaid certaine [   ] to ye the valew of 20 marks.

[To this presentment is appended the following inquisitions touching an affray between the citizens of Waterford and the burgesses of Ross, and a murder resulting therefrom.]

"Inquisicō capta p dño Rege ap^d Roose corā Joħes Taylor supior' ibm 1° die Sept' an° Regni R^s H. 8 x^mo (1518). [Per]subscript' viz. Hen' Walshe, Wiłłm Blake, señ, Thomam Butler, Robt. Dargan, Joħem Lange, Maur' Cleyton, Nicħ Gregory, Joħem Deroose, Robt Lorknane, Wiłłm Taylor, Thomam Badrogane, Wiłłm Owen, Nicħm Barkly, Phillipm Bowens, Jacob' White, Corneliū Thalor, Ricm̄ Brewer & Mathew Catomas; Qui Jur̄ dicunt sup scr̄m suū q^d Nicħus Devereux, David Brewener, Ricūs Walshe, juñ, Nicħus Strange, Ricūs Ayleward, Joħes Rooch, Nicħus Gogh, Wiłłms Busher, Henric' Neale, Patricius Walshe, Nicħ Wadding, Thomam Lumbard, Joħes Shyrlock, Ricūs Browne, Edwardus Shirlock, Jacobus Hoore, Mauric' Madane, Ricūs Fleming, W^ms Fagan, Patric' Comford, Henric' Bryan, Jacobus Leche, Thomam Bayliffe, Thomam Lee, Ricūs Stronge, Jacobus Wodlock, Joħes Whyte, Jacobus Wyse, Robertus Walshe, Roƀtus Bryan, David Whyte, Roƀtus Kenay, Waltus White, Germanus Barbor, cives & Comunes p̃dict' civi^ts ex mandato Patricij Roope Majoris dic' civi^ts cū multis Hispanicis Gallicis Britonib' & Hiƀnicis riotuose venere cū classe Batellor' et naviū more piratico sive guerrino div̄sis armis armati viz paludaments loricis galeis scutis hastis gladijs lanceis balistis telis arcubus sagittis falxis plenarib' et bumbardis sive tormentis ad insultand [et] obsidiend' villam de Rosse 22° die Mayii an° Regni R^s H. 8 x°. Ita q^d ob timore hujus insulti et obsessus sup deind piratore [sic] p conservācone p̃dict ville supior et comūes ejusd̄m compulsi fuerunt delib^uare sup dcis Ballivis et coitat' civi^ts p̃dict maleū* Argenti deaurat ad val' xx^ll. I̧tm dicunt q^d sup^adict' supior et comunes p̃dc' ville occasione hujusmod

---

* In the original this word is written "muleñ;" but as the inquisitions were evidently, from numerous other mistakes, the work of an ignorant scribe, we have ventured to adopt the reading in the text.

insult' dc̄tiorarentur et dampnū hc̄nt ad c" argent &c. In fid' et testiōū
pmissor' sigilla Jurator' sup̄d' p̄sent' sunt appensa &c.ᵃ

"Inquisicō capta p dnō Rege apud Roose corā Joh Taylor supiori ibm
p'mo die Sept anᵒ Regni R˙ II. 8. [xᵒ] p subscript' viz Henric' Walshe,
Willm Blake sen', Thomam Butler, Robtū Dargan, Johem Lange, Mauriciū
Cleyton, Nichū Gregory, Johem de Roose, Robtm Lorknane, Willm Taylor,
Tho. Badregane, Willm Owen, Nichm Barkly, Phillipū Burrons, Jacobum
White, Corneliū Thalor, Ricū Broner, & Mathm̄ Catomas. Qui Juř dicunt
sup sacr̄m suū qd Nichus Devereux, David Brewenes, Ricūs Walshe jun',
Nichus Strange, Ricūs Arleward, Johes Roche, Nichus Guaghge, Willms
Busher, Henric' Neale, Patric' Walshe, Nichus Wadding, Thomas Lom-

---

ᵃ The finding of the Jury may be translated as follows:—" Who say that the citizens and commons of the city [of Waterford] aforesaid, together with many Spaniards, Frenchmen, Bretons, and Irish, came riotously with a fleet of boats and ships, in piratical or warlike fashion, variously armed; to wit, with surcoats, coats of mail, helmets, shields, spears, swords, lances, cross-bows, weapons, bows, arrows, broad axes, and bombards or cannon, on the 20th day of May, in the 10th year of the reign of Henry the Eighth, to assault and besiege, in a piratical and warlike manner, the town of Ross. So that, intimidated by this assault and siege, and for the preservation of the aforesaid town [of Ross], the sovereign and commons of the aforesaid town were compelled to deliver to the aforesaid bailiffs and commons of the city [of Waterford] a mace of silver gilt, of the value of £20. They also say that the aforesaid sovereign and commons of the said town [of Ross], by reason of the aforesaid attack, were damnified to the amount of one hundred pounds of silver."

From the reign of Henry the Third up to this period, and for long after, a state of open war seems to have been maintained between the two municipalities. In the 51st year of Henry the Third it appears, by an inquisition made at Waterford, that at a time when two ships belonging to Richard English, a citizen of Waterford, and William Bouloun, a citizen of Dantzig (de Kadanio), lay in the river below the port of Waterford, about to sail for Dantzig, certain persons, by the consent and at the bidding of the Ross folk, to wit, Henry Breton, and others named in the inquisition, together with sundry persons whose names could not be ascertained, came and seized, *vi armita*, the larger vessel of the two, and ill-used the men therein; and thereon came up Thomas Ketyng, with his followers, in aid of the aforesaid Henry, who, when they saw the larger ship captured, immediately seized the smaller vessel, and then carried them, both by force and arms, to Ross, and caused them to be detained there for seventeen weeks. The Jury then charge the Ross folk with habitually in warlike manner seizing the ships intending to put into Waterford, and causing them to discharge their cargoes at Ross instead; and that the burgesses of Ross had in this way seized more than forty vessels, by each of which the king lost two pipes of wine, or 40s. due to him by way of prisage; and further, that when the Waterford Corporation sent some servants

bard, Johes Shyrloke, Ricũs Browne, Edwardus Shirlock, Jacobus Hoore, Mauric' Madane, Ricũs Fleming, Willms Fagan, Patric' Coũford, Henric' Bryan, Jacobus Lech, Thomas Bayliffe, Thomas Lee, Ricũs Stronge, Jac' Woodlok, Johes Whyte, Jacobus Wyse, Robtus Walshe, Robtus Bryan, David Whyte, Robts Keney, Walt' Whyte, Germanus Barbor, cives, et ceteri communes p̃dict', sūt culpabil' de morte Gervicii Taygm̃ayn de Bristoll qui inffectus fuit cũ tormento sive bumbardo ap^d Roose 22° die Maij an° Regni Rs. H. 8. x^{mo} et postea evictus in Mar' subiñsus de una navi p p̃dict' cives &c. In testimoniũ p̃missis sigill Jurat' sup̃d' sunt p̃sent' apposit' &c.^{a}

of theirs on board a Bristol vessel, one was slain, and another drowned, by the burgesses of Ross, who brought the said ship into that port *vi armata*. Also, they say that the Ross people arrested Henry Coventry, a citizen of Waterford, who had sold a portion of his cargo of salt in Ross, because he had sent his ship to Waterford with the remainder of it, and imprisoned him till he paid a fine of £12, and that the upshot of all was, that, unless a stop was put to the doings of the burgesses of Ross, in a short time there would not be a man found in Waterford,—" villa Wat9ford infra breve tempus videbit' hõib' evacuari."—[Chartæ Statuta, &c., p. 31.] It is a matter of tradition to this day at Ross that one of the corporate insignia of Waterford—a silver mace—was captured by the men of Ross (probably in reprisal for their former loss) from the citizens of Waterford, being the trophy of a naval encounter between the two towns. This mace, which is still in the keeping of the former Corporation, and the smaller of the two belonging to Ross, is 1 foot 8 inches long; its shape that of the ancient military mace; it bears engraved on it the arms of France and England quarterly, and the letters E. R., probably for Edwardus Rex.

^{a} The finding of this inquest—an early example of an Irish bull—is that certain citizens of Waterford therein named "are guilty of the death of Gervice Taygermayn of Bristol who was slain by a bumbard, or cannon, at Ross, on the 22nd of May, in the 10th year of Henry VIII., and *afterwards* thrown into the sea and drowned." On the Patent Roll of the 28 Henry VIII. is entered a pardon for the citizens, inhabitants, and commonalty, of Waterford, *inter alia*, for the death of Geoffrey Fitz Patrick of Ballyhack, probably slain in some similar fray.

THE PRESENTMENTS OF THE JURIES OF THE COUNTY AND CITY OF KILKENNY, AND THE TOWN OF IRISHTOWN, TO THE COMMISSIONERS FOR ORDERING OR REFORMING THE STATE OF IRELAND, ANNO 1537.

HAVING already prefaced the series of State Papers containing Presentments made in 1537 by Juries of several shires and towns in the south-east of Ireland to the English High Commissioners of Reform, it only remains to offer a few remarks on some obscure archæological points in the following portion of these documents. The verdicts already printed relate to the county and town of Wexford, and the town of Ross. Those now published refer to the county and city of Kilkenny. When the entire series, including Presentments from the shire and city of Waterford, the counties of Carlow, Kildare, and Tipperary, and the towns of Dungarvan and Clonmel, shall have been published, they will form, perhaps, the most faithful and complete illustration attainable of the social condition of the people of any country in the beginning of the sixteenth century. Such being the strong and broad light that can be thrown on the state of the ancient inhabitants of this district (that primarily embraced by our Archæological Society), its educated classes may naturally be expected to be ready to advance an undertaking that will so largely gratify their curiosity as to the past of their country; and, indeed, the increasing support extended to this Society is the sure proof that its labours are beginning to be appreciated in a degree as full as that in which most other nations testify interest in their ancient memorials, by preserving and publishing them.

Perhaps the principal points of interest, so far as social history is concerned, derivable from these records—which display the regal customs of both the Anglo-Irish and the Gael of Ireland,—consists in the contrasts afforded between antique Celtic usages and the feudal system ; and in the fact that the condition of rural society disclosed by these documents existed in juxtaposition with an advanced state of civilization in towns; and, moreover, in the reflection that this primitive state subsisted within two centuries of our own time. The progress of civilization has indeed been rapid since 1537, when "Mac-Morrough," the mountain king of Leinster, still compelled the town of Gowran to pay him black rent ; and when "Wrory Amougher" (probably Rory, commonly called Lord O'More, chieftain of the greater portion of the country subsequently made a shire by the name of the Queen's County) exhibited his contempt of English law courts, upon being subpœna'd, by taking the writ and irreverently throwing it into the mire. However much the Government of Dublin Castle may have desired that the Irishry should become subject to the laws obeyed by the Englishry, the power to force them was evidently insufficient. Indeed, these laws were hardly observed outside town walls. Even in the Anglo-Irish county of Kilkenny, no court was held but the shire-reve's or county bailiff's, which was no sessions, for no justices sat. The Statutes or "Actes of Kyllcasshe" seem to have been a code framed for use between inhabitants of town and country, and possibly had been agreed to at a meeting at Kilcash, in Tipperary. These Rules were regularly committed to writing, and the copy in the possession of Rory M'Laughire, my Lord of Ossory's "Irishe Judge, called a Brehon," would perhaps now fetch its weight in gold. The primitive state of Brehon Law, and its professors, may be imagined from the provision of " one hogge, or else 20ᵈ.," rendered by the head of each house every other year to each native rural justiciary, an original stipendiary magistrate, who served as judge and jury, and from whose decisions there was no court of appeal.

Quotations from contemporary authorities, relative to the political condition of the county of Kilkenny, having been given in the first part of these introductory comments, they may be referred to, especially the Report of Chief Baron Finglas, who, having written in the year 1533,[a] seems to have been the first to direct attention to the grievances of the Englishry of Ireland. After the suppression of the Leinster Geraldine's revolt, measures were set on foot for " the reformation of Leinster." Such was then the power of the Earl of Ossory, that, in 1536, the Government of Ireland wrote to the King, recommending that this potentate and his son should be induced to allow government revenue to be levied in Kilkenny, Tipperary, Wexford, and Waterford.

The "Earl of Ostrey, or Ourmond," so frequently alluded to was Sir Piers Butler, first Earl of Ossory and eighth of Ormonde, who had been commonly styled Earl of Ormonde after the death, in 1515, of the English Earl of Ormonde and Wiltshire; but though so denominated, even in his patent of 1522 as Lord Deputy, he was not recognised as Earl of Ormonde until a year after the date of these verdicts. Sir Thomas Bulleyne, then actually Earl of Ormonde, is referred to once or twice.

These Presentments have several notices of the famous Margaret Fitzgerald, wife of this Earl of Ossory, and who—according to contemporary chroniclers, and to tradition—

* MS., State Paper Office.

exercised an uncommon authority in our district. Her
ability to govern was recognised by the Government.
Upon the death of her husband, in August, 1539, the Lord
Justice of Ireland was directed "to draw with the army
into those parts;" and soon afterwards an "order" was
made, "whereby the rule of the counties of Kilkenny and
Tipperary were committed to the government of the Ladie
Dowager of Ormond, Sir Richard Butler, her second son,
and others."[a] A letter, dated at Waterford, in the following
year, addressed by her to the King,[b] is signed in a large and
masculine, but trembling hand, for the writer was aged.
Evidences of the improvement and civilization introduced
by her into the neighbourhood of the city of St. Canice
continued to be remarkable for more than a century, as
affording a contrast to the unreclaimed barbarism of other
districts. She took an active and unusual part in erecting
fortifications, having rebuilt Gowran Castle, and, according
to a manuscript authority,[c] constructed a fortress called
"the Strong Hand." Her son inherited her energy in im-
proving the country, if it is her son, James, the ninth Earl,
to whom the following memorandum in the same manuscript applies:—"James Yrenagh [or Grenagh, one of the
Earl's manor-houses?] built thirty castles, thirty churches,
and thirty toghers, brigges, and cawseyes." This formed
no small work of improvement. She gave her numerous
daughters in marriage to the principal peers in the south
of Ireland, namely, the Earl of Thomond, Lords Cahir,
Dunboyne, Fitz Maurice, Decies, and Curraghmore. And
it will appear by the Presentments from the county of the
the two latter lords, that these her sons-in-law were as much

---

[a] Index to Council Book, British Museum, Add. MS. 4790.

[b] State Paper Office.

[c] S. P. O., Hanmer's MSS.

assisted by her governing talent as the Viceroy Earl, her husband, was. Other particulars regarding this extraordinary dame and her husband will be found in "The History, Architecture, and Antiquities of the Cathedral of St. Canice," pp. 182-249.

It would be curious to ascertain whether some of the duties exacted from the tenantry of the Earls of Ormonde and Ossory were rendered under other names to great lords in England. "Murorum operatio," for instance, the custom under which buildings for the lord's use were erected and kept in repair by the tenantry, although abused by being employed in not only building castles for their defence, but also halls, kitchens, barns, and stables,—and though arising from the Gaelic custom, under which clansmen provided everything requisite for their chief, or official governor,— had also, doubtless, obtained in other and feudal countries.

With regard to the horse and hunt grievances, the studs of a Gaelic king seem to have grazed, by custom, on all waste lands in his country; and the keepers were entitled to meat and drink from the nearest inhabitants during this grass time. To judge by the name of this custom, *gille-cree* (servants of cattle ?), Celtic lords in Ireland, as well as other lords in Spain and elsewhere, had a privilege of depasturing all unenclosed and unoccupied land within their territories. Under the customs called *gille-con* and *dowgollogh*, keepers and huntsmen of a chieftain's hounds were warranted to take food for themselves and hounds for a day and a night with each tenant. Although the Juries complain of " the Earl's hunts" as an evil, they should have remembered that hunting was practised to clear the country of wild animals, such as deer, wolves, swine, foxes, hares, &c., that did injury in various ways; and the Jurors might, perhaps, have admitted that the said hunt was welcomed by the owner of every mansion-house it put up at, as heartily as the splendid packs of hounds that now hunt the same district are received.

The "kerne tighe" of the Earl of Ossory, and of Mac Murrough, were *ceitherne tighe*, i. e. kerne of the house, or the household roof that guarded their lord's dwelling-place. They are represented in the ensuing verdicts as going about the country four times in each year; and it would seem by other records[a] that one of their functions was to accompany the officers who collected rents, which, being in kind, were liable to be either of inferior quality, or exchanged for inferior qualities by the serjeants or rent-takers.

The "galloglacha," i. e. foreign servitors, were also a species of armed police, and, as soldiery, were absolutely required for defence. The accusation, that the Earl exacted "cuddyes," or suppers, and "cosshers," or cess for the king, from certain tenants, and compelled others—whose houses were not large enough to receive him and his train—to send, in lieu of such receptions, a specified quantity of victuals to his mansion-houses, requires explanation. Prior to the general use of money, rent being paid in kind, it was sent in to the nearest castle that defended the district; so that this Earl was customarily entitled to the above-mentioned renderings, the objection to which lay, however, in their liability to be excessively exacted. Such rents being also in process of change into money payments, owing to recent influxes of bullion, their uncertainty was hence also objectionable. The gradual rise of prices, owing to the decreasing value of coin, was a matter of complaint, because the real cause was not understood. Freight of goods by river boats had risen from

[a] Letter of Sir Warham St. Leger, 1589, State Paper Office.

8*d.* to 14*d.* But the rate of workmen's wages, two-pence a day for masons and carpenters, and one penny for labourers, indicates the scarcity of coin as compared with its lower value now. The corn purchased after harvest at two shillings per bushel was, probably, oats, since there is no mention of wheat,—a grain so rare, yet so suitable to this lime-abounding country, that, in 1539, the Earl of Ossory bequeathed a stone of it to the owner of every plough,[a] manifestly with the object of spreading its cultivation.

The reason why Lord Ossory, and other *free*-holders of land, would not allow their farmers to sell anything except to a merchant appointed in each case, consisted in the fact, that as these tenants were in a state of *semi-slavery*, their lords laid some claim to all they possessed. In fact, the condition of the people of Ireland was in a state of transition at the period of these Verdicts, which gives these documents their principal value to historians of social progress.

The Earl of Ossory set himself zealously to the work of reformation. He writes to Viceroy St. Leger, 12th March, 1538 :—

." I have also proclaymed all over the countie of Tipperary that no *caines, allyieys, errikes*, Irish brehons, nether that lawe, *rahownes*, and many like exaccions and extorcions, shall sease, with reformacion for the grey merchunts, and the Libertie Corte to be duly contynued, as the King's lawes require. And as for the countie of Kilkenny, for lack of auctoritie as I have in the countie of Tipperarie of the Kinges Majestie, I, and the inhabitaunts, were, and ar, in falte of admynistracion of justice, to use the abuses hetherto there contynued; the peple being bred in such ignoraunce as they know not justice. Howe be it, I have often perswaded many of them to be converted, which to doo I can scarcely have their assentes, for the

---

[a] See his will in full, " History, Architecture, and Antiquities of the Cathedral Church of St. Canice," p. 245.

lustes they have to caynes and other abuses, torning to their proffit, as it doth to myne. But, fynally, I am thus determyned to drive them therto, so as, whatsoever orders or devises you shall determyne therein to be put in effecte, I shall have such respecte thereto as neither their will, ne any particler commoditie to myself, or to them, shall refrayne me to se the same perfitely executed, God willing."

On the 27th March, 1538, the Earl reports to the King that he has consulted with the High Commissioners of Reformation, and drawn up a series of orders and constitutions to extirp the enormities and abuses accustomed in the counties of Kilkenny, Waterford, and Tipperary, and to plant good civility.[a]

Certain ordinances, drawn up in 1541, endeavoured to remedy two of the grievances set forth in the following Verdicts, namely, the insolence of bards, and impediments to free sale of goods. It will be observed by the seventh item in the first Presentment that the Jury proposed that rhymers should be forbidden to make verses on any person, manifestly in order to prevent the currency of malicious satire, the intimidatory means by which the bards obtained food, lodging, and gifts. The above-mentioned ordinance declared—

"No rhymer (poeta) nor other person whatsoever shall make verses (carmina), or anything else called *auran*" (query *dann?*), "to any one after God on earth except the king, under penalty of the forfeiture of all his goods. Also, no one shall impede the market, nor throw any impediment in the way of any body taking goods and wares to the market, but the governor of a town or castle."[b]

The exactions of coyne and livery, or food for man and forage for horse, frequently complained of in these

---

[a] MS. State Paper Office.   [b] MS. S. P. O., Feb. 7, 1549.

representations, must have greatly tended to keep down the letting value of land. John Bale, the intemperate Bishop of Ossory, in describing the state of the county of Kilkenny in the days of Edward VI., describes coyne and livery as more cruel pillages and oppressions of the poor husbandman than occur elsewhere in the earth, even under Turks and Saracens. The Irish lords, he says, and their under captains, are not only companions of thieves, but also their masters and retainers :—

"After their harvestes are ended there, the kearnes, the galloglasses, and the other breechlesse souldiers, with horses and their horsegromes, sumtyme iii waitinge upon one jade, enter into the villages with much crueltie and fearcenesse ; they continue there in great ravine and spoyle ; and when they goe thens, they leave nothinge else behinde them for payment but lice, lecherye, and intollerable penurie for all the yeare after. Yet set the *rulers* therupon a very fayre colour, that it is for defence of the Englishe pale."[a]

Upon the abolition of these exactions, thirty years subsequently, Mr. George Wyse, in writing[b] to Secretary Cecil, expatiates on the happy effects of that measure; he describes the country people as having, for joy, fallen to play and pastime, as the like were never seen before ; and states that land, formerly letting for a groat per acre, now yielded twelve pence ; and concludes by inveighing against the exacters of those imposts, namely, " the ungodly Irish lords." Justice Fitz Simons also writes, from Kilkenny, that one acre is now more thought of than ten before ; and that pastime is daily used on holydays such as has not been known in the memory of man.

Although chieftains, who were not the owners of the clan-countries, may not have profited by the abolition of

[a] " Vocacyon of Johan Bale." [b] S. P O., June 20, 1567.

these exactions, all feudal landlords must have longed for this abolition, since they absorbed so large a share of the profits of the soil.

But all the above-mentioned and other customary renderings and exactions—which had, when first practised, been requisite—could, of course, be abolished but gradually; and it is remarkable that the Earls of Ormonde, who for centuries had been supported by means levied according to customs similar to those by which Celtic kings were maintained, did not, until thirty-two years after the date of the following representations of the grievances of a few of these levies, relinquish, as a record quoted in a subsequent page says, certain taxes they had been accustomed to raise off the inhabitants of the shires of Kilkenny and Tipperary for their personal expenses.[a]

[a] See note, p. 92.

THE VERDYT OF THE GENTLEMEN OF THE SHYRE OF KILKENNY.

[*October*, 1537.—*MS. State Paper Office.*]

The Verdyt of the Inquest of Gentyllmen[a] of the bodye of the Shyre of Kylkenny, sworen and made before the Justices our Soveraigne Lorde the King assigned for the conservacion of his peace within the saide Countye of Kylkenny at the Generall Sessions holden at the Town of Kylkenny[b] within the saide Countie, the 8 daye of Octobre in the 29th yere[c] of the raigne of our said Soveraigne Lorde.

JOHES GRACE.	JUR.	EDŪS DATOWNE.	
		WILLMS HOWELL.	
JACOBUS SWETEMAN.		PETRUS FORSTALL.	
JACOBUS COMERFORTHE.		EDŪS FORSTALL.	
GILBERTUS DOBYN.	JUR.	JACOBUS PURCELL.	JUR.
JOHES SMYTH.		OLYVERUS SHORTALL.	
EDWARDUS WATOUN.		EDŪS SHORTALL.	
WALTERUS COWIK.		PATRICIUS FORSTALL.	
		JOHES CROKE.	
		EDŪS BLANFELD.	

Fyrst the saide Jurye present and saye upon ther othe, that this present yere the Inhibytauntes of the Towne of Kylkenny have byn chargeid with coygne and lyverye for viii.^{xx} Galloglasseis being in nombre xvi.^{xx} persons,[d] of the Lorde of Ossery, withoute thassent of the saide Inhibytauntes, to ther importunat costes and charges.

[a] See a list of the Gentlemen of Kilkenny at the period, printed at the end of this presentment.

[b] The Lord Chancellor Allen, Sir William Brabazon, and Justice Aylmer, wrote to Cromwell, informing him that on the 2nd of January, 1539, they "kept cessions ther [at Kilkenny], where was put to execution certayn malefactours, some for felonyes, others for murdours by them committed, . . . the like precident whereof have not been seen thies 200 yeres."—[State Papers, temp. Henry VIII., vol. iii., part iii., pp. 112, 118.]

[c] A.D. 1537.

[d] i.e. Three hundred and twenty men. The diet of the Galloglasses was " on

Item, they present that all the saide Inhibytauntes of the saide County byn chargeid with coygne & Lyverye by the said Lord Ossery and all his children,[a] over and besydes the said charge whiche the sustayne for the said Galloglagheis, for all horssemen, kernaghe, horsseboyes and ther horseis, haveing contynuall resort from any countrey or partyes of Irland unto the saide Lorde Ossery or any of his said children, to the greate costes and detryment of the said inhibytauntes and ayenst all right and consyence.

Item, the saide Jurye present that all the Inhibytauntes of the saide Countye of Kylkenny ben chargeid by the saide Erlle to gyve mete, drynke, lodgeing and wageis unto all artyfycers and laborers which the saide Erlle shalle by hymselff or his officers retayne for any his byldeinges[b] untill the clere fynysheing of the same buyldeinges; and also compelleith the said inhibytauntes to carye and bryng with ther garrons or ploughorsseis all maner

fleshe dayes, fleshe, breade, and ale, and on fyshe dayies, fyshe and breade;" but when necessary they could endure great privations, there being none " that will or can endure the paynes and evill faire that they will susteyne." They were "harnessed in mayle and bassenettes [chain armour and steel helmets], having every of them his weapon, called a sparre, moche like the axe of the Towre," " and for the more part ther boyes beare for them thre dartes a piece, whiche dartes they throwe, or they come to the hand stripe; these sorte of men be those that doo not lightly abandon the fielde, but byde the brunt to the deathe." The galloglasses were regular condottierri, ready with their captains to serve any man, or take up any cause for pay.—[State Papers, temp. Henry VIII., vol. ii., part iii., pp. 208, 448; vol. iii., part iii., pp. 383, 444.]

[a] The children of Piers, Earl of Ormonde and Ossory, by his wife Margaret, second daughter of Gerald, eighth Earl of Kildare, whom he married in 1485, were, James, his successor in the title, called Bocach, or the lame; Richard, created Viscount Mountgarret; Thomas, Margaret, Catherine, Joan, Ellice, Elleanor, and Ellen. The Earls of Desmond, Kildare, and Ossory, are charged in the State Papers, that they, with " ther williis, childyrne, and servauntes, do use, alltyr the custumbe and usage off wyld Iryshmen, to come with a gret multitude of peple to monastereis, and gentylmen ys howsis, and ther to contynu 2 dais and 2 nightes, taking met and drink at ther plesurs, and ther horssis and kepers to be sheiftyd or dyvydyt un the pore fermors, next to that place adjoynyng, paing nothing therfor, so as they be found, in in thys maner, in other mens is howsis moo then halff the yere, by the wild Irish custume of extorcion, and spare ther own howsis."—[State Papers, temp. Henry VIII., vol. ii., part iii., p. 185.]

[b] It is a curious fact, that the traditions of the peasantry of the county of Kilkenny mix up the name of Main-

stuff or caryages for the said buyldeinges necessary or requysit at all tymes, withoute any recompence or payment made unto the said inhibytauntes therfor, contrarye to ther duetye and ayenst ther voluntarye myndes to ther costes and chargeis.

Item, the saide Jurye present that the saide Erlle every festyvall daye dureing the tyme of his buyldeinges sendeith unto the inhibytauntes of the saide Countye at his pleasure all his masons, with whome they doo take their mete and drynke, and paye nothing therfor, to ther greate chargeis and ayenst ther wylles.

Item, the saide Jurye present that the said Erlle doithe by his servauntes yerely levye and take of every inhibytaunt within the Shyre of Kylkenny where it shall please hym and other exaccion for his horsseis calleid Somer Otys,[a] paying no thing for the same; to ther great chargeis, and ayenst the myndes and willes of the inhibytauntes.

Item, the said Jury present that dyverse persons, being servauntes unto the said Erlle, callid his hunt, do use to come to the mansion house of any inhibytaunt within the saide Countye, at all tymes at ther pleasure, with ther greyhoundes, houndes, and other dogges of the said Erlle, where dureing ther abode they do take as well mete and drynke for themselffes as fedeinges for the said dogges, withoute any thing paying therfor, whiche is repugnaunt to the wylles of the said inhibytauntes.[b]

Ṡiaḋ nın Ṡeapóıṙ, or Peg Garret, Earl Pier's Countess, with the history, building, or demolition of nearly every castle in the district. It is recorded that she rebuilt the Castle of Gowran.—[Archdall's edition of Lodge's "Peerage," vol. iv., p. 21, n.] In the State Papers the Earl is charged with taking coigne and livery for "his masons, carpenters, taillours, being in his owne werkes."— [State Papers, temp. Henry VIII., vol. ii., part iii., p. 121.]

[a] Nearly every ancient lease held from the Ormonde family covenants that as part of the rent a certain number of sheep, beeves, hogs, capons, oats, &c., should be rendered at stated times; these contributions, technically "Acates" (from achatre, to ransom), being no longer necessary to keep up the profuse hospitality of former days, are now commuted for a fixed money payment. The complaint of the Jury seems to be that this custom was extended beyond the Earl's immediate tenants.

[b] See Introduction, p. 81, supra, and also a Paper by Mr. John P. Prendergast, on "Hawks and Hounds in Ireland," printed in the "Transactions of the Kilkenny and South-East of Ireland Archæological Society," vol. ii., p. 144.

Item, the saide Erlle dothe use to sende to the Inhibytauntes of the said Countye, his younge horseis studdes & horsboyes, who have of the said Inhabytauntes aswell mete and drynke for themselfes as fedeinges for the said horseis dureing all the tyme that it shalle please the said Erlle to have them to tary with suche inhabytaunt, paying nothcing therfor, to no small costes and charges of the said Inhibytauntes, fully ayenst the myndes of the saide inhabytauntes.[a]

Item, they present that ther ar emonges the inhabytauntes of this countrey many harpers, rymers, and messingers, whiche comen at ther pleasures to any inhabytaunt, and wille have mete, drynke, and dyverse greate rewardes ayenst the voluntarye wylles of the same inhabytauntes, of an evyll custome. Wherefor they desyre that it may be ordeyned that suche harpers, rymers, and messyngers maye not take suche exaccions of the said inhabytauntes, nor the said rymers to make any rymes of them, uppon certeyn paynes to be lymytid.[b]

Item, the saide Jurye present that often tymes the saide Erlle his hoole famyly resorteyth to the mansions of dyverse gentyllmen and other inhabytauntes within the saide Countye, and takeith of them cuddyes and cosshers, withoute any thing paying therfor,

[a] In 1542, the Deputy, St. Leger, writes that the late Earl of Kildare always kept from two to three hundred stud mares; and we may be sure the Earl of Ossory was not far behindhand. —[State Papers, temp. Henry VIII., vol. iii., part. iii., p. 379.]

[b] The satirical powers of the Irish Bards was much dreaded, and their laudations valued as well by the native chiefs as by the Hibernicised Anglo-Irish lords. In 1414 we are informed by the Four Masters that Niall O'Higgin, a Westmeath poet, composed a satire against Sir John Stanley, Lord Deputy of Ireland, which caused his death; and about the middle of the sixteenth century a poem was addressed to O'Brien, Earl of Thomond, by his chief poet, Mac Daire, to the effect that he (Mac Daire) had a deadly weapon —a venomous satire—to cast, which would cause shortness of life, and against which neither the solitude of valleys, the density of woods, nor the strength of castles, could protect his enemies—[*Tribes of Ireland*, p. 21]; and in the year 1537 Robert Cowley writes to Cromwell, "that harpers, rymours, Irish cronyclers, bardes, and isshallyn, comonly goo with praisses to gentilmen in the English pale, praysing in rymes, otherwise called danes, their extorcioners, roberies, and abuses, as valiauntnes, which rejoysith them in that their evell doinges."—[State Papers, temp. Henry VII., vol. ii., part iii. p. 450.]

ayenst the myndes of suche gentyllmen or inhabytauntes, and besydes that every of his officers, as his Marssheall, Butler, the Coke, wyth dyverse other his officers,[a] wylle have severall rewardes of suche Gentylmen where the saide Erlle takeith suche coddyes and cosshers, or elles the said officers wille take with them a Table clothe or some other thing, for a plege, whiche they wille retayne untill they be satysfyed of ther demaunde, ayenst right and consyence.

Item, the said Jurye present that the said Erlle compelleith suche persons as be not of abylyte to receyve hym into his house ther to take cuddyes and cosshers at his pleasure, to sende unto one of his manors where he shalbe assygneid, bredde, ale, and other vytayles, contrary to the myndes of suche persons, and whereunto ther habylytie scacely extendeith.

Item, the saide Jurye present that the chyldren of the said Erlle use lyke imposicions uppon the said inhabytauntes, at ther pleasure, to ther greate costes and chargeis.

Item, the saide Erlle, his children, officers, and famylye, exacte and have dyverse other exaccions and extorcions of the gentillmen and other inhabytauntes within the saide Countie, to their greate costes and charges, whiche by contynuaunce wilbe to the utter impovershement and undoing of the said inhabytauntes, oneles reformacion be therof shortly ordeyned and provideid.

Item, the saide Jury present and saye, uppon ther othes, that when and as often as the said Erlle dothe purchase landes and tenementes within the saide Countie, holden of any gentillman or other person or persons within the saide Countye, by fealltye, rent, or other services and customes; and also dyverse tymes onereid with the sessementes to hosteinges, and sundry other taxeis and charges going oute or yerely due of the said landes; whiche

---

[a] The constitution of the households of the nobles seems at this period, and for two centuries after, to have been formed on the plan of that of royalty itself. The comptroller, steward, receiver, treasurer, butler, clerk of the kitchen, cook, &c., were officers in the household of the great Duke of Ormonde, and their accounts rendered in and audited with the utmost regularity, are still preserved in the Evidence Chamber, Kilkenny. Whilst the Duke, in his regal liberty of Tipperary, had his judge, attorney-general, seneschal, and all other officers answering to those of the king's courts.

charges, or any parte therof, the said Erlle, after any suche purchase denyeth to paye, but by his extorte power wille holde the saide lande dyschargeid and exonerated ayenst all persons, as well of rentes as other the said taxes and charges, and wille not suffer the same to be levied of the said land, by reason wherof the owners and fermors of other landes within the said Countye are cesseid and taxeid to a gretter some, to no lytill charge of the said Owners and fermors, and diverse persons abridgeid and barred of ther dueties[a] going oute of the said landes or tenementes.

Item, the saide Jurye present that Edmund Butler, bastard sonne of one Jamys Butler, haveing no certen dwelleing place, but vagarnt within the saide Countye, dothe comynly use to take foyes, cuddyes, coshers, money, and otys of all the inhabytauntes within the saide Countye at his pleasure, withoute any thing paying

---

[a] The number of deeds of purchase of lands acquired by Piers, Earl of Ormonde and Ossory, and Margaret, his wife (the Countess is generally a party in the deed), remaining amongst the Ormonde Evidences, is very great. A presentment of the gentry of the county of Kilkenny, dated April 3rd, 1592, and made in answer to certain articles propounded by Royal Commissioners, a contemporary copy of which is preserved amongst the Ormonde Evidences, states:—" To the thirde article we say that the quantity or number of acres of every the said ploughlands [in the county of Kilkenny] are not to be certainly known, because the said ploughlands or horsemens bedds were (as wee understand) made in the begining by view and estimation, and not according to the quantity or number of acres: we alsoe find that of the said ploughlands or horsemen's bedds, beinge in number eighty-foure, the said Earles [Thomas, Earl of Ossory, the grandson of Piers and Margaret] p'vision in the said sev'all Baronies or quarters doe amount to seaven and twenty ploughlands, and the fourth part of a ploughland, which are now kept free by vertue of her Maties Letters of freedom or tollerance latelie graunted unto the said Earle." In the Irish Council Book, temp. Philip and Mary, and Elizabeth, is entered an order from the Queen, dated June 30th, 1569, directing the Lord Deputy to take measures to free the Earl of Ormonde's lands, in the counties of Kilkenny and Tipperary, from all cesses, other than royal subsidies, in consideration of his abandoning *certain taxes, which he had been accustomed to raise off the inhabitants for his personal expenses;* but allowing him to raise victuals for his house at the Queen's rate of payment.—[" Original Council Book," in the library of Charles Haliday, Esq., Monkstown Castle, Co. Dublin.] The Editors are indebted to John P. Prendergast, Esq., for this important confirmation of the truthfulness of the Presentments. Mr. Prendergast states that Mr. Haliday's invaluable MS. supplies the gap between the published State Papers of Henry VIII. and the times of James I.

therfor; any denyer by any person to him made to the contrarye notwithstandeing.

Item, the present that every of the Iryshe Judges, called Brennes, within the said Countye, doo every 2ᵈᵉ yere take of every towne or hamlet within the saide Countye, 20ᵈ for the price of one swyne, whiche he wrongfully demaundeith of every of the saide Townes or hamletes to be due unto hym, by reason that he is suche Judge.

Item, they present that the Curates for the moste of every Paryshe Churche within the Countye aforesaide, do take for his crysteynynges of every chylde 12ⁱ, and for puryficacion 12ⁱ or 16ᵈ, and other exaccions for the admynistracions of Sacramentes, ayenst the lawe of Godde, and the mere duetye of every suche Curate.

[*Lambeth MS.*, 611, *fol.* 87.]

The names of all the Gentlemen inhabitinge the Count' of Kilkeñi, wᵗʰ theire landſ valewed by Estimation as followeth:*—

Landſ houlden by Knightſ service of the mannoʳ of the Grannagħ by—

	Daton and his kinsmen	c mȓkſ
	James Sherlocke his Landſ	xˡⁱ
	The Bishopp of Osseries Landſ	vjˡⁱ
	Piers Welshes Landſ	xl mȓks
	Thomas Grant his Landſ	xvˡⁱ
THE BARONY OF GRAN-NAGH.	Edmund Grant his Landſ	viijˡⁱ
	Willm̃ Welshe and his Cosens Landſ	xˡⁱ
	James Grantſ Landſ	xxˡⁱ
	Patricke Dobins Landſ	xijˡⁱ
	Peter Strongſ Landſᵇ	ljˡⁱ
	Galleᶜ his Landſ	xxxˡⁱ
	John fitz Willm̃ fitz Adam his Landſ	vjˡⁱ
	Thomas Day his Landſ	xxˡⁱ

* There is no date to this list, but it cannot be many years later than the Presentments. It was transcribed for the Society by W. J. O'Donnavan, Esq.

ᵇ Of Dunkit and Aylwardstown, where the present head of the family, Peter Strange, Esq., resides.

ᶜ The proper name of this family was Bourke, or De Burgo, as appears by an epitaph in the old church of Gauls-

	Mr James Butlers Landſ	xx^{li}
	Redmond Roches Landſ	xx^{li}
	Walter fforster his Landſ	xx^{li}
	Edmond fforster his Landſ . . .	xv^{li}
	Aylwardſ Landſ	xiij^{li}
THE BARONY OF GRAN- NAGH—con.	Archdekens Landſ	vj^{li}
	Gerald fforsters[a] Landſ	x^{li}
	Piers fitz John Butlers landſ	xx m?ks
	Edmond Butlers landſ	xxx^{li}
	James De ffreny his landſ	lx^{li}
	Olyver de ffreny his landſ	v^{li}
	The Baron of Brownesford[b]	l^{li}
		v^c xliij^{li} xiij·iiij^d

Landſ houlden of the Manno^r of Knocktoſer.

	Edmond Welsh and his Kinsmen . .	clj^{li}
	Olyver ffayngſ landſ	viij^{li}
	Robt Tywe his landſ	x^{li}
	David Howlingſ landſ	v^{li}
	James Howlingſ landſ	vij^{li}
THE BARONY OF KNOCK- TOFER.	Edward Howlingſ landſ	iij^{li}
	Nicholas Whitſ Landſ	xl^{li}
	James fitz piers Butlers Landſ . . .	iiij^{li}
	Purcelles of Kilkerely his Landſ . .	vj^{li} xiij^s iiij^d
	Adame Welshes landſ	x^{li}
	John Howell als gilledust hele his landſ	v^{li}
	Wadton[c] his landſ	xx^{li}

kille, and several documents in the possession of Dr. O'Donovan, but they were better known by their Irish descriptive epithet of Gaul, or Stranger. Gaulstown, in the barony of Iverk, was their principal seat. From William Gaul-Bourke, of Gaulstown, descends, by his daughter Catherine, wife of Edmond O'Donovan, John O'Donovan, LL. D., the learned Irish scholar and historian.— See "Transactions of the Kilkenny Archæological Society," vol. i., p. 254.

[a] Walter Edmond and Gerald Fforstall. It was stated in a pedigree, which was in the possession of the late Pierce Edmond Forestall, of Rochestown, that the original name was Forrester. The Rochestown branch is now extinct, and a Mons. C. Forestall, of Paris, is believed to be the head of the Kilkenny Forestalls.

[b] The name of this family was Fitzgerald.

[c] Walton is the correct name of this family.

THE BARONY OF KNOCK- TOFER—*con.*	Poer of porers wod[a]	v[li]
	The churchtown of gerepont and the old towne belonginge to diuerse burgesses	x[li]
		cc iiij''v[li] xiij[s] iiij[d]

Landſ houlden of the Mannor of Calane.

	Willm Swetman his landſ	lxxiij[li]
	Richard Barons[b] Landſ	xxx[li]
	Thomas Comerfordſ landſ	xl[li]
	Richard Comerford & Willm faninge	xxx[li]
	St. Legers Landſ	xxvj[li] xiij[s] iiij[d]
THE BARONY OF KELLES.	ffowlke Comerfordſ Landſ .	xl[li]
	Willm Crokſ landſ	v[li]
	James Butlers landſ	vj[li]
	David Butler and his kinsmen . . .	xxj[li]
	James Tobens Landſ	x[li]
	John Tobens Landſ	xx[li]
	Nicholas Deverony & Willm Lincolt .	x[li]
		iij[c] xj[li] xiij[s] iiij[d]

Landſ houlden of the Mannor of Gawran.

	Thomas Dobens Landſ	xl[li]
	Thomas Den his Landſ	lj[li]
	Patricke fforsters Landſ	lj[li]
	Ryan and his kinsmens Landſ . . .	c[li]
	John Cantwells Landſ	lx[li]
	Edmond Butler of Powleston	xl[li]
THE BARONY OF GAWRAN.	Donell fitz Piers his Landſ	v[li]
	Patricke fitz Geralds landſ	iiij[li]
	Edmond fitz Nicholas Landſ	iij[li]
	The Bishopp of Osseries Landſ . . .	c[li]
	Gerald Blanch ville and his bretheren .	c m?ks
	Robert Sartall his Landſ	xxvj[li] xiij[s] iiij[d]
	John Longe his Landſ	v[li]
	Richard Sartall his Landſ	xij[li]

[a] Le Poer, of Poer's Wood, in the parish of Innistioge; the name is now written Power, but the peasantry retain the old pronunciation, and call the townland Poor's Wood.

[b] Richard Fitzgerald, Baron of Burnchurch; this family, which is now represented by Sir Henry Winston Barron, of the county of Waterford, was as often named "Baron" as "Fitzgerald."

The Presentments of Juries of the

THE BARONY OF GAWRAN -con.

Robert Tobens Landſ	v^{li}
Geoffrey Purcell his Landſ . .	c m?ks
Donell fitz Patricke his Landſ . . .	x^{li}
Robucte Purcells Landſ	x^{li}
James Cowley and his bretheren[a] . .	xiij^{li} vj^s viij^d
	vj^c lxix^{li} vj^s viij^d

Landſ houlden of the Manno^r of Kilkenny.

THE BARONY OF GAWLE.

The viscont Montgarretſ Landſ . . .	c^{li}
Gerald Archedeken his Landſ . . .	xxx^{li}
Richard Archedeken and his kinsmen .	xxx^{li}
Olyver Sartall his Landſ	iiij^{xxli}
The Bishopps Landſ	c m?ks
John Smythe his Landſ	xx^{li}
Richard Grace and Onselle grace . .	x^{li}
Piers Sartall his Landſ	vj^{li}
John Clynton his Landſ	x^{li}
Willm̃ Bourdes his Landſ	iiij^{li}
John Richfordes Landſ	xx^{li}
Lawāt his Landſ	xx^{li}
Richard Shete his Landſ	xx^{li}
David Roth his Landſ	x^{li}
Walter Archer his Landſ	vj^{li}
Edmond Shete[b] his Landſ	vj^{li}
Piers Baron his Landſ	vj^{li}
Piers Ragged his Landſ	v^{li}
Robert Sentlegers landſ	xiij^{li}
Oliver Grace and his kinsmen . . .	cxx^{li}
James fitz Richarde Butlers Landſ . .	xiij^{li} xiij^s iiij^d
	v^c iiij^{xx} xvj^{li} vj^s viij^d

The iij^d pte thereof is to be sett uppon upper Osseries[c] fo^r y^t it conteineth the iij^d pte of the Contrye.

[a] Ancestors of the Duke of Wellington.—See "Transactions of the Kilkenny Archæological Society," vol. ii., p. 102.

[b] Richard and Edmond Shee. The Irish form is O'Seaǧða, anglicised O'Sheth, O'Shea, and Shee, and belonged to a Milesian family originally settled in Iveragh, in Kerry.

[c] At this period the Barony of Upper Ossory, comprising the present Baronies of Upperwoods, Clondonagh, and Clarmalagh, were, in legal acceptation, part of the county of Kilkenny. This valuation would seem to have been made for the purpose of taxation.

THE VERDYT OF THE COMMYNERS OF THE COUNTYE OF KYLKENNYE.

[*October*, 1537.—*MS. State Paper Office.*]

WILLIAM TRODDYE OF CALLAM.[a]	JUR.
PIERS HERFFORD OF THE SAME. JAMYS MOTEING[b] OF THE SAME. RICHARD FANNEING OF THE SAME.	} JUR.
JAMYS MOUNSELL OF THE SAME. WILLIAM HOWLING OF THE SAME. EDMŪD FORSTALL OF INYSTYOKE.	} JUR.
WILLM̃ POWER OF THE SAME. RICHARD WALSHE OF THE SAME. JAMYS ARLAND OF THE SAME. JAMYS KARRON OF THE SAME.	} JUR.
THOMAS POWER OF KNOKTOFER. JAMYS TYWE OF Y^E SAME. NICH̃US FYTZJOHN OF Y^E SAME.	} JUR.
TEYGE LACYE OF THE SAME. WILLM̃ LORKNAN OF THAUNSTONE.[c] JAMYS WHYTE OF Y^E SAME.	} JUR.

[a] i. e. Callan. The "Gentylmen" of the county seem to have answered for their tenantry and retainers, for the Jury of the "Commyners of the countye of Kylkennye" is selected from the small corporate towns of Callan, Innistioge, Knocktopher, and Thomastown. Gowran (equally with others comprised within the county of Kilkenny) is not represented, although of more importance than Innistioge or Knocktopher. To remedy this omission, the complaints of the commoners of Gowran seem to have been embodied in the Presentment of the Corporation of the Irishtown of Kilkenny. There is a fragment of an ancient monument in Callan Church to the memory of "Philipus Troddy quōdā burgēs' ac notarius curialis villē Callanie qui obiit xv° die m . . . . A. D. M. v° lxiii." Another fragment has the name "Jacobus Throdyi."

[b] Nicholas Motyng, Chancellor of the Cathedral of St. Canice, was probably connected with this Callan family. [See The History, Architecture, and Antiquities of the Cathedral Church of St. Canice, p. 266.]

[c] i. e. Thomastown, so called after its founder, Thomas Fitz Anthony.

Fyrste, they present that Coyne and Lyverye is useid by my Lorde of Ostrey[a] upon all the hoole countrey, Port[b] Townes onely excepteid, and yet useid also by all his freholders, every one of them upon his owne tenauntes, and elles where over all.

Item, the saide Lorde of Ostrey useith Galloglassheis, and levieth ther wages upon all the hoole countrey.

Item, the saide Jurye present that the saide Lorde of Ostrey hathe 2 severall companyes of kernes going quarterly, that is to saye, eche of them 4[or] tymes of the yere over all the countrey from one towne to another, and leave none, and ther take mete and drynke withoute paying therfor; and wher they lack mete they take money. And Edmunde Purser[c] and William Purser, brethren, ar captaygnes of the one kerne, and Robert Astyken[d] and Jamys Astyken ar captaynes of thother kernes.

---

[a] i. e. Ossory. All through these Presentments, Sir Piers Butler, Earl of Ossory, is the person so designated.

[b] Possibly towns with walls, and *ports* or gates.

[c] A mistake of the scribe for Purcel. The family of Purcell, or De Porcellis, were of Anglo-Norman extraction, and claimed descent from Purcell, " Lievetenant of the Army [Strongbow's] slaine by the Watefordians." — [Hanmer's Chronicle, Dublin, 1633, p. 137.] The principal Kilkenny branch of the family appears to have been settled at Ffoulksrath, but there were also offsets residing at Ballyfoyl, Lismain, Clone, and Ballymartin. Edmund Purcell, the captain of kerns here presented, died in 1549, and was buried in the Cathedral of St. Canice, where his tombstone still remains, the inscription on which terms him, in barbarous Latin, " Capitanus turbariorum comitis Ormonie." [See The History, Architecture, and Antiquities of the Cathedral Church of St. Canice, p. 250.]

[d] i. e. Archdeacon. Sir Stephen Archidiacon, Knight, is one of the witnesses to William Marshall's charter to Dunbrody Abbey. In 1218 he made a grant to the Prior of Innistioge, which is witnessed by Thomas Fitz Anthony, Seneschal of Leinster [Archdall's Monasticon], whose daughter and co-heiress, Dissere, he married. It appears by Inquisition, No.10, Jac. I., that Archdeacon of Dangan and Denn of Grenan conjointly held a court-baron, " super terram dominicalem," of the vill of Thomastown, as co-heirs of Thomas Fitz Anthony. Sir Sylvestre le Erchedekine is mentioned in the Printed Rolls of 32 Edw. I.

Sir Reymund Lercedekne was summoned as a Baron to Parliament, on the invasion of Ireland by the Bruces, 4 Edw. II., and again, 18 Edw. II. Sirs Edmond and William Ercedekne were summoned to attend the war in Scotland anno 1335. [Rymer.] Sir Thomas and Sir Odo le Ercedekne were among the knights taken prisoners at the Battle of Bannockburn; but they were probably Thomas and Odo le Archdeacon of South Wales, whose pedigree is given in a MS. *penes* the

Item, they present that the kepers of my Lorde of Ostreys studdes and of his houndes[a] do use coyne and lyverye over all, quarterly.

Item, the saide Jurye present that all the saide Lorde of Ostreys freholders use lyke coyne and lyverye, that is to saye, suche of them as have studdes.

Item, the saide Jury present that Edmund Fitzjames of Ormounde,[b] useith to take certein money on every towneship at 4^{or} severall tymes of the yere; and where he can have no money, he takeith mete and drynke to the value of the money, as he lyste to sesse it, that is, of some Towne 2^s and some 20^d, and so more or lesse as the Township is of power.

Item, the saide Jurye present that the saide Lorde of Ostrey useith certen mete and drynke ones yerely, callid guyddye,[c] upon all his owne servauntes and tenauntes, and not elswhere.

Item, the saide Jurye present that the saide Lorde of Ostrey levieth yerely in the tyme of Lent, certen Otes of every Township over all the countrey for his chief horsse.[d]

Item, the saide Jurye present that ther is a lawe useid over all

---

Earl of Cawdor. Theobald, son of Odo, was summoned as an English Baron to Parliament, 14 Edw. II. There was also a family of this name settled in the county of Devon, and another in Cornwall.—[Dugdale's Monasticon Anglican., and Kearsley's Peerage.] Odo le Ercedekne appears to have been the first of the name settled in Ireland; and when the family grew " Irish," it assumed from this Odo the patronymic of Mac Odo, shortened to Cody. Cody and Archdeacon are *aliases* to the present day in the county of Kilkenny, where, especially in the neighbourhood of Thomastown, the names are common.

[a] See p. 89, *supra*.

[b] Probably Edmund, the eldest son of Sir James Butler, and Sawe Cavanagh, his wife, born before marriage, but after betrothal; who, with his brother Theobald, though *muliers* by the law of the Church, in consequence of the subsequent marriage of their parents, was pronounced base-born by Act of Parliament in favour of Sir Piers Butler, the eldest son born after marriage. The only objection to this identification is that, in 1501, Theobald, the son of this Edward, was cited to defend his right, which looks as if his father were dead.—[See The History, &c., of St. Canice, pp. 186–88.]

[c] i. e. Cuddie. *Cuid-oidche*, literally "a portion for one night," was the Gaelic term for the suppers to which a chieftain was entitled from certain occupiers of the clan country.

[d] The " chief horsse" were those used to carry the heavily accoutred knight or man-at-arms. See the " Kildare Rental," in course of publication in the " Journal" of the Society.

the countrey, callid Brehens lawe, whiche is mayntayned by all the Lordes of this lande, and moste specially within the Countie of Kilkenny,[a] whiche Lordes commynly have eche of them one severall Judge under them; the Judges name undre my Lorde of Ostrey, Rory Maklane. Thye whiche Judges shalbe successyvely chosen for the supportacion of the saide lawe.

Item, the saide Jurye present that the saide Judgeis have ones every 2 yeres one hogge or elles 20^d in redy money, for his fee, upon every Township under his jurisdiccion.

Item, the saide Jurye present that the saide Judgeis use upon every accion of dett or detynue or otherwyse, the judgement given, do take the 20th parte of the some judgeid to the recoverer, whiche is levied upon the parte so evicteid.

Item, the saide Jury present that aboutes Midsomer last past one Jamys Kennedy, sonne to the Prior of Knocktover,[b] did burne the house of one Donoughe Makdonell, and therapon taken and imprisoned; upon whiche burneing the saide Irishe Judge, and his sonne with him, compellid the saide Prior and Convent to paye 10 markes to the partie trespased, and to themselffes 40^s, and that payed, delyvered the prisoner at his lybertie.

[a] The prevalence and authority of the ancient Brehon or common law of Ireland, in a county like Kilkenny, which was almost altogether colonized by English settlers at a very early period, is exceedingly curious. When the Commission on the Irish Brehon Laws shall have given its labours to the world, we then, and not till then, may hope to see the subject in all its bearings fully elucidated. That the people preferred the Brehon to the Statute law, we have seen at p. 83 *supra*. The Brehon of the Earl of Ossory is called Rory Mac Laughire in the Presentment of the Corporation of Kilkenny, which also mentions the Irish customs called the "Statutes of Kylcas," conjectured, at p. 78 *supra*, to have been regulations framed at the Earl of Ossory's castle of *Kilcash*, in the county of Tipperary. But when this was written, we did not remember that there was in the Brehonic code a law called "kincogus" (often corrupted into "kylcogus" and "kylcolgas"), from cin, *crime, debt, liability*, and coiħ-ḟocup, *kindred, relations*, which (as we are informed by Dr. O'Donovan) provided that unless the tribe outlawed an offender or debtor of their kindred, they were collectively accountable for his crimes or debts. It prevailed where Irish customs had superseded English Statute law; and a modification of it was subsequently introduced into the Statute Book (11th Eliz., cap. 4). Mac Gille Eain was the old form of Mac Lean.— [Four Masters, vol. v. p. 1364.]

[b] i. e. Knocktopher.—See "Archdall's Monasticon," p. 376, for a reference to the transaction.

Item, the saide Jurye present that when the saide Erlle of Ostrey hathe any buyldeinges or reparacions of any of his castelles or other edyfices or workes to do, he compelleith his tenauntes, or suche other of the countrey as he lykeith, to worke upon the saide buyldeinges and edyfices at ther owne propre costes and chargeis.[a]

Item, the saide Jury present that all the saide Erlle of Ostreis freholders use in lyke maner to compell ther tenauntes to do lyke workes.

Item, the saide Jurye present that upon every murder commytteid, the hole kynred of the partie murderid doo use to compell the hoole kynred of the murderer to come before the saide Irishe Judge, and then the Judge will compell the defendauntes eche of them to be contrybutaries to suche some of money as shalbe adjudgeid by him, and two partes therof to be paied to the principall captayne of the playntyfes, and the 3[le] parte therof to the next of the bludde of the partie murdereid, and so the murderer is quytte.[b]

---

[a] R. Cowley, writing to Cromwell in 1537, states that the Earl of Ossory was ready to build castles to restrain the Mac Murroughs and Kavanaghs, if the King would do the like in Odrone and Mac Murroughs' country adjoining the Earl's lands, and goes on to say—"Such pyles and holdes as the King woll buylde in the marches of the English pale, the inhabitauntes there woll gladly fynde cariadge of stones, lyme, sannde, and tymbre, and labourers to cast hedges and ditches."—[State Papers, temp. Henry VIII., vol. ii., part iii., p. 449.]

[b] The Irish custom of levying a fine in cases of what we now call murder and manslaughter is here very strikingly put forward. A fighting man was of too much importance to his sept and chieftain to exact blood for blood. The custom seems to have been early introduced amongst the English in Kilkenny; for we find by the record of an inquiry and adjudication on a quarrel and affray which took place between the English of Tipperary and the English of the Liberty of Kilkenny, in the neighbourhood of Callan, in the latter county, that it was adjudged that Hugo Purcell, Sheriff of Tipperary, for himself and his followers should pay to the Lord of the Liberty of Kilkenny one hundred and six marks and forty pence; viz., for each Englishman that was slain twenty marks, and for each Irishman slain, five marks and forty pence.—[Plea Roll, 28 Edw. I., membrane 29.] The Liberty of Kilkenny was at that time coextensive with the present diocese of Ossory, and its Lord was Gilbert de Clare, Earl of Gloucester and Hereford. The Irish came in as allies to the English combatants on each side; the O'Shees helping the Tipperary "faction," and the O'Glorys the Kilkenny men. It is worthy of remark that this award was made by the authority and at the command of the royal Justiciary, John Wogan. This Roll is preserved in the Exchequer, Dublin.

Item, the saide Jurye present that Robert Rothe, now Soveraigne of the Towne of Kylkenny, hathe diverse grey merchauntes[a] whiche forstall the market, not onely of almaner of merchaundyseis, but also of vytailles; in suche wise that the market is not duely serveid as it ought to be, ne the kinges poore subjectes can have the saide merchaundyseis ne vytailles soo good chepe as they were wonte.

Item, the saide Jurye present that Gefferey Rothe, Richard Rothe, John Rothe, Piers Rothe, Nicholas Haket, Thomas Purser,[b] Robert Shey, Edwarde Lyner, Robert Dolyng, and manyother merchauntes of the Towne of Kylkennye, whose names the saide Jurye knowe not, have lyke grey merchauntes.

Item, the saide Jurye present that ther ar many other merchauntmen of the Citie of Waterford do use lyke grey merchauntes, whose names ensue, vizt, Patrik Welche, Thomas Lumbard, Henry Welche, younger, Henry Welche, sen^r., Patryk Welche the younger, James Welche, Sherlok, Edward Shyrlok, Jamys Sherlok, jun^r., Richard Lombard, David Baylif, William Madan, Jamys Baylif, Morice Wyse, William Lyncoln, Mallage Tressey, goldesmyth, Piers Dobin, Denys Porsell, John Neyle, John Lee, Nicholas Lee, Robert Lee, and many other whose names they knowe not, and use also to forstall the marketes, and also regrate[c] the same; so that there is not unethes a hide to be boughte in no market ne elsewhere but at ther handes and at ther pleasure, ne wolle, vytalles, ne other thinges.

Item, the saide Jurye present that one John Isam, servaunte to Mr. Scintlowe[d], aboute Midsomer last past, did take and cary awaye

---

[a] Grey merchants (it appears by the Irish Statute, 11 Eliz. cap. 5) were those who, with intent to sell again, purchased " hydes, felles, checkers, fleges, yarne, linnen cloth, wooll, or flockes, in any other place or places but only in the open market or fayre." The term seems to be synonymous with "forestaller." The original Act against Grey Merchants, revived by the above Statute, was passed at Dublin in the 33rd year of Henry VIII.—[Statutes of Ireland, pp. 102, 169.]

[b] i. e. Purcell.

[c] Forestallers were those who bought commodities coming to any market, and before they arrived at same. Regrators were persons who " bought by the great, and sold by retaile."—[Cowell's Interpreter, in verb.]

[d] William St. Loo, Esq., was an English gentleman of family, a younger

the wyfe of Piers Eyloward of Waterford, and sone after she was founde by her husbondes frindes and caried to the Castell of Dungarven,[a] and the saide John folowid herre, and she being defendeid by one of my Lorde Jamys[b] servauntes, whome by the saide John ther was murtherid, and therapon the saide John was attacheid and brought to the Castell of Kylkenny, and afterwarde brake oute of the said Castell,[c] and nowe is at lyberty unpunysheid.

brother of Sir John St. Loo, who came over at the time of Silken Thomas's revolt. He was Seneschal of the Palatinate Liberty of Wexford for several years. The Lord Deputy and Council report, in 1542, that he had been accused of certain murders and felonies, and arraigned in open sessions, when he refused the King's pardon, stood his trial, and was fully acquitted. John Isham was probably a cadet of the Northamptonshire family of that name, of whom Sir John was created a baronet in 1627. In a MS. volume of pedigrees, *penes* the Earl of Cawdor, Sir Nicholas Arnold, Lord Chief Justice of Ireland in 1564, is said to have married Margaret, daughter and heir of John Esam, of [blank], in Dorsetshire, son of Roger Esam, Esq. The office of Seneschal of the county of Wexford was granted to this John, 16th November, 1548.—[State Papers.] He is stated, in the Visitation of Wexford, to have left five co-heiresses, of whom Catherine married Nicholas Stafford, Esq., of Ballymacarne, and Margaret married Nicholas, son and heir of William Hore, Esq., of Harperstown, and secondly, Sir Nicholas Arnold. In a pedigree of Power, of Donisle, county of Waterford, "a daughter to Isam in the county of Wexford" is said to have been married to Piers, second son of Nicholas Power (Baron) of Donisle.— [Carew MS., 635.] The John Isham in question had been in the service of Protector Somerset, and was not a "servant" in the present acceptation of the term, having been a young gentleman-retainer to St. Loo, an English-born knight, Seneschal of the County Palatinate of Wexford. He himself succeeded to this high office in 1548, and died at Bryanston, in that shire, in 1554.—[MS., S.P.O.] He married Ellen Woodlock. Sir Piers Aylward was knight of the shire for the county of Waterford in 1559.

[a] Dungarvan, county of Waterford. This was then a Royal Castle, the custody of which was at this time committed to the Earl of Ormonde.

[b] Lord James Butler, who succeeded his father as Earl of Ormonde.

[c] This was not the first time Kilkenny Castle was used as a prison, or that malefactors escaped from it. Clyn relates that, on the eve of Ascension-day, in the year 1338, Eustace La Poer, then Seneschal of the Liberty of Kilkenny, arrested and imprisoned therein Fulco and Oliver de la Frene, without any ostensible cause; who, fearing his malice and vindictive temper rather than the rigour of justice, Oliver the next day escaped from the fortress, and, assembling his retainers and friends, on the day after, "cum manu valida," burst in the castle gates, and delivered Fulco from durance, in spite of the Seneschal.—[Clyn's Annals, published by the Irish Archæological Society, p. 28.]

Item, the saide Jurye present that where ther is an accion depending betwene Edmund Arsepreche, playntyf, and Thomas Sertall, defendaunt, whiche Edmund of his owne wilfull mynde, and contrarye to the kinges lawes, did forcybly take one horsse as a pledge from the said Thomas, withoute takeing any officer wyth him.

Item, the saide Jurye present that where ther was a wryte of subpena directeid to Wrory Amougher,[a] and delyverid to hym by William Tewe, he not regardeing it, toke it unreverently, and threwe it in the myre from hym.

[a] This was Rory "Ua Mordha," commonly called Lord O'More, Prince of Leix. In Queen Mary's reign (A. D. 1555) his brother, Gillepatrick O'More, invaded Leix, and fought a battle with the adherents of this Rory, who was killed in the conflict. This led to the forfeiture of Leix, which Mary planted with a colony of English. But Rory's widow, Margaret Butler, daughter of Piers, Earl of Ormonde, brought her two sons, Kedagh and Callagh, or Charles, to Queen Elizabeth, and represented to her the injustice done to them, and the Queen sent the eldest, Kedagh, to Cambridge, allowing him one hundred pounds per annum for his maintenance, and Charles to Oxford, with a yearly allowance of sixty pounds. The eldest son died without issue; and Charles [the celebrated Irish antiquary], on returning to Ireland, petitioned the Queen's most honourable Council to represent his case to her. The Queen, unwilling to dispossess a large number of English families planted in Leix, granted to Charles, Ballina, and some other lands in the barony of Carbury, in the county of Kildare, forfeited by the De la Hydes. In the year 1600 Charles married the daughter of Walter Scurlock, Esq. He died in 1620, leaving two sons, Rory O'More, so famous during the war of 1641, who died without issue male; and Lisagh, or Lewis of Ballina, Esq., who was the great grandfather of James O'More, Esq., of Ballina, who died in 1779, leaving one daughter, Letitia, who married Richard O'Ferrall, of Ballinree, in the county of Longford, Esq., the ancestor of Richard More O'Ferrall, of Ballina, Esq.—[See a MS. of the late James O'More, of Ballina, who died in 1779.] Rory O'More, who was killed in 1555, had also an illegitimate son, the notorious Rory Oge, so lauded by the Irish bards for destroying and plundering English towns, who was slain by Brian Oge, son of Brian Mac Gillapatrick, in 1578. He married a daughter of Pheagh Mac Hugh O'Byrne, by whom he had a son, Owny Mac Rory, who defeated Essex in 1598, at beapna na ₅-cleice, the Pass of Plumes, and took the Earl of Ormond prisoner. Three years before his death he had headed a confederacy of the O'Mores and O'Connors Faly; his troops of wood kerns amounted to many hundreds, and they burned and desolated large portions of Leinster, Meath, and Fingal. —[*Id.*, p. 1691.]

Gillepatrick O'More, the elder brother, who killed his brother Rory in 1555, married a daughter of O'Conor Faly,

THE VERDYT OF THE CORPORACŌN OF THE TOWNE OF
KILKENNYE.

[*October*, 1537.—*MS. State Paper Office.*]

RICARDUS SHEE, JUR̄.		THOMAS SHEE.	
RICARDUS ROTHE.		EDWARD RAGGE.[b]	
THOMAS LANTON.[a]		DAVID ARCHER.	
GALFR̄US ROTHE.	} JUR̄.	THOMAS RAAOUR.[c]	} JUR̄.
NICH^s. HAKKET.		WALTERUS LAWLES.	
JOH̄ES WALSHE.		REDMOND SAVAGE.	
JOH̄ES ROTHE.			

First, the said Jurie present that every lorde, gentylman, freholder, & every horseman and Idleman within the countie of Kylkenny use to take coygne & livery, foye[d] & paye at all tymes, at their pleasure, of their tenauntes and other inhabitauntes of the said countie.

Item, they present that Thomas Fitzmorice, Patrik, his brother, & Andrewe, Thomas his sonne, servauntes to the Lorde of Ostrey, doo use to take wood, cole, and al maner vitailes by the high wayes commyng to the market towne of Kylkenny at their owne price, ayenst the willes and myndes of the Inhabitauntes of the countrey, being owners therof.

Item, that the said Andrewe hath taken with force and ayenst

and had a son Callagh, or Charles, who was living at Naples in 1611, and was the senior of his race.

The trait of flinging the Queen's writ into the mire, so graphically described by the "Commyners" of Kilkenny, is very characteristic. The social state of Ireland, at the period, presented no greater difficulty than the impracticability of inducing Gaelic lords to become amenable to English law-courts. Perhaps William Tewe, who had the courage to serve the writ, was a relative of James Tywe (Tighe), of Knocktopher, one of the Jurors.

[a] i. e. Langton.

[b] An old tower at the angle of Rose-Inn-street, Kilkenny, now destroyed, is said to have been called Castle Rag.

[c] i. e. Raghter, now Rafter.

[d] "*Foy* is when idelmen [*edel*, noble or free men] require meat out of mealcs, or when they take money for their *coyne* [refection], and [nevertheless] go a begging to their host's neighbours. It is as much as to say, a benevolence."—[Add. MS. 1328, Exactions of the Irishry.]

the Kinges peace, xii monethes past, in the high waye, from John Amore,[a] bocher of Kylkenny, one kowe of the goods & catell of the said John Amore, & of one Lowghyn Makes.

Item, that James Butler FitzTybod,[b] in like maner, hath taken two kyen from Richard Barys of Kylkenny of the catell of the same Richard.

Item, that the Lorde of Ostrey, the lady his wif, the lorde James Butler & Richard Butler, and their horsgromes, take up certeyn oots every yere in tyme of lent called sommer oots for their chief horse, of their tenaunts and other inhibitauntes of the countie, at their pleasure.

Item, the said Lorde of Ostrey & the said lady his wife, & other their children, doo usually sende their horses to the howses of husbandmen, and with every horse one or two horseboyes, and ar founde at the costes of the said husbondman, and there remayne during their pleasure.

Item, the Lorde Shertell,[c] and the Baron Grace,[d] and all other freholders within the said countie, doo use like exaccyon.

---

[a] i. e. O'More; he is called "More" by the "Commyners" of the town.

[b] Probably a son of Theobald, the *mulier*, or base brother of the Earl of Ossory.—[See p. 99, *supra*.]

[c] "The Lorde Shertell" was evidently James Shortall of Ballylarkan, in the county of Kilkenny. Geoffrey Scortall is one of the witnesses to the charter to Kells, temp. King John.—[Chartæ Privileg., p. 19.] John, son of Simon Shorthall, was one of the sureties in the affair of William Utlaw, the banker of Kilkenny, which gave rise to the story of the Kilkenny witch.—[Patent Rolls, 3 Edw. II.] Robert, son of John Shortall, of Claragh, is mentioned in the Close Roll of 8 Edw. III. Friar Clyn chronicles under the year 1323, "deposissio domini Roberti Scorthals," and that Sir Geoffrey Schorthalis was knighted by Lord Butler in 1336. Geoffrey and Gilbert Shortall were summoned among the knights and gentry of Kilkenny to attend the Scottish war in 1335.—[Rymer, in Appendix to Grace.] Robert Shortall was appointed Sheriff of the county, 20th Aug., 9 Henry V., and as "Armiger" was granted 100s. reward for his services and costs in wars and treaties, anno 4 Henry VI.—[Printed Rolls.] James Shortals, "Lord of Ballylorkan," whose tomb was erected in 1507, is buried with his wife Katherine White, in the Cathedral of St. Canice. Sir Oliver Shortall, Knt. (son of James Shortall and Owney Fitzpatrick) of Ballylorkan, was seised of that manor and of Castle Idough, &c. He married Ellen Butler, and died in 1630, leaving an eldest son, James.—[Inquis., No. 36, Car. I.] The war-cry of the Shortalls was *Puckan-such-abo!* For further information respecting this family, see "The History, &c., of St. Canice," pp. 165-73.

[d] This family has been already suffi-

Item, the said Lord Ostrey and his childern take cuddeys of the inhabitauntes of the countie & of his tenauntes also ; and all other freholders doo take cuddies yerely of their tenauntes & fermors.[a]

Item, Lysaghe M'Conyll[b] & Rosse M'hunedof of Slymagre[c] have spoyled and robbed the inhabitauntes of the towne, and others hav-

ciently celebrated in their interesting history and memoirs, published by Sheffield Grace, Esq. A remarkable grant, and highly illustrative of the above Presentment, was made by Richard II. to Almaric Grace, " Baro de Grace," by which the King gave him permission, for the better peace of the county of Kilkenny, to marry Tibina, daughter of O'Magher, a chieftain of the Irish.—[Patent Roll, 9 Rich. II.] The annalist Clyn records the death of the " noble warrior," Hamond le Grasse, in battle against the Scots under Edward Bruce, anno 1315. John, " Baro de Graas" was appointed Custos Pacis, county of Kilkenny, 3 Henry VI.—[Patent Roll]. Robert, " son and heir of the Baron Grace," stated above to have married a " daughter of Ossory," was probably the same whose wife, Katherine M'Gillapatricke (daughter of the chieftain of Upper Ossory), obtained a grant of English liberty, 29th Jan., 32 Hen. VIII.—[Printed Rolls.] There is a fine tomb in Kilkenny Cathedral to Sir John Grace, " Baro de Courtstown," who died subsequently to 1568.—[See History, &c., of St. Canice, pp. 258-62.] By the list of the gentry of the county in the Carew MS., " Oliver Grace and his kinsmen" held lands to the value of £120 yearly —[See p. 96, supra.]

[a] The profitableness of these Irish exactions made the Anglo-Norman lords of the soil careless about retaining the English yeomanry originally planted on their estates. " The pore Englishe erth tillers," writes R. Cowley to Cromwell in 1537, " who cannot skyll upon penury nor wrechidnes, as the Irishe tenantes doo sustayne and bere, but must kepe honest residence, the lordes and inheritors takith suche a gredy lust of proficte, that they bring into the hart of the English pale Irishe tenantes, whiche neither can speke th'Englishe tonge, ne wer capp or bonet, and expulseth ofte the auncient good Englishe tenantes."—[State Papers, temp. Henry VIII., vol. ii., part iv., p. 449.]

[b] One of the septs of the O'Brenans was called " Clan M'Conill" [Transactions of the Kilkenny Archæological Society, vol. i., p. 240], so that it is likely the spoilers here presented belonged to the O'Brenans, of Ui-Duach, a district of Kilkenny bounded by Slievmargy on the north-east.

[c] This range of mountains separates the county of Kilkenny, the Queen's County, and the county of Carlow. The English Constable of Carlow writes to the Lord Deputy, April, 1549, that, in consequence of Sir Richard Butler building a castle at Garryn Denn, in Slievmargy, the people will not inhabit there, but leave the neighbourhood. That the country belongs to O'More, and not to the Anglo-Irish knight. The constable requested a grant of Slievmargy for himself, stating that " Whale's" (Wale's, Wall's, Veal's, or Calf's) claim is founded on an old record brought over by the High Commissioners, and curiously adds :--" All the profit Baron Lyster [St. Leger]

yng entercourse two or from the market of Dyssert-Dermot,[a] of their goodes to the value of one hundreth poundes and above, and of five yeres past dyd felonously kyll and murther one Laurence Bodell, late of Clarougthe.[b]

Item, that Adam Bremanghen, of Crabale, hath taken three plough horses of Nicholas Hakket, of Kylkenny, by the highwaye with force, and them wrongfully withhold.

Item, the jury present that John Butler FitzTylot[c] dyd take & drive awaye [cattel?] from this towne, of the Inhibitauntes of the same towne, and thereupon freshe sutes were made after the same John, and except the partie making the sute had been rescued by divers inhabitauntes of the countrey he had been slayn by the said John.

Item, Robert Grace, sonne of the said Baron Grace hath by 3 yeres past taken and wrongfully yet withholdeth from Richard Rothe 3 ploughe horses.

Item, they present that Robert Forstell[d] of Kylferrouthe, gente, by 15 yeres past and more, dyd felonously slee and murdre one man in the said countie of Kylkenny, wherefore as the said Jury suppose he hath been indited, and yet remayneth unponished.

Item, that Patrik Forstall, his sonne, hath by xvii yeres past slayne & murdred one Pers Shereman then one of the porters of this towne, therefore the said Jurye suppose he hath been endicted & yet remayneth unponished.

Item, the Lord of Ostrey, and all lordes spirituall and temporall of this countrey of Kylkenny, and also all freholders and

had through Slewmarge in 'hunnaye, corne, butter, catell, and munnaye, by the yere, came not past four nobells Irysh and five pence.'"—[MS., State Paper Office.]

[a] i. e. Castledermot, still celebrated for its fairs.

[b] Claragh, in the county of Kilkenny, bordering on Ui-Duach, the O'Brenan's country.

[c] i. e. Tibot.—[See note, p. 99, supra.]

[d] The Fforstalls were an ancient Anglo-Norman family of the county of Kilkenny. The head of the family held the manors of Kilferagh and Ballyfrunck, by knight's service from the Crown in capite.—[See History, &c., of St. Canice, p. 164.] "The slaughter of Mr. Fowke Comerford and Mr. Peter Forstall, with their company, at Tramore, done upon them by the Poers, the xx day of June, 1452," is related in the Carew MS., No. 632.

tenauntes, doo take canes for theftes, & other offences, and for murdre the take an herik called a salte, that is a fyne.

Item, they saye that the Erle of Ormond[a] hath the possession of the castell, with mylles, meadowes, and pastures perteyning to the same, and doo receave all the cheffry of this towne, which is xviii[li] Irish by yere, whereof his bailif hath xx[s] sterling for keping of the towne courte.

Item, the Galoglaghes of my Lorde of Ostrey, being in nombre for the more parte 2 batelles conteyning xvii score, be contynually kepte at the charges of the countrey, and receave yerely a great somme of money of the Inhabitauntes of the same countrey, which is assessed and levied of the landes of the fermors, inhabitauntes, and other tenauntes.

Item, the Prior of Inystyok, the Abbot of Gerypont, and divers other dwelling nere unto the Ryvre, doo make and set suche weares,[b] from banke to banke in the same Ryver, from Inystyok unto the mountaign of Bleme,[c] that no ferye ne bote may have their course.[d]

[a] This was Sir Thomas Boleyn, created Earl of Ormond by Henry VIII. He claimed the Ormond title and inheritance in right of his mother, one of the daughters and heirs general of Thomas, seventh Earl of Ormond.

[b] Nearly all the "several fisheries" on the Nore are held in right of the lands of the abbeys to which they belonged.

[c] This "mountaign of Bleme," i. e. Sliabh Bladhma, Spensor fables to have been named from the "giant Blomius," the poetic parent of the three rivers Barrow, Suir, and Nore—"the three renowened brethern:"—

"Which that great giant Blomius begot
  Of the faire nymph Rhûsa wand'ring there,
One day, as she to shunne the season hot,
  Under Slewbloome in shady grove was got."

Spenser has here been accused of inaccuracy, inasmuch as the true sources of the Nore and Suir are to be found in the Devil's-bit range over Templemore. But he knew better than the cavillers, for anciently the entire range from Mountrath to Templemore was named Sliabh Bladhma.

[d] The year previous to the date of these presentments an Act had been passed at the Parliament holden in Dublin (28 Henry VIII., cap. 22), as follows:—"Prayen the Commons in this present Parliament assembled, that where at all times necessarie, boates, scowts, wherries, clarans, cottes, and other vessels loden and bestowed with goods, merchandizes, and other stuffe haue beene vsed to passe and repasse through, and in the Kings most excellent Maiesties riuers and waters of the Barrow, the Noyre, the Suyr, and the Rie within this land, which Rie is in the countie of Kilkenny, to and from

K

Item, the Fyshermen of Inystyok, being tenauntes and fermors unto the said Prior, which doo occupie feries and bootes, using to have the cariage of wynes commyng unto this towne by watter, for the which cariage they ar well and trewly paied, yet that notwithstanding the same botemen doo perce the wyne vessels, and drinke a great parte of the wyne of every vessell, and will not suffer the servauntes of the owners of the said wynes to be in the bote with their merchaundyes, to the great losse of the said owners.[a]

Item, the said Fyshermen doo, for the most parte, sell the Fyshe[b] that they doo take there from the inhabitauntes of this countrey, agenst the comen weale of the same countrey.

the Kings citie of Waterford, and the townes of Kilkenny, Rosse, and Clonmel, &c., and yet this, notwithstanding, now of late, diuers wilful persons hauing no respect to the premises, but more rather to their owne wilfulnesse, singular commoditie, and benefite, hauing no ground ne cause reasonable to the same, haue in diuers places of the said riuers and waters made such weres, purprestures, ingines, strites, and other like obstacles, and them and euery of them so do keepe and maintaine that by no meanes any boates, &c., laden and bestowed as is aforesaid can conveniently passe and repasse"—provides that the said weirs may be levelled by any one of the king's subjects in presence of the Sheriff or Seueschal; that sufficient gaps be made in all milldams, and seven feet at each side of said rivers " to bee where they must needs drawe the said boates and other vesselles afore named with strength of horses or men by land, unlesse at the making of this present act there bee a castel, fortresse, orchard, or garden vpon any such land so adioyning to the said riuers, of enerie side of the water, so far and as long as the said riuers or waters doe runne, or haue there concourse for the drawing, taking, loding, and conueying of the said boates," &c. The Nore was by this Act made a navigable river from the " mountaign of Bleme" to the sea, and so it remains to this day *in law*, as established by a late decision on an appeal in a fishery case before the Chairman of the County of Kilkenny at Quarter Sessions, July 1, 1858; although the river has *virtually* ceased to be navigable beyond Innistioge, and is crossed by innumerable weirs. The "hawling" of large flat-bottomed boats, called "lighters," or "clarahans," by gangs of men, from the tide water to Thomastown, continued in use until about fifteen years since, and was witnessed by the writer: gangs of about forty men, at 8*d.* a day each, were necessary to hawl a " clarahan" (the " claran" of the Act) against the rapid current of the Nore.

[a] The Act quoted in the previous note alludes to this fraudulent practice, and forbids it under penalty of forfeiture of the freight or wages, and treble the value of the injury to the owners, and a fine of £5 to the King.

[b] At the present day of railroads and steamers, when the general complaint is that the salmon taken in the Nore finds its way to London, it is curious to learn that a similar grievance was felt in Kilkenny more than three centuries ago.

Item, the Lorde of Ostrey, and all others, being freholders of eny towne within the said countrey, doo use to make statutes upon their fermors, and rule them in suche wise, that no fermor dare sell eny parte of their goodes, vitailles, or other merchaundyses without the licence of their lorde or owner of his tenauncye, to eny persone other then to suche merchaunt men, as shalbe unto them by the said lord, or other freholder assigned.

Item, they doo present that Barnabe Bolger, dwelling at the Bishop's corte,[a] doth forstall the market of this towne, commonly using to bie all suche merchaundises and other vitells commyng to the same market, nere to his dwelling howse.

Item, all the dwellers & inhabitauntes within the Irishetowne, nere unto this Towne, doo bie all suche vitalles and merchaundises which is brought towardes this Towne, & so doo forstall the market here.

Item, the lord of Ostry & his children doo commonly send their masons, carpenters, and kerntighe unto the poore husbandmen of the countrey at their pleasure, and of them have coygne,[b] lyverey, and divers other exaccyons.

Item, all other freholders and gentylmen dwelling within the said countie, doo use to take coyne and liverey, and divers other unlawfull exaccyons, as well by them self as by their servauntes in like maner.

Item, Donough Makeasyre being officiall in this countrey did wrongfully take of Thomas Rector, for sentence giving by hym in a cause of matrymony vi[li].

Item, the said officiall did take of Donyll Higay, for a like matter like sentence iv[li], and of Donough Makloughlyn, for like sentence 20[s].

Item, all freholders and tenauntes dwelling in the countrey have

---

[a] Bishop's-court, or Holmes'-court (now Upper-court, near Freshford, in the county of Kilkenny), was at this time the property of the see of Ossory. Barnaby Bolger seems to have been the Bishop's tenant, at least he was so when Bale occupied the See, who accuses him of having hired certain kerns of the Lord Mountgarret, and the Baron of Upper Ossory, to slay him. — " Vocacyon of Johan Bale to the Bishoprick of Ossorie."

[b] Coinee, or Coinmhe. Coinihe is translated by Dr. O'Donovan [Irish Arch. Misc., vol. i., p. 143], feast or refection.

sensualls,[a] being the more part priests, within their towne or townes, which have the hearing and determynacion of all bludsheddes, fraies, strayes and actes made within that towne or townes; and the partie greved shall not appeale by no meanes from that ordre.

Item, the statutes of Kyleas[b] be commonly used in the countrey by my Lord of Ostrey, and by his Irishe Judge, called a Brehon, and by all other freholders of the countrey, and they use none other lawe but the same, and divers of the bookes of the same statutes ar in the keping of the shiref of the shire of Kilkenny, and the Bishop of

[a] i. e. Seneschals. An Act (22 Victoria, cap. 14) which came into force April 1, 1859, abolishes this office, and the manor courts in which the Seneschals presided.

[b] Sir Edward Fitton, in a letter to Lord Burleigh, dated 31st January, 1571-2, writes of "that old Iryshe law, now long tyme forbydden, called Kylcolgashe."—[MS., State Paper Office.] At p. 100, infra, the true form of this term is given, viz., "Kincogus," from cin, crime, debt, and coib-focup, kindred. The transitions, "Kincogus," "Kylcolgashe," "Kyleas," are easy. We are indebted to Mr. John P. Prendergast for interesting illustrations of the word. The Irish Parliament [11 Eliz. cap. 4] introduced a modification of this Brehonic custom into the Statute Law, enacting that "five persons of the best and eldest of every stirpe or nation of the Irishrie, and in the cuntries that be not as yet shire grounds" should be answerable for the misdeeds of their tribe, and be bound to render the wrong doers up to justice, "or else satisfie of their own proper goods, the hurtes by them committed to the parties grieved." Spenser, in his "View of the State of Ireland," (Ed. 1633, p. 25), speaks in condemnation of this Statute, and terms the Brehonic regulation, on which it was founded "the Custome of Kin-cogish." Elizabeth's Statute was repealed by the 10 and 11 Car. I. cap. 6; but the 13th enactment of the same session, known as the "Statute of Hue and Cry," was identical in principle; enacting, as it did, that all the inhabitants of a barony were liable to make good one moiety of the robberies committed within it, unless they raised the hue and cry, and made pursuit with horse and men, and so of any other baronies the robber might pass through, whilst that in which he was taken or killed was free. The principle also ran through the severe regulations of the Commonwealth in Ireland, and was called indifferently "Kincogas," or "Kilcogas Law," and the assessments under it were called "kindred-money," or "prey-money," whilst the Statute of Hue and Cry was so far modified as to make the Irish and Papist inhabitants repair all the losses. Of this code, the following orders of the Commissioners for the affairs of Ireland, extracted by Mr. Prendergast from the originals in Birmingham Tower, Dublin Castle, and obligingly communicated to us, may be taken as illustrations:—

"Persons transplantable into Connaught, the 8th head.

"Upon reading the eighth head of a Remonstrance of grievances by the persons that are transplanted into the C°. of Clare, setting forth that contrary to

Watterford, and one booke is in the possession of Rory McLaughire, being Judge of the countrey.

Item, where the Kinges writ of alowaunce was directed to the citisens of Watterford for the alowaunce of the grauntes, liberties, and custumes graunted by the kinges most noble progenytors to the Fremen of this Towne of Kilkenny, and confirmed by the Kinges highnes that nowe is; which writ the said citysens receaved, but that notwithstanding they doo denye to alowe unto the said fremen of this Towne their said liberties, grauntes, and custumes, wherfore they

a declarac'on remitting all offences (excepting murthers) to such as w^d conform to the act of Transplantac'on. They are dayly trobled as well for the plunders of the s^d yeare of the Rebellion, as for plunders donn ever since committed by persons in nature of tories, and also by Kincogùs; and, therefore, praying that they might have the benefits of the s^d Declarac'on, and that all orders commenced against them contrary thereunto might be recalled and superseaded, and restitue'on mad of what hath been taken from the Petic'oners on such orders. And upon considerac'on had therof, and of the Report made there upon by the Comittee of Officers, whereby itt appeares that contrary to a Declarac'on of the 14th Oct^r, 1653, remitting all offences (except Murthers), that the Petic'oners are molested upon that account, and they offer it that they ought to be releived therein according to the Act for Transplantac'on, as also that the s^d Kilcogus Law should not follow them into Clare for mischiefes done by their kindred in any of the other Provinces. It is Thought fitt, and hereby Or^d that the premises be referred to the considerac'on of the Lord Chief Justice Pepys, who is desired to report the case (upon perusall of the s^d Act for transplanta-

c'on) unto this Board by munday next, together with the Lo^{brs} opinion what is fitt to be done therein." — *Dublin*, 7 *April*, 1655. — *T. H. C. C.*

"Upon reading the Petition of John Barnwall, and the Certificate of Alderman Tighe and Mr. John Byrne thereupon, Ord^d that the s^d John Barnwall be equally freed from paying any preymonies for the future with any English Protestants:—whereof the Comm^{rs} of Applotment and all others are to take notice." — *Dublin*, 26 *Sept^r*, 1653.

John Jordan, Merchant of Castleknock, was freed from liability to contribute with other Irish Papists of the Barony to reparation of Protestant inhabitants by Tories, and from kindredmonies on account of his civil carriage to the English during the rebellion, and his good affection. — *Dated at Dublin*, 22 *March*, 1652-3.

Plate, money, and goods to the value of £200 belonging to John Williams in Captⁿ Nash's troop were set upon at Bennett's Bridge removing, about the 1st May, from Kilkenny to Waterford: to be levied off the Bar. of Gowran (where the s^d troope hath been continually sheltered) by instalments consistent with the abilities of the inhabitants, and payment of contribution. — *Dated at Kilkenny*, 5 *May*, 1652.

desyre that reformacyon may be had therin by my Lord Deputie and the said Comissioners.

Item, Nicholas Magrewe and Thomas Makeard, and many other priestes of the countrey doo take for the purificacyon of wemen, 2^s; for burienges, 8^d; for weddinges, 2^s. And divers other unlawfull exaccyons, and if they be not paied of the same they doo take pledges by compulsyon.

Item, they present that all the Kinges writtes and processe is duely executed and obeyed within this towne.

Item, they saye that the money which is yerely receyved for murage exceedeth not the somme of 20^s sterling, which money, with moche more, is yerely bestowed for the reparacyon and amending of the gates, walles, and pavement of this towne.

Item, they saye that the Erle of Ostrey hath maried^a one of his

---

The Papist inhabitants of the Bar of Dunboyne to pay Humphry Hills and W. Kennedy of Dublin, Cutters, £185. Decreed by the Court for Administration of Justice at Dublin, and £10 13s. 3d. costs [Instalments fixed]. And the said inhabitants to be at liberty to exhibit their information against the Papist inhabit^s of the Bar^s of Ratouth and Deese through which the enemy who plundered Hills and Kennedy passed at that time; or against any of the inhabitants thereof who entertained the s^d Tories without giving tymely notice thereof. To the end that they who shall be found guilty, may be forced to contribute with the s^d inhabitants of Dunboyne to the payment of the said Decree.—*Dublin, July* 7, 1659. *Edm^d Ludlowe, Miles Corbett, John Jones.*

That there is nothing new under the sun is abundantly proved by the provisions of the modern Act of the United Parliament, which enables the Lord Lieutenant of Ireland to quarter a large police force on the Irish townland where an outrage has been committed — neither the Legislature, nor those who feel the hardship of the law, being in the least aware that the principle had been elaborated by the Irish Brehons, perhaps, before the birth of Christ. Dr. O'Donovan, in a letter before us, says: "I know the law [of Kincogus] in all its phases and bearings, but it would take a good-sized volume to explain it. Unless the tribe proclaimed and outlawed one of themselves, they were accountable for his misdemeanors, or *kin-ta*. But if they went through the process of outlawing him, which was complex, they were for ever freed from his crimes, and he became answerable for his own debts. If he had not wherewithal to pay he was usually enslaved or executed."

^{a} In 1533, Lord Ossory gave his eldest daughter, Margaret, in marriage to Mac Gillapatrick, who is reported at that time to be a "denizen," and likely to become conformable to English rule. —[Published State Papers, vol. ii., part iii., p. 171.] The first "submission of doughters to M'Gello Patrik, being Irishe, and one other, his doughter, unto Dōmough Breme,[a] being also Irishe.

Item, Baron Grace[b] hath maried Robert Grace, his sonne and heire apperaunt, unto the doughter of Ossery.

Item, the lord of Osserey hath the tole of the market of Kylkenny.

Item, they present that [   ] Grace, bastard sonne of the said Baron, is maried to Donogh O'Folyns[c] doughter of Osserye.

Item, they present that Edmond Dof[d] Comerford, and Richard Dof Comerford, dyd steale and cary awaye five hives of the goodes of Richard Rothe, five yeres past, of the whiche he hath restored three hives, and more the said Jury knoweth not.

Mighell Patrick to the Kinges Majestic is obeisaunce, and to holde his landes to hym and his heires, after the due concourse of the Kinges lawes," is dated 8th Nov., 1537. It is printed in the second volume of State Papers, part iii., p. 515; and is an indenture between the Commissioners and "Barnard filium Patrici." He offers to hold and do as do the Barons of Delvin and Slane, and is promised to be created a Baron of Parliament, as Baron of Colthill[Cullehill?] and Castleton. His son and heir is to be educated in the English manner.

[a] i. e. Donough O'Brien, afterward Earl of Thomond. His marriage with Ellen, sixth and youngest daughter of Pierce, Earl of Ormonde, took place before the year 1533.—[History, &c., of St. Canice, p. 277.]

[b] The King (9 Ric. II.) for amelioration of the peace in the county of Kilkenny, granted permission to Almary Grace, Baron de Grace, to marry Tibina, daughter of O'Meagher, an Irish chieftan.—[Printed Patent Rolls.] This use of the term "Baron" shows that even in Henry VIII.'s time, the representatives of the ancient barons by tenure were customarily so styled. "Ossery" here stands for Mac Gillapatrick, chief of Upper Ossory.

[c] i. e. O'Foelan, now Phelan, and Whelan.

[d] Duf, black.—[See p. 119, *infra*.]

THE VERDYT OF THE COMMYNERS OF THE TOWNE OF KYLKENNY.

[*October*, 1537.—*MS. State Paper Office.*]

JOHES LYE.	JOH. LANGTON.	
JOHES BUSSER.	WALTERUS ROTHY.	
FRANC DORMONDUS.	WALTERUS MACHILL.	
JENKYN MARSHALL.	THOMAS GYBBES.	
WALTER CLERY. } JUR.	PATRICIUS RAGGE. } JUR.
WILLS. BRASELL.	TH: GARRARDUS.	
THOMAS PURSELL.	EDWARDUS ARCHER.	
ROBTUS THYVYN.	JACOBUS CAVYN.	

Fyrste, the saide Jurye present that my Lorde of Ostrey, my Lady his wyfe, and children, do charge all the countrey with Coyne and Lyverye, as often as they please.

Item, they doo present that Baron Grace dothe charge in lyke maner all his tenauntes, and dyverse other personnes, with coyne and lyverye.

Item, they do present that Porcell of Ballywhele[a] dothe in lyke maner charge all his tenauntes.

Item, Blannchefilde[b] in lyke maner dothe charge.

---

[a] i. e. Ballyfoyle. Philip Purcell, of Ballyfoyle, was seised of the manor of Mullergge, otherwise Purcell's Inch, the manor of Fenell, and of Mullane.—l-Purcially, &c.—[Inquis. Civit. Kilk., anno 1625.] The ruin of the Castle of Ballyfoyle stands in the glen of the same name, at the foot of the Johnswell mountains, north of Kilkenny about five miles.

[b] The Blanchevilles were settled at Blanchvillestown, &c., at an early period, holding of the King in capite by knight's service.—[See History, &c., of St. Canice, pp. 301-3.] Sir Nicholas Blancheville, Knt., Seneschal of the Liberty of Kilkenny, and Sirs William de St. Leger and Fulke Fraxineto (Frayne) were of the jury at Ross, anno 33 Edw. I., on the lands of Bygod, Earl of Norfolk. Sir John Blancheville, Knt., was summoned to the war in Scotland, anno 1335.—[Rymer.] Isabella Blancheville married Peter, son of Jas. Butler, of Owyll.—[Tomb in Jerpoint Abbey, dated 1490.] Edmond Blancheville, Esq., of Blanchevillestown, married Margaret, heiress of John, brother of Piers, eighth Earl of Ormond. Their son, Gerald Blancheville, Esq., of

Item, they present that Jamys Sweteman[a] dothe in lyke maner charge.

Also they present that Robt. Sertall,[b] of Hyggons Towne, dothe in lyke maner charge.

Also they present that Edmund Butler, of Butler's Wodde,[c] dothe in lyke maner.

Also they do present that Pyers Skantwell,[d] Thobod Butler,[e] his wyfe and children, the Baron of Brownesford,[f] Patryk Porcell of Lowyston, Kaer More Makphoris,[g] do in lyke maner.

Blanchvillestown, was knight of the shire in 1584. There is a printed Inquisition showing the extent of his lands. His son, Sir Edmond Blancheville, was living in 1616.—[Bibl. Sloane, No. 4792.] There are several documents in the S. P. Office relative to the murder of Edmond Purcel by Sir Edmond Blancheville, anno 1629.

[a] Sir Robert Sweetman (the Swedeman?) was summoned as a Baron to Parliament in 1374. His son, John, married Johanna, sister and heir of Robert Meyler, Esq., of Duncormuck. She and her husband were granted livery of her lands anno 1387. The principal seat of the Sweetmans was at Castle-eife, or Castle-eve, and Newtown D'Erley, which they held of the King in capite by knight's service. Edward Sweetman, of Hoodsgrove, died in 1616, seised of a castle, &c., in Gowran, one in Thomastown, and Hoodsgrove, &c., held of the Earl of Ormond, as of his manor of Rosbercon. His wife was Onora Murrish.—[Inquis., Com. Kilk., anno 1619.]

[b] Nicholas Shortall, of Upper Claragh, died seised of the manor of Upper Claragh, alias West Claragh, &c., held of the Earl of Ormond by military service, and of other lands, including Higginstown.—[Inquis. Com. Kilk., anno 1621.]

[c] i. e. Butler's Wood [p. 119, infra,

Inquis. Com. Kilk., No. 79, Car. 1., anno 1636.]

[d] i. e. Cantwell, probably of Cantwell's-court, four miles north-east of Kilkenny. The Cantwells, or De Cantwells, of Kilkenny and Tipperary, were early Anglo-Norman settlers.—[See History, &c., of St. Canice, pp. 180, 181]. The then head of the Cantwells married Mary, daughter of Gerald, Lord of the Decies (brother of the long-lived Countess of Desmond), and widow of Oliver Grace.—[Carew MS. 636]. There are two inquests on the lands of John Cantwell, of Cantwell's-court, dated 1637, among the printed Kilkenny Inquisitions.

[e] Probably the mulier brother of Sir Piers, the then Earl of Ossory.

[f] This proprietor, who was given the title of Baron long after his family ceased to be summoned to Parliament as such, was of the Geraldine stock. The title came at last to be a surname, e. g. Edmond Fitzgerald, alias Barron, late of Brownsford.—[Inquis. Com. Kilk., No. 35, Jac. I.] Brownesford castle is situate over the Nore, below Inistioge. Elenor Butler, one of the daughters of Piers Butler, of Cahir (Wilton), county of Wexford, second son of the first Viscount Mountgarrett, married Fitzgerald, alias Barron, of Brownsford.—[Visit. of Wexf., 1618.]

[g] Caher More Mac-Pheoris is also

Item, they do present that Walter Brennaghe,[a] sen[r]., Edmund, Walter, and Richard, his sonnes, do in lyke maner charge.

Item, they do present that Walter Brennaghe, the younger, Jamys Slygger,[b] Rouland, Baron of Burnechurche, Sheryf of Kyl-

mentioned in the verdict of the county of Wexford as Constable of Carlow Castle [p. 43, *supra*]. His surname is the Gaelic form of Fitz-Piers, i. e. the descendant of Sir Piers Birmingham, the celebrated "treacherous baron." Sir Walter Birmingham owned the manor of Kells, in the county of Kilkenny, and Castle Carberry, county of Kildare.—[Inquis., 34 Edw. III., quoted in Carew MS., 610.] His daughter and heiress, by marrying Sir Robert Preston, took the title of Baron of Kells into the Gormanstown family; but the male branches of the Birminghams disputed the right of female succession and the enjoyment of the estate. Sir William Birmingham was created Lord Carbery by Henry VIII.

[a] Brennagh, alias Walsh, of the Walsh Mountains, in the south-west of the county of Kilkenny. This family, originally from Wales, hence the name Brennach (Britton), or Walsh, was settled in Kilkenny immediately after the Conquest, and held a high position amongst the gentry down to the period of the Rebellion of 1641. Walter Walsh, of Castlehowell, the then head of the family, died in 1619; his son, Robert, died during his father's lifetime without issue, and his nephew, and next heir, Walter, was eighteen years of age in 1619, and unmarried.—[Inquis. Com. Wexford., 25 Jac. I.]

[b] i. e. St. Leger. Sir Thomas Fitz Anthony de St. Leger (see p. 52, *supra*) was the King's Seneschal of Leinster in the reigns of John and Henry III. He incorporated Thomastowne, which is still called in the Irish language *Bally-*

mac-Andan, or " the town of the son of Anthony."—[Lynch's Feudal Baronies, p. 232.] King John gave him the custody of the counties of Waterford and Desmond.—[Patent Rolls, p. 2.] He left five coheiresses, whose husbands paid their reliefs to the Crown, 16 Henry III.—[Reports, Irish Record Com , i. 331], viz.:—

Helen, married to Sir Gerald Roche.

Dionisia, married to William de Cantilupe.

Isabella, married to Geoffrey Calfe, Baron of Norragh.

Margaret, married to John Fitz Thomas, of Desmond, who was slain in 1261.

Dissere, married to Stephen Archidiacon.

Sir William St. Leger, Knight, was summoned among the Anglo-Irish magnates to the Scottish war in 1302. —[Rymer.] He married Johanna, heiress of Hugh Purcell, and her lands were granted to him, 2nd Edw. II.— [Patent Rolls, p. 10.] Her son, Sir Wm. de St. Leodegar, Knt., held the barony of Bargy, county of Carlow, of Margaret Segrave, heir of Earl of Norfolk.—[Patent Rolls, p. 67.] He was summoned as a Baron to Parliament at Kilkenny upon the invasion of the Bruces. Clyn records his death under the year 1328. Clyn records at 1333 that Geoffrey de la Frene, who married Johanna Purcel, heiress of Obargi, was slain by the O'Morthys, of Slemargys. Thomas Seynt Leger, " Baro del Bargy." is mentioned several times in the Patent Rolls of Richard the Second's time. Dr. Hanmer states

kenny,[a] Comberforthe[b] of Ballymak, Richard Comberforthe of

in his Chronicles that Slieve Margie, a mountain reaching along by Leighlin to Butler's Wood, was granted to St. Leger, with the title of Baron, and that of late years a gentleman of the name, dwelling at Danganstown, near Carlow, affirming himself to be lineally descended from Baron St. Leger, made claim to the same. The printed Inquisitions include one describing the possessions of Edward St. Leger, of Tullaghanbroge, who was seised of the manor of that name, &c.—[Inquis., Com. of Kilk., No. 2, Jac. I.] There was also a branch seated at Ballyfennon.—[See History, &c., of St. Canice, pp. 279, 280.] Stanihurst enumerates among the "banrets" who by usage enjoyed the title of Baron without the Parliamentary dignity—"Sentleger, banret of Slemarge, meere Irish ; Den, banret of Pormanstowne, waxing Irish ; Fitzgirald, banret of Burnechurch, &c."

[a] Sir George Carew states traditionally (Carew MS. 635) that the Barons of Burntchurch became to be called Barons because their ancestor was a Baron of the Exchequer, but this is a mistake: see note, p. 117, *supra*. In the 48th year of Edward III. the King's escheator was directed to seise into the King's hands the lands which belonged to William of Morice, late Baron of Burnchurch.—[Rot. Claus.] Roland was his son and heir.—[Rot. Pat. p. 92.] In the 11th of Henry IV., Roland f" Morice, together with Matthew Lappyng, John Gras of Tillaghroan, Robert Shorthals, Richard and Geoffrey Walsh, Gilbert Blanchville, and Patrick Coterel, was appointed custodes pacis in the county of Kilkenny. Roland Fitz Morice is also named in the commission of the peace of the 7th year of the same reign as "Baro de Brantchurch." There is a tomb of . . . . Fitz-Gerald, " alias Baron, dominus de Burinchurch," who died 1st February, 1545, and of his wife, " Anastasia St. Legger," in the churchyard of Burnchurch, four miles west of Kilkenny : his castle at Burnchurch still stands in good preservation. Some time before the year 1532 the "Baron of Brantchurch," who was then Knight of the Shire for Kilkenny, was made captive while travelling to Dublin to attend Parliament, by a retainer of the Earl of Kildare, and kept in irons for a long time in "Beardie's Castle," county of Kildare.—[History, &c., of St. Canice, p. 298.] Rowland Fitz Gerald, alias Baron de Burnchurch, and others (probably trustees), are stated in an Inquisition, No. 41, Jac. I., to have alienated Kiltranyn, otherwise Burnchurch, and other lands, which at the time of the alienation were held of the Crown by knight's service.

[b] This family, said to have come from Cumberford, in Staffordshire, in the time of King John, were settled at Danganmore, Ballybur, Ballymack, Inchehologhan, and Callan, in the county of Kilkenny. By the Statute of the 13 Eliz., cap. 7, "Thomas Queuerford, late of Ballymacka, hauing beene in his lifetime one of the chiefest and principall conspiratours and actuall dooers in this last rebellion," was attainted.—[Statutes of Ireland, p. 204 ; see also p. 115, *supra*.] Richard Comerford, of Ballibur, was descended from Ellen " Freny," one of the co-heiresses of Sir Patrick Freny (De la Freigne), and held the tract of country called Farren-Freny. — [Inquis. Com. Kilk., 4 Eliz., and No. 2, Jac. I.]

Ballybur, Hughe Bakkaham Makkagolde of Danmaghe,[a] John Fitzwilliam of Inchewoldham,[b] do in lyke maner charge.

Item, they doo present that Slyggar[c] of Tolleghan, Olyver Grace of Durles,[d] and Jamys Grace, do in lyke maner charge.

Item, they do present that John Grace of Glasshare[e] dothe in lyke maner charge.

Item, they present that Jamys Ogh Butler of Slewardeghe[f] doyth in lyke maner charge.

Item, they do present generally that all the freholders in the Countye of Kylkenny dothe charge ther tenauntes with Coyne and Lyverye.

Item, they do also present that the Bisshop of Ostrey, th Abbot of Jerypons, th Abbot of Kylleole, the Prior of Kellis, th Abbot of the Hollycrosse, the Abbot of Duske, they Busshop of Leylyn,[g] do in lyke maner charge ther tenauntes with Coyne and Lyverye, and in lyke maner do all other spirituall men of the same shyre.

Item, the Jurye present that Richard Sertoll, Phillip Purcelles, Onell, Conhurlle Odoley, my Lorde of Ostrey servauntes, and my Lorde Jamys servauntes, do in the tyme of Lent take up Otes of every plougheman of the countrey of Kylkenny, not paying money therfor, for to finde his horsse.

Item, they do present that Jamys Oghe Butler of Slewarde,

---

[a] Damagh is mentioned as a manor in the Kilkenny Inquest dated 5 and 6 Philip and Mary, and as having been let by the Earl of Ormond to Lewis Brian.

[b] Probably Inchelologhan, a castle belonging to the Comerfords. Rinuccini, when coming from Limerick to Kilkenny, stopped a night at a country-house three miles from that town, possibly Inchehologhan. — *Nunziatura in Irlanda,* p. 71.

[c] St. Leger, see note p. 118, *supra.*

[d] Correctly, Thurles, in the county of Tipperary.

[e] A castle stands to the present day at Glashare, near Johnstown, in the county of Kilkenny.

[f] Slievardagh, in the county of Tipperary.

[g] The Bishop of Ossory, the Abbot of Jerpoint, in the county of Kilkenny, the Abbot of Kilcooly, in the county of Tipperary, the Prior of Kells, in the county of Kilkenny, the Abbot of Holycross, in the county of Tipperary, the Abbot of Duisk, or Graignamanagh, in the county of Kilkenny, and the Bishop of Leighlin were landlords in right of the temporalities of their sees and convents, and are, therefore, classed with the laity in exacting these oppressive customs, which, however, were the mode of maintaining soldiery for the defence of the country.

doythe in lyke maner, and at the same tyme of the yere, take up Otes of his tenauntes for his horsseis, withoute any thing paying therfor.

Item, they do present that Garrard Fytzpiers, captayn of my Lorde of Ostrey kernetighe, Edmund Purcell, Edmund Gangker, with ther felowes, and Edmundy Butler Fytzthomas, and Rychard Forstall, do enforce peoplle whiche arre Inhabitauntes in the countrey, to prepare and ordeigne mete for ther dynner and suppers, and wylle paye no money therfor.

Item, the Jurye present that my Lorde of Ostrey, the Bysshop of Ostrey, generally with other spirituall Bysshoppes, Abbottes, and Pryors, and all other gentillmen beyng Inhabytauntes in the countrey, do charge theyr tenauntes wyth Codyes and Cosshyes,[a] as often as they wyll, and paye no thing therfore.

Item, the Jurye present that the Baron of Brounesforde and his officers dothe use Blak men, that is to saye, the Baron wille shewe the countrey that he hathe viii^{xx} Gallawglasseis, and require wages of them therfor; where of truethe he hathe not above the nombre of 100 Gallowglassheis, and dothe take and levye of the countrey wages for viii^{xx} personnes, and so kepeith the residue of the money to hymselff, whiche amounteyth to the some of 60 persons wages.

Item, the Jurye present that Pyers Purcell of Ballyen, and his sonne Phillip Purcell, one Onell, and John Rede, consorthe of Doley, Harbengers[b] to thErlle of Ostrey, and Richard Carroughe, harbenger to my Lorde Jamys, do take blak money, that is to saye, when it pleaseyth the said Lordes to take coyne and Lyverye, the said Pyers and others aforesaid Harbingers, go unto townes wyth the said horsseis and themselffes, and wylle charge some of the townes with Coyne and Lyverye, and spareyth one towne, and for the spareing of the same they take money, whiche they converte

---

[a] Cios-Ri, i. e. cess or meat for the King, originally rendered in food consumed on the spot where it was due.

[b] Harbingers were avant-couriers, or men who ran before to announce their lord's approach, and secure pro- per *harbourage*, or lodging and entertainment for him. An Act was passed, 18 Henry VI., against the extortions of purveyors, harbingers, and *aveners*: the last-named officers being, literally, *comers-before*.

and tornne to ther owne use, of whiche use the Lordes theyr maisters knowe not: whiche money so taken is callid Blak Money.

Item, the said Jurye present that the Kinges Wryte of what nature so ever he be, is obeyed as well in the countrey as in the Towne, and that they wylle appere uppon the same. But they saye that ther is useid in the countrey Obrenes lawes, and the Actes of Kyllcasshe, between thInhabytauntes of the Towne and the Countrey; but they saye among the inhabytauntes of the Towne the Kinges lawes be useid.

Item, the Jurye present that where the Kinges moste noble progenitors graunteid afore tymes unto the merchaunt men of Kylkenny, haveing ther course of merchaundyses into Porte townes and cyties in Ingland & Irland, that they shulde be free withoute paying of any customes to the Townes and cyties; whiche grauntes are confyrmeid and ratyfied by the Kinges Highnes our Soveraigne Lorde, and a Wryte of Allowaunce dyrecteid by the Kinges Highnes to the Mayre and Baylyffes of Waterford, whiche redde the same, and wolde not allowe it in contempt of the same the Kinges wrytte; by reason wheroff they to this daye paye ther custome to theyr dyscommodyte, and agaynst the said grauntes and confyrmations aforesaid.

Item, the Jurye present that Patryk Gower Macodye,[a] and dyverse other of my Lorde of Ostrey kernetye, mete with Walter Clerry, one of the Jury, accompenyd at that tyme with his wyf, his suster, and Margaret Drome, wyf unto Frauncyis Drome, one other of the Jury, and Ewstace Drome, doughter unto the same Frauncyis; and they the same Patryk Macody, and other the kerntyghe aforesayde, made assaulte inn the same Walter, and hym did bete and wounde, and 46^s 8^d in money from the same Walter dyd felonyously stele and bere awaye, and ravyssheid the suster of the said Walter, and the doughter of the said Frauncyis. Wherupon they compleyned to my Lorde of Ostrey, the Commyssioners, and they not regardeing the said complaynt, ne wyll not see them have ther goodes agayne, nor punyshe the said felons.

Item, the saide Jurye present that Jamys Purcell, Donogho boy

---

[a] Alias Archdeacon, see note, p. 98, *supra*.

Purcell of Ballywhele, Thomas Makmoroughe and his sonnes, and William and Andrewe, Patryk Makmorroughe, the Lorde Sertall, Lorde Grace, Hughe Bacaghgolde, Thomas Marres th Abbot of Kylleole, Moroughe Bolgyre th Abbot of Jerepon, Blanchefilde, Patryk Purcell of Lowystowne, Leonarde Blannchefilde, Edmunde Butler of Powlestowne,[a] John Sertall of Aghae,[b] Robert Sertall of Higgestowne, the Baron of Burnechurche, do compell ther tenauntes and other the inhabytauntes of the countrey to sell ther vytalles, corne, and other thinges whiche they have to selle, to one only person, of whiche the saide Jamys Purcell and other afore namyd have money to that entent, and wille not suffer them to sell the same to any other personne.

Item, the said Jurye present that Barnaby Bolgyre doythe dayly use to staude and wayte by the waye thoroughe whiche men and wemen have ther resort to the market, and when they come, he byeth the same merchaundyses and vaytayle that so comeyth toward the Market, wherby the merchaundyses and vytaylles in the towne is enhaunceid to ther price, and so is a comen forstaller.

Item, the saide Jurye present that Andrewe Fytzthomas did take a beoff from John More of Kylkennye, as he came to the Mackett warde, wythoute paying any money therfor, and agaynste the wille of the said John More, wyth force.

Item, the saide Jurye do also present that John Troye and his children, Godkelly, Richard Cantwell, John Malmowe, Clement Welche, Patryk Cassyn, Thomas Kelly, shewmaknr, do lye in the waye thoroughe which men and wemen have ther course with vytailles, and the same they and every of them do daylye bye and forstall, wherby the markett is enhaunceid to the higher price.

Item, the saide Jury present that John Lee of Waterforde

[a] Paulstown, in the county of Kilkenny. Edmund Butler was cousin to the Earl of Ossory, being son to Sir James Butler. Sir Walter Butler, of Paulstown, the chivalrous defender of Kilkenny against Cromwell, was descended from this branch of the Butlers.

[b] Nicholas Shortall, of Upper Claragh, was, in 1621, found to be seised in fee, *inte alia*, of the town and lands of Aghe, with its members, which he held of the Earl of Desmond. This was Preston, the favourite of James I., and by him created Earl of Desmond: he married the only daughter and heir of Thomas, tenth Earl of Ormonde.—[Inquis. Com. Kilk., No. 32, Jac. 1.]

doythe forstall in lyke maner and forme, by reason wherof the market is enhaunceid.

Item, the saide Jurye do present that Jamys Sherlokes wyf and John Sherlok Sherlokes sonne, Henry Welche Fytzpatryk Davye, baylyf servaunt [sic] callid Darby, Henry Forstall, servaunt unto Thomas Grannt[a] of Waterforde; Nycholas Dernes & Jamys Porter, do in lyke maner and forme forstall the market, whereby the market is highely enhaunceid; for they saye the personnes aforesayde wille gyve doble the price.

Item, the saide Jurye present that the saide Nicholas Dernes robbed certen fysher men comeing to the market of Kylkenny, uppon the ryver.

Item, the saide Jurye do present that my Lorde of Ostrey hathe forcybly entered in Walter Archers landes, callid Wasesis hayes,[b] of Rose, and hathe & kepeith the possession therof, with force, contrarye to the Statute.

Item, the saide Jurye do present that John Grace, Graceis sonne, hathe forcybly enterid uppon the possession of John Frenge,[c] callid Black Wood, in the Countie of Kylkenny, and the same forcebly witholdethe, and kepeth from the said John Frenge.

---

[a] Sir William le Grant is mentioned by the annalist Clyn as having knighted John le Ereedekne in Desmond in 1342. He was hung in the year 1345, at Castle-island, for adhering to the Earl of Desmond. The lands he forfeited in the county of Kilkenny are mentioned in the Patent Roll of 20 Edw. III.; see also Grace's Annals. Milo Grannt, Baron of Iverk, county of Kilkenny, had, anno 7 Edw. II., three sons, Milo, Roger (married to Mabel), and John.—[Bibl. Cott. Titus, B. xi. p. 78.] "Roger fil' Milonis, Baro de Auverk," is mentioned in the Carew MS. 600, in the Kerry and Slane Controversy, as an ancient baron, not Parliamentary. The "Graunteyns" became a powerful Anglo-Irish sept.—[See History, &c., of St. Canice, pp. 176, 177.] Curluddy, and Ballynebooly, both situate in the barony of Iverk, were the principal seats of the family in Kilkenny.

[b] Washes Hayes, now Sheestown, a denomination of land in the manor of Kilferagh, two miles south of Kilkenny. In 1623 Sir Richard Shee held Washes Haies of Robert Fforstall, as of his manor of Kilferagh, by fealty and 10s. rent.—[Inquis. Com. Kilk., 40 Jac. I.]

[c] The family called De la Freigne, or De Fraxineto, i. e. of the ash-wood, was of high distinction in the county of Kilkenny. Fulke de la Freigne is placed first on the list of gentlemen of that shire who are named in Rymer as having been summoned to the war in Scotland, anno 1302. The others are: —Oliver fil' Eynon (probably Walsh,

Item, the Juery present that Robert Sertall, Lorde of Higgenstowne, hath forsybly entred into the Parke of Lyrace, and there

of the Walsh mountains, Einon being a Welsh Christian name), William le Grant, William de St. Leger; Anselm, David, Edmond, and Hamond le Gras; John, Silvester, William, and Maurice le Ercedekne; Robert de Sorthales, and Milo (Grant), Baron of Overk. Among the jurors in the inquisition on the lands of Gilbert de Clare, Earl of Gloucester, are Sir Fulke de Fraxineto, Sir Robert Shortall, and Sir Adam Purcell, with Philip de Comerford, Edmund le Gras, Geoffrey Coterel, and Adam fil' Adam le Blund.—[Inquis. Tur. Lond., 8 Edw. II. No. 68.] Friar Clyn records, at the year 1320, that Sir F. de la Frene was slain by the satellites of Edmund the Butler in saving his country from spoliation. The same annalist notes, sub anno 1335, that James, Earl of Ormonde, knighted Fulke de la Frene on the occasion of an incursion into the Duffry in the county of Wexford, against the O'Brynnis, or O'Breens. Other notices of this valiant knight occur in these annals, which, indeed, close with a eulogy of his character. The Anglo-Irish force which joined Edward III. at the siege of Calais was under his leading and that of Maurice, Earl of Kildare. He was slain in the year 1349. His son, Sir Patrick de la Freigne, is mentioned as a knight in the Patent Rolls of 48 Edward III., and his wife, Eleanor Ercedeken, in those of 7th Henry IV. Sir Patrick's son, Fulke, married Katherine, widow of Edward le Botiller. —[Patent Rolls.]

Dowling, the annalist, accuses Sir Patrick, as Seneschal of Leinster, of having made oppressive inquisitions into tenures of land and charter-uses, and free customs:—"He made fayre wether with a vile reach, sed anno sequenti rex propter suas exactiones et cetera, et eo quod deposuit plures injuste ex suis dominiis et libere tenementis, revocavit autoritatem, cum incarceravit fecit cum facere restitutionem probantibus et juste accurantibus, et imposuit super eum muletam pecuniarum."—[Clyn and Dowling's Annals; Dowling, p. 24, sub. an. 1372.]

Sir Robert de la Freigne was summoned as a Baron to Parliament, 49th Edw. III. Clyn notes at the year 1347 that both Roger and Oliver de la Freigne died whilst holding the office of Seneschal of Kilkenny. John, son of Oliver de la Freigne, was made Escheator of the county of Kilkenny, 29 Edw. III.—[Rot. Pat.] The Four Masters record, under the year 1421, that Mac Gillapatrick and the son of Libned (Oliver) a Frene, one of the English, set out with twelve score soldiers on a predatory excursion into Leix, but they were attacked and defeated by O'Conor Faly.

The De Freignes, or Frenys, of Ballyreddy, were the heads of this family at the period of the Presentments. Robert Freny, of Ballyreddy, died in 1611, leaving four daughters, coheiresses. Oliver Freny, son and heir of Edmond Freny, succeeded as next heir to James Freny, grandfather to Robert, and entered on the possession of Ballyreddy, &c. He died in 1613, and left a son, Robert, twelve years old. The premises were held of the King by knight's service.—[Inquis. Com. Kilk., 28 Jac. I. Ballyreddy is situated in the barony of Ida, and county of Kilkenny.]

cute 3 trees of the Parsone of Callan, and the same trees so cut downe did cary awaye with force.

Item, they knowe not that eny musters be kepte, but they be omitted in defalte of the Officers and Lordes of the countrey; but they saye they duely kepe 2 musters in the yere within the towne.

Item, the Juery sayen that they have no Quarter Sessyons, but they saye they kepe Sessyons in the Towne when they thinke it requesyte; but in the countrey they saye there is none kepte, as farre as they here, but that the Sheref sytteth 2 tymes a yere; but they thinke it be no Sessions, for there be no Justices.[a]

Item, the Jurie present that Hugh Makeagowne, Kateryn Braye, in the kinges strete, being in Goddes peax and the kinges, the same Macagowne, dyd with force and armes make assaute in the said Kateryn Bray, after Midsomer last past, and her violently did strike upon the hed with one swerde, so that she nowe lieth in perill of dethe.

Nota. That wordes were bitwene them.

Item, the Jury present that . . . ., servaunt unto William Doghmate, by the commaundement of the said William, his maister, dyd entre into the barne of Thomas Pursell and John Routh, and there did steale whete, & was taken with the maner, and that taken from hym ayene. And afterward they loste owte of the same barne a sak of ootes, but they knowe not whoo had

---

[a] The Commissioners write to Lord Crumwell, 2nd January, 1538 :—" In oure survay of the counties of Kilkenne, Typerare, and Waterforde, we perceived the great lacke of thoes parties was lacke of mynystracion of justice; and thoes countres being distant from the other four shyres obedyent to the Kyngis lawes, the justices of the same cowlde not convenyently repaire to the said other three sheres." They therefore recommend that two learned justices be made resident in Waterford, and that others be appointed to ride circuit yearly in those shires.—[Published State Papers, vol. ii., part iii., page 538.] That appliances for the administration of the laws were neglected even in the metropolis may be seen by the following passage in a letter of the year 1537, from Alen, Master of the Rolls, to the Commissioners :—"And in any wyse some ordre to be taken immedyatly for the buildeing of the castell hall, where the lawe is kept; for yf the same be not buyldeid, the majestie and estimation of the lawe shall perrysh, the justices being then enforceid to minister the lawes upon hylles, as it were Brehons or wylde Irishemen, in their Eriottes."—[Id., p. 501.] The Irish Council write 8th Feb., 1539, that assizes had been held at Kilkenny, one malefactor hanged, and divers " put to their fynes." " The like precident whereof have not been seen thies 200 yeres."—[Id., vol. iii., part iii., p. 118.]

them; but they suspecte the boye therfore; it were good they thinke he were examyned therof.

Item, they present that Rowry the Taylour felonously hath stolen a horse of Thomas Garrard of Kylkenny.

Item, the Jury present that Robert Fitzwilliam Thobyn[a] hath stolen 60 kyen from Thomas Langton of Kylkenny, out of Brownston, besydes Kylkenny.

Item, the Jury present that Bryan Bolgyre tooke from Thomas Garrard, in the Kinges high waye, by colour of dystres, a horse; the consyderacyon of the dystres was for that he said that a brother of the said Thomas Garrard was indetted unto hym, and he wold not deliver the horse unto hym unto suche tyme as he had two spones of the said Thomas Garrard in pledge for the said money.

Item, the Jury present that one whiche was servaunt to Edmond FitzRichard Butler, by the commaundement of the said Edmond, his maister, tooke felonously in the kinges high waye from Nycholas Goyland, servaunt unto John Lye, one of the Jury, 33ˢ 4ᵈ [1] of the goodes & catalles of the said John Lye; the name of whiche servaunt they knowe not.

Item, the Jury ferther present that Davy and Garrald, sonnes to Kateryn Blanchefeld, did take felonously from the said Nicholas Goyland, servaunt unto the said John Lye, of goodes and catalles of the said John Lye 13ˢ 4ᵈ in Makmorrough countrey.

Item, the Jury present that Morough Ballough Makdonough tooke from the said servaunt, & John, sonne of the said John Lye, felonously in the Kinges high waye, of the goodes of the said John Lee, one beaf, to the value of 10ˢ Irishe, and 4ˢ of money Irishe.

Item, Edmond Mabody hathe forsebly taken in the Kinges high waye, one horse, from Edward Archer; but he hathe it ayene.

Item, they present that Garrard tooke away a horse with force from Malyffynbane, but he saith that he hath hym ayene.

---

[a] Tobin, originally St. Aubin. The St. Aubins were titular Barons of Compsey, in the county of Tipperary; a junior branch seems to have been settled at Ballaghtobin, in the county of Kilkenny.

Item, they present that Richard Sertall, Philip Pursell, did felonously in the daye tyme breke the house of Davy Tobyn, and there stale 2 horses.

Item, they present that Davy Purcell dyd burglarly and felonously, in the night tyme, breke the shop of Piers Welche and Piers Scotes.

Item, Morough of Fogurd[a] hath felonously stolen one horse from William Clyrry of Kylkenny, at the faire of Benetes Bridge.[b]

Also the Jury present that the said Morough and Edmond Graunt, his servaunt, have felonously robbed in the kinges high waye, the kinges subjectes repayring to the Market.

Item, they present that the said Morough hath felonously stolen the beastes of John Maghen, and taken the purse of the servaunt of the said John.

Item, they present that James Grace and Patrik Walle stale

---

[a] i. e. Fothart, the barony of Forth, in the county of Carlow, bordering on Kilkenny. It was the clan country of the O'Nolans, who were often troublesome neighbours to Kilkenny.—[O'Donovan's Annals of the Four Masters, vol. i., p. 5, note '.]

[b] A bridge over the Nore, four miles south-east of Kilkenny. This early notice of the fairs there is curious. They still keep up their fame. This pass, as lying on the marches of the turbulent MacMorough's, O'Ryan's, and O'Nolan's countries, must have been of early importance. The bridge there was of ancient date, but we have been unable to discover the origin of the name. As there was a chapel on the bridge, it might have been so called if St. Benedict were the patron, but such was not the case, as the chapel was dedicated to the Blessed Virgin. In the 16th year of Richard II., Thomas Middleton, clerk, custos of the chapel of the Blessed Mary, received a license to "crenellate" or fortify a tower on the bridge adjoined to the chapel. "turrim super Pontem vocat' Benety's brigge, adjunctam capellæ." —[Rot. Pat. Tur. Lond., quoted in Gent. Mag. October, 1856, p. 473.] Midleton was afterwards outlawed; and from the Exchequer Records it appears that the rectory of Benetsbridge, " Rectoria de Benetesbrigge," was worth £40 per annum. He made fine of 40s., and was exonerated from the outlawry on the 5th April, in the 6th year of Henry V.—[Rot. Memor. Scaccar. Hibn. 5 Hen. V., 1ª pars, m. 43, dorso.] The chapelry was in the King's gift, for John Lydington was presented to it by the King (Henry V.). In the presentation, entered on the Patent Roll of the 7th year of that King, it is termed a free chapel, "liberam capellam beate Marie de Benetsbrige, Ossor' dioc', vacuam et at Regis donacionem spectantem."—[Rot. Pat et Claus. Canc. Hib. Calendar., p. 215, col. b, No. 13.] All trace of this ancient fortified bridge and superpontane chapel have long since been

4 hives of Thomas Langton and Patrik Kanton; and they present that Thomas Fitzwilliam of Butlers Wood knowing them to have committed the felony aforsayd, them receayed and comforted.

Item, they present that the pannage and murage is bestowed aboute the reparacyons of the Towne walles, gates, pavementes, and holding up of the Bridge.

Item, they present that the Erle of Ourmond[a] hath been of longe tyme seased of the Castell,[b] and howe that nowe the same is in the possession and seasyn of my Lord of Ostrey; but by what title he hathe the same, they knowe not.

Item, they present that to the same Castell belong 4 mylles, 2 medowes, 4 howses, 4 or 5 acres of pasture, 4 or five acres of arrable lande, a garden called the Great Archard, and a garden at Saynt Johnes, and a culverhouse[c] in the medowes aforsaid.

Item, they present that there be many men in the towne whiche

---

obliterated by the impetuous winter floods of the river which it spanned. We have, however, an interesting notice of the ruins of this ancient bridge as they appeared upwards of a century ago. William Colles, of Kilkenny, the founder of the well-known marble works there, in a letter to the Rev. John Perry, of Dromore, November 15th, 1743, describing the course of the Nore, writes: "After it leaves the citty, It runs S. E. thro' a Beautiful Country to Bennetts Bridge, where there is a stone Bridge over it, and a few yards below ye present the Ruins of an old bridge wch had a small Castle at ye End of it to defend ye Passage."—[Original Letter Book, penes Alexander Colles, of Kilkenny.] In 1794 the tourist Holmes observed at Bennetsbridge, " near the river, a small ancient building, now part of a mill."—[Sketches of some of the southern counties of Ireland," p. 207.]

ᵃ See note ᵃ, p. 109, *supra*.

ᵇ The Castle of Kilkenny, originally built by William, Earl Mareschal, in the reign of John, descended through co-heiresses to Sir Hugh le Despenser, from whom it was purchased in 1391 by James, third Earl of Ormonde. From this period it became the chief residence of the Butlers, Earls of Ormonde. The deeds of purchase and release, with the seals of Le Despenser and Ormonde, are still preserved amongst the matchless collection of family and historic manuscripts at Kilkenny Castle.

ᶜ i. e. A dove-cot, from culfre (Saxon), a dove, or pigeon. In the deed whereby the Duke of Ormonde, in 1684, endowed the school at Kilkenny, he gives to it " all ye large mansion house in Kilkenny, now made use of for a school-house, &c., and meadow thereto adjoining, commonly called Pigeon-house meadow." This meadow is the field or lawn in front of Kilkenny College. We have not been able to identify the four mills; the Ormonde Woollen Factory and Jenkins' Mill, near Francis Abbey, were two of them.

paye chyvery[a] unto the Castell for their houses and gardens which they have in the Towne, which chyvery amounteth to the somme of £14 or more.

Item, they say they knowe no persone within all the Countie of Kylkenny that holdeth of the kinge eny manours, landes, or tenementes; but they say that my Lord of Ostrey hath many wardes, and the proffites of the mariaiges of the same; but by what title he hathe them they knowe not; whether he hath them as Garden in right[b] or Garden in dede, as committe of the kinge, they knowe not.

Item, the doo present that the Bisshop[c] taketh for the probate of Testamentes, that is to say, if the goodes be worth £40 he will take for the prof thereof £12, and of every pounde he will have 18[d] for the Probate.

Item, the saide Jurye do present that the Bysshopes Officiall[d] will not gyve any judgement ne sentence, but that he wylle have, if he be a poore man, 6ˢ 8ᵈ, and if he be a Gentillman or Grete man, 40ˢ, for gyveing of the same sentence.

Item, the saide Jurye present that the Paryshe Preist of Seint Johns and the Clerke will not crysten a chylde oneles they have of the frindes of the same childe for the christynyng, ther dynnar[e] or 6ᵈ in money.

Item, the saide Jurye present that the Priestes & Clerkes of Seint Patrykes in Kylkenny, and all other priestes of the same countrey, do in lyke maner.

Item, the saide Jurye present that when the Fryers[f] be in the countrey, men use to ride to the same Friers where they be useid to be kept, and the Constable of Leylin, the Constable of Athye, and the Counstable of Grelaghe,[g] will not suffre them to passe thyther, but that they paye Customes where they shulde pay none.

---

[a] i. e. Chiefry, or head-rent.

[b] i. e. "Guardian" of the ward. The Earls of Ormonde *did* hold, of right, the wardship of their sub-infeudatories.

[c] Milo Fitzgerald, or Baron, one of the Fitzgeralds of Brownsford (see note [d]. p. 117, *supra*) was Bishop of Ossory at this period.

[d] i. e. Vicar-General, the Judge of the Consistorial Court of the diocese.

[e] See note [c], p 134, *infra*.

[f] Perhaps the stations held by the Dominicans are here meant.

[g] Perhaps this word should be read

Item, the said Jurye present that Thomas Makmorroughe, toke Custome of Edwarde Archer, and Richard Clerry, to passe thoroughe the highe waye at Bellygragen.[a]

Item, the saide Jurye present that there be greate weares buylded in the Ryver of the Newre thoroughe whiche men have ther passage with botes, so that by reason of the same weares they cannot passe wyth ther botes as they have useid heretofore, & specially in the Ryver of Belligragen.[b]

Item, the Jury present that at suche tymes as th'Erle of Ostrey, or the Lorde Butler, his sonne, or any other by his commaundement gothe into England, the said Erles sergeauntes sesse upon the countrey certen sommes of money at their pleasure, for his or their costes.

Item, when the said Erle maketh any buyldinges or fortres, then he doth also charge the countrey with mete and drinke, hollydaies and workedaies, and 2^d by the daie for the masons and carpynters, and to the Maisters Masons 4^d the daie, and to every laborer 1^d by the daie.

Item, they present that John Goyry, Code Kellye, Richard Cantwell, Thomas Kayly, David Burnand, John Monand, and 2 hundreth other in the Countie, yerely come to the poore mennes howses and bye the corne in the feldes, feldes, and barnes, in the begynnyng of the yere at 2^s the busshell; wherby almaner grayne is regrated in their handes, so that no corne can come to the market but is bought at their handes; which they will not sell but for 10^s the busshell, to the undoing, &c.

Item, the present that there be iii[xx] botes belonging to Innerteak [or Inverteak][c] where the cariage of every bote was ever wont to be but 8^d Irishe; and nowe is enhaunced to 12^d or 14^d ar more at more at pleasure; and also they drinke their wynes and fill it

---

[a] Probably an attempt at the Irish name, Bel-atha Raghat, now Ballyragget. Grenagh, a strong castle of the Earl of Ormonde, on the Suir, near Waterford. There was, however, a pass called Greallach on the River Liffey, in Kildare.—[Four Mast., vol. i., p. 180, note.]

[b] See previous note. Ballyragget is on the Nore, nine miles above Kilkenny.

[c] Innistioge, a town on the Nore, fourteen miles below Kilkenny. The tide comes up to it, and it was, in consequence, the port of Kilkenny. See note [d], p. 109, *supra*.

ayene with watter, and divers other exaccyons to their undoing. The names that occupie the botes ar, John Astekell, Richard Astekell, Nicholas More, Richard Belgyn, and all other that occupie botes.

THE VERDYT OF THE CORPORACŌN OF THE TOWNE OF IRSHTOUNE.[a]

[*October*, 1537.—*MS. State Paper Office.*]

JUR̄ VILLE DE IRISHETOWNE.

THOMAS WALL.		JOH̃ES MOWNAM.	
WALTERUS ROTHE.		THOMAS KELLEY.	
JOH̃ES POWRE.	JUR̄.	WILLĪS BROWNE.	JUR̄.
JOH̃ES KELLEY.		JOH̃ES NASSHE.	
JOH̃ES MALVY.		NICH̃US STANTON.	
RICARDUS CANTELL.[b]			

First, the Jury present that the constable of the Towne of Garon[c] dothe daily charge the Inhabitauntes of the said towne with coyne and livercy to 4 men appoynted by the said constable.

Also, they doo present that my lorde of Ostrey dothe at his pleasure charge all the towne of Garon,[c] and all the countie of Kylkenny with coyne and lyvercy, as well his tenauntes.

Also, they doo present that the lorde Sortall, lord Grace, lorde Sleggar, the lord Swetman, the baron of Burnchurche, the lorde Pursell, lorde Blanchefeld, and all other the freholders of the said

---

[a] Irishtown was an ancient corporation, deriving its privileges from the Bishop of Ossory, and quite independent of the Corporation of Kilkenny proper, although forming together but one town. This separate jurisdiction continued down to the time of the late Act for the reformation of Corporations, when the Corporation of Irishtown merged in that of Kilkenny.—

[See History, &c., of St. Canice, pp. 22, 23.]

[b] i. e. Cantwell.

[c] i. e. Gowran. It has been already observed that Gowran, not being represented on the Jury of the commoners of the county, seems to have rather incongruously been included, as to its grievances, in the Presentment of the Irishtown of Kilkenny.

countie of Kylkenny, doo use at their pleasure to charge their tenauntes, and all other the Kinges subjectes within the said countie, with coyne and lyverey.

Also, they doo present that my lorde of Ostrey doth in the tyme of Lente, levie and take of his tenauntes, and all other inhabitauntes within the said countie, otes for his horses, without paieng anything therfore.

Item, the Jury presente that Makmurrothe[a] doth take blak Rente of the Inhabitauntes of the Towne of Garon, and for bicause the same inhabitauntes wold not at his commaundement paye the said Rent, he forsebly dystreyned the same inhabitauntes, to thentent to compell them to paye the same, whiche dystres was 2 plowes of horses, and they doo also present that the Kernetythe of the said Makmurroughe have felonously stolen 2 horses, colored red, out of the pasture of Redmore, besydes Garon, of the goodes and catalles of John Nasshe, the names of whoose servauntes been, Piers Reau and Patrik FitzEdmond.

Item, the saide Jury present that Garralte Makart with force and armys in the kinges highe waye, betwene Benettes bridge and the towne of Garon, made assaulte in Nycholas Staunton, and hym did bete, and evyll entreate; and £10 2^s 8^d Iryshe, and a stone called a precyous stone, of the goodes and catalles of the said Nycholas, did felonyously stele and bere awaye, contrary to the Kinges pease.

Item, the Jury present that the Bysshop of Leylin did forcybly enter upon the possession of Sweteman, that is to saye, into xx acres of lande lying besydes the towne of Garon, and the same detayneith and kepeith with force.

Item, the saide Jurye present that the vycar of the towne of Garon wyll not crysten ne baptyse a childe, oneles the frindes of the same childe gyve him his dynnar or money.

---

[a] The Mac Murrows, or Cavanaghs, were subsidized by the English crown, temp. Richard II., and regularly received their "black rent" from the Royal Exchequer. This recognition of their power had ceased long before the period of the Presentments, but the sept was still unsubdued, and levied black-rent on the neighbouring English settlements. The town of Gowran lay near the frontier of the Cavanaghs' country of Odrone.

Item, the saide Jurye present that the Vycar of Garon will take porcon-kanon, that is to saye, after the deathe of a mannes wyf, if the goodes of herre husbond be under the value of 20^s, he will take the fyfte peny, and if it be above the said value of 20^s he wille have v^s for all the hoole goodes, and leve the fyfte peny.

Item, the saide Jurye present that Fargaunanne O'Corin[a] doithe take the admynistration of a woman goodes, that is to saye, a woman, *covert de baron*, dye, he wille have of every xii^d of the goodes of the husbond 1^d and 3 fartheinges, and saye that they be the goodes of the wyf where indede she was, *coverte du baron*, at the tyme of herre deathe.

Item, the saide Jurye do present that Henry Oxxe doithe levy the same, and so is a trespaser, in respect that the vycar hathe no coloure to have the same, and by the same reason nor the saide Henry by his comaundyment.

Item, the saide Jurye do present that Sir Morris nowe paryshe pryste of Seynt Kylkenny,[b] doithe take for the baptysing of a childe his dynnar,[c] and money for the christenyng of the said chylde.

Item the saide Jurye present that the vycar of Castell Doughe[d] doythe in lyke maner forme take for the xp̄enyng of chyldren.

Item, the saide Jurye present that the vycar of Cashel Doughe is a Senciall[e] and Judge, and useith enormall actes and fassions, that is

---

[a] We have here the name of the "official," or vicar-general, presented by the Jurors of the Corporation of Kilkenny.

[b] Probably one of the Vicars-Choral of the Cathedral, licensed by the Bishop to the cure of the parish of St. Canice, of the tithes of which they were and are, as a body, impropriators.

[c] The Corporation of Irishtown, at the Dern Hundred holden on 8th of January, 1579, enacted " thet noo man ne woman shall come heraft^r to enny christening of children, or churching of women brought abed, butt the gossobs for ye time being, fathers and mothers, brothers and sisters, uppon payne of forty shillings Irish . . . . . and y^t it shall be lawfull for enny y^t spieth such men or women coming from ye feast to take away there hatts, or rolls and mantles, and ye same to forfeyte, and to take away the mydwife is roll and mantle y^t goeth to warne the people, oth^r than those wch by this statute are allowed, and y^t the parish priest shall have none in his cōpany but his clercke."—[The Most Aucient Book of the Corporation of Irishtown, fol. 39.

[d] Now Odogh, a parish in the diocese of Ossory, about four miles north-west of Kilkenny, part of Ui Duach, the tribe district of the O'Brenans.

[e] i. e. Seneschal. Castle-doughe, or

to saye, if any affraye be made betwene men aboute him where he dwelleith, so that ther be bluddeshodde, he wille assesse a grevyous fyne or amercyment upon the persons that so made thaffraye, and the same fyne so assesseid he wille levye by waye of distres, if they have landes or goodes in whiche or wherby they maye be dystrayneid to thuse of the lorde of Sertall; and over that he wille have 12ᵈ himself of every blodshodde which he dothe his owne self without inquyre of the affraye so made by Inquest, and taxeith also the fyne himself.

Item, the saide Jurye present that Edmund Sertall, Donoughe Makhewgan, by the commaundyment of the lorde Grace, Richard Sertall, and Malayhan Ogge Clerry, do use the same in lyke maner.

Item, the saide Jurye present that Obrunes^a lawes ben useid in the countrey, and the Actes of Kylkasshe.^b

Item, the saide Jurye present that Barnaby Bolger, Edmund Leweis, Patryk Macode, William Maghtegge, William Welche, Malache Oboy Cornewall of Doley, Burgeyn of Seint Johns strete in Kylkenny, do dwell in the countrey, and do interupte men and wemen whiche ar comeing to the markat with vytayles, and bye them, and wille not suffer them to come to the markat, wherby the market is enhauneeid to the higher pryce, and so is a comyn forstaller.

Item, the saide Jurye present that there be graye merchauntes in the Towne of Kylkenny, that is to saye, Nicholas Hekket, Walter Lawlesse, pyers Welche, Edwarde Archer, Thomas Savage, do sende men into the countrey to bye all manner thinges as well vytaylles as other merchaundyseis, and the same men bring it to them, and they kepe it, and after sell the same agayne.

Item, the saide Jurye present that Thurlok Fytz Davy did forcybly make assaulte upon Walter Routhe of Kylkenny, at the saide towne in the Highe strete, and hym dyd bete and grevyously did wounde, so that he was in greate perill of deathe.

Odogh, was an ancient manor. In 1359 David de Stradbolgy, Earl of Athol, was its lord (Rot. Claus., 33 Ed. III., m. 31). About 1381 it belonged to the De la Laundes (Rot. Pat. 5 Ric. II., m. 19). How it came into the possession of the Shortalls does not appear.

^a i. e. Brehon Laws.
^b See note ^b, p. 112, *supra*.

Item, the saide Jurye do present that Richard Slyggar,[a] in the Kinges highe waye, within the lybertye of Kylkenny, did with force and armes make assaulte upon Tegge FytzJohn, of the Iryshe towne, and hym did bete and wounde so that he was in greate perylle of deathe.

Item, the saide Jurye present that Jamys Grace in the Kinges highe waye, besides Kylkenny, dyd make assaulte upon Derby Casshye and Robert Keyly, and hym dyd bete, and xvi[d] in money, nombre of Iryshe, and 2 beoffes, felonyously from the saide Robert Keyly dyd stole and here awaye contrary to the kinges peace.

Memorandum.—The gentylmen with all the comoners of the said counte, the Soverelne with all the heddes and comoners of the towne of Kylkenny, ben very desirous to be obedient to the Kinges lawe, and to lyve in gode cevylite; and albehit the Kinges lawes in the said counte be not only clerly voide and frustrate, but allso all the exaccions, suppressions, and other enormytes before presentyd, with many mo, be mayntened and enforsed only by the Erle of Ossery, my lady his wyff, the lorde Jamys Buttler, Richarde Butler, and other the said Erles childerne and kyne of his name, wherfor to provide that thes persons[b] may be reduced, and the countie wyl be immediatly prosperous, and of gret strenght to defende there self ageinst ther enemyes.

---

[a] i. e. St. Leger.

[b] The chief of the Butlers was evidently looked on as the great supporter of the oppressive Irish customs complained of. Sir Thomas Masterson, a Cheshire gentleman, and Seneschal of the county of Wexford, writes to Sir F. Knolles, 10th August, 1566, from Kilkenny :—" Ye wolde not beleve what great joye is here emong the Commons [people] for putting away of coyng and lyvery, and how much they pray for the Queen's Majesty, and be redy to imbrace and obey her laws. Some of those that have lived by it dothe report it shall come up agayn by my Lord of Ormond's suit made to the Queen. God forbyd that that noble man, whom I love and honor so much, should be the auctor of so synfull a dede; by which a great part of his own landes hath bene hitherto wasted, and begyn now to be inhabited and yelde him rent."—[MS. State Paper Office.] It shows a considerable independence amongst the inhabitants of Kilkenny when so bold a recommendation as the above was put forward.

THE REPRESENTATIONS OF DAVID SUTTON, ESQ., FOR THE COUNTIES OF KILDARE AND CARLOW, ANNO 1537; THE RE-PRESENTATIONS OF OLIVER SUTTON, ESQ., TO THE ENGLISH PRIVY COUNCIL IN 1565, RESPECTING THE EXACTIONS OF THE EARL OF KILDARE ; THE PRESENTMENTS OF JURIES FOR THE COUNTY AND CITY OF WATERFORD, THE TOWN OF DUNGARVAN, THE COUNTY OF TIPPERARY, AND TOWN OF CLONMEL, TO THE COMMISSIONERS FOR REFORMING THE STATE OF IRELAND, ANNO 1537; AND THE PRESENTMENTS OF JURIES FOR THE COUNTY OF CORK, ANNO 1579.

IN our view, the most remarkable feature in the Presentments now in course of publication is the peculiar nature of the duties, services, or renderings obtained from the occupiers of the land. The collection of evidence on this important matter was a main purpose of the Commissioners. Nothing is plainer than that these services were levied in a very uncertain and arbitrary manner; and in this uncertainty consisted the abuses attending their exaction. But the Reformatory Commissioners would have been extremely perplexed had they attempted to bring about a system of commuting those renderings into fixed money rents. The truism, that ancient customs cannot be changed by sudden effort, is especially applicable to those usages on which the rights of property depend; and this country was then unripe, by a whole century, for such a change. In England, the requisite alteration of somewhat similar feudal services and exactions into cash payments had been already generally effected; but this salutary reform, though it had received impulse by the insurrections of Tyler and Cade, simultaneous with the Jacqueries of

France and Flanders, had occupied more than a century and a half in its development. Sir Thomas Smith, writing his "Commonwealth of England," about the year 1560, observes, that the yeomen and husbandmen of that happy country are no more subject to taile or tax than are the gentlemen. Every phase of slavery, even respecting the lord's claim on the property of his serf, had vanished. But such was not then the case in either France or our own country. Of this fact, as regards the latter kingdom, we could add largely to the proofs contained in these Presentments.

Originally, in Ireland, the country of a clan was held in common, and there were neither landlords nor tenants. In process of time tenancies commenced, but the very denomination of a Gaelic farmer indicates the public object of his tenure. He was called a *biatagh*, or "public victualler," from keeping a house in which he was bound, in certain cases, to provide food; his name being derived from *biad*, food, and *tagh*, a house. Sir John Davys observes, that a bally-betagh, i. e., a biatach's townland, was "in the Irish tongue a town [dwelling] able to maintain hospitality." Probably, the term designated a house adequate to receive a chieftain and his train. It has been denied that the betaghs of the Pale resembled the tenantry of the same name in the Gaelic districts, yet, on the contrary, the similarity of these two sorts of land-holders seems to extend beyond their denomination. For centuries after the Conquest, the former caste remained in a state of slavery, from which they were gradually emerging at the time under view. But the latter do not seem to have lived in so complete a condition of the slavery called villeinage.

The "Four Masters" style some of the descriptions of betagh tenantry in the Celtic countries, " general biatachs ;"

but this was in later times, and perhaps implies that the "houses of general hospitality," or food-houses they kept, had assumed the character of "public-houses," in which more than mere "dry lodging" could be had for money, if not for love of hospitality. Originally this class of tenants appear to have held their lands on the condition of entertaining the chieftain and his troops, and all visitors and messengers; their tenure was, in effect, holding by free-quarters. Another and inferior class of farmers were the *brughaidhe*, who, besides rendering a small stipulated rent, originally in kind, were liable to perform various agricultural and other services. The difference between this caste and the other was probably owing to the distinction between servile and free races. While the *biatagh* was of free descent, and was himself generally the *ceann-cinè*, or head of a pastoral sept, occupying land, or hiring summer pasture as a "free-holder," privileged to remove and bargain for some other pasturage within the clan country, the *brughaidhe*, or victuallers, seem to have descended from enslaved races. Similarly among the Saxons, the distinction between an "edel," or noble or well-known man, and an "ignoble" one, was marked by the former rendering fixed tributes, while the latter rendered services. Among the Gael, it was the "noble" families that were liable to provide coyne or "refection." Our disquisition on this point may close with the remark, that the practice of paying small certain rents, and rendering large refections, with occasional unlimited aids in kind, was inevitable in a pastoral and uncommercial country.

The charges brought against the hierarchy and clergy of the see of Cashel require more explanation than our space affords. Undoubtedly many of the fees and exactions they took were equally customary and due to them as coyne and cuddihy were to the temporal lords. As to undue exactions of bishops and ecclesiastical officers, in extortions, talliages, aids, and visitations as guests, see "Register of All Saints,"[a] pp. 7 and 113.

The ordinary Irish exactions were, of course, as much demanded in other borders of the English Pale as in those now under notice. According to an Exchequer Record of 3 & 4 Philip and Mary, the farmer of the estates of Darcy of Platten complained that Thomas Tyrrell, of Fertullagh, Gent., had intruded into the manor of Lyn, &c., county of Westmeath, and had disturbed the tenants by taking from them "Coynees, Cooyshers, and Coodyes."

These extraordinary "cesses"[b] (cıoɲ, rent) and "cuttings," or unusual charges, called "talliage" in English law, were submitted to by the humble Irish tenant without repining, provided he was defended from being plundered by strangers; and his willingness is apparent in the proverbial reply to his lord's demands:—" Spend me, but defend me!" One of the lords of Fermanagh, Philip Maguire, head of a family celebrated as surpassing all others in the virtue of hospitality, is styled by the annalists[c] "the spender and defender of his territory." In every clan there were two castes, freemen and bondsmen. The first traced their descent from the same stem as the head of their name; the latter represented slaves purchased in early ages, or subjected aborigines. All "idel-men" were essentially "swordsmen." They disdained to be aught but warriors. If poor, they carried darts and skeins as kerne; if in possession of horses, they bore staves or lances, but all wore swords. Those near in blood to the Rıᵹh (Rex or chief) had fertile districts allotted for their support, and bore themselves in war with the gallant impetuosity

---

[a] Published by the Irish Arch. Soc.
[b] The term still lives in the Grand Jury "Cess" of the present day.
[c] Four Masters, *sub anno* 1395.

Edmund Spenser ascribes to the Irish chivalry. While the servile caste did the work of the country, the free class performed the duty of defence. This division of labour is thus alluded to in an ancient poem :—

"What country is there," asks the bard, "in which its own king and prosperous chief does not appoint with full consent—

  Toparchs (Caıpıʒ) over districts (Cuaċlıp)
  And farmers (bpuʒhaıolıp) over townlands ?
  The sons of kings guarding them !"

Edmund Spenser explains that the exaction of ordinary customs by Irish landlords was no injustice to the tenantry, on the maxim in law, "to the willing there is no wrong done." It was usual, he says, "amongst landlords of the Irish to have a common spending upon their tenants," of whom, being for the most part at will, they used to take " what victuals they listed, for of victuals they were wont to make small reckoning. Neither in this," observes Spenser, " was the tenant wronged, for it was an ordinary and known custom, and his lord commonly used so to covenant with him, which if at any time the tenant disliked, he might freely depart at his pleasure. But now by this statute [interdicting coyne and livery], the said Irish lord is wronged, for that he is cut off from his customary services, of the which this was one ; besides many other of the like, as Cuddey, Coshery, Bonnaght, Shrah, Sorchin, and such others." And the writer concludes by remarking that the Irish " were never wont, and yet are loth, to yield any certain rent, but only such spendings, for their common saying is—' Spend me and defend me.'"

The inconvenience to the public arising from the interdict of old country customs by the above-mentioned newfangled Statute, by which taking coyne and livery was made treason, is also adverted to by Spenser :—" Now," says he, " no man can goe into another man's house for lodging, nor to his owne tenant's house to take victuall by the way, notwithstanding that there is no other meanes for him to have lodging, nor horse meate, nor man's meate, *there being no innes,* nor none otherwise to be bought for money, but that he is endangered by that Statute [to be charged] for treason." So severe a penalty being attached by enactment to receiving refreshment in the old hospitable fashion, the wants of travellers soon made it necessary to establish regular hostelries, and accordingly many licenses for keeping country taverns were granted during the reign of James I. But the habits of a nation were not to be hastily abolished by Act of Parliament; the doors of houses which are recorded by annalists[a] as well known in their day to travellers and the poor as abodes where welcome and relief were certain, remained open; and, in virtue of the lingering tradition of that universal hospitality, the needy wanderer still enters freely and unforbidden into every Irish peasant's house.

Inns or hostelries were deemed by the Irish an English invention and innovation. These serviceable institutions for merchants and travellers were established instantly after the Conquest, Strongbow having granted an *hospitium liberum,* " a frank house," in Wexford, another at Ferns, and another at Kildaran, on the road to the metropolis.[a]

It is easy to show that the exaction of coyne and livery was rendered necessary by the circumstances of the time and country. Protection was the most sacred duty of a chief to his followers; but they had to pay for being de-

[a] Four Masters, 1586, &c.   [b] Pat. Canc. Antiq.

fended. Of the exactions enumerated in these representations, many more were for the general benefit than for the lord's peculiar profit. Although it seems strange that an Irish "king" should have occasionally sent his house-kerne round his country "to take up six weeks' victuals" for a campaign, it is likely that he had political reasons for doing so. In ages when payment of rent and taxes in money was impossible, he could not feed even his household without some power of levying contributions in kind. In 1559, the Earl of Ormond, apprehensive, it would seem, that Government would enforce the enactments against exacting food, petitioned the Queen "to have a sufficient authority to provide victual within his own rule for his house." We are sure that he himself could consume but one man's share, and may believe that the subsistence so supplied was expended in the service of his people. Primarily, the rendering of *cuid-oidche*, i. e. a portion for a night, was the sole rent a Celtic king received, for his birthright was no more than a mess of pottage. The rights of his order grew with the increase of his clan's requirements; but whenever the clansmen were oppressed by his exactions, they had their remedy, for, in their proverb, "stronger than the chief are the vassals."

Endeavours were frequently made by churchmen to free their land from renderings to the king of the country in which it was situated. Thus, an ancient Irish charter, as "the freedom of Cill Delga,"[a] specifies that this land was dedicated, "no king or chieftain having head rent (*cen cis*), tribute (*cen chobach*), hosting, coigny (*choinnim*), or any other claim on it, for no chief durst touch it while staying in the territory." Another charter asserts the freedom of

[a] Irish Arch. Miscell., vol. i. p. 137.

Ardbraccan, now the seat of the Bishop of Meath, because the king of the surrounding territory had sold the tribute due to his clan from this churchland, viz., one night's *coinmhe* every quarter of a year, for ever, in consideration of three ounces of gold. The "general freedom of all churches" is also arrogated in this charter. A case can be adduced in which a chieftain, in the fifteenth century, extended his prerogative to receiving a leader and his men, who had been expelled by their own tribe, and to giving lands whereon his cattle should feed, and entitling his men to use "the coigny of the country."[a]

Such was the ravenous conduct of the age, that it was esteemed a proof of virtue in the popular eye, if a prelate could, by mere force of character, let his cattle graze in remote pastures, on finding them considered sacred. Thus, "Mac Sir Morris," Bishop of Leighlin in 1512, a native of Idrone, was, according to the annalist-writing Chancellor of that diocese, Dowling, "commended for hospitalitie, and *for the number of cowes that he grazed without losse* (so well was he beloved) upon the woodes and mountaines" of Brandon, Moilglas, Ballycarew, and Aghcarew. In such times, when a native hierarch was judged to be popular because of the immunity vouchsafed to his kine, how long would beeves belonging to the Sassenach soldier, Sir Peter Carew, Constable of Leighlin, have depastured the lands, called, indeed, after his surname, but which he had recently recovered from a Gaelic clan that had wrested them from his ancestors? From Bale's Memoir of his Life as Bishop of Ossory, we know that, on one occasion, his servants were cruelly murdered by the Irish, on being found making hay not seven miles from the walls of Kilkenny.

[a] Irish Arch. Miscell., vol. i. pp. 247, 295.

All research warrants us in agreeing with the ensuing sentiments expressed by Strafford, regarding the beneficial change effected for the lower orders in this country by their emancipation from clan government—a change not less evident, because this viceregal despot was bent upon taking power from the Irish nobility and strengthening the Crown. He writes in 1637 :—

" 'The people in general are in great quietness, and, if I be not much mistaken, well satisfied and fast delighted with His Majesty's gracious government and protection; it being almost sure, that the lower sort of the Irish subject hath not, in any age, lived so preserved from the pressures and oppressions of the great ones, as now they do, for which, I assure you, they bless God and the King, and begin to discern and taste the great and manifold benefits they gether under the shadow of, and from their immediate dependence upon, the Crown, in comparison of the scant and narrow coverings they formerly borrowed from their petty yet imperious lords."

Having carried notices of some consequences of the Commissioners' labours down to a century subsequent to the date of the High Commission, we may now close these observations by alluding to the opinion expressed by several learned archæologists, viz., that the series of documents now published presents an unusually lucid picture of the social state of a mixed and remarkable people. The future author of a civil history of Ireland will, therefore, find in these Verdicts large materials for genuine history.

PRESENTMENT BY DAVID SUTTON TO THE KING'S HIGH COMMISSIONERS, AS TO OPPRESSIONS SUSTAINED BY THE COUNTIES OF KILDARE AND CARLOW, FROM THE ILLEGAL EXACTIONS OF THE LATE EARL OF KILDARE AND HIS SUBORDINATE OFFICERS, 20 SEPTEMBER, 1537. AND THE REPRESENTATIONS OF OLIVER SUTTON TO THE ENGLISH PRIVY COUNCIL, DATED 1565.

THESE Presentments were emphatically directed against the exaction of "coyne" (*coin-meadhe*) and "livery," or requisition of food for man and horse, whenever a military force had to be maintained. The Earls of Kildare, as defenders of their own territory, and governors of Ireland, were often compelled to enforce this levy, in order to defend the Englishry. The impost is of Irish origin, and was suitable to ages when, in the absence of money, taxes were paid in kind. Some of the early English governors vainly endeavoured to substitute the unobjectionable system of a money cess; but it was reserved for Sir Henry Sydney to accomplish, in 1575, this reform. In the middle of the fourteenth century, Viceroy Rokeby used to say (says the annalist Grace), "that he had rather eat and drink out of wooden vessels, and expend gold and silver on food, clothing, and hired soldiers," evidently desiring that mercenary troops should be paid and fed by means of cash payments than that they should be quartered on the country. This "just and prudent man," as the annalist terms him, died in 1356, in Kilkea Castle, probably while engaged in protecting the Pale. It had not been easy for him to keep his resolution of paying in cash, for he was, on one occasion, obliged to borrow "in magnâ necessitate, pro commodo Regis et maintenencia pacis." At his suggestion also, a curious royal ordinance was issued, to suppress the abuse of imposition of coyne and livery under the form of "King's Cess;" and an unpublished Statute of Henry VII. is levelled against this exaction in general, which is declared to be the principal cause why the most part of the old English freeholders and tenants had deserted the land, "whereupon," says the preamble, "the lords and gentlemen using the exaction have intruded into those inheritances, and do set them to the King's Irish enemies."

The Gaelic chiefs, and their *clanna*, or children, secure in their glens and forests, and constantly increasing and multiplying, *crescentes in occulto*, had almost overwhelmed the Englishry, somewhat by the methods by which the semi-subjugated Canaanites overcame their ancient conquerors, until but a small remnant was left. "So wonderfully," says an old writer, "had these Irish lords encroached upon the English Pale, that when Henry VIII. came to the throne, and took in hand the general reformation of that country, it was found that the Pale was restrained into four counties onlie, viz., Dublin, Kildare, Meath, and Louth; and those also not to be free from the Irish invasions, but so weakened withal and corrupted, that scant four persons in any parish wore English habits, and coince and livery as current there as in the Irish countries, which [exactions] were first brought into the Pale by Sir James of Desmond,[a] in the time of his government."[b]

It is observed in a "Memorial for winning Leinster,"

[a] If we could ascertain who this was, the date of the introduction of coyne and livery into the Pale would be fixed. Chief Baron Finglas, in his Treatise on the decay of the Anglo-Irish, says that "James, Erle of Desmond, grandfather to the Erle that now is (and it is a little above 51 winters sithence he died), was the first man that ever put coyne and livery on the King's subjects." But the date of this treatise is uncertain.

[b] Bibl. Cotton, Titus B. xii.

dated 1537, that because the Irish septs of this province were decidedly under the dominion of the great houses of Kildare and Ormond, " the moste of them" having been under tribute to the former, and " part of them" to the latter, this had been the reason why these natural enemies had not been extirpated ; and " also," observes the writer, " as far as could be perceived, the Geraldines preserved most of them for scourges to the Kynge's subjects," for such times as the Earls were displeased with such subjects, " and for other causes, knowing well that if these parts [of Leinster] had been reformed, they sholde not have borne the rule, nor enjoyed the advantage they had."

The publication of the "Kildare Rental Book" by this Society will throw new light on the service of these Gaelic clans to the Earls of Kildare. From various other records, it seems that the Earls of Ormonde also availed themselves of the support afforded by the septs that were under their power. In some instances, lands which had been recovered by the Irish were again taken from them. Piers, Earl of Ossory, writes, anno 1531, that Thomas, the late Earl of Ormonde, having given him the manors of Tullow and Arklow, with their appurtenances, to hold by paying one-fourth of the profits :—

"Which manors were in the possession of Irishmen the space of these 200 years, unto such tyme after the obtaining of the said deed of gift, I, with force, daungier of my life, and great charge, recoveryd the possession of the said manors out of the Irishmen's hands, and made thereupon great byldings and raparacions, to make them strong and defensible . . . . which manors be the very keys of the country."[a]

The letter earliest in date (1509), among the Irish correspondence in the State Paper Office, is an announcement

---

[a] Printed State Papers, vol. ii., part iii., p. 154.

by the Council of Ireland to the King, that they have entreated the Earl of Kildare not to depart for England, but to abide and protect them from the Irishmen. In 1514, the Archbishop of Armagh describes, to Wolsey, the perilous state of the Pale, and insists that the King is as much bound to reform this land as to maintain good order and justice in England. At this epoch the power of the Crown in Ireland had sunk to its lowest ebb, and the tide of dominion did not rise again until the rebellious conduct of Kildare's son compelled the sending of English troops hither, and proved the necessity of reformatory measures. In 1515, during that Earl's government, the author of the first printed State Paper on the condition of Ireland, with "A Plan for its Reformation," declares:—

"Some say the Kinge's Deputie is cause that all the common people be so poore, so feeble, and so Iryshe; for when somtyme, in our dayes, the Kinges Deputye useid alwaye to have aboute him, wherever that he dyd ryde, a strong garde on horseback of sperys and bowes, well garnysheid, after the Englyshe maner, that payde trewly for ther meate and drynke, wherever they dyd ryde; nowe garde of the Kinges deputie is none other but a multytude of Iryshe galloglagheis, and a multytude of Iryshe kernne and speres, with infynyt nombre of horsseladdes; and with the said garde, the Kings Deputye is ever moveing and styreing from one place to another, and with extortion of coyne and lyverye consumeith and devoureith all the substaunce of the poore folke, and of the comen peoplle of all the Kinges subjettes."[a]

In the same year the Dowager Countess of Kildare, exhibiting articles of complaint against her stepson, the ninth Earl, declares that he, though Lord Deputy, has suffered her lands to fall into the hands of the wild Irishmen,

[a] Printed State Papers, vol. ii., part iii., p. 12.

excepting some part, which has been taken by Sir Walter Delahide, his steward ; and she further states that the estate of her ward, Rochfort, of Kilbride, is made waste by daily oppression of coyne and livery.

This coyne and livery, or free quarters for man and horse, formed the war tax of the time, and this terrible tax was incessant. In 1520 the Earl of Surrey came over as Lord Lieutenant, but, being always in want of money and cavalry, was recalled after two years, and a native nobleman, Piers, Earl of Ormonde, was intrusted with the colonial sword. In point of fact, such was the distracted state of the country, and such the apathy in England, that the government naturally devolved on an interested and powerful native party.

In 1524 the King entered into an indenture with Kildare, by which, on this great nobleman being constituted Lord Deputy, he agreed to the following restrictions on his power of demanding food for man and horse :—

"The same Erlle granteth, that as oft as he shall passe throughe the Englyshe pale to any osteinges, or journays, or to parlle with any Iryshe man, he shall not sett his men too coyne uppon the Kinges subjectes within the Inglyshe pale, but by bille made by the arbinger by thadvyse of too gentillmen of every baronye where the saide coyne shall be sett; and that every of his men, so lyveryd, shall be content to have such meate and drinke as folowith; that is to saye, every horseman and captayne of kerne and galloglasse to have, in flesshe days, flesshe, bredde and ale, and in fysshe dayes, fyshe or butter; and his kyrnne and boyes, such as the husbond hathe; orelles to take but for every horsseman 2*d*. a meale, every foteman 1½*d*., and for every horsekeeper 1*d*.; every chief horsse 12 sheives for a nyght and a daye, every bereing horsse cyghte sheives, and but 1 boye for a horsse. And allso the saide Erlle graunteth that at suche tyme as he shall sett his men to coyne in the marches, that they shalle not take noo coyne, but after the said rate; and also but oone boy to oone horsse. And also the said Erle graunteth, that he, being at any Parliament, counsaill, or in his private busynes, in the Inglishe pale, shall not take coyne or lyvery of any persone, but onely upon his owne tenauntes; but for to pay for mannes meate, and horsemete, of every of his men and their horses, in maner and fourme folowing; that is to witt, for a horseman two pens every meale, and for a horseboy a peny, and for every six reasonable sheves of oates a peny, and for a bushel of oats 8*d*.; and that his said horsemen, yemen, and horseboyes shall be contente with suche meate and drynke as the husbondes have, paieing 1*d*. for a meal therfore. And also the said Erle graunteth, that at suche a tyme as he shall ride through the Englishe pale to parlle with any Irisshe man, or otherwise, that he shall take with him as small a company as he may convenyently for saufgard of his persone."[a]

The entire counties of Kildare and Carlow are declared, in a printed Report of 1534, to be under the rule of the Earl of Kildare, his brothers and kinsmen; and curious details are given in the Report as to the exactions levied by him. It appears that, for twenty-eight years previously, all law had been administered by his officers, under plea of a grant of palatine liberty to De Vesci, formerly Lord of Kildare, but resumed by the Crown, yet usurped by this Earl's father since the twentieth year of the reign of Henry VII. In the year 1317 the office of hereditary sheriff of Kildare had been conferred upon the second Earl, and it would seem that this office was continuously exercised by his successors. In consequence, the King's subjects in this shire had traditionally given their obedience to these Earls, throughout whose dominions the Crown received neither allegiance nor revenue.

In the same year that the High Commissioners commenced their work of reform, the principal officers of the

---

[a] Printed State Papers, vol. ii., part iii., p. 115.

Irish government wrote State Papers of suggestions, and, in one of these, by Justice Luttrell, the ensuing detailed account is given of the first imposition of coyne and livery in the Pale :—

"Item, the fyrste coyne of galloglasseis, callid Coyne Bon, that was ceassid in thes quarters within this 50 yeres, that Geralde, fader to Geralde, late Erlle of Kyldare, cessid in the countye of Kyldare which was one Barret haveing but 24 spores; which came to him, being exiled oute of Conaght. Item, the said galleglasseis soo encreasid, in the tyme of the said Geralde the fader, that, in his time they came to 120 speeres; moste parte to the charge of the saide countye whiche his sonne Gerald cessid on Iryshe oftentymes, and dyschargeid muche the said countye of them and ther charge. Item, the saide twoo Erlles, being Deputyes, took no coyne in the hert of thEnglyshe pale of the countye of Dublin, Meathe, ne Louthe, but comeing thoroughe the same, for one nyghte and one daye, to be in one place. Item, the Baron of Delvin, being Substitute Deputye under the said Erlle, then being in England, was the first that, going throughe the said parte, tooke coyne for twoo nyghtes and twoo dayes, which was never before seen. Item, the Erlle of Osserye after being Deputye, in the first rebellyon of the traytor this O'conour, and the Garaldynes, after toke coyne within the said quarter, for fower dayes and fower nyghtes in one place, whiche was never before seen ther. Item, after, the said Erlle of Kyldare, upon the said presydent, toke ther coyne and lyverye, as is aforesaid, following the president of the said Baron, for 2 dayes and nyghts; and nowe the same folowith mor and more, whiche wylle make the said quarters, that hathe byn unto this time preservid after some Englyshe sort and maner, to be lyke to the rest of the merches, if hastye remedy thereof be not hadde. Item, I do remember my self, being of thage of 40 yeres, when at the cesseing of 120 galloglassheis in the countye of Kyldare, in exchewing of the Erldom thereof, many Englyshe husbondes of the same countye came to inhabit in the countye of Dublin, and Meathe at one tyme, and soo yerely others followid, so that nowe in the said countye, whiche was more parte Englyshe, as the countye of Dublin now is, ther is

not one husbondman, in effect, that spekeith Englyshe, ne useith
any Englyshe sort ne maner, and ther gentyllmen be after the same
sort; all by reason of coyne and [lyverie]: and the conversation with
the Iryshe sort that taketh it, and the poverte that men is brought to
by the same, causeyth ther gentyllmen, oncles be fewe that takeyth
the same extortion, or have gayne therby, that they are not well
able to set an Englyshe garment about them. Item, the saide
countye of Kyldare, and elleswhere, in marches, where the said
contynuall coyne, otherwyse called Coynowe Bowne, is taken,
was extendeid to beare the same after no indyfferent sortte; for
for some 20ti acres many placeis is chargeid with asmuche as 100
acres in many other placeis: so that ther landes in favour, or hadde
wylle under the Erlles of Kyldare, and other marche captaines,
have that fredom, and others not, so long as coyne shalbe thought
of necessyte to contynue, wold be remedied, so that all landes in
the same mercheis to be lyke chargeid, were reasonable."[a]

Three examinations, dated May, 1557, taken of the
M'Donnell gallowglasses, acquitting the Earl of Kildare of
putting *bonaght* upon Irishmen, except when he was Lord
Deputy, and then for the King's service, are given in the
introduction to the "Kildare Rental Book."[b]

The "supplication" addressed by the Earl to most of
the lords and gentry of the counties of Kildare and Carlow
would be a curious document. His use of the phrase, that
he proposed to be their "defender and spender," shows that
he intended to assume much the same relation to them
that an Irish king stood in to his clan. To be the "defender and spender" of his people was the best eulogium
bestowed on a chieftain. The Gaelic customs this Earl
followed, which will be amply illustrated by the publication of the "Kildare Rental Book," require some remarks

[a] Printed State Papers, part iii., vol. ii., p. 502.
[b] Journal of the Society, new series, vol. ii., p. 275.

in elucidation of the representations under view. Friar Clyn, writing in the middle of the fourteenth century, mentions the head of the Leinster Geraldines of the preceding century as "chieftain of his nation," showing that this feudal family had already assumed the independent condition of a clan. Their cousins of Desmond became so completely Celtic, that Mac Thomas, as each Earl of Desmond was styled, claimed tribute from his race, less as their feudal lord than as their senior, as appears by the dedication of an ancient Irish manuscript volume in the Stowe collection, the scribe of which, Sighraidh mac Thorna O'Mulconry, a *filedh*, or poet, states that the book was composed "for Maurice Mac Thomas, Earl of Desmond, and the Senior" [emphatically], "to whom belongs the primary right of Baal's fire, after the tribute of the south of Ireland may have been paid to him, as well by foreigners, as by the Irish."[a]

Kildare's option of enforcing either the Brehon law or the King's law was very objectionable. Yet the Irish, under his rule, had no cause to complain if their own code was dealt out to them; while the English naturally preferred that *their* laws should be administered to themselves. By a strange "order made in the Parliament of 1541, any person stealing over the value of fourteen pence was to lose one ear on conviction of the first offence, the other ear on the second conviction, and to be put to death for a third offence."

Some considerable activity in enforcing the "King's laws" might be expected to have followed the Commissioners' labours. However, but a single instance can be quoted, so far as the State Papers throw light upon such

* Dr. O'Conor's Rerum Hibernicar. Script.

legal proceedings—this unique case being an indictment in Latin, dated May, 1538, against Peter Fitzgerald, late of the Great Grange, near Cloncurry, Maurice *Bacagh* Fitzgerald, Edmond Asbold, of Maynooth, servant of Lord Leonard Grey, and James Fitzgerald, of Ballysonan (who is mentioned in the ensuing representation as a great succourer of thieves), for instigating Kedagh O'More, of Stradbally, Shane M'Coyn, of Kildare, and Neale Lalor, of Disart, gent., to steal cows and horses from the Earl of Ormond and Alexander Fitz Turlough, of the Great Grange. By this indictment it appears that Stephen-ap-Harry, of Rathangan, gent., a Welsh captain in command of certain of the royal troops, actually received ten cows of the said Kedagh " for comfort and favour."

The old rooted customs of the country were long in eradicating. Even James, the noble ninth Earl of Ormonde, who led the age in this land, could not divest himself of usages that were essential to his power; and he was frequently obliged to employ force to quell the disturbances consequent on the suppression of the Leinster Geraldines. In 1546 the Archbishop of Dublin writes to the King, inveighing against the Irish extortions of Earl James, who, says the prelate, is more like a prince than a subject. "Although," continues the writer, " this Earl repairs to your Majesty's Council in English apparel, with a retinue of yeomen, yet is there more Irish order, more Irish rule, and more stealth now in the lands given him on this side the Barrow than was in the Geraldines' time."

These haughty Geraldines did not submit tamely to the overthrow of their pride of place, and to the deprivation of their patrimonies. We read in O'Donovan's edition of The Four Masters:—

1546. "Many disaffected persons" [or rather ɒɪbƒeɑpᵹɑɔ, i. e. outlaws given to plunder and revenge] "of the Geraldines rose up against the Saxons, in revenge of their expulsion from their patrimony, namely, William, the son of James, son of the Earl of Kildare, Maurice-*an-feadha*, [i. e. of the wood], son of James *Meirgeach*, son of the Earl; and many other youths besides these. They did indescribable damages, among which were the plundering of Ballymore-Eustace, the plundering of Rathvilly, and of all the country around them; as the plundering and burning of Rathangan, from which they carried away on that occasion many thousands of cows, a number [in fine] that could not be enumerated or reckoned."

In the next year, these rebels were defeated at Three Castles; sixteen were taken, including Maurice of the Wood and his brother; and being conveyed to Dublin, were hanged and quartered. Thus, say the Annalists, were these plunderers and rebels dispersed and scared; and although their career was of but short duration (one year only), they committed vast depredations.

Gerald, brother of Silken Thomas, being restored to the Earldom of Kildare, gradually assumed much of the port and demeanour of his forefathers; and, when employed in arms in the service of the Crown, used, for want of regular pay for his troops, the old system of coyne and livery. Gross abuses obtaining in the army, the captains making false musters, so as to receive pay for "black men," William Bermingham, "lord of Brymycham's country," gave information in a bold spirit, quite uncommon in that age, of this and other public grievances; and in consequence, Sir Nicholas Arnold was sent hither to take musters, and, being made Lord Justice, effected, in May, 1564, reductions in the garrisons. This measure of economy was very displeasing to the Earls of Kildare and Ormonde, who, as commanders of the forces, were in receipt of high pay. In the month of September, the first-named Earl was in the field against rebels, at the head of the whole disposable force of the realm. The last-named nobleman, the loyal Ormonde, had issued a proclamation, abolishing coyne and livery in Tipperary. Yet there is ample testimony to prove that no other means were available for the support of an army. At a time that the Crown, when making war on public grounds, had no other mode of feeding its troops than the old exaction of cess in kind, how could private men, such as Kildare, Ormond, and Clanricarde, whose territories the Crown was utterly unable to protect, do otherwise than employ the customary means for defence? The attacks, in the year above mentioned, of Desmond upon Sir Maurice Fitzgerald, and the losses sustained by Clanricarde from the O'Briens, show that private wars were frequent and prevalent. On the latter occasion, Lord Clanricarde boldly demands redress of the Queen, or "at least to be allowed to take redress after the country fashion."

In the meanwhile, William Bermingham continued his exertions to procure reform in the army; while another Anglo-Irish gentleman, Oliver Sutton, of Richardston, county of Kildare, directed himself to the no less patriotic, but more perilous task of drawing attention to the growing exorbitancy of "the great" Earl of Kildare.

Some account of the public-spirited author of the earliest of these representations, namely, David Sutton, is requisite, since, indeed, his labours seem to have led to the other presentments being now of record. He was of a Strongbonian family of knightly rank in the shires of Wexford and Kildare. The curious letter from the gentry of the Pale, sent, in 1454, to the Duke of York, is signed by a member of this family. This David Sutton was of

Rathbride; he was mayor of Dublin in 1543; and, during the Geraldine rebellion, had, according to Holinshed, taken a loyal and steady part. Robert Cowley writes to the Duke of Norfolk, in 1540:—

"Where a good gentilman callid Davyd Sutton who kepith at his charge divers horsemen and fotemen, had the constableship of the Kinges castell of Kildare, the said Robert [Brabason] did put him oute, and for lucre took uppon hym self to bee constable of Kildare, keping in his handes the constableships of Carclingford, distansing asunder lxx myles; and left not in the castell of Kildare any manner of pese of ordynance, somoche as a hand gonne or any pese of artillery, not oon bowe, but likking up the proffut; and OConnor beeing thereof monysshed, entered into the towne and burnyd it, and entered into the castell and ryfeled it of all the cattaill therein put for refuge, and toke horses out of the Castell. And oon hand gone may have kepte theym out and saved the Castell and all that was therein.

"Item, that part of the Armye may bee content to departe from suche charges of constableshippis, that wol take no paynes, but take their passe tymes in good townes pleasantly, permitting their castelles to bee takyn and prosterated behinde theyme, as on Dewke constable of Castle Jordan, in the borders of OConnors cuntrey, this last woke, was passing tyme whiles the Castell was takyn, brokyn, and ryfeled, and the warde like feynte cowardes gave over the Castell and rendered theymselves prisoners to OConnor, who had vj. half hakes, a redd pese, a passvolant, ij. hackbusshes, and a shipp pese, with all their pellets, moldes, and powder, which OConor kepith to the great daunger of the Kinges subjectes."[a]

In 1544 the Government wrote to the King, recommending that David Sutton, a gentleman of the county of Kildare, who has rendered very acceptable service, be appointed a member of the Irish Privy Council, and be al-

[a] Ellis's Letters, vol. ii. pp. 98, 100.

lowed to purchase the lands of the late Commandery of St. John's, called Tully.

The office of belling the cat descended hereditarily to Oliver Sutton, who, bravely daring the displeasure of the Earl of Kildare, addressed several memorials (one of which we print) to Queen Elizabeth, disclosing the Earl's "enormities." This gentleman had been imprisoned by Lord Justice Arnold during sixteen weeks, for complaining of having been despoiled; and he drew up, at the close of 1565, A book to be exhibited to the Lord Lieutenant against coin and livery, which the Earl of Kildare taketh, with other the said Earl's enormities and abuses. This document, which is longer than the one now published, seems to have been written in Ireland. On December the 2nd, having come to London, he exhibited "Articles" against the Earl, which agree in substance with the former accusations. The writer states that he has been compelled by the Earl to forsake his ploughing, and abide in Dublin or England, for safety of his life. On the 11th the Queen wrote by him to Lord Deputy Sydney, desiring this high officer to report on what is convenient for her Majesty to judge of in Sutton's "exhibition of disorders," which, the Queen observes, "too directly touch the Earl of Kildare." Security was to be provided to protect this bold accuser's life from persons he was in fear of, on account of his information; and Sydney was to send his opinion as to Sutton's suits for leases of crown lands. Little seems to have been done in favour of this public-spirited Anglo-Irishman. In April, 1568, he supplicates the Privy Council, stating that he has been injured by the Earl to the value of £2000; is in continual danger of his life for having disclosed this magnate's disorders; and prays that his causes may be determined.

His representations as to the grievance of the exaction of coyne and livery aided, however, the measures soon adopted for its abolition. The Earl himself headed a movement in this direction, since there is an entry in the Kildare Rental Book of " The ordyr takyn at the Solanis the last of Maii, 1567, by the Ryght Honorabyll the Erlle of Kyldare, and the rest of the gentyllmen of the same syre, for the setting forthe of the rysing out to the generall Ostyng ;" in which order special regulations are laid down for levying the necessary commissariat.

The following is David Sutton's Presentment, dated 1534:—

P'SENTED BY DAVID SUTTON FOR THE COUNTYE OF KYLDARE.

This Booke made the 20th daie of Septembr, The 29th yere of the reigne of o^r sou?aign Lorde the Kinge that nowe is, by comandment of the Kings comissioners then being in Ireland; which had me sworne to declare the trothe how the countie of Kildare and Carlagh was used by the late Erle of Kyldare, and sithens and nowe, which I trust trewly shall appere hereafter.

First thErle sent to all or the most parte of the Lords and Gentylmen of bothe the said counties for to have had the defense of them, and also to spende them, as he said in his supplicacōn or writting, but at their owne pleasure, wherunto the most parte of the forsaid gentylmen put to their hands to the aforsaid writting, as of trothe durst not saye the contary.

Itm̄, after the forsaid writting be used bothe the counties as his owne, but onely he suffred the gentylmen to levie their owne rents.

Itm̄, he wold put upon them to finde hym as many horsmen, horses, and boyes as went comonly wth hym aboute.

Itm̄, he wold sesse on them in like maner, if eny straunger Irishe or Englishe cam unto hym, all their horsmen, horses and boyes at all tymes.

Itm̄, whatsoev? tyme he kepte his Ester or Cristmas, which he wold doo wth a great numbre of people, then wold he sesse all their horses and boyes and his owne upon the countrey to have horsmete and mannesmete duryng the feast.

Itm̄, he used to give many horses to gentylmen, and to ev?y man w'in the said counties that he gave eny suche horse, if the man were able to receave hym, he wold be wth hym ii daies and twoo nights, to have bothe mete and drinke with hym.[a]

Itm̄, he used to have vi^{xx} kerne and xl^{ty} boyes to have their mete contynually upon the said counties and upon the borders of the same, but when they bare gallowglas.

Itm̄, when he sessed them wth Gallowglas[b] in the said counties he set his kerne in Lonne, Moishlagh, and Moy Innorragh, and in the Barony of Desse and Westmeth.

Itm̄, he used to sese the counties a while but w^t vi^{xx} speres of Gallowglas and that is xii^{xx} men, and other whiles w^t viii^{xx} speres, that is xvi^{xx} men.

Itm̄, he used to have a hunte w'in the forsaid counties, and ev?y dogge to have bothe bred and butt? like a man.

Itm̄, his men that kepte his stode had their mete upon the said counties.

Itm̄, he reared a carte w^t ii men and iiii garrons one weke in the yere upon ev?y plough within the said counties, to cary stones to the castels on the Borders, upon their owne mete and drinke and wages.

It? in another tyme of the yere he wold have a workeman one weke of the yere upon ev?y plough w'in the said counties and a man upon ev?y iii cotages w'in the same counties, one weke in the yere

---

[a] This custom of giving *tuardsdala*, or retaining fees, was Gaelic, and the recipient became the vassal of the donor, who thereupon was entitled to take *ciosa-ri*, coshery, (i. e. king's rent) at the dwelling of the retainer, for the usual term of two days and nights. The Kildare Rental Book, now publishing by this Society, proves how fully the Earl practised this custom.

[b] Cessing with *gall-oglasha*, i. e. foreign servitors, was imposing *bonacht* or hired men, termed in Latin *Scotici*, because usually of Scottish extraction.

upon their owne mete and wayes to cast diches and fastnes upon the borders.

Itm̄, he used ons in the yere to rere an axe upon a plough and an axe upon ev{}^?y thre cotagers, to cutte passages[a] upon the Borders of Irishmen sometyme foure daies together, and sometymes two daies; and the gentylmen and horsmen of the countrey to goo to defende them, they havyng horses and boyes mete of their tenants and their owne vitelles upon themselves.

Itm̄, he used most comonly to have iii[xx] horsmen to ev{}^?y hostyng upon the said counties and oute of the Nas vi yemen,[b] Carlagh, Dese, Darmot, Kylka, Athie, Kyldare, Rathangan to bere his owne boyes for they bare nothing with the contrey.

It̄, the said Erle used in eny manor of his that lacked eny house of office, as hall, kitchyn, barne or stable, that the ten[a]nts of the same manor shuld make it upon their owne charges and to bringe the stuf to hande, but onely the said Erle to fynde the carpenters and masons.

Itm̄, he used two lawes, o[r] p[rin]ce's lawes and brehens lawes, which he thought most beneficiall, as the case did require. Brehennes lawe is for stealing of a shepe or like thing v m̄ks tociens quociens and not to be hanged, for drawing any wepen out of the scabard xx[s]. If he drawe bludde w[t] the same it is v m̄ks, If he cut eny joynte c[s], & if he dethwounde hym though he kill hym not, his ramesome,[c] & all the forsaid forfaitures to come to

---

[a] These were passes cut through the woods that often divided "the Maghery," or plain ground, from the countries inhabited by the Irishry, who sometimes converted such a pass into a "fastness," as it was technically termed, by "plashing the wood," or making fence-works across and along the passage; thus making it a *bearna baogail*, or pass of danger. In Ireland, such roads through forests were the "passes of danger," whence incursions were made by one clan upon another, as mountain passes were in Scotland. In 1548, at the beginning of the coloniza- tion of Leix and Offaly, so important was the cutting of passes in the "great wood of Leix" and the forest of Offaly considered, that the Lord Deputy writes, it were better than forsake it, to lose most of the harvest of the county Dublin.

[b] Yeomen, representing the ancient English freeholders.

[c] This *eric*, or blood-money, was received by the king of a clan to compensate for injury to or loss of a clansman. When Maguire became tributary, in 1542, to O'Donnell, he conceded to him half the eric paid to him for killing

the forsaid Erle, & nothing to the partie, wherby ther fell many gentylmens lands to hym by meane of suche forfaitures. And ev'y comandement or pclamacõn that he caused to be made it was taken for a lawe.

Itm̃, of this forsaid booke there is no man useth it nowe as to set coyne and liu?ey upon eny other manes ten^a nts but onely the Lorde of Kylcullyn,[a] which doth set coyne & liu?ey upon the kings ten^a nts as well as upon other Gentylmens lands, for he is not able to kepe half the men he hath upon his owne lands & there is no man in the countrey that hath men of warre but he in effecte for the defense of the countrey; howe be it he hath some noughty men and ill doers, and if they were not w^t hym or put to execucõn they wold be doing hurts, as Piers Fitzgarrates sonnes doo nowe.

Item, William Brymycham useth alman? exaccõns worse then eu? dyd the Erle of Kyldare & as having coyne & liu?y, as well upon the kings lands as upon other gentylmens lands, and alman? works upon the ten^a nts upon their owne charges, as aforsaid of the Erle of Kildare.

Itm̃, he causeth the ten^a nts to give xvi q^a rtes to the galon

men throughout Fermanagh. So recently as 1554. Gerald, Earl of Kildare, levied a *boraimhe mor*, or great fine of cows, viz., 340, on Delvin-Eathra, as an eric for his foster-brother, slain by M'Coghlan. A curious account of this levy is given in the Kildare Rental Book. "Ramesom" is ransom, or the sum paid to deliver from rapine.

[a] The Lord of Kylcullyn was Eustace, Lord Portlester, created Viscount Baltinglas. This family are understood to derive from Sir Eustace le Poer, and this descent is warranted by their war-cry having been *Poeragh-aboo*. They may have become entitled to part of Offaly from this knight having married a coheiress of Birmingham, Earl of Louth; and they acquired four knight's fees in Kildare by an heiress of Le Bret, one of the representatives of the Fitzgeralds, Barons of Naas. There is a curious letter to the Duke of York, dated 1454, in Ellis's Letters, Second Series, vol. i., p. 121, mentioning an attack on Rathcoffy Castle, then inhabited by a Eustace who had espoused the widow of Wogan, of Rathcoffy. James, third Viscount Baltinglas, owned half the manor of Naas, and chief-rents from the Eustaces, St. Los, Flattisburys, Suttons, and Missets' lands, and from Clinton's Court; and also owned the old manor-house of Kilcullen. He was attainted for treason, 27 Eliz., by the special Act known as the "Statute of Baltinglas." In the time of Henry IV., the town of Kilcolyn was burnt by the Irish, upon which the King granted the burgesses a regular market day, with certain tolls. — [Rot. Pat. 4 Hen. IV.]

whither it be ale or butt⁹ as in paieng hym his vitailes or mets.ᵃ

Itm̃, he hath a galon of butter upon ev?y cowe in his lordship.

Itm̃, he giveth cōmandement and maketh it for a lawe throwe out the Barony of Carbre, calld Brymych^am countrey,ᵇ that no man shall [bring] eny man⁹ thinge that they have to eny m̃ket, but onely to his wif, and she to make the price.

Itm̃, William Brymycham taketh theves and letteth them goo at his pleasure, so as they fyne with hym.ᶜ

Itm̃, nowe of late there was two stronge theves taken by the kings tenants in har'st, of which one of them is nowe with my Lord

---

ᵃ Rent was paid in kind in the west of Kildare at this period. On the other hand, in the east and more fertile parts of the county, money rent, averaging sixpence an acre, was paid. Sixteen quarts to the gallon may have been customary in measuring ale and butter. Comparative with modern payments for the grass of a cow, sixteen quarts of butter were not much for the summer's grass.

ᵇ The county of Offaly, or of the O'Connor-Failghe clan, which was originally granted by Strongbow to De Birmingham, had become divided, before the reign of Edward II., between the latter's descendants and the Fitzgeralds, barons of Offaly, while the western and woody parts of the country remained in the possession of the O'Connors. In 1524, "Brymmyngham," captain of his nation, was one of the principal Anglo-Irish lords marchers. At the period of these presentments, it was advised that the portion of old time inhabited by the "Brymmyniames," extending as far east as Tower Trowan, be restored to them; that "William Brymmyniame, because of his activitie, be made lord thereof," to him and his heirs; that the rest of the country be granted to Cahir O'Connor in fee-tail, at the same time creating him Baron of Offaly (a peerage recently forfeited by the Fitzgeralds); and William Birmingham, a lord of Parliament. This latter active representative of this anciently distinguished family was knighted, and created Baron of Carbery, at the time of the creation of the earldoms of Tyrone, Clanrickard, and Thomond.

"Sir William Birmingham, Knt., Baron of Carbery," was, in August, 1541, appointed an arbiter of differences between O'Conor of Offaly (Brian) and his brother Caher. The others were David Sutton of Connall, gent., James Fitzgerald of Osbardston, gent., and Richard M'Kenegan, brehon or judge to O'Conor.—[Printed State Papers, vol. iii., p. 316]. The clan country around Carbery is styled, on a map of *circa* 1569, "Clan Iores, *alias* Bremachane." They had resisted the feudal law that would have entitled Preston, lord of Gormanston, to part of the estate on marriage with a co-heiress. With reference to this, the senior line of this eminent Anglo-Irish family, see Lodge's Irish Peerage, vol. iii., p. 51.

ᶜ That is to say, the thieves paid him *caina*, or fines for being relensed.

Deputie, and the other the strongest thief and a gentylman borne, which William Brymycham sent for hym, and let hym goo, bycause he was Cayre Occonners s'v'nt.

Itm̃, the said William keepethe of the Connors with hym, which be better spies in this countrey then they that be borne here.

Itm̃, Philip Morice[a] setteth coigne & liv'y upon all the ten'nts w'in Allon as though they were his owne, and he is but chief Lord ou'l them, as well upon my Lord Bishops lands there as others.

Itm̃, he kepeth of the Doneyes[b] with hym daily, which be the best spies in o' countrey, and when they go home doo take the goods of the countrey with theym by means of his men and they together.

Itm̃, James M'Gerald accompanieth with the Deneys & w' the strongest theves of theym which doth hurte oftymes.

Iẽ, the Gentylmen put all man'l charges that come to the countrey upon their tenants aswell to the hostyngs as otherwise & no charge upon themselfs.

Itm̃, ev'y gentylman gen'ally putteth coyne & liv'ey upon their owne ten'nts.

Itm̃, there goo many of the Lord of Kylcolyns men, James Geralds sonnes men, to aske and to take foysse, and Richard Fitz-Edmonds sonnes ev'y night (a foye is to saye to aske mete) and there as they goo, the folks ashamed, or affraied to saye them naye, for feare of burning by night.

Itm̃, Piers Fitz Garrats sones been socored & their men w'th the baron of Noragh[c] ofttymes they being oute upon the countrey.

---

[a] Philip Morice, lord of Allon, was, probably, of the Geraldine family. "Gerod fyz Fyllype, of Allon," was cessed with one horseman to general hostings in 1567.—[Kildare Rental Book.] Gerald, son of Philip Fitzgerald, late of Allon, died in 1611, was seized of this manor, and of Baronston.—[Inquis. Lag.]

[b] Probably some of the O'Dempsy's, of whom the chief was subsequently created Viscount Clanmalier.

[c] Norragh was granted by Strongbow to "one Robert," who seems to have been ancestor of the De Valle, Le Veale, or Calfe family, barons of Norragh, whose heiress, Elizabeth, was espoused by the celebrated Arthur Kavanagh, the M'Murrough, of Leinster. The barony went, however, by a subsequent heiress to a branch of the Wellesley family, of whom one was the Baron of Norragh above-mentioned,—[Inquis. Lag. Kildare.]

Itm̄, ev'y man comonly maketh pledges by their owne hands for their demaunds.

Itm̄, another ivill ordre is, that when we be at peax with Leysse & the Donsyes they come in companies to aske mete & take the best that the poore ten'nts have, so so that they have ympoufished the borderers, so that the kings ten'nts[a] have given warnyng to go from their holdings.

Itm̄, the s'geaunts[b] have for their labor, bicause they have no fee s'teyn, oute of ev'y xx carts that ar rered or levied to the hostings, one carte & of ev'y xx horsemen one horsman, in like maner of fotemen one hoope of whete & one hoope of oats upon eu'y plough & a henne upon eu'y cotage. And the countrey saith they rere this sometyme double in the countrey.

Itm̄, every borderer useth to rere the forsaid v m̄ks for the effects doon upon them or upon their ten'nts.

Itm̄, James Fitz Gerot of Ballyssannan[c] and his brother ar great socorers of the theves of Leyse, and his brother Piers leadeth them thorough the countrey to steale; and the theft to be taken the first night to the Blak Wood, and in the second night to Balysonnan & in the third night to Lexe, and so from place to place of their owne tyll they be quite out of the countrey, so that it is hard to pve them.

Although of later date than the foregoing presentments, the "booke" of Oliver Sutton naturally comes in here. It is numbered 55 in the lately published Catalogue of the Irish State Papers, and is evidently the draft of the paper numbered 56, which is much longer. It runs as follows:—

[a] Probably the takers of the lands newly in the hands of the Crown by the forfeitures of the Geraldines.

[b] Serjeants were servants who collected rents, and allotted cess, and hosting taxes, &c.

[c] Ballysannan was the seat of a branch of the Geraldines. A curious picture-map, representing the siege of the Castle by the Parliamentary forces, was published in the Journal of the Society, vol. i., New Series, p. 110. By printed Inquest, Sir Piers Fitzgerald, Knt., of Ballysonan, was found to have died seised of two castles in this manor; also of the Blackwood, and of other manors. He died in 1593. Sir James was his heir. This place was taken from its owners in 1649, and attempted to be restored to them by James II.— See Archbishop King's State of the Protestants of Ireland.

AGAINST THE EARLE OF KILDARE TAKING OF COYNE AND LIVERIE.

[*December*, 1566.]

A Booke to be exhibited unto the Righte Honorable the Lord Lieutenant agaynst Coyn and Livery which th'Earle of Kyldare takethe by extorte power of th'inhabitants of the countie Kyldare, with other the sayd Earle's enormities and abuses.

<small>Coyn and Livery disalowed by Kynge Ric. the second, and Edward the IVth.</small>

Fyrst it was enacted in the tyme of Kynge Ric. the secunde at his personall beinge here in this realme of Ireland that Coyn and Livery should be abolyshed th'Englyshe Pale, as Methe, the countie of Dublin, the countie of Kyldare, and the countie of Catherlaghe, wch acte was newly confirmed by Kynge Edward the 4th, as dothe appere by recorde &c.

<small>An Acte in Kynge Henry the VII^{thes} rayne, approvyng this exaction to be felony.</small>

Item, in the rayne of Kynge Henry the 7th ther past an act within this realme of Irland (this Earle of Kyldares graundfather being then Lord Deputie) wch is called thacte of Marches and Maghery, that suche as tooke coyn in the Maghery, or Englyshe Pale,^a shoulde be esteemed felons, except it were uppon their owne lands in the borders.

<small>Order taken by Fitz Harbard Commissioner agaynst the same.</small>

Item, Sir Anthony Fitz Harbard, Knyghte, and other Commissioners sent hither by the late Prince of famous memory Kynge Henry the 8th, tooke order that the actes aforesayde shoulde stand in force.

<small>An Acte in print by Skevyngtons tyme disprovinge the same.</small>

Item, in the tyme of Sir Wylliam Skevyngton, being Deputie of this realm, ther past an acte for th'extinguishment of the sayde coyne and livery, as playnly maye appere by the same acte in print confirmynge lykewyse thactes aforsayd, &c.

<small>^a This shows that the Pale consisted of the *Machaire*, i. e. plain land, of the central eastern part of Ireland, while the mountainous districts remained still with the unconquered native tribes.</small>

Item, it apperethe by a graunt made by the gen̄t of the countie Kyldare that the sayde c^{yn} and l^{ivery} was graunted unto the late Earl of Kyldare but for a certayne tyme limited in the sayde graunt towards the sustenance of his chardges for the defens of the same countie, till farther ayde were sent from the Prince, lyke as nowe houldings are graunted (uppon occasion) by all shires durynge a tyme for ther better defens till they be ayded by the governoure &c.

A grant of coyn and livery for a tyme.

Item, so longe as the Queens Majestes progenitours held thErldome in ther owne hands by thattaynder, for observyng thacts aforesayde, they nether required nor had eny suche duties of thinhabitants of the same shire. So as this Erle, clayminge in by them, can be in no better case then they were, albeit he had never so ample words in his creation, &c.

ThErles prerogative surmountinge the Princes.

Item, his auncestours were bound by indenture to the late Kinge Henry th Eyghte (amonges other covenants apperyng by the same indenture) not to take this exaction within the Englyshe Pale, uppon penaltie of a thousand pounds &c.

His ancestors bound by Indenture to forgo this exaction.

Item, the Governours, with the most parte of the army, sins the late Earles attaynder untill this mans creation, without takynge eny suche exaction, laye within this shire for the defens of the same and thEnglyshe Pale, to the great relief of thinhabitants as well tuchinge ther safeguard as also ther prosperitie and welthe of lyvynge, with suche good government that (all causes of complaynt being supprest) the subjects lyved pleasauntlie. Yet, sins the comynge of this Earle, throughe his intollerable extortion, they are quite fallen from that welthe into extreme povertie and ruine. And that as well in the countie Kildare as in all other shires whear he hathe so avayled sins his comyng, &c.

The subjects prospered when this exaction was left.

Item, the contrey sherede the chardges continually with no lesse than 200 of his horses, with 2 boyes appoynted for every horse, takyng 24 sheaves for every chief horse, and 26 sheaves for every hackney.

The number of his horses & boyes charged uppon the contrey.

Also his boyes must have a tester[a] for every meale, or a distresse thryse worth the same, and never to be delivered the partie agayne. Lykewyse uppon a denyall of eny thies his exactions, he sendethe his power to the partie that so denicthe to leavy of his cattell what he wyll for satisfaction thereof, and killethe the same presently for the provision & furniture of his kytchen &c. As for example, he tooke from Mr. Aylmer[b] 16 beoves, from Oliver Sutton 2 beoves, from Rocheford of the Laraghes 4 beoves, and from divers others, without makeyinge eny restitution or satisfaction of the same, &c.

The countrey charged yerely with meat for his great horses.

Item, the contrey is chardged in the tyme of otesede at least with 300 pecks yerely, whiche he callethe otes for his great horses. So that a score of boyes and horsmen appoynted to levy the same must have coyne and livery whearsoever they go &c.

He oppresseth the contrey with strangere horses.

Item, at suche tymes as Iryshe Lordes or other his alyances do visit him, the contrey must stand chardged comonly with all they[r] horses and boyes durynge theyr abood in his howse or in the shire.

An ordinary dutie to charge the contrey at tydes.

Item, on every Christmas and Easter the contrey is opprest with no lesse than 5 hundrethe horses, as well of his owne as strangers, which purposely resorte unto him to kepe theyr tydes. And this he claymethe as an ordinary dutie; ye and thoughe they com not themselves, yet som send ther horses. Also his servaunts plowe horses must be ceassed under colour of his owne to make up a number, &c.

He oppresseth the contrey as well in his absence from home as otherwyse.

Item, at suche tymes as he listethe to absent himself from home by disport of huntyng or eny other occasion, or when he liethe at any gentlemans howse, he appoyntethe his horses and idle boyes into the contrey. Also his officers, otherwyse called lyvrous,[c] take for ther unreasonable duties at least 200 marks yerely, &c.

[a] Tester, a coin impressed with the king's *teste, tête*, or head, commonly a sixpence was so called up to the present.

[b] Aylmer, of Lyons, in Kildare.

[c] Liverers, perhaps serjeants, or collectors, wearing the Earl's livery.

Item, he retaynethe towards the kep-
ynge of his horses 200 hable men at least,
as boyes, borne in thYryshe pale, whose
progenitours have been alwayes enemies
unto Englyshemen, continually spoylyng and robbynge the shire.
So that being threatened for the same they fle into theyr contreis,
wheare they remayne untill they thinke ther offences be forgotten,
and then they returne without eyther warrant or protection; as
Ulstermen, the Brenny, the Farrols, Connors, Doyns, Laghlens,
Dempsyes, Moores, Kerrols, Cavanaghs, and suche lyke, whose
offences beinge complayned to the Erle by the farmor or any other
whom they trespas, his answer is, take you the offendors and I give
you leave to execute the lawe uppon them; and thus with frivolous
answers the partie is without remedy, &c.

He retayneth for his boyes suche as be alyed to the Queenes enemies.

Item, he keepethe 40 fote boyes at
least, wch runne in his carrands and affayres in all wheares, and duryng absens
must have daly growynge unto them 2 grots a daye; and they with
the rest do gyde into the Inglyshe pale other malefactours to spoyle
and pilfre the countrey, &c.

The number of his messingers, and of ther duties.

Item, there be 8 score ketynge kerne^{a}
wch by his mayntenaunce have coyn and
livery 2 dayes and 2 nyghtes quarterly in
every barony in the countie Kyldare, Lune, Micbare, and My-
laghe, with other baronyes and lordships in the borders of the Englyshe pale, doyng no service for the same, but pilfre and steal, con-
ductyng the enemies lykewyse to suche places wheare they se is
best oportunitie to spoyle the subjects, &c.

Kerne mayntayned by hym uppon the contrey.

Item, as often as he hathe comission to
pray eny Iryshemen for his own private
cause, he drawethe at least 3 or 4 hun-
drethe strangers into the English Pale (as Moores, Connors, Cavanaghs, Farrols, Doyns, Laghlens, Dempsyes, Kerrols, Tooles,

He draweth strangers to endomage the contrey.

---

^a The Earl of Kildare's "ketynge kerne," commanded by William Keating, were mostly of that family, which evidently, of old time, supplied the Earl's *kern-tigh*, or household troops. See p. 175, *infra*.

Byrnes, and Kynchelaghs), wheare they muste have coyn and livery by force of his comandment; whereby the Englishe Pale sustaynethe more damage then do the place whear tendethe his revengment, by reason of suche booties which they take from the subjects in jornyeng too and fro, pretendyng the same to be well gotten under thErles former pretense. &c.

The contrey chardged with his hounds and huntesmen.   Item, his houndes and huntesmen must have meate as often as he dothe appoynt, to the number of 40 or 3 score, which is a more prerogative then eny Christian prince claymethe, &c.

His boyes do steall the subjects corne by nighte.   Item, his boyes in harvest tyme doo stell by nyght the corne lyenge in the felde to sell the same, complaynt whereof beinge made to thErle, he fedethe the partie with some dilatory answer and threatenyng words, so that he dares not make further complaynt, be his occasion never so just, &c.

Thimpostions of the couutie Kildare exceedinge other shires.   Item, notwithstandyng this his grevous extortion, which is directly agaynste the lawe, and therfor not alowable, yet this poor shire, sins his comyng to therldome, hathe bene as muche charged with the governours provision, the forts and all captayns and souldiours as eny other of thEnglyshe shires which beare nothing so muche impositions. So that of righte it should be removed, and so much the more for that it situatethe betwixte the forts[a] and thEnglyshe Pale, and for that hathe more accesse of travaylers, with whom it standethe not a little chardged, consideryng the want of innes or victualyng howses[b] toward ther further entertaynment, &c.

Distresses taken for coyn and livery to poor subjects great damages.   Item, it is comonly sene that suche his boyes as can not have coyn and livery do runne unto the farmor or husbandmans ploughe or carte in the feld to take a horse for their distresse, insomuche as the poor subject is letted of

---

[a] The forts erected in the reign of Edward VI. in Leix and Offaly, when the plantation of these countries with English colonists was first effected.

[b] Called by the Irish *biadtagha*, i. e. food-houses, kept by Betaghs.

sowynge his sedes or tyllynge his ground, ye sometimes for the space of a sennyghte or more, and wotes not whear to pursue his destres and sumtymes never recoverethe the same, &c.

He claymethe coyn and livery for defens of the shire which he defendeth not.

Item, wheras under colour of our defens he claymethe this exaction, yet is it sufficiently knowen howe the contrey was never so sore impoverished with spoyles and robbryes as it is nowe and hathe ben sins this Earles comynge to the realme:—ye and thoughe the poor dothe crave his assistans therein he strayghtwayes directs them to the Governor, affirmynge that forasmuche as he is not Governor, he oughte not to seke the redresse of eny suche enormities. So that by thies his answers and wrongfull impositions he hathe inforced thinhabitants so to forsake theyr dwellyngs that the shire is in a manner clene broughte to desolation &c.

Other inconvenienses growynge uppon the Countie Kyldare by thErle of Kyldares impositions.

The subjects decayed by his extortion.

First, whearas thinhabitants of the barony of Saut were wont at every muster to make the number of a thousand fyghtinge men[a] well appayraled for the warre, wherof should be of archers and gonners 5 hundrethe at least, yet nowe a man shall scarse pick out a dozen good archers and gonners by reason thimpositions. And nightly robbryes are so intollerable that the poor inhabitants are fayne to sell and gage ther sculles, haberchens, bowes, arowes, and suche other munition, sekynge with the gayne therof to sustayne ther offesprings, so that nowe it is a rare thing to se a pyke, fork, or eny suche weapon within any inhabitants howse. Wherof this hapnethe it is sone understood. Also it is the practise of suche idle persons as he dothe ceasse uppon the contrey to take nowe and then for theyr destresses suche warlyke munition as they can find, meanynge therby to disable the shire, that they myghte with lesse dread attempt the spoyle thereof &c.

[a] This proves the great strength of the ancient English colony.

Item, sone uppon his entre into the possession of his Earldome[a] (Sir Anthony Sentleger beinge then Deputie) beinge at Rathangan and Kildare for the space of a monethe ther come unto him Shane O'Neyle, Donnoghe O'Connor, Caher McArte, Morghe Cavanaghe, and divers others of their countreys, with whom he companyed marvaylous frendly and pleasantly, and so departed. Yet is it not knowen that they, being rebels a little before, came in uppon eny protection. But it is manifest that sone after they became ranke traytours, and have continually sins endamaged thEnglyshe Pale, which to resist he never coveted &c.

<small>Thassemble of Shane ONeyle, Donnoghe OConnor, Caher Mc Arte, and others with thErle.</small>

Item, it is to be noted howe many pilfres and spoyles have bene all thies yeres past comitted in the countie Kildare and thEnglyshe Pale, and the same conveyed by the Moores and Connors with thayde of the bastard Geraldins[b] throughe Athy and other the Earles lordships; yet was their passage not interrupted by thErle his constables, nor other his officers: complaynt wherof made to thErle, he answerethe the parties willing thym, in derision, to seke the remedy therof at the Lord Lieutenants hands, affirmynge he hath nothing to do withall.

<small>Spoyles passinge throughe the Erles lordships and thenemies not apprehended.</small>

Item, about December last, he being sent in commission to parle with the Moores, the Viscont of Baltynglas[c] beinge then present dyd challäge one Kedaghe O'Moores sons for certayne spoyles and other injuries don by them to him and his tenants. Wherefor desyring restitution thereof, els he woulde seke a further remedy, they answered openly that they were at de-

<small>He bears with the rebels in Parliament against the Vicont of Baltinglas.</small>

---

[a] This was in 1554. His visitors were his near relatives, who naturally came to welcome him home on his restoration. Shane O'Neill induced him to lead a hosting into the Earldom of Ulster, where he claimed large possessions, to chastise Red Felim, Lord of the Clandeboye O'Neills. Donough O'Conor was his relative, of the Offaly sept. Caher Mac Arte was a chieftain of the Clan Kavanagh, and created a peer of parliament in the same reign.

[b] The bastard Geraldines are noticed by the Four Masters.

[c] A curious list of the possessions of this nobleman is to be found on the back of a map in the State Paper Office.

fyans with the sayd Vicond and all his helpes, which the Erle hearynge dyd not once reprove, to the great encouragement of the sayde Kedaghes sunes and such other rebells, and to the great discoragement of the subject.

Gentlemens tenants spoyled and the Erles tenants spared.

Item, the Moores and O'Connors somtymes to the number of a hundrethe and more do comonly take meat within the shire, and are not once disturbed by the Erll nor eny of his. So that they cary away peacably the spoyles of gentlemens tenants, but never of the Erles owne tenants or lordships, wherin semethe to be a partialitie &c.

Christofer Fitz Oliver placed in Gryffen Rathe to plague the country.

Item, he placed in Gryffenrathe within a myle to Maynothe one Christofer fitz Oliver, a bastard kynnesman of his, who is notably knowen to be a currupt person; Insomuche that many spoyles and booties taken out of the Englishe Pale have bene found with him; yet could he never be broghte to triall for the same, his alians is suche. Also the spoyles of kyne and garrans are posted by him and Gerald m^c Shane from the countie Kildare to Westmeethe and to Morghe O'Toole, who are confederated to worke what mischief they can, meatynge sundry tymes at the sayd Gryffenrathe to confer their intents, &c.

Gerald Mc Shane and the Moores ayded against Mr Marshall.

Item, at suche tyme as Mr Marshall[a] squared with Gerald Mc Shane for retaynyng of 200 riotous persons, being of the Moores and other rebels, Mr Marshall covetinge to apprehend them, the sayde Gerald came for refuge into the countie Kildare (after he had committed sundry tresspasses in Westmeathe worthy of deathe) and was supported in the same countie Kildare untill he almost undyd the same with his robbryes. Redresse wherof being soughte at the Erles bands, he posted the same to the chief governour, affirmynge that he had no authoritie to correcte such offenders. Further it can be witnessed that certayne of the sayd Moores affirmed they and Gerald Mc Shane would or maye even sett on fire the towne of Trym about Mr Mar-

---

* i. e. the Marshal of the Lord Deputy's hall and of the troops.

shall's cares; and that theyre should be none within the realme of Irland of stronger power then a Geraldin within shortetyme; and thys is the common reporte of suche idlemen as com from theym abrode the contrey, &c.

The bastard Geraldins ayded and danger ensueng to ther poor accusors.

Item, he mayntaniethe in suche sorte all bastarde Geraldins that be his kynnesmen, and borne to no enheritance (but supported by him to work his feats), that be they accused of ever so heynous an offens yet will he labour so that they shal not be broghte to triall, but ether the same shal be prevented by a pardon out of England or else by some suche frendly shift, that the poor men whom they do spoyle and rob dayly, dare not once accuse theym fearyng to incurre th' Erles anger or displeasure. Also it is sufficiently knowen that thoughe thiese bastard Geraldins be borne to no possessions, yet can eche of them lyve by sheyr pilfering and shiftes as well as can eny gentleman of £200 inheritans, &c.

Ketyngs and Geraldins (under pretence of servitors) do rob the Englyshe pale.

Item, suche as be appoynted comonly by thErle for the defens of the shire are Ketyngs and bastard Geraldins, who are and have bene alwayes secreat enemies unto the same, which under pretens of true servitours range from howse to howse, as spies ready to mischief the contre, and specially suche as cannot favour thErles proceedyngs. Lykewise in tyme of prayer they reprove all such as do not chiefly commend the Erle in their prayers, and humbly thank him as theyr only defender, althoughe the poor commons do knowe the contrary, &c.

Geraldines would have the Erle to be Governour.

Item, they bost throughcout the controy that tis thErle and not thEnglyshe power that preservethe the same from burnyngs and other mischiefs, affirming that the subjects shall never lyve quietly untill thErle have the governauns of the realme, &c.

Theyr pryde.

Item, they glory so muche in theire blood, that in respect of theymselves they sett all others at noughte, thinkyng therby to make the whole realme slaves unto them, as they have always done.

The Erles negligens in service. "Item, wheras he is able to make the number of two thousand persons at least at suche tymes as he is bound to praye or spoyle eny Iryshman for his owne private commoditie, yet, when the O'Conors and others, accompanyed with the bastard Geraldins, fyred the towns of Kylheale and Owghterinny, which are not past two myles distans from his manor of Maynothe, also spoyled other villages and slewe the inhabitants, he did not once with his power seke to rescue the same, nor yet eny other enormitie committed in this shire sins his coming to thErledome. Which enormities are esteemed by the poor more hurtful then all th'exactions and censses borne to the queens majestys army, or other her officers &c°. And for confirmation as well of this as of the premises, the gentlemen, farmours, and other thinhabitants of the countie Kylydare being called to examination are ready to verifie the same, and chieflie the poore, whose dayly exclamations are righte sorrowful to heare."

On the 11th December, 1565, Queen Elizabeth sent Oliver Sutton back to lord deputy Sydney, with his "books of disorders, which," her majesty observes, "too directly touch the Earl of Kildare." It appears, from an enormous mass of manuscripts in the State Paper Office concerning the conduct of this Earl, that he was playing the game of his forefathers. On one occasion he let fly Viscount Baltinglas, as a precursor in revolt. The high character he had gained when in Spain and Italy, and his exalted position in Ireland, induced Elizabeth not to proceed to extremities with him.

THE PRESENTMENT OF THE COMMONS OF THE COUNTY OF
WATERFORD TO THE ROYAL COMMISSIONERS, A. D. 1537.

The theme of the ensuing Verdict of the Commoners of the County of Waterford evidently consists in setting forth the list of exactions and impositions used by Lady Katherine Poer. The members of the reformatory commission, to whom these grievances were presented, had, no doubt, become versed in the topic of Irish customs; but in the present day, when traces of these obsolete usages are only to be found in rare books and scarcer manuscripts, it is difficult to explain their distinct natures. I may, however, briefly attempt to do so, and include in the footnotes, and in these introductory remarks, some additional original information on the subject.

The exaction of coyne and livery, the general and most pressing evil, heads this list, as it does all contemporary complaints. The term itself is half Gaelic, half French, the first word being a corruption of *coinnmeadh*, i. e. refection for men, and the second a corruption of *livrer*, i. e. to deliver, or give out food, for horses, whence the modern terms, " to stand at livery," and "a livery servant," whose coat was supplied to him.[a] This imposition, so customary in Ireland,[b] and which often amounted to free-quarters for as

[a] Chaucer alludes to the origin of this word:—" That is the connaisance [cognizance] of my livery, to all my servants delivered."

[b] How customary it was, more than half a century later, appears by a letter, A. D. 1598, from Thomas, tenth Earl of Ormonde, to John Liston, whom he had commissioned to raise a company of foot for the Queen in the county of Kilkenny, in which he says—" in yo' travell y' shalbe lawful for yo" to take meate and drynke for one

many men and horses as the chieftain could force his people to receive, was an inevitable mode of providing for soldiery in an uncivilized land, which was divided among clans that were always predatory and were therefore so constantly fighting, that, as stated in the verdict, this war-tax, in comparison with which an income-rate of ten per cent. is a trifle, was " continual upon all the King's subjects."

The grievance of the exactions imposed by Gaelic chieftains and Anglo-Irish lords consisted in the uncertain and arbitrary degree in which they were levied. Additional imposts, also, were exacted by the latter class on the authority and precedents of the feudal system. For example, John le Poer, of Dunoyle, obtained a writ from the crown (dated 18 Edward II.), directing that he should have aid from his knights and free servants towards making his eldest son a knight.ᵃ This levy, which had no corresponding one among the Irish, was for the purpose of defraying the costs of feasting, &c., attendant on the ceremony. Another writ, of the same date, commanded the sheriff of Cork to enable David fitz Richard to have aid from his knights and freeholders towards the marriage of his eldest daughter. This impost, which was to provide a portion for the young lady, was somewhat similar to the custom in Gaelic countries, by virtue of which Baroness Poer, of Curraghmore, endowed her daughter, Lady Devereux, with the portion mentioned in this presentment. In feudal cases, however, an act of parliament limited and defined the levy.

The Lords Le Poer had, by degrees, obtained an enor-

nyght, and a breakefast, in ech place, in competent manner, not usinge of extorcõn or other oppression on the countrey."—" Transactions,'' vol. iii., p. 323, first series.

A trace of the custom still remains in the billetting of marching soldiers on householders, who are bound to find beds and light.

ᵃ Calendar, Pat. Rolls, p. 32.

mous power over this county. Descended from a companion of Strongbow, who received a vast fief here, they usurped entire dominion, excepting in the Decies, an ancient barony of the house of Desmond.

Among the magnates of Ireland summoned by Edward the First to attend the Scottish war, in 1302, no less than seven of this great family appear on the list. The Le Poers of Donhill, or Kilmaiden, appear to have been the senior line, according to Sir George Carew, who was versed in Irish genealogy, and who notes in their pedigree:—" Out of this house all the Powers of Ireland, and the Fitz-Eustaces, Viscountes of Baltinglass, descend."—*Carew MS.*, 635, p. 145.

Sir Arnold Le Poer, Baron of Donhill, was one of the four patriotic nobles of the Englishry who made firm and gallant stand against the invader, Edward Bruce. In the 33rd year of Edward I., the crown appointed John le Poer, Baron of Donhill, to be sheriff of the county of Waterford; and the reasons for the appointment are stated to be, that much damage was done by divers malefactors running through that county, some of whom were of the family of the Poers, and others under that family, whom neither the sheriff nor the people could resist; wherefore the Baron of Donhill, *who is fully able* to chastise all such malefactors of his family and their accomplices, is made sheriff there.*

The story of the feud between the first Earl of Desmond and Sir Arnold le Poer is told by all our annalists. The knight had mortally insulted the great chief of the western Geraldines by calling him "a rhymer" in some public assembly. Although the later earls of the house of Desmond were remarkable for their acquirements, and their

---

* Lynch's "Feudal Dignities," p. 236.

patronage of learning, during very ignorant ages and in an unlettered country (for instances, the fourth earl was styled "the poet," and the eighth, beside being able to write his name, founded two colleges), yet the *soubriquet* of "rhymer," so publicly given to the first Earl, enraged him, being the term the Englishry were accustomed to apply contemptuously to a Gaelic *fhiledh* or bard. This story is borne out by printed records. Writs were issued on the 28th June, 1325, to Le Poer and Maurice Fitz Thomas (Desmond), commanding them to desist from congregating men-at-arms for the purpose of attacking each other. In the following year Fitz Thomas, and John, Baron of Donhill, received permission to treat with the felons of their separate families, surnames, and followings; and the sheriffs of the neighbouring counties were ordered not to arrest the said felons. All these royal writs were, however, of no avail; for soon afterwards the defamed lord assembling his forces, plundered and burned the countries belonging to Le Poer in Ossory, Kells, and Offa, so that the old baron and his son Sir Arnold were forced to take refuge in the city of Waterford—and when the latter sailed to England, in order to complain to the king—his enemies took advantage of his absence by laying waste "every thing belonging to him."[a] The quarrel probably originated in a more serious cause than the bestowal of a nickname, viz., in depredations committed by numerous and predatory "Poerines" in Lord Desmond's barony of Decies. In the following year, 1328, a still more formidable enemy arose to Sir Arnold in the person of the Bishop of Ossory, who brought a charge of heresy against him, and he was committed to Dublin Castle, where he died

[a] Grace's Annals.

a prisoner. His son, Sir Eustace, became a firm adherent to the very Earl of Desmond who had been so hostile to his family; and when that nobleman's remote territory in Kerry was entered and attacked by the Lord Justice, Sir Eustace had the hardihood to defend the strong fortress of Castle-Island. But the castle was taken, and its defender ignominiously hanged. An idea of the extent of the possessions of this head of the Le Poers may be formed by enumerating the lands forfeited on this treasonable occasion :— viz., the vast Waterford estate ; the manors of Dunbryn and Grenagh, in Kilkenny, held of the Earls of Ormond ;[a] the barony of Kells, in Ossory (afterwards granted to Lord Birmingham) ; the manor of Ardee, in Louth, held in right of his wife, a coheiress of Birmingham, Earl of Louth ; and the manor of Kilmchide, near Athy.[b] Donhill and the Louth estate were afterwards restored.[c]

The Powers of Curraghmore appear to have branched from the main line of Donhill in the person of Nicholas Le Poer, who was, towards the close of the 14th century, summoned as a baron to several parliaments.

Sir Richard Le Poer was created baron of " Coraghmore" by Henry VI., in 1452. The following notice of this great Anglo-Irish chieftain curiously illustrates the theme of the presentments for this county and city. The record is from an unpublished Act of Parliament of 1476.[d]

" Whereas, Richard Power is sheriff of the county of Waterford, and has been so for more than twenty years past, and he out of his insatiate malice, as an enemy to God, and a rebel to the king, has by himself and people and other rebels made assault on the

---

[a] Patent Roll of Chancery, p. 91.
[b] Idem, p. 55.
[c] Idem, p. 73.
[d] " Tracts Relating to Ireland," Vol. II., Statute of Kilkenny, p. 18, published by the Irish Arch. Society.

mayor, bailiffs, and commons of Waterford, both by sea and land, murdering and slaying divers of the citizens, and spoiling and robbing them of their goods, and has put many of them to fine and ransom, and not only the citizens, but also foreigners resorting to the city for trade, as English, French, Spaniards, Portugals, Britains, and Flemings, to the utter destruction of the said city; and as in all the countries round about said city there live no lords, gentlemen, nor commons, arrayed in English habit, nor submitting to the king's obedience, nor governed by his laws, but only the wicked and damnable law called Brehon law, contrary to divers statutes made against Brehon law; and as about the said city there is no rule or goverment, but murder and spoiling, robbery, and an universal rebellion; therefore it is enacted, that the mayor and common council of Waterford, for the time being, shall from henceforth have the full election of a sheriff of the county of Waterford for ever, annually, and that said Richard Power shall, from this time, be entirely divested of the said office."

Sir Piers, his successor, acted during his life-time as sheriff of Waterfordshire, and assumed authority over the entire county as if it were his own; an assumption promoted by his marrying one of the Ladies Fitzgerald, of Decies; and, secondly, a daughter of a still more potent house, that of Kildare. His heir, Sir Richard, was, in 1535, created Baron of Coraghmore. This nobleman was husband of the lady who figures so conspicuously in these presentments, Lady Katherine Butler, daughter of Piers, Earl of Ossory, and his Countess, Lady Margaret Fitzgerald. Lord Power had died shortly before the date of these representations; but his widow governed her son's country with as much vigour as her mother, when also a widow, had ruled the Ormond territory. It seems, however, that the Baroness was much supported by the wide-spread authority of the Countess, whose *soubriquet*, as given in the presentment, viz., "Magheen," or Little Margaret, is an amusing instance of the Irish practice of giving nicknames, which were usually antiphrastic; for it cannot but be imagined that this Countess was as great in body as in mind. According to the peerage-book, Sir Richard was slain in service against Irish rebels in 1539 or 1541; but the date is an evident mistake, for he had lately " disseassed" when the county of Waterford drew up their " verdict," and when his masculine widow, " Dame Katherine," ruled the county in the name of their son and heir, "pretending the King's county was his by succession of inheritance." Sir Richard was slain by " the traitor," Connogher O'Callaghan, before the year 1538.[a]

Such was the extravagant dominion exercised by the house of Curraghmore, as evidenced in these verdicts, and many years elapsed before the authority of the crown was recognized. In 1543, indeed, a subsidy of £30 yearly was agreed to be paid to the royal revenue out of the " Poorine county;"[b] but, in June, 1548, the freeholders of the county addressed a complaint to the Lord Deputy, that Lord Power had, without right, cessed and distrained upon them six shillings upon every ploughland, reserving all lands that hitherto have been free.[c]

---

[a] Published State Papers, vol. ii.
[b] Additional MSS., British Museum, 4790, p. 99.
[c] State Paper Office.

THE VERDYCT OF THE COMMYNERS OF THE COUNTYE OF WATERFORD.

PETRUS DOBBYN,[a]		WILLIUS BROWNE.	
NICHLAS DEVEUX,[b]		WILLIUS MACK SHANDOLE.	
JACOBUS MADAN.		DAVID BROWNE.	
T. SHYRLOK.[c]	} JUR.	JACOBUS GOUGHE.	} JUR.
PETRUS AYLEWARD.[d]		WILLIUS FITZ ROBERT POYER.	
MAURICIUS WYSE.		WILLIUS FITZ NYCHOLAS POYER.	
RICHUS BROWNE.			

De Comit' Watford.

We fynde that the Countie of Waterforde belongeth onely to oure Sovaigne Lorde the King, and that all the baronyes and freeholdes of the same immediatly be holden of his goode Grace and of none other, ne of no Poer, Butler, nether Geraldyn, nether beryth to none of them no sute nor service.

We fynde also that Sir Pyers Poer and his father, Rychard Poer, the later, were, and evy of them, was the Kings Sheryf of the foresaide Countye of Watford, and evy of them ruled y[e] same by thauctorite of ther office; and after, by contynuance of tyme they usurped on the Kings auctorite, and toke them to be as Lordes of the saide countye, untyll Maghyn[e] and they ruleid the hole countye at ther pleasures by extort power oppressing the king's subjects.

---

[a] Mayor of Waterford in 1541.
[b] Mayor of Waterford in 1548.
[c] Mayor of Waterford in 1549.
[d] Sir Piers Aylward was knight of the shire in the second year of the following reign. The estate of Faithlegg was granted in the year 1172, by Henry II. to "*Aylwardo Jureni,*" as "King's merchant," an office then well known; and the property remained with the Aylwards until the year 1691 [Lynch's Feudal Dignities]. Ailward (El-ward, a Saxon name) may have been one of the Ostmen merchants of Waterford.

[e] i. e. *Mageen,* or Little Margaret, the nickname, *per antiphrasin,* of the Countess of Ormonde (née Margaret Fitzgerald). She still lives in the traditions of the Kilkenny peasantry as Máiŋǵiaḃ nın Ǵeaṗóıḃ.

And Dame Katheryn Butler[a] daylye useith lyke extorc̅o̅n, imposyc̅o̅ns, and unlawfull exacc̅o̅ns, as useid the foresaide Poers by ther tyme: and nowe, in the name of younge Pyers Poer, sonne unto the late deceassed Sr Rychard Poer and Katheryn Butler, pretendeing as lorde and inherytor of the Kings countye by succession of inherytaunce.

Exacc̅o̅ns and Imposico̅ns useid by the foresayde Poers, and nowe by the Lady Katheryn Poer, alias Butler.

Fyrste, coyne and lyvye, bothe horsse and man, contynually upon all the Kings subiects.

Itm̅, the kernthye[b] in lyke maner to the nombre of xvii. and sometyme more, and the countye not the better.

Itm̅, iiiior kepers of ther stedes[c], dryveing ov evy mannes grounde, and wylle have meate and drynke for themselffes of the kings subiects.

Itm̅, xiiii. psons kepeing ther hounds, besydes ther owne meate wylle have bredde and mylke for evy hounde.

Itm̅, to all mañ of buyldeings[d] to have a man or a caplle oute of evy vyllage, to the charges of the village.

---

[a] Lady Catherine Power, daughter of Piers, Earl of Ormond, and his wife "Mageen," and widow of Sir Richard, Lord Power, of Curraghmore.

[b] Kernthye; *kerne-tighe*, i. e. the kerne of the house, or household troop of the chieftain, which formed his regular force, and performed functions somewhat resembling those of the police of the present day, viz., assisting the lord's serjeants or bailiffs in collecting rent and all exactions, apprehending criminals, and guarding the chief and his house. The complaint in the text, that the county was "not the better" for Lady Power's kerne, is explained in subsequent passages, showing that some of the band, and indeed its very captain, occasionally turned highwaymen.

[c] *Stedes*, studs, standings, or establishments of horses. Great exertions were made in Ireland in the beginning of the sixteenth century to increase the breeding of horses, which were much valued in England, as shown by "the Rental Book of the Earls of Kildare," now publishing by this Society.

[d] Buildings.—The technical name for this exaction was *Musterown*. As the residence of the king of a clan appertained to his office, all its buildings and repairs were made at the common charge. It was obviously of importance to the inhabitants of a district defended by a castle, that the building

Itm̃, all masons, carpintors, and taylors haveing any worke to doo with the lorde at the countrey, is founde on hollydayes at coyne and lyvye.

Itm̃, the lorde at Cristemas and Ester to have meate for as manye as him lyste to bring, and incase he be refuceid at Xp̃mas he wylle have of the tenant lxˢ, and at Ester xxˢ, wyth greate favoʳ wylle the said monye receyve.

Itm̃, if the lorde Deputye, or any greater man be conveevyed by the saide Katherin, but she wylle com̃aunde a subsydye to be levyed apon the countrey for meate, drynke, and candel llyght, to the lords pleasoʳ.

Itm̃, if the lorde or ladye marye theʳ doughters, eṽy husbondᵃ in the countrey that have shepe shalle paye one, and a cowe of eṽy vyllage.

Itm̃, if the Lorde or Lady send ther sonne into Inglande, a subsydye to be levied apon eṽy acre, or viˢ and viiiᵈ apon eṽy village or ploughelande in the countrey.

Itm̃, ther is with the lorde or lady callid Foye, that is to saye xxᵗⁱ. or xxiiiiᵗⁱ. psons to take meate and drynke, wyth horssemete.

Itm̃, they take vp and levye some otys for theʳ horsseis, viz. a b5 dī. of eṽy plougheᵇ.

Itm̃, yf a gentyllman haveing iiiiᵒʳ. m̃ks rent, the imposicõns to be double to the lorde or lady, and oftentymes treble.

Itm̃, the kings lawes be not useid, but the Yryshe Lawes; soo that if a quarell be pyked to a trewe man, and yf the p'tye defendaunt be quyte, he shalle paye the hole fee of sentence, to be devided betwyxt the lorde and the Judge.

Itm̃, ther is Kane goddeᶜ, whiche is that the lorde or lady takyth of the pore theffe v. m̃ks, and of the riche thyfe muche more; and if

---

should be sustained; but the grievance was, that the mustrons were employed notonly in building castles, but also halls, kitchens, barns, and stables, as is stated in David Sutton's representation as to the exactions of the Earl of Kildare.

ᵃ Husbond, i. e., husbandman.

ᵇ i. e. a bushel and a half.

ᶜ " Kane godde."—Cain godde seems to have expressed the ransom rendered by the kindred of a thief to redeem him from being hung. A "guddihang" was the Anglo-Irish term for a man fit for nothing but the gallows.

he have noothing, he shall be hangeyd; his frinds shalbe warneid to redeme hym by a certen day or elles to be hangeyd.

Itm̃, yf a mannes sᵣvannte take from his Mʳ ii. or iii. shevys of otys, or other lyke thing, the Lorde wylle have of his Mʳ v. m̃ks, and the malefactoʳ not excepted for his trespace but in xxˢ, and the Mʳ for the rest.

Itm̃, yf a man haveing a lease for tme of yeres of the freholder, and if the yeres be expyred, an other shalle not have xl more in a newe farme, upon payne of forfeteing v. m̃ks to the lord.ᵃ

Itm̃, yf the lords horsse be kept fasteing one night, the tenant shalle forfeyt w'oute any grace; and yf it be any horseman of her companyeᵇ, he shalle forfet di b̃5 of otys.

Itm̃, in cesseing vytaylles or wages for the Kings osteingsᶜ noo restitucõn is made of any relyf, and a certen nombre of horsemen and foteman shalbe appointeid comenly, the half of them shalle goo forthe; the resydue of vytaylles and wages remayneing to the lords advantage, yf they passe oute of the countrey if it were but a myle.

Itm̃, all mañ felonye, robery, and extorcõn, cõmytteid by any pson or psons w'yn the said countye of Watford shalle make his fyne for certayn money wᵗ the lorde or lady, and so shalle goo quytte unpunysheid from the due form of lawe.

Itm̃, my lorde Butlerᵈ came into this countie by the sufferannce of my lady Katheryn and eyde of certen psons, viz, Whelans, and toke awaye forcybly certayne kyen and catall from the kings subiects, and frome them that was doing the kings sᵣuice, as Poer of Kylmedan; as Mr. Seintloweᵉ and Mr. Wyseᶠ maye testyfie ferther at lengyth.

ᵃ It was evidently, by this penalty, the design of the chief lord to prevent the subletting of holdings without his permission. An interesting proof is afforded that leases were still in use among the Anglo-Irish, although not yet adopted by the Irish.

ᵇ That is, if any horse of the Lady Power's was so kept fasting.

ᶜ The hostings or military arrays and expeditions which the Englishry were bound to attend by feudal tenure.

ᵈ James, Lord Butler, Lady Catherine's brother, son and heir of Piers, eighth Earl of Ormond, and afterwards ninth Earl.

ᵉ William St. Loo.

ᶠ Sir William Wyse, of Waterford.

Itm̃, nowe this p'sent tyme, the forsayde Lady Katheryn, entendeing to goo to Dublyn, cesseyth the countrey for her going thyther, and for the conviveing gyven by her to her fader, to the some of xxi. li̇ks, and this to be levied of the kings subiects.

Itm̃, it is enacteid by the said Lady Katheryn that no beoffe, ne mutton, hogge, ne butter, hony, ne whete, nor malte, shalle come to the cytye, but suche as the countrey shalle refuce; the p'misseis to be bydde to salys at Churche, vpon payne of vi^s viii^d, and forfeture of the goods.[a]

Itm̃, Nicholas Deṽex of Ballymagir[b] horseis and horsegromes and other horseis was lyṽied in the countye the last nyght past, by the assygnation of Katherin Butler.

Itm̃, the foresaide Nicholas Deṽex receveith in wards mariage a shepe of eṽy croo or shepehouse, and a cowe of eṽy village, other the value of yt in money.

Itm̃, yf any pson or psons swere by the lords or ladyes hande[c] as an othe, and pven to the contrarye of his othe, he forfeyteith to the lorde or lady c^s, and any pson forswereing any solemne othe shalle clerely goo unpunysheid.

Itm̃, the saide Lady Katherin did levye and toke up of the subiects xviii^{xx} shepe[d] for her hande maydens.

---

[a] This right of preemption on the part of the lord was enforced by *cain-eacht*, i. e. penalty for sale. See Introduction to Kildare Presentment.

[b] "Nicholas Devereux, of Ballymagir," seems to have been a ward of the late Lord Power, according to the statement that he received his curious portion "in ward-marriage" with this nobleman's daughter. This dowry is also mentioned in the city presentments. The young bridegroom was representative of one of the most considerable Norman-Irish families in the Co. Wexford, as grandson and heir of John Devereux, who is mentioned in that county's verdict. He was originally a ward of the Lord of Wexford, the Earl of Shrewsbury, who put him to school in England, where he was a schoolfellow of Lord Burghley's; and he had livery of his estate, 21st May, 1540. He was knighted for distinguished services in protecting his native county, and died in 1576. The marriage portion his wife received was customary among the Gaelic clans. Other instances of the same exaction are mentioned in the presentments for the county of Cork. Feudal lords had a similar privilege, limited, however, by law.

[c] For a clansman to swear by his chief's hand was the strongest oath he could take. Spenser notices this custom, and considers it of Scythic origin. Nicholas Walsh, writing from Waterford in 1573, states that "forswearing of lord's hands is almost given over."

[d] i. e. Eighteen score sheep.

Sone after, by the peurem^t of Dame Katheryn Butler, certayn psons of the countye of Kylkenny and of this countye of Wafford inwadeid and preyed one Richard Lunde, and forecbly toke awaye from him certen kye, to the nombre of c., and feryed the same at Portglashe by Wafforde into the countie of Kylkenny, and pte thoroughe this countrey to Katherins Castell, and ther sett to herre use; moreo^r none dare be so hardye to wytt her, or any of hers of the foresaide prey : the p^rmisseis by Walsheis, alias Brenaghe, in the countye of Kylkenny.[a]

Itm, where as the Lady Katheryn owyth displeaso^r unto any in the countre, she entyseyth and drawyth certen psons oute of other countres as Smashaghe,[b] viz. Tobins,[c] to spoyle and robbe all thoo that she owyth any dyspleaso^r unto.

Itm, murder and manslaughter comytteid by Richard Fytzdavye Poer, Walter Mac Shanrowe, Thomas Evall, Moryshe Mc Shanrow, Patryck Mc Shanrowe, the whiche psons was then and is nowe Katheryn Butlers s^ru^nts, and the saide psons kylle and m^rdre Walter Fytzwillm Poer, Edmund Fytziohn Poer, Edmound FitzWalter Poer.

Itm, no Courts no^r Cessyons be not duely kept after the form of the Kings lawe in all the countrey, but by the Iryshe judges and maner.

Itm, the hyghe waye is kept by certeyn psons, viz. Robert More Fytz Thom^as Poer, and his brother Nycholas, and toke Patryk Brenne and his syster Ellyn, and spoyled them to the value of xv^s.

Itm, also Donyll O'Bryen,[d] of Geralde McShannes countrey, and the servants of Katheryn Butler alias Poer, being in ther com-

---

[a] These Walshes, of the Walsh mountains, in the county of Kilkenny, were of British or Cimric extraction, as their *alias*, Brethnaghs, implies ; and pure Welch names were common amongst them down to the times of the Edwards. They were special followers of the house of Ormonde, and hence were employed by Lady Power.

[b] "Smashagbe," apparently a designation of retainers used for coercion.

[c] The Tobins, *recte* St. Aubyns, were a degenerate Anglo-Irish family of Lower Ormond and Kilkenny.

[d] O'Brien, of Cummeragh, descended from Turlough O'Brien Maol, King of Thomond, deposed A. D. 1370, for siding with the English. Turlough's children received from James, Earl of Desmond, in 1413, the lands of Cummeragh,

panye, viz. Nicholas Fytz Thomas Folan,[a] captayn of her karntye, kept the highe waye, and toke onest psons of Watford as p[r]soners at Boghill.

It[m], Will[m] M[c] Hee, one of the foresaide kernthye, and his company, kept the highe waye betwyxt Watford and Passage,[b] and toke certen psons of Watford as p[r]sons.

It[m], David Browne, gent. kept the highe waye, and toke Richard Browne of Watford as p[r]soner, and gyveid[c] hym iii. dayes.

It[m], Teyge O'Kenedy and Thomas Kenedy, and Moroghe Keregan, and Richard M[c] Teige ne Karege, and Walt Frene and Will[m] Grace, harpengers[d] to the foresaide Katheren, do mysuse the in cessem[ts], and take muche more then ther duties, and useid blakbedds.[e]

It[m], Katheryn Butler denyed and dysobeyed the Kings auctorite, forbyddeing Jamys Wyse to execute the office of seneyallship, in whiche office the said Jamys was auctorysed by the Kings Deputye, whiche auctorite he declarid to herre and to herre audyence.

It[m], Thomas Poer[f] useid coyne and lyverye and all expenseis on the countye, and nyght meats at X[p]mas and Ester, and also iiii[or] tymes by the yere, as ii[de] pson after the lorde or lady, useid all other cha[r]ges.

which had been granted him by King Henry V.—Lodge's Peerage (edit. Archdall), vol. ii. p. 21.

[a] Felan, or O'Faelain, was lord of the Deisi (Decies) at the time of the invasion. The families of Phelan or Whelan are descendants of this sept.

[b] i. e. the passage or ferry across the river at Ballyhack.

[c] That is to say, put him in gyves, or fetters.

[d] Harbenger is a term derived from the German *Herberger*, i. e. one who looks out for a harbour or lodging for another; and thus came applicable to a forerunner, and by consequence an announcer of something coming. Chief Baron Finglas speaks, in his *Breviate*, of the king's harbingers, whose duty consisted in billeting the Lord Deputy's guard or retinue, and who were used to stamp their billets with a seal bearing the sign of a horse's head, and hence, perhaps, "the nag's head" became a common sign of hostelries.

[e] Black-beds may have been a charge for the entertainment of men who had not been entertained, just as "blackmen," in a military roll, were dead or absent men. The term "bed" is here used in some sense analogous to its use in the term "a horseman's bed," anciently designating a townland charged with maintaining a horseman.

[f] Probably Thomas Power, eldest son of Edmond, a natural son of the second Lord Le Poer. His brother, Nicholas, married a daughter of "Redmond of

Itm̃, Thomas Poer toke in the Kings waye an Englysheman, one Thomas Beck[a] of Chesĩ, as p^rsoner, and put him to fyne for his ramson.

Itm̃, Nichas Poer of Kyllmedan[b] do use coyne and lyṽye, srahe, and bonneh, in his owne lands, of his tennants, the Kings subiects, and also nyght-meats, and fyne for thevis that robbe and stele of his ten^ants.

Tower Hook." Another natural son (Nicholas) of the same lord married a "da. of Thomas Tobin of the Cumshie, (she ma. secondly, Murrough ballagh M'Shee, and thirdly, William, Knight of Kerry), and had several sons.—[Pedigree compiled by the Earl of Totness.]

[a] Edward Beck, of Manchester, had a grant of free trade in Ireland, 5 & 6 Henry VIII. In 1535, he writes to the King's secretary a letter of Irish news.

[b] Nicholas Power, hereditary Baron of Dunhill, who is styled of Kilmedayn in the Presentment, married Shela, daughter of Sir John Fitzgerald of the Decies, sister of the celebrated long-lived Countess of Desmond, and had issue:—

I. Robert.
II. Pierce, " of Caninge-Philipp" (Carew MS., 635), who married a daughter of Isham of the Co. Wexford, and had :—
   John, m. a da. of John Roe, of Hacketstown in the Decies;
   2. William, m. the heiress of Fitz-Edmond, of Kilbolane, in Cork; 3. Pierce; 4. Thomas; 5. Katherine, m. Sheran [?] in Roche's country; 6. Ellen, m. to Hackett, at Howth.
III. Giles.
IV. Honora, m. to Gerald fitz James Fitz-Gerald, of Ballyoyestie, in the Decies.

Robert Power of Dunhill married one of the daughters of the Baron of Burntchurch, and left issue :—
Nicholas; 2. Richard, m. a da. of Redmond McOdo; 3. Rowland; 4. John, and others.

Nicholas Power was of " Douneyle," and "lyvinge" in 1600, according to Carew, and had one son, Walter, by his wife, a daughter of Thomas Purcell, Baron of Loughmoy.

The following are a few of the names of men who received state pardons in the year 1318, for certain transgressions, at the instances of John fitz Piers, Baron of Dunhill, and his son Sir Arnold :—Geoffrey le Poer, of Ballydurne, Maurice, John and David, his sons; Jordan, Rowland, Silvester, Tancard, John, Gregory, Patrick, Emoun fitz Edmond, Edmond, John, Roger, Andrew, Robert, Maurice, Walter, Henry, Piers, and Durand, all bearing the name of Poer; William O'Callych, Neel O'Donnyll, Richard Oboille, John O'Dinevan, Donald M'Cuy', Gregory O'Donwelyth, Cormok O'Malmorthe, Walter O'Kety, Adam le Waleys, Thomas Ocuyn, Philip Omaleassill, Ragunyld O'Conyl, Henry le Botiller, Roger Brithwolde, Dionysias Obokil, Malmury O'Douenyld, Sutbry M'Quir, John Ocelly ; Thomas Griffin, Philip and John Christofre ; Nicholas and James de Courcy, Reymond de Caunteton, Gilbert O'Brasill,

Itm̃, Geralde Mc Shan[a] do use all mañ of charges, Iryshe lawes, and all mañ of imposicõns on the Kings subiects under his power in this countye of Wafford.

Itm̃, my Lorde of Ossery[b] useith the same in this countrey, and also letts the resort of peoplle comeing to the m̃ket of this cytye w^t fleshe, vaytayles, and m̃channdyseis.

Itm̃, he letteith the Scolers,[c] and others comeing hyther wyth lynnyn clothe, and takyth them to fyne, and taskeid them by the Barron of Berron s^{e}horith,[d] his fermar.

Itm̃, tharchebysshop of Casshell[e] w^t a companye, and specially Philyp Hennebre, toke a bootye of Clonmell men and goods wythin this ryver.

Itm̃, the saide Philip Hennebre, my Lord of Ossory s^{r}ieannte, toke, and dayly takeith tymbre woode sett on the banks of the ryver by the Kings subiects to be broughte to the cytie.

Itm̃, Thomas Butler of Kaher do use all mañ extort imposicõns, exaccõns, and charges on the Kings subjects in the countrey of Tyberrarye, w^t Iryshe judges.

Itm̃, the fooresaide imposicõns be useid dayly in Fytz Pyers countrey, w^t Irishe judges, by the Lorde of Ossery.

Itm̃, we fynde that my lorde Archebysshop of Casshell, my lorde Bysshop of Wafforde, the Bysshop of Ossery, ther com̃yssaris, officialls, deanes, levien and taken of the Kings subiects pfe of testam^t, contrarye to the Kings ordre taken upon the same, and preyseyth the testator goods to the value of the tresshors.

Also if any pore man other riche of the countrey dye, the Bysshop wille take [*a blank*] pte of his goods, and the curate willetake v^s of porcõn cannon, and his best arreye, w^t his armys, sworde, and knyfe; and yf the wyf dye, they take the same the husbonde being alyve.

---

[a] Edmond, Reymond, and Richard de Nangle, William Stalith, Roger M'Gillemurry, John and Adam O'Culan, and John and Nicholas Odolith.—Rot. Pat. 2 Edward II., p. 24.

[b] Gerald Fitz-Gerald, Lord of the Decies, son of Sir John Fitzgerald.

[c] Piers, 1st Earl of Ossory and 8th Earl of Ormond.

[c] *Scolers:* wandering scholars were known to the last generation under the name of "poor scholars"; but here the connexion must be with trade.

[d] i. e. Fitz Gerald *alias* Barron, Baron of Burnchurch, in county of Kilkenny.

[e] Edmund, natural son to Piers, Earl of Ormond and Ossory, then filled the see of Cashel.

Also they taske the fee of judgm^{ts} of matrymonye causeis after the substannce of the pson, contrarye and above the^r owne statutes pvynciall, to the greate impo^{v}ysheing of the Kings subiects, and takeith ii^s for the allowaunce of the fyrst record, and xii^1 for e^{v}y other recorde examyned to mayntayne the rightfull cause.

Also the curates take for the mynystring of the Sacraments, as Baptysm, Puryficacõn, and Weddeings, sertayn ducties by compulsion, as well meate and drynke and money, for them and for thers.

Itm̃, as often tymes as my Lady Katheryn goo, or is goyng, in to Dublyn she cesseith the countrey w^t soore charges of money ;* and at herre last being at Dublyn she borowid of the Deane of Watford, for whiche money the pore men or subiects were compellid by her officer, Teyge O'Kennedy, to pay the foresaide Dean in whete at ii^s Yryshe the b5., where as yt was worthe iiii^s Iryshe.

The p^rmisseis consyderid, it maye please yor M^rshippes to chose and apoynte a sufficient pson, bothe of auctorite and strengyth, to be Shyrif of the countye of Watford; and also a Seneyall and other offycers necessary to rule and governe the same. And to execute justice, and to mynistre the same indyfferently to e^{v}y pson, accordeing to the ordre that shalbe taken, orderid, and stabyllysheid by yor wysedoms for the reformacõn of the saide countye, and thes officers to be Englyshemen, and none of the by^rthe of this lande. And to o^r estymacon Mr Seyntloo is moste meteist and able, wyth the King's supportacõn and ayde, to be Shyrif. And we the freholders of the saide countye wille gladly bere all suche charges as shalbe thought necessarye by yor wysedoms, and by theadvyse of Mr Seintlowe and Mr Wyse and others the freholders of the countye, as shalbe thought moste meteist for the assesseing of the foresaid charges for the defence and mayntenance of the saide countye and officers of the same.

---

* This exaction, which defrayed the expenses incurred by the chief of a clan in going to the seat of government, was levied on the plea that he went thither on the public business of the community.

THE PRESENTMENT OF THE CITY OF WATERFORD TO THE ROYAL COMMISSIONERS, A. D. 1537.

More than ordinary attachment to English privileges was felt by the citizens of Waterford, who boasted a specially loyal attachment to the Crown. The "Urbs intacta" was founded by a Danish viking, and has a Scandinavian name; and its inhabitants partook in the desire, felt by all commercial communities, for preservation of the purity of law, and for maintenance of peace. The descendants of the Norse sea-rovers, by whom the old town was built, and whose small circular towers were standing,[a] in testimony of the rude, insecure life of the first settlers, had mostly been displaced by the posterity of the merchant race established by Henry the Second. For four centuries this port had ceased to be a resort and perhaps even a nest of pirates; but its shipping was sometimes the prey of sea-robbers, whenever piracy flourished on the wild south-western coast. The O'Driscolls, a maritime and fierce Irish clan, used their creeks and castles to shelter their own and other piratic vessels; and the trade of Waterford having often suffered at their hands, this city more than once fitted out expeditions in retaliation. The State Papers contain a curious narrative, dated April, 1538, of the treachery of Finnin O'Driscoll, Conochor his son, and Gille Duff, his base son, in seizing a Waterford ship, which they had captured when in distress; and the document describes the revenge taken by the Waterfordians. But this old feud was slight in comparison with the long and lasting animosity between the citizens of Waterford and the great

[a] Carve, Lyra Hib.

county family of Le Poer. It would seem that this enmity arose when the Lords le Poer, discarding feudal law, assumed the position of Celtic chiefs, and permitted their loose men to plunder the town traders, to make good a claim of yearly black rent upon the city. Several interesting documents respecting the combined attack, in 1368, of the Powers and O'Driscolls, upon the citizens, and subsequent similar assaults, evidencing the settled rancour borne by the Power family to the inhabitants of their county town, are published in the Miscellany of the Celtic Society. So deadly was this animosity, that verse was enlisted into the service of the townsmen, in order to warn them of their danger, by means of a ballad, which, we are told became a household song. Sir James Ware has this note at page 94 of Lansdowne MS., No. 418 :—

"There is in this book (the Book of Ross or Waterford) a longe Discourse in meter, putting the youth of Waterford in mind of harm taken by the Powers, and wishing them to beware for ye time to come. I have written out ye first staffe only :—

"Yong men of Waterford lernith now to plai,
For 5ur mereis plowris ilad beth a way[a]
Scure 5ur hafelis y^t lang habith i lei[b]
And fend 5ou of the Powers that walketh by the way,
    For rede.
For if hi takith 5ou on and on
From him scapith ther never one
I swer bi Christ and St John
    That off goth 5ur hede.
Now hi walkith" &c.

Archæologists will deplore that Sir James Ware confined his transcript to copying the "first staffe only." The original "long discourse in meter" is now lost, having been

[a] For your mares and plows are led away.
[b] Secure your oats that lieth too long in the field.

abstracted from the original parchment volume. Sir James evidently attached little literary or historic value to this ballad, which, however, would now be deemed very curious, if merely as a specimen of early metrical composition in the English language.

Henry the Second, when excepting, in his feudal grants to great barons, the districts around seaport towns enjoyed by "Ostmen," or Easterlings, those *sterling* traders who founded the commerce of this kingdom, particularly accorded to the Ostmen of Waterford that they should be judged by English law. The district they held round the city retains the name of Gaultier, or the Foreigners' Land. That the Ostmen of the county Wexford had peculiar rights is shown by the record published by our Society. Their best franchise was, that, subject to paying certain poll taxes, they were free to hold land of what lord they pleased within the Liberty of Wexford.

Sir William Wyse, the 'squire who was foreman of the city jury that drew up the ensuing presentment, who was afterwards knighted, and who was granted the house and estate of the Hospital of Knights of St. John at Waterford, took a worthy part in exposing the grievances under which his fellow-citizens and the frankleins of the county laboured. Holinshed's Chronicles give an anecdote or two of this distinguished man, who stood in high favour with Henry VIII. In 1539, the Council of Ireland write in the following terms :—

"Mr. Wise of Waterford, the king's servant, a sadd" [sedate], "wise, discrete gentleman, being heretofore appointed to be sherif of the county of Waterford, hathe discretelie used himself in that rome, as he hathe trayned the people theraboutes to a moche better order and obedience than they have been in theis many yeres past; so as we judge him very meet among others to be in rule in theis parts."

In 1545, Sir William Wyse[a] excuses himself to the Lord Deputy for not levying a tax for galloglasses in the shire of Waterford, alleging that he could not raise it, owing to the arbitrary conduct of Lady Catherine Power; and he afterwards writes, 5th January, from Waterford, that, Lord Power having died, the Earl of Ormond and his sister, Lady Catherine, will be at the Abbey of Mothel, beside Curraghmore, where they intend to celebrate an obsequy for the soul of Lord Power, and that much "devotion" of meat and drink is prepared there. "The poor people are like," he says, "to sing *Requiescant in pace*, but the more they cry, the more sorrow increaseth."—See Hamilton's "Calendar of State Papers, Ireland," p. 70.

[a] This Sir William Wyse, fitz John, fitz Maurice, married, and had issue:—

I. Henry ob. s. p.; 2, John, *de quo infrà*; 3, Andrew, who was knighted, and became Privy Councillor and Vice-treasurer of Ireland; he m. a sister of Sir W. Brabazon, by whom he had one d. Mary, wife to Sir Alex. Fitton, K[t]; 3, George, Sheriff of Waterford, 1571.

II. John fitz William, m. Mary Anne Walshe of Co. Dublin, by whom he had issue:—

III. James fitz John, m. Alson Finglass of Westphalton, by whom he had issue: 1, John, *de quo infrà*; 2, Andrew, Knight of Malta, Prior Angliæ, 1593; 3, Henry, ancestor of the Wyses of Virginia and Maryland; 4, Thomas, Mayor of Waterford 1605; 5, Nicholas, Sheriff same year.

IV. John fitz James, m. Mary Lincoln, and had issue: 1, Robert, m. Mary Wadding, Mayor of Waterford 1630; 2, Francis, m. Genette Walsh, ob. 1647; 3, Andrew, *de quo infrà*.

V. Andrew fitz John, who had issue:

VI. Thomas Fitz Andrew, Mayor of Waterford, 1688, ob. s. p. m.; 2, Robert, m. Anastasia Le Poer, of Guilea, Co. Waterford, and had issue:—

VII. Francis fitz Robert, Lord of the Manor of St. John, by settlement of his uncle, 1695; m. Mary Masterson, of Moneyseedy and Castletown, Co. Wexford, and had issue.

VIII. Thomas fitz Francis; m. into the English families of Bourne and Lacon, and by first wife had issue: 1, Francis, ob. s. p. 1739; 2, John, *de quo infrà*.

IX. John fitz Thomas; m. Mary Anne Blackney, of Ballyellin, Co. Carlow, by whom he had issue:—

X. Thomas fitz John, m. Frances Mary Bagge, of Dromore, Co. Waterford, and had issue:—

XI. Sir Thomas fitz Thomas, K.C.B.; m., 1821, the Princess Letizia Bonaparte, by whom he had issue:—

XII. Napoleon Bonaparte Wyse, Esq., of the Manor of St. John, J.P., *nunc vivens*, twenty-fourth in descent from Sir Andrew Wyse, a younger son of a Cornish or Devonshire family. Arms, sable, three chevrons ermine.

THE PRESENTMENT OF THE CITE OF WATERFORD MADE BEFORE THE KINGS COMISS̃ THE [XII] DAY OF OCTOBRE ANNO XXIX°. R̃'S. H. VIII.

Civitas Waterford.

WILL̃S WISE ARMIGER.	JACOBUS WISE.	
PATRICIUS WALSHE.	DAVID BAYLIFF.	
WILL̃S LYNCOLÑ.	JACOBUS WHITE.	
JACOBUS WALSHE.	ROB̃TUS WELSHE.	
EDWARDUS SHERLOK. ⎬ JUR̃.	RIC̃US BUSHER. ⎬ JUR̃.	
JOÑES BUTLER.	THOMAS GRAUNTE.	
NICÑUS STRONGE.	PATRICIUS COMFORD.	
JOÑES SHERLOK SEÑ.	NICÑUS ROWE.	
HENR̃ WELSHE SEÑ.	HENR̃ WELSHE.	

First the said Jurie p'esent that as touching coygne and liṽey the lady Kateryn Butler usurpeth a domynyon upon the kings subiects in pcell of the countie of Waterford called by her Powers countrey, w'out title or graunte of the kings magesty or his deputie of this his land of Ireland, and that contynually from yere to yere.

Item Thomas Power of Balycanvan[a] used to take coyne and lyṽey as tanyst, That is to wit, the second capitaigne of his nacyon,[b] and is ₱claymed t̃ knowen a cōen extorcyoner oṽ all this countrey, and hathe taken many of the kings liege people, emp'sonyng them t̃ setting them at fyne t̃ raunsome and hathe diṽs theves retaigned to dystres the kings peax. He tooke p'soñ Thomas Abck[c] ñchaunt of manchestrf & tooke of hym v^{m'cs} for his Raunsōme t̃ also lay in awayte t̃ tooke the deane of fernes horse going bitwixt the citie of Waterford t̃ the passage, which he kepeth as yet.

Itm̃ they p'sent that the said Thomas for like extorcyon was

---

[a] Ballycanvan was, perhaps, "Confin," the residence of a branch of the family. See note, p. 70.

[b] This denomination is curious evidence of an instance in which a Norman-Irish family became a "nation," which, adopting tanistry, or succession by election, chose their chiefs and tanists, or secondary thanes.

[c] Or Beck. See note ª, p. 191, *supra*.

taken by Mr William Sayntlowe 't kepte prson by the said Mr. Sayntlowe in a handlok 't delived after unto my lord Thresaurer who tooke a Recognysaunce for the kinge of dame Kateryn Butler 't Edmond Power prior of Saynct Kateryns besides Waterford, to be forthe comyng at all tymes.

Itm they prsent that the said Thomas sonne, called Edmond Power, nowe remayning in the Mayres gayle, brought in by Mr Sayntlowe, a coen extorcyon 't kep of highwayes, robbing the kings people, 't hathe burned a howse full of corne belonging to patrik Comford mchaunt of Waterford.

Itm they prsent that what tyme the lorde deputie departed a Seneshall 't other officers [were appointed] to see good ordre kepte in the countie of waterford, whiche they enterprised to execute accordingly. The said lady Kateryn with all opprobry 't rebukefull words comaunded the said Seneshall to be disobayed 't none offic there to be alowed but onely hers, wherby the said Seneshall for jupdy of his lif was fayne to entremedle no ferther.

Itm they prsent that the said lady Kateryn kepeth kernty at the charge of the countrey to the nombre of lx 't sometyme more.

Itm they prsent that the said lady Kateryn subftithe the kings lawes, as hanging men w'out auctoritie, pdonyng Theves by takyng canes 't letting felons at libtie.

They fynde also that she hath ordeyned an Irishe Judge called Shane McClaunaghe, and that the said Shane useth Brehens lawe 't ordreth the matts of variannce of the countie moche aft her will 't comaundement and taketh for thuse of his Judgement called Oylegeag^a xvi^d stt of ev'y mk st, and taketh asmoche of the playntif as of the def'.

It they prsent that the said lady kepeth co'te of the Galtyer^b aft an Ireshe extorcyonous man, and maketh sfgeaunts & offics to take up freyes 't bludsheds at her will thorowe all the countrey.

It they prsent that there be keps of her stode founde of the

---

^a From the Irish *oilegh*, a Brehon, and *cag*, payment. See note, p. 70.

^b The Gall-tir (now Gaultier barony), i.e. Foreigners' Land, was originally colonized by Scandinavians, or Ostmen, who were specially admitted by Henry II. to the privilege of English law, and whose descendants were, therefore, wronged by the imposition of an Irish court of judicature.

countrey, the said stode pastureth o' e'y grounde payeng nothing therfore, likewise her hounds 't doggs w' their keps fonde at the charges of the said countrey.

Iĩ she taketh ℥ten psons oute of e'y villege called in Irishe mostroen at their owne costs to buylde her manors & howses payeng nothing therfore.

Itm̄ all masons carpento's 't taylo's which she retayneth to her works take coyne & ly$ey e'y holly daye.

Itm̄ she taketh yerely of e'y village for Ester & Cristmas a coydhy[a] otherwise called a nights mete w't as many as she list to bringe. And he that is not mete or redy to receave her 't her company be set to xl^s Cristmas 't xx^s for Ester & others more.

Itm̄ they p'sent that as ofte as the lorde deputie or the lorde her father and suche great men as come to her mano^r of Co^{r}ags more or any other mano^r she hath, that what is spente in mete 't drinke is sessed upon the countrey besides ly$y$yng of all their horses and genets 't money by the cessyng of the same which is cōmitted w't in iii. yeres.

Itm̄ they p'sente that the said lady marieng her daughter to Nicholas De$y$eux of balymegy$^{r b}$ tooke ℥ten kyen 't shepe towards her mariage of e'y village of the countrey, which catell her daught Kateryn Power had awaye to her use.

Iĩ they p'sent that the said lady Kateryn hathe taken 't exacted of the kings people for the fo^{r}nisshing 't sending forthe of her sonne, piers Power, into England in company w't the lord Thresaurer, a ℥teyn sōme of money the ℥tenty wherof they knowe not.

Iĩ the said lady taketh foye which is is [sic] mete 't drinke for a pety company of xx. or xxiiii^{ty}. 't horsmete w'all di$y$s tymes of the yere paieng nothing therfore.

Itm̄ she taketh of e'y plough ℥ten oots in lente called sōmer oots. And where she taketh ii, Thomas Power taketh one not onely in oots but in all cudies.

Itm̄ she useth to take of hym that hath his horse or catell stolen v$^{m'es}$ because he watched not his owne good.

Itm̄ she putteth her p'ce horses or yonge colts to ly$y$ey for xii.

---

[a] *Cuid-oidhche*, a night's portion.   [b] See note [b], p. 188, *supra*.

Itm̃ she taketh for disobayeng her sgeaunt, o'r offič, be it right or wronge v marks 't of hym that refuseth to give her horse oats 't their keps mete for nought, one beaf called kyntroisk.[a]

Itm̃ she useth no indifferency in the cessing for them that goo forthe to s͠ve the kings deputie, 't p͠s͠veth 't dischargeth all the lands that she or her sonne hathe in possession from almaň ymposicions, leieng their charges o͠v other mennes lands.

Itm̃ that she cesseth her chargs upon the kings people of this country at any tyme she goeth to Dublyn aboute her p'vate cawses.

Itm̃ that a s͠vant of the said lady Kateryn called Robert More constable of her castell of Kylnetomasyn[b] hath robbed 8teyn vitaillors which used to bringe this citie vitells from the combragh[c] 't this cōmitted in the kings high waie.

Itm̃ w'in this iii weks the said lady brought ii galleglas of the Retynue of the lord of Osserey into this countie of Waterford to take coygne 't lyfey for ii daies 't ii nights called Soren.[d]

Itm̃ they p͠sent that Nicholas Powre of Kylmydan[e] hath taken coyne 't lifey, 't his brethern likewise John Morice 't Benet Powre, 't useth the same contynually 't hath ioyned in tyme past w't Geralt McShane and p͠cured hym to robbe this countrey 't hath cōmitted in revenging his quarell agaynst Sr Richard Power dif͠s felonies as manslaughter robbing 't burnyng.

Itm̃ that Gerald McShane of Drōmaneagh[f] gent[n] usurpeth upon the kings subjects 't mysgofneth the kings subiects in his q͠rters called the Decyes, 't taketh that q͠rt͠s to be his owne, saieng his father 't his auncetors used coyne 't lyfey; 't all dampnable exactyons' rehersed hath been and is daily used 't cōmitted by hym, 't hath by Sr Richard Povers daies envaded robbed 't dystroyed thenh͠itants of this countrey, 't daily doo robbe 't spoyle thies q͠rtrs by night, 't useth brehenns lawe.

Itm̃ the said Geralt of late disobeyed the kings tres of cōmiss di-

---

[a] Kyntroisk, i. e. a fine.
[b] Now Kilmacthomas.
[c] The Cummeragh mountains.
[d] Soren (query *sruan*, a measure of oats) was the original rendering, from arable land, of food to the chief and his troop of followers.
[e] Kilmedan is the name of the parish in which the watering place, Tramore, is situated.
[f] Gerald fitz John Fitz Gerald, of Dromana.

rected out of England to Mr William Scyntlowe 't William Wise 't wold in no wise appere before them to be iustefyed of suche wrongs as is moneyoned agaynst hym, 't maketh peax 't warre w'out licence of the kings deputie.

Itm they present that power of Donvill[a] being constable of the castell of Dongarvan under the Erle of desmond having in the said castell his wif 't his brother Shane Pover in his absens he then being p'soner here within the citie of waterford for Sr Richard povers cause, at which tyme a ship of Rosse was wyndriven by stres of wether into dongarvan aforsaid, wherein were m̃chants of Lymerick Rosse Waterford 't Kylkenny havyng good substance of div̊s kinds of m̃ch^andises, the said m̃chaunts then being taken p'soners by the said p'soners Povers wif 't his brother, suche as the said Pover wold were deliv̊ed by his p'vey token 't the rest remayned p'soners to their great ympov̊ishement.

Itm we fynde that Sir Thomas Butler of the cahirgh[b] in the countie of Typary knight useth 't taketh coyne 't lyv̊ey throut all those q^arters w'like dampnable exactyons 't mysgov̊n^ances 't maketh peax 't warre w'out licence of the kings deputie, 't hath taken by his retynue a šv^ant of Harry Walshe of Waterford m̃chaunt in the kings highwaye going to the faire of Casshell 't robbed hym of x^li 't useth brehens lawe.

Itm they p̃sent that one Richard Rothe Butler of pollekere[c] is a cõmon extorcyeno^r, 't hath taken 't ymp'soned ofte 't div̊s tymes the kings subiects 't cõmitted infinyte heynous offences agaynst the kinge 't his lawes, and his brother Water Butler as great an extorcyoner.

Itm that in the same q^art of Typary howe James butler Abbot of Inislonaght 't deane of lysmore hath sondry tymes disobayed the kings writ 't is a man of odyous lif, taking yerely and daily mennes wifs 't burges doughters, 't kepeth no devyne švice but spendeth the goods of his churche in veluptuousytie 't morgageth the lands of his churche 't so the house is all decayed, 't useth coygne 't lyv̊ey.

---

[a] Now Donisle near Annestown: there are here the remains of a strong castle seated on a steep rock.

[b] Now Cahir.

[c] Now Poulakerry, Poulakerry castle stands on the Suir, below Clonmel.

Itm they p̃sent that Edmond Archbishop of Casshell riotously
t wt a company of malyfactors being in a bote on the river of Waterford, a° xxiiii^to R. II. VIII. qui nunc est, hath spoyled t robbed
a bote of Clōmell charged wt clothe sylke t safron t other m̃chaundise to the value by estymacyon above one hundreth pounds sł, t
tooke t ymp^soned the owners of pcell of the said goods t kepte
them in p^sonc tyll they made fyne t rannsome, t is an open maytayn^r t berer of causes, t manassed to trouble them that wold tell
trothe, t useth coyne t lyv̂cy in all thies parts in such forme that
he paieth no money for horsmete nor mannesmete.

Itm the said Archebishop useth extorcyon in his visitacyon
sometyme cessyng his charges wt great somes of money, t suche
as refuse to compounde wt hym for a ĉteyn unreasonable some must
fynde mete t drinke t lodging for as many as he list to bringe with
hym, t hath retayned one called Dyrmond Doff for his officiall t
counsaillor or cōmissary which en̂stayneth the kyngs people by
color of canon lawe that there can be no more extorcyon cōmitted
by any Irishe brehowne, t polleth the kings subiects as he list, t
taketh for fee of sentence of a devorce xli or more.

Itm they p̃sent that the bishop of waterford lyv̂eth his horses t
his boyes upon his owne tenants paieng nothing therfore contry to
the kings statutes phibiting that no coyne ne lyv̂cy be had in lieu
of rente or by any condycyon res^lved.

Itm he useth hym in his visitacyons wt suche exacyons for his
charges as the said archebishop doth.

Itm he taketh by hym t by his mynisłs for the fee of sentence
of devorce vli, t of some more, t for the diffinicon or iudgement of
ev̂y matter brought before hym or his officiall taketh a fyne at his
pleasure, t for correccyon of synne taketh money, and taketh xxd of
ev̂y pounde of the soules pte for pbate of testaments, t so dothe the
forsaid Archebishop'.

Itm the deane of waterford in one moneth of the yere useth
visitacyons, t exacteth of the people as the bishop doth in testamentory causes punishement of synne t matters of devorce t other
matters of judgement, t maketh the parties to paye hym unreasonable somes of money contrary to gods lawe the kings, wherupon
the kings subiects make sore exclamation.

Itm̃ they p̃sent that the bishop of Ossercy is culpable in like extorcyons, t̃ the bishop of Fernes was, havyng no vertuous qualities ne obedyence to any good lawes.

Itm̃ they p̃sente that the house of Saynct Kateryns besids Waterford, where is a pᶦor t̃ iii chanons which ar at suche divisyon that they sepate themselfs asundre t̃ have divided their Revenues in two porcyons contrary to the rules of their pfession t̃ sore ruyn of their place.

Itm̃ they p̃sent the pᶦor of Kellys in the countie of Kylkenny hath taken p̃soners in the kings high waye one John Sherlok t̃ William Welshe mͬchᵃunts of Waterford t̃ kepte them in Irons longe tyme t̃ after sent them to the cvmssyᵃ the kings Rebell, there kepte to their sore ympoṽishement, t̃ that the said pᶦor is alwaye fugetif t̃ alwayes dysobedyent to the kings pcesse t̃ lawes.

Itm̃, they p̃sent that Piers Erle of Ossercy t̃ bothe his sonnes use coyne t̃ lyṽey t̃ brehew lawes t̃ chargeth ofte the countie of Kylkenney wᵗ. gallowglas t̃ Kahernty and mustron, t̃ all other parties of their rule use the same, and charge the said countrey also agaynst cristmas t̃ Est̃ wᵗ finding mete drinke t̃ candle lyght to the manors where the said Erle is resydent, and that the said Erle t̃ his sonnes take up yerely sōmer otes of eṽy plowe for their horses t̃ manyfold other exaccyons as Cudyes coucheries stode t̃ dogges, by whom the countie of Waterford t̃ Typary take p̃sydent t̃ ensaumple, eṽy capitayn saieng for their excuse let the lorde of Ossery give oṽ extorcyon t̃ we will, els not.

Itm̃ he taketh canes t̃ heriks called souldsᵇ throut the said countrey.

Itm̃ he setteth at libṽy diṽs Theves t̃ Felons takyng sōmes of money for their setting at libṽty wᵗout satysfaccyon to the ptie greved, t̃ maketh all his castels t̃ mañs to be gayles to his owne cōmodytie.

Itm̃ they p̃sent that the constable of Dongarven, the constable of Thourles, t̃ for the more parte eṽy suche constable belonging to the said Erle or his sonnes, taketh up into their hands all the

---

ᵃ i. e. Tobin or St. Aubin of the Compsy in the county of Tipperary.

ᵇ Soulds, query from the Latin *soldo*, to pay? hence *soldier*.

mͬchͣundyses in circuyt aboute them, 't no subiect of the kings shall not bye nor sell but suche as shall please the lorde or them, all the abbotts of the said countreys use like p̃sydent to the undoing of all cities 't townes adiacent.

Itm̃ the said lords offic̃s oftymes give ympedyment to diṽs psones that bringe mͬchͣundises 't vitelles to the citie of waterford which ympoṽisheth sore the ynh̃itaunts of the same.

Itm̃ they p̃sent that contrary to the kyngs statutes 't phibicōns the said lorde 't the lady his wif ladeth great store of woll 't floks oute of this lande into England Fraunce 't Flaundres, which is the sore decaye 't occasyon of Idlenes for all our crafty men, so as for lak of their accustumable bieng of woll in their parts, 't also the pⁱses so reysed, by the great occupieng 't takyng into the same ladies hands, that our craftsmen ar like to fall to Idlenes 't decaye, for restraynt wherof none dare attempt to forset or sease their wares so laden on payne of their lives, 't take up all other mͬchͣundises likewise into their hands wherby the kings subiects be sore hyndred.

Itm̃ fynally we se 't fynde that the counties of Kylkenny Typary 't of Waterford ar all mysgoṽned by the lady of Osserey 't the lady Kateryn her dought̃, and that the lord Butler mayntaigneth his sysť the said lady Kateryn in her extorcyon.

Itm̃ that there was an office taken in the countie of Waterford for the kynge after the dethe of Sʳ Ricᵈ Pover, 't fonde that Pers Pover being wᵗⁱⁿ age is the kings warde, 't the said Sʳ Richard dyed seased of the manor or castell of Carraughmore, the castell of Clonhey, the castell of Kylmᶜtomassyn wᵗ their app'tenͣnces Knokdyrry Balylogh, Knockmyles, the Crosse 't dyṽs other villages as Calleghan 'tᶜ.

Itm̃ that upon the feeferme of waterford xˡⁱ Irishe is the kings right by reason of therledom of Ourmond, which was given hym towards his creacyon, and also the litle Iland in the hands of James White is nowe in the kings right longing to the said Erledom.

Itm̃ that Durbards Iland called the great Iland to be the kings right wherin dwell diṽs burgeses.

Itm̃ the Carryig MᶜGriffyn is the kyngs by reason of the said Erledom, 't that the castell of Dongarvan is the kings right.

Itm̃ that the mare t̃ cõmons of waterford holde the mañ of Kyloran of the kynge by the yerely s̃vice of a sparhawke as of his honor of Dongarvan.

Itm̃ they p̃sent that in the countie of waterford ar, besids all that is written, iii notable extorcyoners more, viz old Nicholas Pover of Corroduf, Water t̃ Davy Pover.

Itm̃ the said Jury takyn for our sov̂aign lorde the kynge before his highnes Cõmissioners confesse all the p̃mises to be o^r verdyt, delivered unto the said Commissioners the xii daie of Octob̃r in xxix yere of o^r said sov̂aigne lords Reigne.

BYLLES OF COMPLEYNTE FOUNDE BY THE SAYDE JURYE.

To the kings highe Cõmission^rs

Compleyncinge shewen unto your Audyence yor orato^r t̃ s̃uaunte Nichas Poer of Donnyll^a that where as he being in the kings s̃vyce wayteinge on William Wyse as then being Shyryf in the countye of Wafforde t̃ one' William Scintloo the kings Captayne at warres in Irlande, at ther goyng unto Geralde Fytziohn of Desmounde the wyke before xp̃mas in the xxvii. yere of king Henry the viii^th, one Jamys Butler sonne to Pyers Erle of Ossery and the kings highe Tresorer in Irlande came into the sayde Nychas Ten^unts t̃ robbeid them, wyth suche companye as came wyth hym of dame' Katheryn Butlers s^ra^unts, of the some of ix^xx kyne iii^xx capelles w^t householde stuff. The p̃misseis consyderid it maye please youre Audyence as well to cause the said lorde Tresorer to make restytucon of the saide hurts as the foresaide Katheryn and this done for the lawe [love] of godde t̃ in the waye of Charytie.

The saide Jurye fynde that the saide Jamys Butler toke this praye the saide daye t̃ yere, the nombre wherof the saide knowe not.

To the right worshipfull the kings highe Cõmission^rs.

Humblye complayneing shewith unto yor wysedoms yor dayly orato^r Nichas Poer of Donnyll that where as he coming from the kings plyament from the citie of Dublyn by the lord Deputye that nowe is kept in Maye anno xxvii° R. H. viii., was taken by Jamys

---

^a Power styles himself "Baron of Donnyll" in his subsequent petition.

Butler sonne to Pyers Erle of Ossery and the kings lorde Tresorer s̄vᵃnts at Glanrenalde,ᵃ and was guyveid and his casket dyscloseid t̃ some householde stuffe lost by the saide s̃ữuᵃnts and never hadde no amendes therof for his greate slander being in the kings humble s͠duice. In consyderacn̄ wherof it maye please your wysedoms to see a remedy in the p̃missels unto yoʳ orator to be hadde, and this don for the love of godde 't in the waye of Charytie.

The said Jurye fynde this byll to be true.

To the kings highe C̄omissionʳs

In moste humble mañ cōplayncing shewith unto yoʳ dyscreat wisedoms yoʳ dayly orator 't s̃ữuᵃnt Niclias Poer Baron of Donnyll that where as the s̃ữuᵃnts of dame Katheryn Butler vydowe came into Goran-trowale in the nyght upon iii wyks past, 't toke from yoʳ said orator oute of the same vyllage x kyne besyds householde stuffe 't lefte yoʳ supplyannts doughter in poynte of deathe, wᵗ one more besyds her, 't apon a certayn [day] before the saide hurts was donne certayne of yᵉ saide dame Katheryn s̃ữuᵃnts came unto yᵉ foresaide towne 't caryed wᵗ yᵉᵐ in householde stuffe the value of iii. m̃ks, 't wonedeid sore a good husbondman, 't before yᵉ said hurts don theʳ came of her s̃ữuᵃnts a company into the saide towne 't toke wᵗ yᵉᵐ xL. shepe by force, wherof yoʳ said oratoʳ besecheith yoʳ Audyence to cause the saide dame Katheryn to make restytucõn of the hole p̃miss unto yoʳ said suppliant 't his poore tenᵃnts and this don for the love of god 't in the waye of Charytie.

The saide Jury fynde this byll to be but for the certentye.

To the Right Worshipfull the Kings highe Commyssioners.

In moste grevyous maner compleyncing unto yoʳ Audyence yoʳ orator Niclias Poer of Donnyll that whereas the s̃ữuᵃnts of dame Katheryn Butler laste wyfe unto Sʳ Richard Poer came iiii yeres paste unto the saide Donnyll and kylde of yoʳ saide orator is best Gentyllmen and s̃ữvannts iii psons, after the peace made attuix the saide Niclias and dame Katheryn, and aboute midsomer anno xxixº R. II. viii. the saide s̃ữuᵃnts came unto Kylbrydye and robbeid yoʳ supplyaunte oute of the churche yarde of the same ii horseis, 't

---

ᵃ Probably Glen-Ranellagh, in Wicklow.

ne͡v hadde restor*ᵃ*unce. The p̃myssels consyderid yoͬ orator humbly besecheith yoͬ dyscreat wysedoms to see a remydye herein to be hadde for the love of godde t̃ in the waye of charytye.

The saide Jurye finde that the saide men were kylled by Sͬ Riĉ Poers s͡Juᵃnts viz Riĉ Fytz Davy Poer t̃ others.

"Bonneh." According to a statement as to Desmond's rents and customs, dated 1589, Bonnybeg and Bonnyban were "soldiers kept in readiness, as well in peace as in warr, at the charge of the country, with meat, drink and wages." "Bonaght-bun," says O'Donovan ("Four Masters," p. 1686), "was the fundamental or original bonaght. Bonaght, which signified free quarters to soldiery at the discretion of the chief, came to designate the soldier so sustained. The term appears to derive from *Bun-eaght*, the original payment, or rendering; signifying the first charge upon land, and the most important, being for defence."

"Caine Eaght" was a fine upon sale without the lord's permission, in times when serfdom gave lords right of property in what serfs possessed.

"Sraghe" would seem to have been a primary rendering from land; for, by a note in the S. P. O., dated December, 1589, the rents of *sraghe* and *marte* are the only ones mentioned as chargeable on the Connollaghe country.

City of Waterford, etc.

THE PRESENTMENT OF THE TENANTS AND BURGESSES OF THE MANOR OF DUNGARVAN, IN THE COUNTY OF WATERFORD, TO THE ROYAL COMMISSIONERS, ANNO 1537.

DUNGARVAN formed the south-western point of the wide territory sheared off by Henry II. from the rule of Roderick, the last monarch of Ireland. Its castle, which is said to have been built by King John, and which, as commanding the seaport, was long deemed of much importance, became the *caput baroniæ* of the barony of the Decies, a district granted to Thomas Fitz Anthony de St. Leger, whose eldest coheiress brought it to John Fitz Thomas, ancestor of the Earls of Desmond, and to whom Edward I. committed the custody of the counties of Waterford and Desmond.

An Inquest of 10th Edward I., No. 21, preserved in the Tower of London, shows the extent of lands held by "John Fitz Thomas" around Clonmel, including the hundred of Decies excepting the barony of Donuil. Among the jurors were three knights named Le Ersedekne, and the document contains curious lists of tenants to Mac Thomas. The grant of 1260 to him excepts the advowson of Dungarvan church, and provides that the castle be given up to the Crown, in cases either of war, of sure suspicion of the said John or his heirs, or should the lands fall to a female heir. This important fortress was repaired by Earl Thomas, the great lord who was beheaded in the reign of Edward IV., and a statute of this reign states that Dungarvan is "*del auncient temps le tres pluis graund auncient honour perteignaunt au Roy en Irlande.*" The Desmond noblemen retained the barony of the Decies until James, the seventh peer, conferred it upon Gerald, his younger son, excepting

Dungarvan town and manor. After the beheading of the elder son, his brother, the Lord of the Decies, assumed the titles of MAC THOMAS and Earl of Desmond, and thenceforward, after that his usurped power was defeated by the eighth Earl's heirs, mortal enmity subsisted between the Desmond stem and Decies branch. The fall of the sixteenth peer originated in his attempt to enforce his rights as supreme lord over this barony. Of early instances of this family feud, it may be noticed that there are two unpublished interesting letters from Sir John Fitzgerald, and his son Gerald, to the King, dated 1528, at the manor of Dromany, stating that they have obeyed his commands, and aided Lord Butler; in consequence of which, James Earl of Desmond has come with a great host and burned and destroyed the most part of their country; but that they have driven the Earl to sea, and slain many of his men. This was the eleventh or traitor Earl, who, dying 18th June, 1529, was succeeded by his uncle Thomas, who, repudiating his first wife, and marrying a daughter of this Sir John, namely, Catherine, the celebrated long-lived Countess of Desmond, made the following confirmatory grant of the Decies to his father-in-law:—

[*MS. Cotton, Titus B.* xi. *fol.* 102ᵇ.]

The FEOFFMT of THOMAS EARLE OF DESMOND of his LANDS in DESIES.

Sciant pntes 't futuri quod nos Doms Thoms Comes Desmoñic dedimus concessimus 't hac puti carta indentat' confirmavimus Johi filio Geraldi Fitz Jeames quod [*sic* evidently for " quod', quondam] comit' Desmonic milit' 't Geraldo ejusq filio hered's suis et assign' õnia messuag terr Doma tent' reddit' 't servic cum suis ptinen q̃ ter' in Desia una cum villis Ballinmaghe 't Cnoknau Anñtoriam nᶜnon cum oibus cessibus redditibus de Monotryc 't duabus ũcis in Dungarvañ vel in Baillinmcarty in com Waterford ac totam Baroniam de

Killsyllan in coṁ Tipperary tᵃm in Doṁo cum omnibus eorum juribus 't ptin' universis. Necnon dedimus concessimus remisimus relaxamus Sloticos seu Bwonabeḡ si addes qṅdo dc̄a prian [*sic*, perhaps for "pr̃ia" patria] decianaū obligabatʳ Hēnd' 't tenend' oṁa p̃dēa messuag' terr̃ tenement' redd' 't servic̄ p̃dico Joḣi Geraldo hered' 't assign̄ suis de me meisq̨ hered' 't assign̄ imppetuum redd inde nobis 't heredibus nr̃is onera debit' 't de jure consuet' put in cartis p̃decessorum nostrorū inde confect' plenius continet' Villa et maneria nr̃a de Dungarvan cum suis burgag̃ except Et. nos vero p̃dc̃i Dn̄s Thoṁs hered & assign̄ nr̃i oṁa p̃da tenementa Villas Baroniam terras redditus statuoɹ remissoɹ [*sic*] 't servitia omnia cum corund̃ ptinen̄ p̃dc̄is Joḣi Geraldo hered 't assig̃ suis contra oēs gentes Warrantizabimus acquietabimus 't imperpetuum defendemus. In cujus rei testimonium sigillum ūrum quo in talibus utimur apponi procuravimus. Dat' apud Cork in cr̃o Lucæ Evangelistæ Anno Regni Regis Henrici octavi xxi° 't Doṁ nr̃i Jesu Christi 1529.ᵃ

Exᵗʳ' p Nichum Courties deput' Miċhis Appesley
Protonotar' totius provinc̄ Momonie.

It will be observed that the imposition of Scottish mercenaries, called Bonnaghtbeg, is relinquished. It does not appear how this deed, which left the Lords of the Decies subject to their original rents, was so set aside as to emancipate them from vassalage to the Desmonds. On the revolt of James, Fifteenth Earl, his great enemy, Piers Butler Earl of Ormonde, was commissioned by the King to recover from him the honour and castle of Dungarvan. It seems that the victualling of this fortress by any of these Earls was deemed their signal for war. In 1534, Earl Thomas had, with this object, seized a Spanish ship, then in the port, laden with wine. A curious letter published in Ellis, "Original Letters," gives an interesting account of the ir-

---

ᵃ This 16th century transcript of the charter, preserved in the British Museum, is in many parts obviously very corrupt.

ruption into Pembrokeshire of numbers of Anglo-Irish, who were repelled from our south-eastern shores by the war consequent on this rebellion, and who sought, upon plea of kinship, being of Pembrokeshire extraction, shelter and support from their Welsh cousins. Captain Ap Harry, a Welsh officer, gives in October, 1535, an interesting account of Lord Butler's proceedings for the recovery of Dungarvan Castle. On the way the expedition was met by his Lordship's brother-in-law, Gerald Mac Shane of the Decies, who, though a "a very strong man in his country," could speak never a word of English, but made the troops "good cheer, after the gentilest fashion that could be." The fortress surrendered, on which the expedition passed on to Youghal; "Here," observes the Captain, "they sell a gallon of Gascoigne wine for fourpence." Thence a circuit was made by Cork, Mallow, Kilmallock, Limerick, Cashel, and Clonmel. The natural richness and beauty of the country drew the warmest terms of encomium from the Welshman, who writes:—"All this journey, from Dungarvan forth, there is none alive that can remember that ever English man of war was ever in those parts. Some days we rode sixteen miles of waste land, the which was Englishmen's ground; yet saw I never so goodly woods, so goodly meadows, so goodly pastures, and so goodly rivers, and so goodly ground to bear corn; and where the ridges were, that hath borne corn, to my thinking there was no beast did eat it, not this twelve year; and it was the most part such waste all our journey."

Dungarvan was annexed to the Crown by statute, passed in the year 1537; yet the wild power of the Celto-Norman nobles west of the Barrow was but little suppressed. Nicholas Comyn, Bishop of Waterford, writes in the year 1538 to Secretary Cromwell, offering to surrender certain livings and manors adjoining to the western Geraldines, in which the King might place discreet captains, so as to subdue the "protervity" (rudeness) as well of the Lords Barry and Roche as of Gerald Fitz John, Lord of the Decies, and Gerald of Desmond's sons. This Lord of the Decies, who was brother to the celebrated long-lived Countess of Desmond, appears by the ensuing paragraph, to have repudiated all loyalty save to his liege lord, the chief of his name. In 1539 the Irish Council write to the King's Secretary,—

"Of all the hooll shire of Waterford, ther aunswered the cessions the inhabitauntes scantelie of thoon half, which is called the Powers' landes or cuntrie; th'other parte oon Gerald Mac Shane of Desmond, oon of the Geraldines, a kyndisman of James pretended Erle of Desmond, possesscthc, and kepethe the same; who woll neither obey the King, his lawes, ne officers, but adhereth hollie to the said pretended Erle, albeit that all the landes which he hathe in the countie of Waterford been of the kingis oolde inheritance, as parcell of his honor and lordship of Dungarvan."

In 1552, James, fifteenth Earl, addressed a curious statement to the Lords of the Privy Council respecting the circumstances under which the manor and castle of Dungarvan had been taken from him, and supplicated for their restoration. His ancestors, he says, had enjoyed this valuable property by grant from Edward III. He proceeds to narrate how his grandfather, Earl Thomas, falling under the displeasure of the Queen of Edward IV., was beheaded at Drogheda for treason; and how Piers, eighth Earl of Ormonde, and his son and successor, being at enmity with the complainant, procured an Act of Parliament to evict him out of possession of Dungarvan, which was then conferred on Ormonde. The custody of the castle was then committed to Mr. Robert St. Leger, afterwards to one Matthew Wykyng, and lastly to James Walsh, "a servant of the late Duke of Somerset, and who," continues the Earl, " hath presentlie the charge thereof, not without burdening the King as well with men in extraordinary wages, as with sondry other like charges, standing to small effect either for the service of His Majestie or defence of the country thereabouts, the same being chieflie at this day by the said Erle" [of Desmond's] " pollycy and power kept in the stay it is, by having his men and constables planted everywhere upon those borders." This boast of the Earl's is somewhat borne out by a letter, dated ten years subsequently, addressed by the Corporation of Youghal to the Queen, commending the Earl for the protection he has afforded them in rooting out a den of thieves, who maintained a castle four miles up the river. At the beginning of the turbulent conduct of the sixteenth Earl of Desmond, his authority over the Decies was frequently a subject of examination; and there is a curious petition, dated 1565, from Sir Maurice Fitzgerald, of "Dromaney" (Dromana), to the Queen, against " the impositions, services, exactions, and demands made by the Earl of Desmond on his territory called the Decies," which, the knight alleged, he held in fee, answerable only to the Crown. Dungarvan Castle is mentioned by M. Boullay Le Gouz, in his tour through Ireland, A. D. 1644, as a considerable fortress. The Fitzgeralds of the Decies are represented in the female line by the present Lord Stuart de Decies, who takes his title from their old seigniory, and resides at their ancestral seat, Dromana.

Coúnty of Waterford.

NŌIA TENENCIŪ ET BURGENC̄ MAN'IŪ DE DUNGARVAN
CUM CASTRO IBIDEM.

MOYSES TAYLLOUR.		JOH̄ES FITZ WILLIAM.
MATTHEUS HORE.[a]		JOH̄ES COLLAN.
WILLS NYGENT.[b]		PATRICIUS GERE.
EDŪS HORE, SEN̄.	JUR̄.	JOH̄ES RUSSELL.
WILLS HORE.		TEG O MOLGAN.	JUR̄.
THOMAS HORE.		EDŪS HORE, JUN̄.
JOH̄ES NOGULL.		EDŪS DAVYS.
JACOBUS NYGENT.		WALTUS POORE.

Fyrst the said Jury p̄sente that the Vicar of Dungarvan taketh coyne and livey of his tenants when the Bishop repaireth thether and his s̄uants ev'y Sunday in the yere have mete and drinke of his tenants.

Itm̄, they p̄sente Garald Fitz John[c] and as many gentylmen as be under hym doo take coyne and livey and their kernes and gallowglas ꝗ hunte at their pleasure.

Itm̄, they p̄sente that the said Garrald and all the gentylmen in the countrey doo custumably take one daies labor of the Kings tenants or ii daies, at their own pleasure w[t] their plowe.

Itm̄, they p̄sent that Morys Fitz John dyd breke the house of Morys Taillor to take his piggs to the nombre of xviii the which shal be ii yeres at Candlemas next com̄yng.

[a] This branch of the Hore family is said to have descended from one of the name who was seneschal to an Earl of Desmond, and who obtained Shandon Castle and lands, near Dungarvan, as a hereditary fee. James Hore was knight of the shire for Waterford in 1497. John Hore, of Shandon, was M. P. for Dungarvan in 1634 and 1639. His son, Matthew, was restored, in 1688, to 1423 statute acres in the Co. Waterford, and received 2864 in Galway and Roscommon. He was M. P. for the Co. Waterford in King James's Parliament. His son, John, was M. P. for Dungarvan, and left three coheiresses, married respectively to Donnellan, of Ballydonnellan; Aylmer, of Lyons; and Sir Patrick Bellew, Bart.

[b] Nugent, of Cloncoskoran, descended from the second Baron of Delvin.

[c] Gerald, son of John Fitz Gerald, (son of an Earl of Desmond), of Dromana, Baron of the Decies, and there-

Itm, they p̃sente that John Thobyn was slayne by one of John Isam's[a] company at mydsoñ last past, and one man of the company of the said John was hurte w^t· a hand-gonne by Morrys Power and they knowe not what justice was mynisthred for the same murthre but that the said felon was kepte a small season in p^rsone in the castell of Dungarvan, and so deliv̄ed from thens.

Itm, they p̃sent that where there was ětcyn comon belonging to the towne of Dungarvan by suffraunce of the Lorde there, paieng rent therfore, is nowe occupied by Deonyse O'Brien and his brethren and if the townesmen doo put eny cattell theron they take pledges.

Itm, they p̃sente that ev̄y Munday if they nede they have a corte kepte in the said towne and if eny man make a fraye or bludshed, they have a queste of xii men to enquire upon the said bludshed and fraye and if it be upon the watter or where the tyde runnethe he that is condempned shall paye xi^s that is to saye x^s to the constable and xii^d to the waẗ bailife and if it be in the strete vii^s that is to say vi^s viii^d to the Lorde and iiii^d to the sr̃geant.

Itm, they p^rsent that ev̄y bote of fishermen being straungers paye for their custume ons in the year vi^s viii^d also of ev̄y bote one hake as well of the townes men as of the straungers as often as they come to lande if they have it, and of ev̄y drover that goeth to take hering as well of townes men as of straungers ons in the year a mese of hering that is to say v^c aft̄ vi^xx to the hundreth, and from Cristmas to Est̄ as often as they come in with fishe that is w^t white fishe to paye one linge when they have it and if they have none but haddoks to paye one haddok to be taken as well of townes men as upon straungers, and of ev̄y ship comȳng with wyne having above x tonne paieth for p^rsage ii tonne wyne paieng to the m̃chaunt XL^s st̄ and if the lorde doo refuse the said payment then to have but one tone wyne, and of the custume of hids of straungers for evv̄y dyker xiii^d st̄, and for the custume of ev̄y hundreth haks of straungers iii^d st̄, and for ev̄y barell of hering i^d ob st̄l, and of

fore lord of the surrounding country. He was an Englishman, captain of a
[a] See a former notice of John Isam. company of soldiers.

eẽy burthen of white fishes iᵈ sᵗ, and eẽy barell salt ixᵈ sᵗ, and of eẽy waye of whete and malt viᵈ stl of straungers, and of eẽy waye of beanes iiiᵈ stl, and of eẽy mantell caried from this towne iᵈ sᵗ, and of eẽy habdashe amounting to the some of xxˢ sold there doe paye viᵈ sᵗ, and of eẽy wrek that is fonde there one half therof goeth to the fynder and the other half to the Constable of the Castell, and the admyrall[a] to have a share therof, and all wreks of fishe that cast themself upon lande, the one half to the fynder and the other half to the Constable, the said custumes be taken on straungers, and none other.

It', they p̃sent that the Constable of the Castell paieth the masons their wages for makeing the towne walles or repaering therof, and the burgeses of the towne fynde mete and drinke to the masons doing reprations upon the said walles, and the Coḿons of the towne there fynde workemen at their owne costs and charges to make morter and cary stone, and the Lorde to fynde a lighter or bote, and also horses to cary stones from the said lighter.

Itm̃, they p'sente that the owner of eẽy house in the said towne and also in the countrey taketh of his tenant ymmediately afᵗ his dethe viˢ. viiiᵈ.

> Dungarvan.
> Libʳe tenētes.

Itm̃, they saye that the burgeses of the towne shall paye at Ester vi m̃ks, and at Mighelmas as moche for their fre lande viiiˡⁱ xiiiˢ iiiiᵈ sᵗ p annū.

It', the rest of the frelande which was some tyme in tenants hands is nowe in the hands of the Constable, that is to saye, when a tenant dieth w'out issue his lands shall remaigne to the Castell: by the yere } LIIIˢ iiiiᵈ

Itm̃, there is a 8tayne grounde belonging to this Castell which was given by the Erle of Desmond to the pishe churche there, which is by the yere } viˢ viiiᵈ

---

[a] Probably the admiral or captain of the fleet of fishing boats.

It', they saye that there is ẞtayn lands called Croughton Claischy licing beside the West gate, assigned to a carpenter by the said Erle, for that he shall give his owne worke to the Castell, as often as nede shall require, and is worthe p annū   viii^s s$^?$

Itm̄, they saye that a ẞteign lande in the towne of Ballaghoo lieth in pledge to Donell McRagh^a for the p^{i}se of a horse, which land is worth by the yere   viii^s

Itm̄, they saye that Deonise Rynyen kepeth by force xx acres of lande, pcell of the demeanes which shuld belong to the smyth of this Castell; and is worthe by yere   xiii^s iiii^d

Itm̄, that Gerald Fitz John w^{t}holdeth a towneship from this Castell called Ballym^{c}mawen, what value they know not; it conteyneth one plowe lande and more.

Itm̄, that a ẞten lande and a warreyn of conyes, called Congard Pointe, is witholden by the said Gerald Fitz John, con' in lengthe iii q^{a}r^{t}s of a myle, and in bredthe one boweshot, well replenished with conyes.

Itm̄, there belongeth to this Castell a hundreth great acres of land, licng in the south west syde of the Towne, cont' by estymaṫon, in the hands of the Constable at viii^d the acre, LVI^s viii^d.

Itm̄, that Morrys Fitz John holdeth lande called Co^{r}te Towne by force from this Castell, and is worthe xxvi^s viii^d s$^?$.

Itm̄, Gerald Inchdowne w^{t}holdeth lande called the Chanon-hill, conteyning by estymaton xx acres of Fyrse grounde, the value unknowne.

Itm̄, Denys Abrien kepeth lande and underwood from this Castell, the value unknowen, cont' by estymaton iiii great acres.

Cotagers. Itm̄, none that paeth any rent to the kynge, but they paye to the free burgeses which is conteyned w^{t}in the some above said.

psonage. Itm̄, the psonage is a faire house, and hathe vi teñts^b

---

[a] Mac Graith, or Magragh.
[b] This may read "tenants," or "tenements;" " "tylling" (see p. 219) may be an error for "tything."

to the same, no lande, but the tylling of xvi pishe churches, and is worth by yere c. ñlks s̄t by estym̄.

It', they saye that the Vicar hathe buylded xx houses upon the churchyarde grounde, and taketh rente to his own use.

It', the same Vicar taketh ev'y mannes or womans best good for a mortuary[a] aft their dethe, that is to say of their appell.

It', a vally called the great vally of pasture, being a com̄on to the said towne, cont' by estymaton in lengthe from the mountaigne one myle, and in brerthe one qr̄t, which belongeth to the Castell.

TO THE RIGHT WORSHIPFULL THE KINGS HIGHNES
COM̄ISSIONERS

Grevously complayneth unto your M'rships, one Hewe M'errell, dweller in Bridgewat in England, who dyd come to Dungarvon in the xx[th] yere of the reigne of our sov'aigne Lorde Kinge Henry the eight, and there dyd put into the house of one John Horre Steyn whete and beanes to the som̄e of a pipe and ii hoggesheds whete, and one hoggeshed of beanes, and one bushell and a peck whete besides; and one Gerrard Wegynton, then being Constable to the Erl of Desmond, dyd forcebly take awaie oute of the house of the said John Hore the said whete and beanes w'out paieng therefore, and nowe supposing because y[e] said towne is in the Kings awarde and keping I have desyred my corne of the said Gerrald, and he denyeth me playnly that hee nev' tooke my corne; and nowe, by the meanes of Nicholas Browne, Under Constable of the same Castell, [there were] fonde Steyn honest men and dwellers in the same Towne of Dungarvan, the which was sworne on the iiii Evangelies that they sawe the said Gerrat and his wyf and their s'geant, conveyeng the said corne into the Castell, whose names heraft folowen, first, Thomas Tobene, William Tobene, John Russell, John Mernyng, t Germyn Tuke, being portrif the same yere, w[t] many mō; and also the Erle of Desmond, being that

---

[a] The "mortuary" was an ancient ecclesiastical customary mulct. Dean Swift mentions the "tithe pig, and mortuary guinea."

tyme, did send the said portrif unto the said Gerrald, comanding hym to paye me my said goods; and besides this, the said Gerrald went aboorde the ship where my coffer laye and brust the lok and tooke w{t} hym a doʒ clothe, the whiche coste me xx{s}.

And nowe I desyre you in the waye of charitie, and for the love of God, that I may have a remedy of the same, and I shall daily pray for your m{r}ships.

THE PRESENTMENTS OF THE GENTLEMEN AND COMMONERS OF THE COUNTY OF TIPPERARY, OF SUNDRY MERCHANTS AND OF THE HEADS AND COMMONERS OF THE TOWN OF CLONMEL, TO THE ROYAL COMMISSIONERS, ANNO 1537 ; TOGETHER WITH THE PRESENTMENT OF EDMUND COMY AND HIS ASSOCIATES, AND JAMES FLEMYNE AND HIS ASSOCIATES, AT THE SESSIONS HELD AT CLONMEL BEFORE SIR WILLIAM DRURY, LORD PRESIDENT OF MUNSTER, ANNO 1576.

THE representations made respecting the state of Tipperary describe, as may be expected, a peculiarly lawless condition of society. During a period of nearly two hundred years, the Earls of Ormond had not only, as palatinate lords of this shire, stood in place of the Crown, but had, for the most part, been absentees. In 1347, Earl James had been granted, "for life," the regality, knights' fees, and all other liberties in this county. His successor, the fourth peer, appears to have exercised extraordinary authority. Among complaints preferred against him, he was charged with admitting some of the native Irish to be knights of shires, " the which," says the remonstrance, " wolde not in no wyse assent to no good rule, nor to nothing that should profite and avaylle to you, Soverein Lord."

Thomas Earl of Wiltshire and Ormond died in 1515. Meanwhile, Sir Piers Butler, eldest heir male of the family, inherited the entailed estates, and sought to strengthen himself by following " Irish," or independent " order." In the first, and not least remarkable printed State Paper of this date, the name of " Sir Pyers Butler" stands conspicuously at the head of " all the Captaines of the Butlers of the countyes of

Kylkenny and Fyddert," as that of a great Anglo-Irish lord who held "Irish order," ruled his vast territory by native usages, and made peace or war as he pleased. Yet, so reduced in power were the inhabitants of these counties (Fethard is an ancient town in Tipperary), that they were compelled by O'Carroll to pay him an annual black rent. The King's laws were unknown within their limits; for Brehon law was rife throughout degenerate Kilkenny, and palatinate or feudal law followed, or, more probably, discarded for native justice, throughout wild Tipperary. In 1527, this knightly chief of the House of Butler was elevated to the peerage as Earl of Ossory, but was generally styled Earl of Ormond, a title which he claimed as heir male to Thomas the 7th Earl. The grievances connected with his exactions are the subject of printed State Papers in 1525, the Earl of Kildare having exhibited certain "Articles against the Erl of Ormond," which set forth complaints of a nature similar to these presentments. Among other acts of alleged oppression, he is said to have exacted coiny and livery throughout Tipperary and Kilkenny not only for his soldiery, but for his masons, carpenters, and tailors, and even for "his sundry hunts, that is to say [saith the document], 24 persons with 60 greyhounds, and hounds for deer hunting; another number of men and dogs for to hunt the hare, and a third number to hunt the martin." Yet, as this was an age when all wild animals were unpreserved, our readers can understand that a county hunt, which lessened the number of wolves, martins, and wild deer, was a public benefit, and therefore deserving of public support.

In May, 1534, a notable indenture was drawn up between the King and the Earl of Ossory, and executed on the day of this nobleman's departure from England, immediately preceding the revolt of the Leinster Geraldines which broke out in June, 1534, perhaps much in consequence of this commission of enormous power to the head of the rival house of Butler. By this instrument, the King granted the Earl and his son "the leading and governance," as his Majesty's lieutenant and deputy, of the King's subjects, and the inhabitants of the counties of Kilkenny, Tipperary, and Waterford, and "the countie of Ossorie and Ormond," the Earl engaging to assist Skeffington, the new Viceroy, and not, without his assent, to make, or maintain the making of, any Irish lord or captain, but aid the Viceroy in admitting such persons to those "roumes" or lordships; to maintain, everywhere above the River Barrow, the King's laws; to recover Dungarvan castle; aid in reducing Thomas twelfth Earl of Desmond; and to resist the Bishop of Rome's usurped jurisdiction.

In October, 1536, the Dublin Government advises the King to induce the Earl of Ossory and his son to *permit* Crown revenue to be levied in the shires of Kilkenny, Tipperary, Wexford, and Waterford, as it is in the four counties of the Pale. This proposition demonstrates the independence and wide authority of the House of Ormond.

As lords palatine of Tipperary, their charter entitled them to exercise all judicial privileges, except the four pleas of the Crown, within the pale of that liberty; but during their absence in England, their delegated authority had, doubtless, frequently been abused. The High Commissioners report that, in their survey of the shires of Kilkenny, Tipperary, and Waterford, they perceived "the great lack of those parts was lack of ministration of justice." These counties were, in fact, without the pale of the King's law, and, as such, had lost their title to be called shires—a term derived from having been sheared off from the unsubjugated wilderness. The reader will find, in some notes to my edition of Sir Henry Sydney's memoir of his government of Ireland, published in the "Ulster Journal of Archæology," comments on this Viceroy's exposure of the evils attendant on the enormous authority given by the grant to the Earls of Ormond of the Tipperary palatinate liberties.

Lord Ormond writes, 12th March, 1538, to the Lord Deputy :—

" Hitherto, though I have bene as willing, as any erthly creature, for reformacion of many abuses in thies parties, where I have the rule under the Kinges Highnes ; yet, in that, to this tyme, I have had somoch busynes, aswell agaynst the Geraldynes as the Irishry, I was enforced to give, in maner, to the inhabitauntes of the same their owne talentes and willes, applieng to their appetites, or otherwise could not defende the countie, neither be able to resist the malignacion of myn adversaries, having alonely therby numbre of men, with which power I have alwaies so served the Kinges Highnes, as I trust hath bene to His Graces good contentacion. And nowe, in that partely the occasion of lak of a more civile ordre, or conformytie of obedyence some deale is seassed, and haveing also to hart moch your good and holsome exortacion for that purpose, I have bene in thies parties, with other the Kinges Commissioners, where we have assessed the first frutes, and 20^{ti} parte of all spirituall promocions, to be annually levied to the Kinges use. Therto thies counties of Waterford, Tipperarie, and Kilkenny. I have also proclaymed, over all the countie of Tipperary, that no caines, allyiegs, errikes, Irish brehons, nether that lawe, rahownes, and many like exaccions and extorcions, shall seasse, with reformacion for the grey merchuntes, and the Libertie Corte to be duely contynued, as the Kinges lawes require. And as for the Countie of Kilkenny, for lak of auctoritie, as I have in the Countie of Tipperarie of the Kinges Majesty, I, and the inhabitauntes, were, and ar, in falte of admynistracion of justice, to use the abuses hetherto there contynued ; the peple being bred in suche ignoraunce, as they knowe not justice. Howe be it, I have often perswaded many of them to be converted, which to doo I can scarsly have their assentes, for the lustes they have to caynes and other abuses, torning to their proffit, as it doth to myne. But, fynally, I am thus determyned to drive them therto, so as, what soever orders or devises you shall determyne therin to be put in effecte, I shall have suche respecte therto, as neither their will, ne any particler commoditie to myself, or to them, shall refrayne me to se the same perfitely executed, God willing; but in stede therof must be devised first, howe justice shalbe otherwise mynistred emongest them. I have also mocyoned them to be contributaries to the charges of officers, to have justice resydently executed here. And albeit the like ignoraunce therin maketh them dull and deffe, as their wittes be not open, or can perceive the benefite that may followe: yet having chiefly in myn ies my dutie to the Kinges Highnes, and next that being enclined to their utilities, I will put in effecte suche reasonable thinges to that purpose, and other like, as you shall will me to put in excecucion."

Lord Ossory and his son, as the leaders of the Reformation movement in Ireland, and as instruments of the fall of the Geraldines, rose high in the favour of their royal kinsman, Henry VIII. The claim to the Earldom of Ormond was allowed, in addition to that of Ossory, and he and his sons were loaded with grants of lands and high offices. In 1545 the Lord Deputy writes :—" There is now a great matter concerning the same Earl, for such liberties as he pretendeth to have in all the hoole countrie of Teperary, which, as he makes the shere now to be, is a great countrie." The Earl claimed all jurisdiction, or the regality, save in the four high pleas of the Crown, and thereby the right to give pardon for offences, and showed a grant by Edward III., "and fair books of usage of the same."[a]

In 1555, the clergy of Cashel presented a bill to the seneschal and justice of the liberty of Tipperary, complaining of certain exactions by sergeants and others under the

[a] Printed State Papers.

Earl of Ormond, the Baron of Dunboyne, and divers other persons, who cessed the manors of the bishops, and the manses of parsons and vicars, with horses, galloglas, kerne, hounds, and other impositions contrary to the liberties of the holy Church; upon which an order was passed at Clonmel, by the seneschal, Viscount Mountgarret, the justice, David Roth, and other officers of the liberty, commanding the sheriff and under-sheriff of the liberty to see the requests of the bill put in execution. On the 10th May, 1567, the Lord Deputy Sydney, and Council, ordered that the prelates and clergy of Cashel should have the benefit of this order.[a]

The following original document, on the theme of these presentments, will undoubtedly be read with interest:—

"THE HUMBLE PETITIONS OF THE EARL OF ORMOND TO THE QUEEN'S MOST EXCELLENT MAJESTY.[b]

"Wheare Sir Edward Bellingham being Deputy of Ireland placed certain soldiers in a house of the said Earls called Leighlen Bridge, and partly at his tenants charges fortified a frerie thereunto adjoining which the said Earl holdeth for years yet to come. The occasion of which charge of soldiers 't fortifycation proceeded upon respect of the said Earls tender years, after the death of his father the late Earl, by reason whereof those frontiers wanted the accustomed defence; so as ever since the said Earl (your highness faithful subject) could not enjoy his inheritance of that house, ne yet his term of years in the other, in consideration whereof and to the intent your highness may be disburdened of a thousand pounds yearly charges, which presently your Majesty sustaineth, and yet your service as much advanced for the good and quiet stay of your highness subjects there as hitherto hath been, he most humbly beseecheth your Majesty to grant unto him as well restitution of his

---

[a] Calendar of State Papers. 45. The date is before the 16th of
[b] State Papers, Ireland, Vol. i., No. July, 1559.

said inheritance and the custody of your highness house edified there, which shall be nevertheless at the commandment of your Majestys Deputy for the time, yielding unto your Highness yearly such rent as the same hath been surveyed at, as also to appoint him as Captain of Leinster, that is to say of the Kavanaghes, Twolles and Brynnes (for the most part rebells and disobedient to your Majestys laws) being no charge to your Majesty but a great furtherance of your Highness service.

"Itm̃, for-as-much as the greatest mischief to the public weal of that poor realm groweth of an unreasonable imposition called conny and livery continued time out of mind, which the said Earl utterly detesteth and seeketh by all means the abolishment thereof and the increase of civile order according to his education in England, and for that his attempt of such reformation may give example and incouragement to the rest of the Lords there to embrace the like, he most humbly beseecheth your highness to give him sufficient authority to take and provide victuals and other necessaries within his own rule for the furniture and maintenance of his house and residence, at such prices as the Lord Deputy hath used to pay for his provision, and that therefore the people inhabiting within the said Earl's whole rule may be exempt from all other like provisions, cesses and bonaghtes for gallowglasse, as in the time of his ancestors hath been accustomed, and also for the further relief of your highness said subjects to grant unto him the fee-farm of certain parcel of land called Onaght, surveyed at 6^{li}. 13^س. 4^d. sterling by the year, standing upon the borders of the Irish countreys and very necessary for the defence of the said Earls liberty of Tipperarie.

(*Marginal note in Burghley's hand*):—

"To be recompensed with some other piece of land in Kilkenny or Tipperary or Waterford.

Dorso.

"The Earl of Ormonds requests to the Queens Majesty."

This tenth Earl of Ormond, a profound statesman, as well as a vigorous general, was so anxious for the abolition of coine and livery, that, although, owing to the want of a circulating medium, the country was not ripe for change from exactions in kind to payments in cash, he made efforts in this direction, to the extent of issuing a proclamation, dated 1st July, 1654, " for taking away the mischievous custom of coine and livery in the county of Tipperary, with the orders necessary for the preservation of the country." On the 22nd November, however, he informs the Queen's Secretary that, when on the very point of abolishing it, the invasions of the Earl of Desmond " have forced him to continue one disorder, to withstand the other." Here we have the excuse for the practice, in its necessity. The abolition of this convenient custom was much disputed. There are documents, dated 1568, in the State Paper Office, showing the inexpediency of such a measure, and appointing certain provisions instead, for the defence of the country; also notes of the horsemen, galloglas, and kerne, supplied by the Earl of Ormond, and the counties of Kilkenny and Tipperary, at hostings, and a list of names of the freeholders[a] in these shires. At length, during the eventful government of that admirable statesman, Sir Henry Sydney, an Act was passed, by the Parliament of 1569, "for taking away Captainships, and all exactions belonging thereto, from the Lords and great men of this realm." The preamble of this important statute sets forth, that the chieftains of Ireland had, in times when the execution of justice fell into decline, arrogated unto themselves, on pretext of defending their possessions, " absolute and regal authority, within large circuits," each chief assuming "as much right as force would give him;"—that these seigneurs, "in

---

[a] The Kilkenny list will be found at p. 93, *supra*, transcribed by John Maclean, Esq., and not, as there erroneously stated, by W. J. O'Donnavan, Esq.

drawing to them all inferior states, to be of their several factions, fell to such strife for greatness of rule and government," that all fear and obedience, due to the Crown alone, was wholly converted to them; and yet that they themselves were "not in so good a state of life, both for honour and revenue, as their ancestors had been, as appeareth by ancient records and monuments of this realm." Accordingly, the assumption of the title of ruler of a country was forbidden, as also were exactions for sustaining chieftains' " horsemen, footmen, galloglasse, kerne, hackbutters, horses, horseboys, hunts, studkeepers, officers, or adherents." Neither were clans or septs to be assembled for the purposes of making peace, raids, forays, granting of taxes, benevolences, finding armed men, or for offensive invasions. A statute enacted in Dublin was, however, of no avail in remote regions, where it could not be enforced. According to Dowling, the annalist, in 1575, the Earl of Ormond repudiated the exaction of coiny and livery in his country. In 1576, Lord-Deputy Sydney abolished, say "The Four Masters," the taxes of coigny, kernetty, bonaght-bun, and bonaght-bar, in the "two provinces" of Munster.[a]

Let me now give some original papers, which evidence the antiquity of disturbances in this county.

In February, 1539, the corporation of Limerick address a remonstrance to the Earl of Ormond against the conduct of the garrison which Donough O'Brien has in Carrickogonel, in plundering the neighbouring country; and in the next month, Sir Thomas Butler writes, from "the Caghir," (Caher, Co. Tipperary) to the Government in Dublin, praying them to use their influence with the Earl, that he may not be extremely handled, nor his lands plundered, by the

---

[a] For a curious account of these taxes and exactions see No. 617, p. 212, and No. 611, p. 139, Carew Collection, Lambeth Library.

230 *Presentments of the Gentlemen, etc., of Co. Tipperary,*

officers of the liberty of Tipperary. The ensuing letter, hitherto, I believe, unpublished, is copied from the original in the MS. marked Titus B. xiii., p. 81, Cotton Library[a] :—

PIERS BUTLER, LORD CAHIR, TO THE EARL OF SUSSEX, COMPLAINING OF THE OUTRAGES COMMITTED UPON HIS PEOPLE BY THE EARL OF ORMOND AND THE BUTLERS. CAHIR. 11. OCTOBER. 1563.

"My most humble ductie to your Lordship premised. Thies are to advertise your honour that Sir Edmond Butler, Mr. John Butler, James and Edward Butler, my Lord of Ormonds brothers, came in warlike array with their trayn the second of this present month of October, and invaded and spoyled my poore tenants and countrey under the Queens Maiestie, of the value of one thousand pounds in cattell, houshold stuff, and apparaill, as thoghe they were mortall enymies, alledging that I have caused the White Knights sonne to take the pray of a villadge called the Grage, and that my sonne and others of my men were assisting him in so doing. And the same allegacōn being made by him, the said Sir Edmond, after the said enormous spoyle, was by me annswered in this maner; that I wold not myss to deliver suche persons as he should name of my men, or at my leading or comandment, offending, into the hands of the Sufferein of Clonmell, or Maior of Waterford, or any other indifferent men, to be tried according to justice; which he did refuse, and refused also to restore any the goods to the poore men, onles he had pledge into his hands for the contentation of his owne deasyr, which I thought not indifferent, using me after the like extreme sorte, as he is accustomed to serve me. What further disorder or spoyle shall be committed by him I knowe not. Therefor, my good Lord, for asmoche as, God knoweth, I am giltles in any matter the said Erle or Sir Edmond do chardg, yet I am pleased to deliver suche persones, as shall be named to me, of my servants and men, to have offended, to the said Sufferein or Maior, or other

[a] Irish Correspondence, State Paper Office.

indifferent men, to answere for suche things as shal be objected against them, which I think to be sufficient, and yf it be not, I will be alwayse prest and readie to do anything your honour will think reasonable, humbly beseeching your Lordship for asmoche as I and all my men must be fourthcoming to answer before all suche Judges and Commissions as you will thinke indifferent for me ; beseeching your Lordship, therefore, to command my said Lord of Ormonde to cause the said Sir Edmond and the rest of his brethren to restore the poor men to their goods, but also to see correction done for the said disorders, and even so to comand them to comit not any the licke offences herafter, yf it will stand with your honors pleasure, the rather that the said Sir Edmond is the bolder to comitt the licke, for that no order is taken with him for his manifold injuries, and one to me without occasion ministered of my side, as knoweth the Lord who have your honorable estate in his preservation. From the Cahir the xi of October, 1563.

"Your Lordships assured to comande

(Signed in autograph,) "PIERS CAHIR."

The county of Tipperary seems to have been fully colonized soon after the Invasion, and to have subsequently been little overrun by the Irish ; yet, still, its inhabitants anciently warranted the proverb, being *Hibernis ipsis Hiberniores.* On the other hand, however Irish in mind and manner the Prendergasts, Purcells, and Tobyns, may have become, it is to be believed that they entertained much national antipathy to the people they imitated. Little love was wasted between the Butlers of Ormond and the O'Briens of Arra ! The "mortall mislyke" borne by the Macgillapatricks for their *gallaibh,* or foreign neighbours, in the shire of Kilkenny was so strong, down to the latter days of the reign of Elizabeth, that their chieftain, Lord Upper-Ossory, "would not suffer any tryalls of his country to be made in the county of Kilkenny, but in the Queen's County," of which, he insisted, his country was a member (see Carew MS. and Dymock). After all, these presentments do not depict a state of society worse than all accounts, whether in prose or poetry, give of the contemporary condition of the Scottish Border, where old Celtic customs, such as clanship, with its train of "deadly feuds," and old hostilities and revenges, kept both internal and external enmities fiercely burning. The misery and misfortune, however, of this state of affairs in Ireland were, that it gave opportunity for aggression on the part of covetous English courtiers, who were enabled to plead—in excuse for extirpating families descended from the ancient conquerors of Ireland—their degenerate and lawless condition. Thus, as a case in point, in the year 1630, the districts of Upper and Lower Ormond were declared to be "wholly wild Irish," and, for this reason, demanded to be granted out and replanted, being, as was also alleged simply for the above cause, wholly in the King's right!

[*State Papers, Hen. VIII., Ireland, Vol. V.—Oct.* 1537. *N°.* 39.]

THE VERDYT OF THE GENTYLLMEN ⁊ COMYNERS OF THE COUNTYE OF TYPAR?.

THOMAS P̃NDERGAST.   JUÑ.

RICUS BUTLER.	} JUÑ.	JOÑES ENGLYS.	} JUÑ.
JACOBUS KETEING.		JOÑES MOCLERK.	
JACOBUS VALE.		JACOBUS WALSHE.	
WILLM̃S WOYDELL.	} JUÑ.	PÑIUS VALE.	} JUÑ.
JOÑES BUTLER.		WALTUS VALE.	
JOÑES DE STO JOÑE.		NICÑUS KETEING.	

Fyrste the saide Jurye p'sent that the lande is wasteid ⁊ desolateid by Thom̃s Butler ther lorde takeing ⁊ opp'seing them wyth horse and men ⁊ knavis ⁊ c^{on}yes [companies] of xxv men eṽy night yerely on the sayde countrey called Karren tyee.

and of Head Men and Commons of Town of Clonmel.

Itm̅ the saide Jury p'sent that the Erylle grayes[a] fyndeing them by opp'ssion at the saide Thom̅ᵃs commaundyment.

Itm̅ they p'sent that they ar opp'seid by workemen to the said Thom̅ᵃs, whatsoeᵘ̃ opacon, buyldeing or other worke he hathe, that nothing therof shal be at the saide Thom̅ᵃs coste, but onely at the ꝑpre costs 't expenceis, sendeing workemen therto callyd mostrons, 't to fynde meate for the machones,[b] holy dayes dureing the worke they ar compelled.

Itm̅ they p'sent that when the said Thom̅ᵃs Butler hathe a castell or any other substanceyall worke to be made or amakeing, his subjects poore and riche haveyng shepe must gyve hym to the saide worke eṽy of them a shepe, yf they have any.

Itm̅, they p'sent that he compelleith them and eṽy of them haveing a flok of shepe to gyve his doughtis a shepe for ther dowrye when they ar marryed or to be married.

Itm̅, they p'sent that if the said subjects be any yere w'out haveing galloglassheis or speremen in ther countrey, that then they muste paye 't gyve the saide Thom̅ᵃs at Ester x m̅ks to the wyne.

Itm̅, they p'sent that the coyshyr wherwᵗʰ they ar moste greveid 't desolateid, by abundaunce and multytude of people whiche the said Thom̅ᵃs bryngyth to them 't eṽy of them of habylytie, by the whiche they ar wasteid, 't ther substaunce, whiche many dayes 't nyghts finde them, is in ii dayes 't nyghts spent, 't this is useid iiii tymes in the yere of men haveing any substaunce.

Itm̅, the saide Jurye p'sent that Richard Butler was opp'seid and wrongeid by the saide Thom̅ᵃs Butler, in takeing from hym 't his feloweis viii m̅ks xiˢ iˡ ob, bycause he wolde not obey the saide, as to bryng hym capullesᶜ to carye 't convey sclattsᶜ to the said Thom̅ᵃs castell in the Cahyr.

Itm̅, they p'sent that the saide Thom̅ᵃs useid, 't dayly hathe, dyṽse Juges 't S͏ʳgeants in his coun̅trey opp'seing and compelleyng the peoplle at ther owne wille, 't not to lawe ne Justice, complayn-

---

[a] Perhaps we should read "present that the Erylles grayes," that is, the Earl of Ormonde's *gray* merchants, already so often complained of.
[b] Machones, i. e. masons.
[c] Capulles, i. e. horses.

cith them, and thes ar the names of the Juges, Rery McClaneghyc, Oyne McClaneghe, Thom^as McClaneghe. And thes ar the names of the s^rgeaunts, Edmūd m'ke Donogho, Derby m'ke Edmūd, John Duff, haveing after hym vi S^rgeaunts 't dy͡se othe^r S^rgeaunts.

Itm̃, they p'sent that c͡vy somer they muste paye to the saide Thom^as oute of c͡vy colup, whiche is iii or iiii^or tenne, a bushell of otys by compulsion, that is of e͡vy ii or iii horseis, or iii or ii kyen a bushell of otys.

Itm̃, they p'sent that therle, Pyers Butler, useid yerely to opp'se the saide subjects w^t boynes[a] contynually, and at his resortcing in thes pties opp'seid them w^t horsemen, horseis, 't hounds.

Itm̃, they p'sent that the said Thom^as is s/u^a nte, Arte Odonyll, have killeid John Condone, s^rvaunte to the Moclear, and this supposeing us wrongfully don. And we the said Quest choscin, electeid, 't sworen, to declare and testyfye the p'misseis humbly besecheing youre highencs to take compassion 't pytye on yor said subiects, so that all the said compleyn^ants and opp'sions be redressed 't reformid, 't that we may lyue fro the said tralldom accordeing to o^r gracious prynceis wyll, king Henry the viii^th.

The names of Thom^as Butler s^rju^aunts of this countrey,

John Tobyn, Morice Tobyn, Edmund Tobyn, Davy Tobyn, William Tobyn, Richard Tobyn, Nicholas Tobyn.

The names of the lorde Ossery s^rjeaunts in the countrey of Typar,

Tayke McLee, Thom^as McTayke, Patryk McConogher, John McConogher, William Kaylle, Edmund Kaylle, Donyll Omayll, Denyse Boye 't manye other.

Itm̃, the saide Jurye p'sent that Walter Butler in Ratheronane kepeith the vycaryge of Ratheronane, whiche he p'cheseid oute of Rome xx wynter agone, which vycarige belongyth to the kings highnes.

Itm̃, they p'sent that the saide Walter hathe taken of the lorde

---

[a] Boynes, i.e. Bonaghts. Bonaght was an imposition levied at the pleasure of the lord for the support of his Galloglas and Kern, &c.

of Rathronan, Jamys Walys, the remēnt[a] of his father decesse, by reason that he was pson of the saide towne, 't kepeith from the saide Jamys xxiiii acres of his lande, saying that it cons'rneith to his churche.

Itm̃, they p'sent that the churche of Kyllshevan[b] is in decaye, and the pson takeyth the pfits, 't syngith no masse ther, and Denys Moryce is vicar ther, and my lorde of Ossery hathe psonage there.

To the right honorable the king's high comĩissioners of this lande of Ireland.

Theis Bylles are founde to be trewe by the verdy[t] of the gentyllmen 't comỹns of the countye of Typar'.

Greveusly complayning sheweth unto yo[r] hono'rable wisedomes the kings trewe subiect yo[r] trewe oratrix Mawde Goldyng, borne woman of the citie of Waterford, That whereas yo[r] said [orators], laboring to cōme by her lyving in trewthe, hath gonne 't rowed bote towards the towne of Clōmell in the kings river. And one of the s'uants of Edmond Butler, decessed, called Derby Fitz Edmond which was then the said Edmond Butlers s'geaunt, and nowe s'uant to S[r] Thomas Butler, knight, the said Edmonds sonne, have riotously taken yo[r] said cōplayn[a]nt forsebly oute of the bote, and tooke her p'soner 't tooke with hir a m̃ke s[r] in money, 't a crosse worthe vi[s] viii[d], 't kepte her p'soner half a yere 't more. And afterward he paied for her raunsom to the said Edmond Butler a pipe of wyne worthe xi marks Irishe and ii[s] in Irs. to the said S[r] Thomas Butler, besids yo[r] said complayn[a]nts costs and losyng of her pfits during the said ymp'sonment, And also yo[r] said complayn[a]nts mother, decessed, was taken in the kings highwaye riding towards Clōmell forsaid by the said Derbyes father, called Edmond Fitz Donagh, being then also s'geaunt to Edmond Butler, 't nowe s'u'nt to Thomas Butler forsaid, and took then of yo[r] said complayn'nts mother app'ce horse,[c] And

---

[a] Remēnt, perhaps raiment, which, by the Canon law, belonged to the parson, as a mortuary, in case of death.

[b] i. e. Kilsheelan, near Clonmel.

[c] App'ce horse, perhaps a horse of price or value.

all this done to yor said complayn^{a}nt and to her mother for v yeres gayne. The p^{r}misses consydered therefore that it may please yo honorable wisedomes to cause and lawfully compell the forsaid Sr Thomas Butler, sonne and heire to the said Edmond Butler, which Sr Thomas hathe the saide malefactors t̃ extorcyoñs in his s^{r}vice t̃ domynyon, to satysfye yor said cōplayn^{a}nt t̃ her mother of the forsaid damages susteyned, els to showe sufficient warraunt to barre yor said complaynnt of the said exclamacoñs as shall stande w^t right lawe t̃ conscience; and this in the way of Justice t̃ charitie.

Wee knowe and testefy that the said Mawde Goldyng of the citie of Waterford was taken by the said Derby Fitz Edmond, offic̃ of Edmond Butler in the kings lyṽey as tofore written, t̃ this without any lawfull cause.

[1537. Oct. N°. 40.]

To the right honorable the kyngs highnes cōmissioners of this land of Ireland.

Grevously complayning, sheweth unto y^r honorable wisdomes the kings trewe subjects yor trewe orators, James Braye t̃ Ric. Wedlok, m̃chaunts t̃ borne in the towne of Clonmel; where as they went by the kings highwaye, accompanyed w^t other yonge men, half a myle oute of the towne of Clōmell, one John Duf, s^{r}geu^{a}nt to Edmond Butler deceased, and nowe to Sr Thomas Butler knight, fellowe with Wal̃ Flemyng,^{a} m̃chaunt, of the towne of Cosshell, as he went by the said highwaie w^t a pipe of wyne in a carte, t̃ wold have arested the forsaid wyne t̃ horses, The forsaid m^{r}chu^{a}nt of Cassell owing no dewty unto the forsaid s^{r}geaunt nor to his lorde or M^r, defended hym t̃ his goods t̃ tooke it to his towne. Then the forsaid s^{r}geu^{a}nt reto^{r}ned into the towne of Clōmell, and cōplayned to the suffrayn that the said cōplayn^{a}nts had forfeit the forsaid m̃chandises t̃ goods. The soṽaign belevyng this open false s^{r}geu^{a}unt, cōpelled yor forsaid complayn^{a}nts to abide the

---

^{a} i. e. were in company with Walter Fleming, no doubt to protect him and his merchandise from the dangers here complained of.

judgmēt of iiii men chosen by the forsaid Edmond Butler, 't by the suffrayn, to whom Edmond Butler said openly that his Judges shuld here 't agre w¹ them of the towne, The forsaid Judges w'out delib'acon awarded that your fornamed cōplayn*nts shuld paie unto the forsaid Edmond Butler x¹, 't to themselfs iii¹, and to the forsaid s*geu*nt for his fee xx*, 't then sent your cōplayn*nts to Edmond Butlers place, where they were kepte in p*sone xii weeks, 't then paied xv* iiii*d* for jaylo* fee 't other, besids the forsaid somes; one of yo* forsaid cōplayn*nts hath attached the forsaid Judges to the lawe whiche been named William Fagan, burgeys, John Haryhan, clerke, 't the matē was brought tofore a 'quest whose names folowen, vz. Th. White, Ric. White Fitz John, Ric. White Fitz Thomas, burgeses, Robt Butler, Edmond Braye, James White Fitz Henry, m*chu*nt men, who were sworne after the use of the towne, dyd here and receave yo* cōplayn*nts true evydences, 't then dyd not agree supposyng yo* forsaid cōplayn*nts that the forsaid iii burgeses were not egall, for they went abrod 't brought no verdite, And thus yo* complayn*nts 't true orators can have no right syn the xxiiii yere of the kynge o* sov̄aign lorde the kings reign unto this tyme. It maye therefore please yo* hono'able wisedomes to see a lawfull ordre in this matter, 't thus in the waie of Justice 't charitie.

> We knowe that the said James Butler brother[a] and Richard Wodloke of the Towne of Clōmell & Water Flemyng of Casseyll were inv̄upted by the said John Dufs su*nts when they passed in the kings highwaie, and this unlawfully doon not accordyng to the kings will.

The following Presentments, though of a later date, may well be appended to the foregoing, bearing as they do on the general grievances of the county of Tipperary :—

---

[a] Brother is here evidently a mistake for Braye. See the commencement of the petition, where the name is written Braye.

The p'sentment of Edmonde Comyn and his associetts, at the Sessions houlden at Clonemell, befor Sr Will'm Drewrye, knight Lo. president of Mounster, and other his assistanc', in November in anno 1576.

We p'sent that the xth of Jan^{ry}., the xixth of o^r soūaigne laidie that nowe is, one Tybott Hanckuth, of Moyldrome, wth diverse others, malefactors, came to Shippston wth in the countie and libertie of Typperrarie, and then and theire traiterouslye did burne xxx houses, the valewe of one hundrith pounds of houshold stuffe, bysides the Bur[n]inge of a womane and a mane childe, contrarye to o^r Soūaigne Laydye the Queens Ma^{ts} peace, and the statute pvideth in that case, of the goods and cattelles of Edmond Hanckuth and his tenants of the same: p Edmond Comyn cm̄ socii[s] sui[s].

We p'sent that the xxth of August, the xvi yere of o^r soūaigne laidie that nowe is, one Quaghe McConogher nessiny, of mon Roo, came to Dowhe, wthin the countie and libertie of Typperrarye, and then and theire traiteriously burned ix houses, one hundith shiepp and swyne, and the valwe of xx^l. in houshould stuffe of the goods and cattell of Teigg Ofogirtie Dowepe, aforsaid, countrarye to the Queen's Ma^{ts} peace and to the statut in that case providid: p Edmond Comyn cm̄ socii[s] sui[s].

We p'sent that the xxth of September, the ix yere o' raigne o^r soūagne laide that nowe is, Phillip Comyne Fitz Geordge, Willm Comyn Fitz Gorge, Art McDiermoth McShane glefe, rorie Begg, w^t diūse others malefactors, came to Camkeyle, wthin the said countie and libertie, and then and there traitorishousely burned eight ricks of corne in fild of Camkell aforsaid, of the goods and cattells of Edmond Comyne, of Kilcomell, and that Mr Edmond Butler, of Cloghensie and supre, traitorouslye supported, mantained and peured the said traitors to tak them to his Core Rick^a traitorinously and contrary to statute in that case pvidid: p Edmond Comyn cū socii[s] sui[s], &c.

^{a} Comeric, i. e. protection

We p'sent that the xxth of Janu^{ry}. the ii yeare of o^r soûayne laydie that now is, Phillipp Comyne Fytz John, of Grayglewane, horsmane, Philip Comyn Fitz Gordge, lat of Raylstowne, Wiłłm Fitz John, Odower Keylne Manighe, horsmane, w^t divers other malefactors, did sett her Ma^{ts} highe waye and wilfully murdred one Art McBrien, Galiglashe, wonded Edmond Comyne, of Kill konell, traitoriousely in his right hand, and contrarye to the statute provided in that case: p Edmond Comynge cū socii[s] sui[s].

We p'sent that in the tenth yere of o^r soûayne laidie that nowe is, one Gellenenewe McTeigg McShane, of the Bores Lighe, wthin the Crosse barth come to Wiłłm Oge Faninge Mobamane, wthin the countie and libertie, and then and there traitorinously murdered one Conogho^r O Kelle, of the same house, contrarie to the statute pvideith: p Edmond Comyn com' socii[s] sui[s].

We p'sent that the last of October, in the xviiith yere of o^r soûaigne laidie that nowe is, one Shane McGarrald, horsmane, Riē Melebe, s^{r}vant to Mr Pires Butler, Shericft, came to Shirpstō, and then and their feloñusly, to[ok] a caple, price xl^s of the good and cattell of Wiłłm Bowy, of the same house, felonusly contrary to the statute in that case made: p Edmond Comyn com socii[s] sui[s].

We p'sent that all the weares on the ryver of the Suir by Clonemell do stopp the concorse of boats and fyshes to come alonge the ryver, and specially the weare that is caulled Crowck wear: p Edmond Comyne cum socii[s] sui[s].

We p'sent that the iiith of December, the xviii yere of o^r soûayn laidy that now is, one Tyboied Burke, gent, and Tybodd Fytz Richard Burke, Donole O Henege, w^t twoo cam to Moclristowe, wthin the libertie, and then and there [took] iii^c sheaffs of otts, price xvi^d, wth meat and drinck to the valwe of x^s, feloniuously and contrarie to the ordinance and statute made: p Edmond Comyn cū socii[s] [suis].

The p'sentment of Jacobe Flemyne and his associetes, at the Sessons houlden at Clonemell, before Sr Will'm Drewrie, knight, Lo. President of Mounster, and other his assistance, in November, 1576.

We p'sent that in the yere of o^r Lord 1568, and the xxv day of Auguste, Edmond the Whit Knight sonne, John Fitz W im Makened, and Tegg, brother to the said John, Darbie Coroickem O Hupinn, s'vant to Margeret Poo^r, of Ballilogan, at that tyme wthin the countie and libertie of Tipparie, wth others dyverse unknowē psons, John McShane and Darbie McShe, sonne to the said John Dowlinge, in Bally Drowt, wthin the countie of Liberteck,[a] captaines of the Galliglasses to James Fitz Moris, at that tyme came to the barrony of Cahir, wthin the countie and libertie of Typperare, and their vilonusly burned and spoyeled the said barrony to the nomber of xvi townes of Sr Tybbot Buttler, knight, iii raynges of the Queen's Ma^{ty} land of the Abbe of Cahir, and after this fact committed by those psons aforewriten, they weare receved by Margeret Powr and her ten^{a}nts in Gart tardon, wthin this libertie, and there she and her ten^{a}nts, John Ban, James Ohes, and John Rous, w^t others unknown psons of her ten^{a}nts, rec^d to the nūber of xii kin, ii shepp, xxx hogis and geat, of the forsaid spoyel, violently and contrary to the Queens Ma^{ts} lawes.

We p'sent that in the yere and day aforsaid, Richard Fitz Ullic Burk, of Bally Vadic, wthin the libertie of Typperarie, did receve iiii^c shepp, ii in kalf kyne, of the psons afore writen, of the forsaid spoyell, violently and contrarie to the queens ma^{ts} pice, after the comittinge and bur[n]inge aforsaid.

We p'sent that in the yere and day aforsaid, Rory Moile Omowledane, of Keilerfekelty Malag Bray, other same goner did violently receve of the psons afore writen, thre sco$\cdot$ sheppe and geat, ii in kalf kyne of the aforsaid spoile, after the bur[n]ing comitted by them aforsaid, &c.

---

[a] *Sic* in the original, evidently a blunder of the scribe for Limerick.

We p'sent that in the yere and daye aforsaid, Walter Fits John Burke, of the Cappack, wthin the said libertie, and John Fitz Walter Burke, of the Gotten, wthin the said libertie, and his sonnes, Walter and Tyboth, did receve iii in kalf kyne, iii^{xx} shepp, of the aforsaid spoill and psons, violently after comittinge the aforsaid buringe, &c.

We p'sent that the bridge of the Gowlin was repared in the tymes past by the pson, vicer and pricioners of a Tashill,^{a} &c.

We present that the bridge of the Cahir owght to be repared right by Sr Tybott Butler and others, as is a costomed frome Cnockenaie to Reachee, and for Cnocklowetie to Cahir.

We p'sent that the bridge of Ardfinan ought to be repared by the lord Bushopp of Watterford and Lessmore, &c.

We p'sent that the bridg of Bally Drout ought to be repared by Knockgraffin and Glane Gowlane, otherwise cauled Baly Drowit, &c.

We p'sent that all the weyres uppon the Shoure, frome Korke Ileny to the Carige, be hurtfull to the comon welth.

We p'sent that Mr Edward Butler and his mē, John Burk, of Kenlefeckelly, wthin the county and libertie of Tipperarie, horsmane, Pires Comyne, of Lalyn Rayle, wthin the said libertie, kernaghe, Brene Moriеck and Teigg Nenaroghe Odaremond, Philip Ospellan, Wittm Opollin, Moris More, Shean McDermond Oge O'Flahirt, do daylie ceasse uppon the countrye w^t convie and liverie, coudhie, horsmen, and foottmē, galiglasses, goners, doggs, and boyes, contrarie to Her Ma^{ts} statute in that case providid, &c.

We p'sent that Mr Sherief of this libertie and his men, Henis Omoris, kernaghe, ceassor of his fott mē, Thomas Walle, kernaghe, Walter Walle, kernaghe, Garrill McSheane vallw, horsmane, John Fitz Garrold, horsmane, Richard Pursell and James Purshell, horsmen of the com of Kilckeny; Feillemboy McHeis Canctag, horsmeñe Hony O'Dower, kernagh, Jeffery Fitz James Pengirdas, kernaght, Tegg Oquorick, Jonoick Englio, of Solachod, w^t many other unknowne psones, do daylye cesse the cuntry w^t convie, and liverye,

---

^{a} i. e. Athassel.

and codhie, contrare to the Queens Ma^{ts} peace, and statute vidid in that case, &c.

We p'sent that my lord of Woremonde his men, Donoch McDowe, otherwise called Machenoach Dermod McDac McHonye, Shane McDac, wth Hen .... James Moore galdowse and Turlaghe Oge, do dayley ceasse the cuntry w^t convic and liverye, contrary to the statute pvidid in that case, &c.

We p'sent Sr Edmond Buttlers men, James Welshe, of Garre Hodie, Robert Welshe, sonne to McAdam, Holliver Welshe, of the countie of Kilkenelln,[a] Gille Duffe Fitz Waulter [of] Baylly Vony, and Richard Fitz Waulter of the same, and Far McDermond, of Keyle Moor, in the county of Typparye, Shane O Lalowr, servant to Sr Edmonde Buttler, do daylie cesse the cuntry w^t convic and liverie, contrary to statute, &c.

We present that Richard Butler and Tibott Buttler, sonne to Pires of the Grallaghe, do cesse the country against statutie, &c.

We p'sent that Hony Duff Omoris, servant to Mr Peirs Butler, sherief of the countie and libertie of Typpare, came to Bally Hack, and to Ballie Castell, and to Mowe Careck, and to the Caboragh, and to Bally Homarin, and to Pople O'Fogortie, and to Pople Drom, and to Cowle Crowe, and there and thies lead and toock awaie w^t them to the nūber of xii caples, the firste of December, 1576, forcsabley and contrarye [to] the Quenes Ma^{ts} peace, &c.

We p'sent that the L. P^rsident of Mounster, that nowe is, do cesse the cuntre w^t horsmen, and horses, and boyes, contrarye to the statute.

We p'sent that the churche of Temple BallyDowle, wh^{th}in the count' of Typparie, is not kept according as it owght to be, the church not built but standing in waste, to the great hindrance of the pariosoners, and contrarye to the statute pvidid in that case, &c.

[a] A blunder for Kilkenny.

THE PRESENTMENT OF THE HEADS AND COMMONERS OF THE TOWN OF CLONMEL TO THE ROYAL COMMISSIONERS. A. D. 1537.

The Clonmel Presentment concludes the representations laid before the Commissioners of Reformation. The picture it affords of the state of the adjacent districts differs little from those given by the juries of the adjoining counties and towns. A single unusual word arrests our attention—the term "franklein," now obsolete, but which designated a considerable freeholder. To judge by the well-known description, by Chaucer, of the English franklein, from whose class justices of the peace, sheriffs, and knights of the shire were chosen, he was a lordly squire, a fine old English gentleman of the olden time.

The state of the monastic establishments near Clonmel is elucidated by this Presentment. They were often in the hands of men whose lawless relatives exacted succour and sanctuary within abbey walls. Chief Baron Finglas, writing about the year 1533, says:—"To alleviate the kyng's chardges to this reformacion of Leinster, there be divers Abbeyes adjoining to these Irishmen, which doe gyve more aid and supportacione to them than to the kyng or his subjects, parte against their wills; as the abbie of Donbrothie & Tintern, in the Co. of Wexford; Dowthe, in Catherlough; & Grane and Baltinglas, in Kildare; which may be suppressed, and given by the King to young lords, knights, and gentlemen out of England, which shall dwell upon the same." Baltinglas Abbey, he observes, was "a living for a lord;" and so was the Fassagh, or weald, of Bantry. Some of the monasteries and great manors he enumerates were soon afterwards bestowed on gentlemen of English birth, who took up their residence in Ireland, as the Colcloughs, at Tintern, and the Itchinghams, at Dunbrody.

THE VERDYT OF THE HEDDES AND COMYNERS OF THE TOWNE OF CLONMELL.

[1537. *Oct.* 18. *N⁰.* 38.]

BENNET WHYTE, JUÑ.
RICHARD FYTZ THOMAS WHITE. WALTYR POER.
WILLIAM FAGAN.   JUÑ. JOHN MOLERNY.   JUÑ.
RICHARD FYTZ JOHN WHYTE.   TYBALDE WHYTE.
JOHN STRYCHE.   WILLIAM LAYMAZ.
JAMYS WHYTE.   JUÑ. CORNELL BRATHE.   JUR.
WALTYER WALLE.   JOHN CORRE.
NICHAS MITHYE.
MORYCE QUYRKE.   JUR.
JAMYS QUYRKE.

This Inquyre is for thes ii yeres past above the date above wrytin, and so we gyve o' Ʋdyt.

Fyrste, as twicheing coynes and lyƲyes sesseid, we have inquyrid and founde that the Erle of Osserye and the lorde Jamys Butler doo assesse coyne and lyƲye w'oute thassent of the freholders.

We fynde that Sr Thom^as Butler, knight, useid t assessid coyne t lyƲye, and that the sayde Thom^as useith to assesse his hounteris t kerne to coyne t lyƲye upon the countrey, horsse knavis t horse boys w'oute paying any monye to the Inhibytaunts of the same, all the funnkelins and gentyllmen under protexion t govern^ance useith the same.

We fynde t psent that when tyme as pleaseith thaforesaide lords and gentyllmen to be at any buyldeing of any castell or works they do assesse the' tennts under ther goƲnaunce to have workemen and horseis to labor w'oute gyveyng of meate or paying any money, and they set ther masons and carpinters to coyne upon the ten'nts eỹy holly dayes.

Itm̃, they fynde when it pleaseith the said lords and gentillmen to have any tayllors for to have worke or garments to be made, they use to sett them at coyne upon ther ten"nts in holly dayes.

Itm̃, they fynde that the Erlle of Osserye 't Sr Thom^as Butler usith takeith 't assesseith upon eỹy ploughe a bushell of otys in somer tyme for ther pryncipall horseis.

Itm̃, they fynde that idell men 't vacabounds goyth in the count^rye and takeith meate 't drynke, paying no money therfor.

Itm̃, they fynde that therle of Ossery and his sonnes, and also Sr Thom^as Butler, useith 't takeith supps callid cuddyes^a, 't, as well the lords spuall 't under ther governaunce, as all others useith thē in comyn.

We fynde that the Blackbedds^b, when tyme any assesseing of coynes and lyỹye is sett by the foresaide lords advyce as to saye to the lord of Ossery's marshall, namyd Geffery Mawelorke 't Jamys McDavy, for the galloghis and marcialls for Sr Thomas Butler, namyd John Mawelorke 't Walter P'ndregast useing blackbeds.

Itm̃, the sayde jurye fynde that thoffiēes of the lybertie hathe not executed the kings lawes agaynste Waltyer Butler whiche was endytied in the assyse, wherof growith muche inconvenyensye 't injurye don by the said Waltyer Butler of Polkyr,^c which ewas wyth them, and mought be taken yf the senyshall 't shryfe wolde have don ther office and ductye, for the said Waltyer dayly was under ther jurisdiccōon.

Itm̃, they finde that all lords 't others haveing domynion w'in this Quarter useith to have Iryshe judges for ther advantage.

Itm̃, they fynde that Shane Fytz Tybbalde of Mowskry makyth his pclamations that no m̃ket may be solde nor shalle not be solde out of his shyre but to Jamys White and Edmūd Quyrke, and then paying eỹy of them a fyne x^s yerely.

---

^a Cuddye. *Cuid-oidche,* i. e. a portion for a night, or supper. The word supper seems to derive from supping a mess of potage, or soup.

^b Blackbeds, i.e. charges for dead or non-existing men.

^c The Castle of Poulakerry, on the Suir, about three miles below Clonmel.

Itm̃, they finde that Jamys White, m̃ch^a unto, useith 't hathe graye m̃chants regrateing the m̃ket; Thom^a s White 't John M?thyc useyth the same.

Itm̃, they fynde that dy^v se of Wafforde 't others goen from vyllage to vyllage, so that the m̃kets be hynderid 't lost in this Quarter, that no vytaylle nor m̃chandyse may be gotyn for any money, p^a ying youre dyscrete wysedoms of a remydy breffely.

Itm̃, they fynde that Donyll Mc Kraghe^a of the Mountayn hathe ordyned 't establysheid that none of his ten^a nts shalle selle nor bye any hyds but to hymself at a certen pryse for his owne avantage.

Itm̃, they fynde that Sr Thomas Butler, knight, Nychas Keteing, 't Nychas Town, Jamys Keteing of the Mortown, Jamys Englyshe of Whytchurche, the Pryor of the Kaghes, the Prior of o^r Lady Abbey, John Mawelorke of Donnes Town, Thomas P^e ndregast of the new Castell, Robt Mc Shane P^e ndregast, Robt Keteing of Ardysman, 't all others w^t in this shyre in the cantred of Clonmell that have any town or village under his go^v naunce, w^t one assent 't assembleing before Sr Thomas Butler as go^v ner of them, hathe affyrmed 't establysheid 't enacteid that none under ther go^v naunce nor jurisdycc̃on shall sell or bring any wolle, fleshe, or other m̃chandyse oute or fro any towne or vyllage to m̃ket towne of the kings, wythoute speciall lycence. And so this acte made by com̃andym^t 't penaltye to be leved of the seller w^t oute grace.

Itm̃, they fynde that when tyme any greate capytayn or gentillman repayre or is lodgeid w^t gentyllmen of the countrey, that it is useid to take bewer of the tenants of the countrey callid m?tyeght,^b and paying no money therfor.

Itm̃, they fynde that Sr Thomas Butler hathe 't levied a subsydye or trybute upon all his tenants to be dely^v yd to the lorde Jamys Butler for his affayres into England, and more they fynde by credence 't hereing that suche trybuts was cesseid 't levyed in the countye of Kylkenny and Slawardaghe.

---

[a] Magrath? Probably Magrath. chief of a bardic family.

[b] Martyeght. *Mart-tighe*, i. e. beef for the lord's house.

Itm̃, the saide jurye fynde that this p̃sent yere the viii[th] daye of Julye Waltyr Butler of Polkyn, and Shane Bretnaghe, Waltyr Bretnaghe of Rochystown is sonne, w[t] a Rowte of kerne and thevys by nyght forcebly toke oute of a bote laden w[t] m̃chandyseis in the ryver besyde the key of Clonmell a fardell of clothe and m̃chaundyse valued at xvi[l] costs and all.

Extorcyoners,

Shane Duffe of the countye of Typar̃.
Shane Grasse of the countye of Kylkenny.
Tybalde Hooyr of Kyltenan.
Shane Fytz ps of the Rowskaghe.
Richard Butler of Polkyr.
Sowen Okyve pryst.
Remounde Fytz Garrot of Glanchoyr.
Richard Englyshe of Kylkhoran.
Edmũd Archebyshop of Cashell and his folowers hathe com̃ytted ryoute.

Itm̃, they finde that the cessions is kept at the lords wylle, 't not at iiii tymes by the yere.

Murder.

Itm̃, they fynde that Arte Hoge m[r]therid Shane Conden, Mawclerk is s͡uant this p'sent yere in the moneth of July.

Itm̃, they fynde that Geffery Mawclerk is towne hath m[r]therid the said tyme, in revengeing of the aforesaide m[r]der, a husbondman of John Mawclerk of Bayllykhleryan.

Itm̃, they fynde that Donyll M[c]Swayne hathe m[r]therid one William Morowzo.

Itm̃, they fynde that Edmũd Ivoyr hathe shlayne George Baron by chaunce this p'sent yere.

Itm̃, of the enormyties, they fynde that S[r] Thomas Butler do use 't assesse and levye a shepe of ev̄y flock of shype in his countrey when tyme that any of his doughters is maryed, thes enormytyes ben useid paying nothing therfor, and this is useide xxx myles rounde aboute w[t] ev̄y lorde 't gentyllman.

Itm̃, of the werys made from Clonmell to the Carryk the greate daunger 't enormyties of them, that bothe men 't goods byn dayly in daunger of loseing, 't by west toun into the cahyrd.[a]

Itm̃, they fynde that Carryk takeith unlawfull customes dayly, cont^arye to all goode ordre 't right of all suche bootys w^t m̃chandyseis not chargeid nor dyschargeid w'in the fruncheis of the towne, whiche the kings deputye awardeid agayne them, whiche one Fitz Wiltm. as custymer to the lorde of Ossery, polleyth 't takeyth dayly the said wrongfull customes.

Itm̃, they fynde that the Byshop of Lysmore 't Waſforde and Robert Remon, clerke, and Mr Moryce hyerlyez, the said byshop is officiall, hathe takyn in one mater 't cawse of matrymonye for fee of sentence viii^l of money.

Itm̃, they fynde that the Abbaye of Innyslawenaghte besides Clomell of great enormytie usethe no devyne s?vice, but fewe masses by verbe; And the Abbot of the same using hys leman or harlot openly by daie and night to his pleasure, and ev̂y monke of his havynge his harlot and houshold; And the said abbot is possessed of xx^l lande erable, besids mountaignes and woods, also we ar not 8teyn whether the Abbot holdeth by pvision or not.

Itm̃, we fynde the p^iory of the Cahir having no devyne s?vice, 't we be not 8tayn of his possessions but v plowe lande, and is a visor out of Rome.

Itm̃, the p^ioresse of Mollaghe, holdeth p̃ndregast of the newe castell w^t coyne 't liv̂ey 't a nights supp, afſ the man̄ 't unlawfull use of the countrey, havyng a plowlande.

Itm̃, we fynde that the p^ior of o^r lady Abbaye of the freors karmys useth to have his leman and harlot openly, and no devyne s?vice, having a ploughland.

Itm̃, we fynde the p^iory of Athashell, Edmond Archiebishop of Casshell, hathe pvided oute of Rome, 't we know not whither it be by the kings licence or not, And the said abbaye, as by hering of o^r p'decessors, is infeffed of xiiii knights lands 't ccc^lin tythes oblacyons, having no devyne s?vice, but fewe masses, w^t iiii chanons, and some of them using 't having wifs and childern.

---

[a] i. e. They complain of the weirs built in the Suir, west of the town, up to Caher.

Itm̄, we fynde that the Abbay of the holly crosse is of xx plowlande, and may spende ccc¹ in oblacyons 't tythes.

Itm̄, we fynde that the Abbaye of Hooghuyr on this side of Lymerik is of more possession of lands then we can fynde by enquery. And this to put yoʳ high auctorities in remembraunce.

To the kings hyghnes Cōmissioners w'in this lande of Ireland.

Thies Bylles are founde to be trewe by the verdyt of the hedde 't Com̄yns of the towne of Clonmell aforesaide.

Grevously complaynyng, sheweth unto yoʳ discrete wisdomes 't high auctorities yoʳ poore humble 't daily orator, Robert Donyll, freman 't dweller w'in the kings towne of Clonmell w'in the said lande, That where as he laboring trewly for his living in England cam home wᵗ his living, and at his goyng towards his dwelling place of Clonmell aforsaid in the river of Waterford agaynst Kylmydan, w'in foure myles of the said citie, cam the Archiebishop of Casshell wᵗ force, and tooke riotously yoʳ poore suppliaunt (wᵗ many others) with his goods to the value of viii¹ 't more, 't ympˡsoned hym the space of ix weks, to the utter undoing of yoʳ said poore suppliaunt his wif 't childern, And this contrary to lawe 't right, as ye shalbe credybly heraft? enformed by sufficient recorde.

It maye therfore please you of yoʳ charytable goodnes to see yoʳ poore suppliaunt restored to his trewly begotten goods, 't the damages that he hath susteyned by reason of the said ryot, and this in the waie of charitie, seeing that yoʳ said suppliaunt is not able otherwise (as by lawe) to obtaigne his goods. And your said suppliaunt shall praye to God for yoʳ pspous estats longe to endure.

The some of the goods taken by the said Archiebishop from yoʳ suppliaunt the xvii daie of August, in the xxiiii yere of the kings reign that nowe is, viii¹. viˢ. viiiᵈ.

We fynde this bill trewe.

To the kyngs highnes Comissioners within this land of Ireland.

In most humble wise complayneth unto yor wisdomes yor daily orator, Patrik Busher of Waterford, m̅chaunt, That where he hathe been taken cōmyng from the faire of Cassell in the kings high waie, the xxiiii yere of o^r so͡vaign lorde kynge Henry the eight, by thes͡u^{n}nts of Sr Thomas Butler, knyght, 't his brother Piers Butler, 't by them deli͡ved 't sent to their father[s] garyson called the Kahir, and from thens removed 't sent to the said peres castell named Kylma-Hemerey, and there kepte 't retaygned in irons both o͡f hande 't foote xxi weks, unto suche tyme as he paied xxvi^l vi^s viii^d for fyne 't raunsome, as he shall affirme [au] thentykly, in money 't m̅chaundises besides the damages 't losse of tyme that yor said suppliaunt hath susteyned duryng his said ymp^{i}sonement, which he submitteth unto yor wisdomes, besecheth the same to considre, and thus in the waie of charitie.

We fynde that Patrik Bussher paide a tonne of wyne 't ii hundreth iron.

The advyse for the redresse of the enormyties aforesaide devysed by the saide Jurye.

Oure best advise, after o^r symple dyscrecyons 't most diligent and faithfull maner, please it yor right discrete wisdomis accepted, of the good ordering of the lande of Ireland, if by your wisedomes maye fynde the meanes.

That first coyne 't li͡vey be put bake, and the Inglishe lords 't trewe subjects of Ireland be brought at one peax, and that none may be at no se͡vall peax$f$ w^t eny of the Irishe nacyons, but w^t suche Irishe nacions as is trewe 't faithfull to the kynge and to his subjects, 't that then all Irishe nacyons under the kyngs lawes be obedyent to the statutes 't lawes pelaymed affyrmed by the kings deputie 't his counsell, and that the bigge Irishe sherts[a] be dampned 't put bak and brought to lasse making 't facyon, And when tyme

---

[a] "The big Irish shirts" are described by Campion.

is and may be by leasure after yor discrecyons that all Inglish nacyons of Inglishe and Irishe be brought to one appell as nigh to the Inglishe maner and facyon as may be, and that e̔vy man be so charged to soco^r ne favo^r no thieves nor Irishe rebelles, and that e̔vy lord within his dominac̄ōn be charged to have weapon after the best mañ according as he maye occupie best, and e̔vy man after his degree answere the crye, 't defende his neighbo^r the kings subjects, 't that e̔vy gentylman annswere for his s̔uant in the countrey, that useth Irishe mañ. God save o^r so̔vaign lorde kynge Henry the eight.

To the right worshipfull the kings highnes Cōmissioners.

In most humble wise complayneth 't sheweth unto yor worshipfull m^rships y^r daily orato^r 't poore bedeman, Richard Graunte of Fetherd, Burges, that where as afore tyme he was in the s̔vice of Sr John Arundell, of the countie of Cornewall, knight, and so being in s̔vice with the said Sr John, for that he was willing to see his frends 't the countrey where he was borne, he obtayned licence to goo into Ireland where he was so borne to the entent before rehersed, and after that he had been there to retorne into Cornewall ayene from whens he cam, wher upon he tooke shipping 't arived at Dungarvan, in Ireland aforsaid, and there at the same tyme, that is to saye about ii yeres nowe passed, met wythe Edmond Mawrice, gent, who for a ȝteyn some of money bitwene the said Edmond 't Richard agreed, upon communycacon had bitwene them, the said Richard retaigned the said Edmond saufly to conducte and bringe the said Richard 't ȝteyn goods which the said Richard had then in his possession to Clonmel, of which conducc̄ōn 't hire yor said orator hathe sufficient recorde 't witnes. After which said conduccyon 't hire, the same Richard, upon the truste and confydence that he had in the same Edmond, went hymself with his goods toward Clōmell w^t the said Edmond Mawrice, which said goods amounte to the value of xl^l, And the said Edmond, notw^tstanding the confydence and truste which the said Richard had in hym, in the way bitwene Dongarvan aforsaid and Clōmell, dyd w^t force 't

armes assaute the said Richard, 't hym dyd beate and grevously
wounde, and the same goods then being in the possession of the
said Richard, dyd felonously steale 't bere awaye, 't after the same
robery dyd convey the same goods so stolen to the towne of Rckyll,
And the said Edmond, with other company to yor said orator unknowen, dyd bringe yor said orator w^t force to the said towne of
Rckyll, where Sir Thomas Butler, M^r to the said Edmond, then
inhited, 't there the same Sir Thomas Butler imp'soned yor said
orator 't hym reteyned in p'sone by the space of half a yere, and by
force of the same ymp'sonement copelled yor said orator to give hym
eight pounds 't x^s Irishe for a rannsome or fyne, for the payment of
which rannsome 't fyne yor said orator was enforsed to morgage his
lands, to his utter undoing 't ymp'sonement. In consideracyon of
all the p'misses it maye please yor worshipfull ñship as well to cō-
m^{a}unde the said Sir Thomas Butler to come before you to make
aunswere to the p'misses and to repaye the same viii^l x^s to yor
said orator, and to make hym amends for his fals and wrongfull
ymp'sonment, as also to cōmanude the said Edmond in like mañ to
come before you to annswere to the p'misses 't to enjoyne hym to
make restytucyon of the same goods so by hym stolen from yor said
orator, and that he may further be punished for his offence as shal
be thought by yor worships worthy for suche offences, and your
said orator shall daily praye to God for the p̱spitie of yor worshipfull ñships long to endure.

> We fynde 't knowe that the fornamed Richard G^{a}unte was taken
> by one Edmond McMorish, and hym conveyed to Sr Tho-
> mas Butler, 't so ymp'soned 't lost 8teyn goods by bothe of
> them, 't suppose the said Ric' to be trewe, and moreo͡f we
> fynde that the said Sir Thomas Butler hathe taken a pipe
> of wyne and a noble of money for the w'in named Ric', be-
> side what the forsaid Edmond Fitz Morice hath taken.

and of Head Men and Commons of Town of Clonmel. 253

The following List of the "Gentlemen" (i. e. men of blood and arms,) of the county of Tipperary, will serve to illustrate the foregoing presentments; it is later in date than the presentments made to the Commissioners of Henry VIII., but as little change took place in the landholders of the county between the reign of that monarch and of Elizabeth, it is equally applicable to both. The Association is indebted to W. J. O'Donnavan, Esq., M. R. I. A., for the transcript of this interesting document. The presentment of Kilkenny county was illustrated by a similar list, also taken from the Carew MSS., but copied for the Association by John Maclean, Esq., F. S. A. By a slip of the pen it was stated at p. 93, *supra*, that the Kilkenny list was also communicated by Mr. O'Donnavan.

[*Lambeth, Carew MS.* 611, p. 91.]

The Names of the Gentlemen inhabitinge the Cont. of Tippary wth the extente of theire Lands by estima$\overline{co}$n as followeth:—

Lands houlden of the Manno^{rs} of Knockgraffen and Kilshielan.

James Tobin and his kinsmen the comsic in the canthred of Clonemell	cl^{li}
Richard Loūt his lands	v^{li}
Willm̃ Vale his lands	xl^{li}
Barnaby O'Nele	xl^{li}
John Nele his lands	viij^{li}
Donell O'Nele	iiij^{li}
Edmond Vale	viij^{li}
Willm̃ Meydole	xl^{li}
Richard Butler and his kinsmen . . .	lxvij^{li}
James Butler his lands	lxvij^{li}
Willm̃ Fitz Richards lands	xiij^{li} vj^{s} viij^{d}
Edmond Butlers lands	v^{li}
Philipp Vale his lands	v^{li}
David Welsh -	l^{li}
William Poer	xx^{li}

Patrick Sherlocks lands	x^{li}
Edmond Fitz Richard	v^{li}
Theobald Haked his lands	xiij^{li} vi viij^{d}
Walter Fitz Thomas	x^{li}
John Corre	x^{li}
Geoffrey White	xx^{li}
John Strich and Henry White . . .	xx^{li}
John Fitz Piers his lands^{a} . . .	vj^{li} viij^{s} iiij^{d}
John Moukelerke his lands . .	v^{li}
Thomas Trevers and his kinsmen . .	xl^{li}
Sir Theobald Butler his lands, . . .	cccl^{li}
Piers English and his kinsmen	xl^{li}
Thomas Fitz Theobald and his kinsmen .	xxx^{li}
Robert Ketinge and his kinsmen . . .	xxx^{li}
James Prendergast and his kinsmen . . .	cl^{li}
Morish English and his kinsmen . . .	xx^{li}
Edmond English and his kinsmen . .	xxx^{li}
John Ketinge and his kinsmen	l^{li}
Richard Ketinge and his kinsmen . . .	xl^{li}
The Bishopp of Waterford	xx^{li}
	m^{li} cccc xxxij^{li} vj^{s} viij^{d}.

Lands houlden of the Manno^{rs} of Nenaghe, Roscre, Templemore, and Thurles.

The White Knight his lands there . . .	c^{li}
Walter Bourke and his kinsmen	c^{li}
John Bourke and his kinsmen . . .	xl^{li}
Onaght by the yeare	x^{li}
Odowire and his kinsmen . . .	ij^{c} ij$^{c li}$
The Ryans theire lands	cl^{li}
McBrien arre his lands	cl^{li}
Ormond and all the Kenedies . . .	iij$^{c li}$
O'Caroll and his kinsmen in Ely . .	iiij$^{c li}$
O'Meagher and his kinsmen in Ykyrin .	c^{li}
O'Kahill his lands	xx^{li}
John O'Forgertie and his kinsmen . . .	xl^{li}

^{a} To make the sum total of this division correct, the amount at which these lands were valued should read vi^{li} xiij^{s} iiij.

and of Head Men and Commons of Town of Clonmel.

Walter Bourke and his kinsmen . xl^{li}
James Ashpole[a] and his kinsmen . . l^{li}
Thomas Purcell and his kinsmen . . . . c^{l}
Richard Reaghe Buttler . . . . xx^{li}
James Fitz Richard Butler and his cosen . xxx^{li}
Walter Archer his lands . . . . xl^{li}
Edmond Fitz Thomas Heding and his kinsmens lands . . . . xl^{li}
Thomas Fitz John Butler and his cosen . . . xx^{li}
Miles Cantwell his lands . . . . . . x^{li}
Piers Cantwell his lands . . . . . . xxx^{li}
Piers Butlers lands . . . . l^{li}
The Archbishopp of Cashell . . . . x^{li}
mml^{li}.

Lands houlden of the Manno^{r} of Kildenale in the Barony of Slieve ardaghe.

James Butlers lands . . . . lx^{li}
John Cantwell . . . . x^{li}
Richard Cantwell . . . . xv^{li}
Richard Cantwell . . . . vj^{li}
Thomas Stoke . . . . xx^{li}
James Laffen and his cosen . . . . . . xxx^{li}
William Fitz James . . . . iij^{li}
Thomas Butler and his kinsmen . . . . viij^{li}
Richard Marvell . . . . xv^{li}
Willm Fanninge . . . . l^{li}
William Fanninge . . . . xiij^{li} vj^{s} viij^{d}
James Mories . . . . v^{li}
ccxxxv^{li} vj^{s} viij^{d}.

Lands houlden of the Manno^{r} of Knockgraffen.

The Baron of Donboyne his lands, . . . iij$^{e\ li}$
John Butler his lands . . . . xl^{li}
Theobald Butlers lands . . . . . . xxx^{li}

[a] Probably Archbold.

Robert Saint Johns lands	xl^{li}
Richard Saint John	x^{li}
Richard Vale	xiij^{li} vj^s viij^d
Piers Oge Butlers lands	x^{li}
Willm Bryth his lands	vj^{li}
John Brythin his lands	vj^{li} xiij^s iiij^d
James Brithin his lands	vj^{li} xiij^s iiij^d
Edmond Mouckelereke	xl^{li}
Edmond Comen and his kinsmen	xxx^{li}
James Comen his lands	v^{li}
Melaghlin O'Carran	x^{li}
The Archbisshopp of Casshell	xl^{li}
Richard Salle his lands	x^{li}
Patrick Hackett	x^{li}
Piers Hackett his lands	x^{li}
John Hackett	viij^{li}
Edmond Hackett	xv^{li}
Edmond Comen and his kinsmen	xxx^{li}
Redmond Aylward	xxx^{li}
Richard Hackett	x^{li}
Tho: Vyn	xv^{li}
Robert Sawte	xx^{li}
Theobald Fitz Thomas Butler	viij^{li}
Thomas Fitz Theobald Butler	x^{li}
John Bromingham his land	v^{li}
Willm Moncell	viij^{li}
Darby O'Carran his land	vj^{li}
O'Kearny his land	x^{li}
John Kearny his land	x^{li}
Theobald Ashpole	xx^{li}
Andrew Hackett	x^{li}
James Fleming his land	x

viij^c xlij^{li} xiij^s iiij^d
Sū^a tot^{lis} vj^m ix^c lviij^{li}

[*Carew MS*. 635, p. 55.]

Woodes and Fastnes in Leinster.

Glandalour,[a] a fastnes in Pheagh Mc Hughes country.
Shilelagh,[b] S[r] Henric Harrington, in the countie of Dublin.
The Duffrin[c] in the countie of Wexford.
The Drones[d] and Leucrocke in the countie of Catherlagh.
The Great bogg in the Kinges countye which reacheth to Limericke.
The Fuse,[e] in the county of Killdare.
The woods and boggs of Mounster Euan.[f]
Gallin,[g] and Slewmarg[h] in the Queen's county.
The Roury[i] nere S[t] Mullins, where the Nur and Barrow meet together and make yt halfe an Island.
Parte of Couslcrarke,[k] joyninge upon the countie of Killkenny.

---

[a] Glenmalure, in the county of Wicklow.

[b] Shillelagh, now in the county of Wicklow, was famous for its oak woods, hence the proverbial name for an oak stick, "sprig of shillelagh."

[c] The Duffrey, lying between Enniscorthy and the mountains.

[d] Idrone. Leucrocke has not been identified.

[e] That is "the woody districts," from the Ir. ꝼeaḃa, woods.

[f] Monasterevan.

[g] Gallen, in the King's County, a district surrounded by bogs.

[h] Sliemargie, the hilly district between the Queen's County and Carlow.

[i] The Rower, county Kilkenny, naturally a very strong fastness shut in by the rivers Nore and Barrow and Brandon Hill. The name is derived from the Irish an ṛoḃaṛ, the red land, probably from the colour of the soil.

[k] Not identified.

PRESENTMENTS FOR THE COUNTY AND CITY OF CORK, MADE IN THE YEAR 1575.

THE county of Cork, lying remote from the metropolis, was naturally reached later by any measures of reform than the shires nearer the seat of Government. Although this region had been sheared off from Gaelic rule, and erected into a county at an early period, the Irish clans had so overwhelmed it, that in the fifteenth century its Anglo-Irish lords were nearly extinguished, and the King's laws were only known within the walls of its chief place, the city of Cork, and of Kinsale and Youghal. It appears from Spenser [p. 24], that these advances of the Irish were made under the leadership of a great warrior, named Murrough O'Brien en Ranagh. However, by mistaking the Duke of Clarence, brother of Edward IV., and Lord Lieutenant of Ireland, for a former Duke of Clarence, he has committed a wide anachronism of about a century. Murragh en Ranagh, or na Reithinidhe, of a junior branch of the O'Briens, lived in the reigns of Edward III. and his successor, as may be seen in Lodge's pedigree of the family, and in the Annals of the Four Masters. Spenser's relation is remarkable, but perhaps on account of the above error it has been overlooked by all the compilers of Irish history. He tells us that Murrough overran all Munster and Connaught, subverting all corporate towns that were not strongly walled, as Inchiquin, Killalow, Thurles, Mourne, Buttevant, and many others, and made himself king, and was called king of all Ireland. The peasantry about Mourne Abbey ruin have a curious version of the destruction of the place. They say that the town of

Mallow, five miles distant, was formerly there. There is an inquisition relating to Mourne, taken in the reign of Elizabeth, which might allude to these events. The Annals of the Four Masters make comparatively slight mention of Murrough, and say he died of the plague in 1383, but he is mentioned some years later in the Close Rolls. Leinster escaped his ravage by payments of money. The government seem to have been entirely powerless before him. (See five orders on this matter in the printed Close Rolls of 1 Ric. II., and others at the 8th and 17th of the same reign.)

The fact of the great decay of the English power in Munster is curiously evidenced by the ensuing passage from Campion's "Historie of Ireland," quoting an ancient and remarkable letter, from the Records of Christ Church, Dublin :—

"In this Kings raigne, [Henry IV.], the inhabitants of the county and towne of Corke, being tyred with perpetuall oppressions of their Irish borderers, complained themselves in a generall writing, directed to the Lord of Rutheland and Corke[a], the King's Deputy, and to the Councell of the Realme, then assembled at Divelin, which letter because it openeth the decay of these partes, and the state of the Realme in times past, I have thought good to enter here as it was delivered me, by *Francis Agard*, Esquire, one of her Majesties privy Councell in Ireland.

"'It may please your wisdomes, to have pittie of us the Kings poore subjects, within the county of Corke, or else we be cast away for ever, for where there was in this countie these Lords by name, besides Knights, Esquires, Gentlemen, and Yeoman, to a great

---

[a] Edmond Plantagenet, grandson of Edward III., was created Earl of Rutland and Cork, 13 Ric. II. (1390). He was killed at the battle of Agincourt, in 1415; and does not appear to have been viceroy of Ireland. He left no issue. Richard Plantagenet, Duke of York, bore the same titles, and was Lord Lieutenant of Ireland in the year 1449.

number, that might dispend yearlie 800. pounds, 600. pounds, 400. pounds, 200. pounds, 100. pounds, 100. markes, 20. pounds, 20. markes, 10. pounds, some more, some lesse, to a great number, besides these Lords following.

"'First, the Lord Marquese[a] *Caro*[b] his yearely revenues was besides Dorzey Hauen and other Creekes, 2200. pounds sterling.

"'The Lord *Barnevale*[c] of Bearehaven, his yearely revenues was, besides Bearehaven and other Creekes, 1600. pounds sterling.

"'The Lord *Vggan*[d] of the great Castle, his yearely revenues was, besides havens and creekes, 1300. pounds sterling.

"'The Lord *Balram* of Emforte, his yearely revenues was, besides havens and creekes, 1300. pounds sterling.

"'The Lord *Courcy* of Kilbrotton[e] his yearely revenues, besides havens and creeks, 1500. pounds sterling.

"'The Lord *Mandevil*[f] of Barrenstelly his yearely revenues, besides havens and creekes, 1500. pounds sterling.

[a] This term was applied to Barons, who were lords marchers, or governors of frontier districts.

[b] Sir George Carew, Earl of Totness, mentions his Anglo-Irish ancestors as Marquesses Carew; and Sir Warham St. Leger, of Kerrycurrihy, observes, in a state paper of 1589:—"The Great Cogan, the Marques Caroo, Yfee Stephens, Desmond, &c., some enjoyed 40,000 marks yearly revenue."

[c] The Barnewelles came from the place of that name in Western Normandy, and were settled at an early period in the Pale. They seem to have emigrated from the Pale into Cork. We find Barnewelles of the Pale mentioned long before those of the County Cork. (See Lodge, vol. 6, p. 22.)

[d] *Cogan* became *Goggin* and *Gaggin* in many branches, some of whom have resumed the form Cogan. Holingshed spells this name "Wogan," but erroneously. Sir John Wogan, the well-known Lord Justice of Ireland in the time of Edward II., was probably an Englishman. Among the barons summoned to the Parliament of Kilkenny by writs, tested by Wogan, was John de Cogan. (See Lynche's "Legal Institutions of Ireland," p. 312.) The Lords Cogan of the County Cork descended from the famous invader, Myles de Cogan, whose name was taken from the place of this name in Glamorganshire. The "great castle" was Carrigaline, alias Beauvoir, as to which there is a curious legend, illustrative of the extinction of these Lords Cogan.

[e] Kilbritton Castle passed from the Lords Courcy to the Irish sept, M[c]Carty Reagh.

[f] There was also a baronial family of Mandeville in Ulster, but almost extirpated by Bruce's invasion, which was bravely opposed by their chief.

"'The Lord *Arundell*[a] of the strand his yearly revenues, besides havens and creekes, 1500. pounds sterling.

The Lord *Baron*[b] of the Guard his yearly revenues, besides havens and creekes 1100. pounds sterling.

"'The Lord *Sleynie*[c] of Ballimore his yearly revenue, besides havens and creekes, 800. pounds sterling.

"'The Lord *Roche*[d] of Poole-castle[e] his yearly revenue, besides havens and creekes 1000. pounds sterling.

"'The King's Majesty hath the lands of the late young *Barry* by forfeiture, the yearly revenue whereof, besides two rivers and creekes, and all other casual ties is, 18000. pounds sterling.

"'And at the end of this Parliament, your Lordship with the Kings most noble Councell may come to Corke, and call before you all these Lords and other Irish men, and binde them in paine of

---

[a] The name of Arundel is hardly met with in our archives. Smith says, in his "History of Cork," that the remains of Arundel Castle, on the strand of Ibawn, are still to be seen. Spenser notices the decay of this lord.

[b] Lord Barrett, of the Guard. This family came from South Wales. Some settled in Connaught. This Cork house is that of which the anecdote is told of Hugh O'Neill, Earl of Tyrone, who, on his being pointed out the residence of Barrett, as of an Anglo-Irish Catholic lord, whose ancestors had come over four hundred years before, replied that he hated the churl as much as if they had come but yesterday.

[c] Lord Sleynie, of Baltimore, may have been Steinie, or Fitz Stephen, a descendant of the first invader, Robert Fitz Stephen. Gerald Fitz James Mac Sleyney, captain of his nation, in the cantred of Imokilly, County Cork, sold Rostellan Manor, in 1565, to John Geraldine. [Patent Rolls, 5 James I. p. 117.] Certainly, this surname, however spelt, was identical with the "Yfee Stephens" mentioned, in 1589, by Sir Warham St. Leger as the name of one of the ancient magnates of Munster. Stephenson became one form of this family's surname. We find an Edward or Edmond Stephenson, of Dungarvan, County Waterford, whose daughter was second wife of Sir Robert Carew, of Garrivoe Castle, in the County of Cork, Knight, living temp. Car. I.

[d] Roche of Poole Castle was Viscount Roche of Fermoy.

[e] Shippool Castle (?), near Innishannon, now the property of the Henicks. Philip Roche, of Kinsale, obtained a licence from Henry VIII., in 1546, to bring provisions from England, "to the intent that the said Philip Roche, &c., should buylde a castle near unto the ryver Glasselyn, in Co. Cork." This castle, a great part of which is still standing, was completed within three years. It is called by the Irish, Poul-na-long.

losse of life, lands and goods, that never any of them doe make warre upon another, without licence or commandement of you my Lord Deputy and the Kings Councell, for the utter destruction of these parts, is that onely cause, and once all the Irish men and the Kings enemies were driven into a great valley, called Glanehought,[a] betwixt two great mountains, called Maccorte, or the leprous Iland,[b] and their they lived long and many yeares, with their white meat[c] till at last these English Lords fell at variance among themselves, and then the weakest part tooke certaine Irish men to take his part, and so vanquished his enemy, and thus fell the English Lords at variance among themselves, till the Irish men were stronger then they, and drave them away, and now have the whole country under them; but that the Lord *Roche*, the Lord *Courcy*, and the Lord *Barry* onely remaine, with the least part of their auncestors possessions, and young *Barry* is there upon the Kings portion, paying his Grace never a penny Rent. Wherefore we the Kings poore subjects of the Citty of Corke, Kinsale, and Yowghall, desire your Lordship to send hither two good Iustices to see this matter ordered, and some English Captaines with twenty English men, that may be Captaines over us all, and we will rise with them to redresse those enormities all at our owne costs, and if you doe not, we be all cast away, and then farewell Mounster for ever. And if you will not come nor send, we will send over to our Liege Lord, the King, and complaine on you all.' Thus farre the letter.

"And at this day the Citty of Corke is so encumbered with unquiet neighbours of great power,[d] that they are forced to watch

[a] Glanarought, viz., Glenaroughty, the great valley near Kenmare.

[b] The Lepers' Island, where lepers lived secluded, as in the many "Lizard's Points," i. e. promontories set apart for lazars. This demonstrates the seclusion of this last fastness of the Munster Irish.

[c] White-meats is a term still in use to express milk and butter, which are allowed during Lent.

[d] In August, 1548, the Mayor of Cork writes to the Lord Deputy, informing him, among other particulars, that one Tyrry, a bailiff, on going to Lord Barrymore to claim lands withheld by his lordship's clan, was "murdered by 23 foynes of an Irish knife, given him into the very heart." In reply, the Viceroy says he "will speak to the Earl of Desmond," to see the murderers punished. A some-

their gates continually, to keepe them shut at service times, at mcales, from sunne set, to sunne arising; nor suffer any stranger to enter there with his weapon, but to leave the same at a lodge appointed. They walke out for recreation at seasons, with strength of men furnished, they match in wedlock among themselves, so that welnigh the whole city is allyed together. It is to be hoped that the late sent over Lord President of Mounster, Sir John Parrott, who hath chosen the same place to abide in, as having greatest neede of a Governour resident, would ease the inhabitants of this feare, and scourge the Irish outlawes that annoy the whole region of Munster, pp. 94-96."

The citizens of this splendid sea-port town, who so what similar case occurred in the Co. of Cork, so lately as 1740, when Mr. John Swete writes from Greenwich as follows:—" Dear Brother—My uncle has ordered me to signify to you he had a letter lately from our sister Ann, complaining of the barbarous treatment her husband met with at Killglass, where, upon only demanding the interest due to him in right of his wife, Cousin Ben Swete fired a pistol loaded with ball at him," &c. This Ben Swete's son was High Sheriff of the County of Cork, in 1799. It does not appear, however, that the shot took effect. The recipient of the letter transmitted a copy of it to the delinquent, among whose papers it has remained. The brother of the latter (John Swete) in the same year applies to him for interest money, and as he was Mayor of Cork in 1758, and also father-in-law of the famous Henry Sheares, we add what he writes:—" Cork, 23rd February, 1740.—Dear Brother—As Mr. Winthrop is so kind as to offer me a sum of money at the current interest, if he was secured, and as it's high time for me to look about and do something for myself in order to get an honest livelihood, that I should not be an incumbrance to my relations (for without a sufficiency, one has but a dull reception to visit on courtesy to most friends), therefore I must beg the favour of you (if you regard my interest), that you will bring when next you come to town your account with me in order to settle, as I'm sure it's high time. It's hard to have neither interest or principal paid me. You're sensible my calling requires a stock, and that I cannot put myself forward in the world without having my fortune paid me or some part of it, as I can put it to much better advantage than to have it at interest. I can't tell if my uncle will give me more than he has, so I intend to carry on my business with what I can put together of my own stock, and pursue the world for a maintenance. I am, with great regard, your affectionate brother, John Swete.—Addressed to Mr. Benjn Swete, Killglass."

boldly threatened to complain to the Crown against the Lord Lieutenant, did not improve their character for loyalty by the part taken in the matter of Perkin Warbeck, whose cause was warmly espoused by their Mayor. The true surname of this official, who is styled in history, O'Walter,[a] is mentioned in the ensuing record. Other old surnames in this city became naturally corrupted. The Myagh family, originally it would seem Celtic, changed their name to Meade;[b] and Golys became Gould. The original record of the oath of fealty, taken by the citizens of Cork after Perkin Warbeck's affair, is preserved in the Public Record Office, London. The document commences :—

"The othe of the Citesyns and cōes of the Cite of Cork and the Towne of Kynsale, made unto our soʃayn Lord Kyng Henry the VIIth, the xv day of October the yere of the reyne of our said sov lord, the xiii, before the right noble Lord Gerald, Erle of Kyldare, Depute Lieutenant of Ireland and the Kynges Counsell of the same."

The signatures are "John Wat', Mauric' Roche, Armig', Thomas Sheperd, Edw' Tyrry', Joh' Lawallyor, Jac',

[a] "Walter," was the name. It is now "Waters." In the great island on Cork harbour, on the ruins of a castle called Waterstown or Watertown. 38 Eliz. James Water a!s. M[c] I Watiarig de Ballinwatiarig, in the Great Island, Co. Cork, granted to Mainea Romayne, Ballinwatiarig and Kelemuckerie, in said Island, on a bond for twenty-three pounds. October 1, 1595.—A controversy arose between Moris Ronayne of Cork, gent., and James Waters a!s. Mac I Watiarig of Waterstown, gent., touching the right of Ballinwatiarig a!s Waterstown, Kilemuckerie, Bally M[c]Rorane in Barries Island, Co. Cork. Both parties submitted to the award of Thos. Sanfield of Cork, Ald., and Edmond Barry of Ballynegall, gent., &c.

[b] Yet there is very early mention of this name in Latin documents as "de Midin," the name of the province of Meath.

Myagh, Will' Golys, Edw' Golys, Will Tyrry, Gerald Golys, Ric' Galwey," &c.

Several feudal and Gaelic exactions, once customary in this shire, are noticed in certain documents published in 1853, in the "Gentleman's Magazine." These records are ancient deeds between the Lords Barrymore, and one of the Tyrrys of Cork, containing freedom from, and reservation of, certain exactions, such as "Cwmry" or "Curnry," "Aghyny," "Soryhyn," or "Sorghyn," "Conhyrt," "Srach," "Rahgrynty" or "Kehyrycy," "Ryell Serviss" (viz. royal service), "Kynduoff," and "Kehyrynty."

The first Earl of Desmond was the first nobleman of his rank that rebelled against the Crown, and raised himself and family to great power by adopting Irish exactions. In 1345, Lord Justice Ufford subdued "Mac Thomas More," Earl of Desmond, and seized the person of his Seneschal, whom, having exercised, held, and invented many grievous, foreign, and intolerable laws, he caused to be hung, and his quarters suspended in divers parts of Munster,[a] in memory of his tyranny.

According to Dowling, the eighth Earl of Desmond was the first who burdened the counties of Waterford, Cork, Kerry, and Limerick, with Irish impositions, such as "mercuniis, carragiis, pedagiis, et customis;" and this annalist says, that the Earl was executed in 1462, on account of these exactions, and for outrages against the King's peace and laws. The following copies of two documents in the State Paper Office, written at the time of the extinction of that great house, elucidate the nature of the various exactions levied by these Earls and other Anglo-

---

[a] Clyn's Annals.

Irish chieftains, and thereby explain the general scheme of these presentments :—

> 1587. *Names of Rents, in money, victuals, and customs, which were due to the late Desmond.*

Shraughe. W^{ch} is a yearlie rent in sterlinge mony.

Marte. It is a yearelie rent of beofe.

Cheeffrey. It is a rente certaine uppone lande, paienge halfe face money, wch is the third p^t better then sterlinge.[a]

Choyney. A charge of meate & drincke for the time *sans nomb*.

Lyvery. A charge of horse wth otes, corne, haie, and strawe, *sans nomb*.

Kearnety. A charge [of] iii^s iiii^d or iiii^s uppon a plowlande, towardes the maintenance of the Earle's kerne, c. cc. or ccc. men, more or les.

Sorren. A charge set uppon the freeholders landes for a nomb certaine for certaine daies in a qarter, of galloglasses.

Galloglas. A nomb of soldiers, to put the contrie to charge, bearinge axes.

Kearne. A nomb of soldiers to aide & assist the Justices, seneshalls, receavors, stewardes of courtes, & serjeantes, in the execuc͠on of the lawes and customes of the contries and terretories of the said late Earles, for the rule and governement of his people and landes, and the receavenge, leauienge, and gatheringe of his reveewes.

Bonnibeg & Bonugbar: were soldiers kept in readines as well in peace as in warre, at the charges, wth meate, drinke, & wages.

Musteroon. A charge set uppon the contry to helpe the Earle in his workes, wth cappells, garrons, & men at his owne will.

Taxe & Tallage, als *Southe.* A connuocac͠on of all tenantes, freeholders and inhabitantes, to helpe to paie the Earles debtes or to helpe him to mony at his neede.

---

[a] i. e. The silver shillings and groats with the profile of Elizabeth, 9 oz. fine to 3 alloy, coined in 1561, before which year her "sterling" half-face money was of the same standard as the base money of Philip and Mary, viz., 3 oz. fine and 9 alloy. The latter weighed 130 grains, and the former only 70, however, which would make the relative value about as stated above.

Reecton. Is only repast and away.
Cosshery. Is a chardge of the Erle's people for lodginge xl., lx.. or c. together under one roofe.
Cuddy. Is a charge of meales meate and drinck, the time he hath his people in Coshery.
Gillicree. Is as muche to saie in Englishe, as a stoode-keep allowed, to be maintained by his tenants.
Gillycon. Is as muche to saie as dogg-keep, or huntseman, in like manner allowed.

These exactions are more fully explained in the following State Paper, drawn up in May, 1589, by Sir Warham St. Leger:—

The Nature of Sorowhen landes and other chargeable lands in Ireland.

Sorrowhen doth warrant the Lorde to come once in everye foorteen daies with all his company without lymitation of an certeyn number, to the lands and tenements founde by Office to be charged therewith, and to take meat and drinck for him, and his said Company of the inhabitants 't freeholders of the said lands the space of xxiv howers.

Gullycon, viz. the keepers 't huntsmen of the Lords hounds are warranted by that tenure to take by waye of cesse sufficient meat and drink for themselves 't their said hounds of every the freeholders inhabitants of the said country, so that they remayne but one daie 't night with every inhabitant or tenant.

Gullycree, viz. keepers of the Lords stoode are warranted, with their said stood, to come to the wast lands of the said country, and to pasture and graze upon the said wast land, 't to take meate 't drinck of the next inhab^ds for themselves, and to be in number so many as please the Lord to appoint.

Cuddye, called a night supper, doth warrant the Lord with such company as pleaseth him to come to the lands charged with that tenure, and to take meat 't drink for him and his company of the inhab^ts thereof the space of iiij meales at iiij tymes of the yere.

Kerntye viz. the overseers 't controwlers of the Sargeaunts, of which Kerntye there should be xii in number. They to examine the demeanours of the said Sargeaunts whether they deceive the Lord of any part of his rent and duties, 't to cesse his horsemen 't footmen from tyme to tyme, and in consideration thereof they may take meat 't drinck of the inhabitants of the said country.

South is that the Lord, towards his maynteynaunce eyther to Dublyn or to any corporat townes, he may impose his charges upon the inhabitants of his country, and in like sort he may distribute among them his chardges bestowed in receiving the Governor, or anye other straunger of countenance, into his house.

Mustron is when the Lord hath any wourck to buyld, then every inhabitant so to help with his own laboure during the said wourck.

Connewe 't *Lyvery* is to exact impose 't take horse meat, 't mans meat, 't boyes meat of all the inhabitants in the countrye, so long as please the lord.

Besides xiij^s iiij^d sterling out of every plowe land inhabited, 't vi^s viij^d cesse of every waste plowland.[a]

---

[a] It is to be observed that the above exactions were the only rents which tenants paid for their land. Spenser (p. 53), says, "they were never wont, and yet are loath to yield any certain rent but only such spendings, for their common saying is, '*spend me and defend me.*'" He remarks that the statute against these exactions was unjust to the landlord, and truly enough, as he was entitled to no other rent. There were somewhat similar exactions in England at that time from copyhold lands.

The Presentment of James Ronane and his associates at the Sess[ions] houlden at Corke before S^r W[illiam] Drewry Knight Lord President [of] Mounster and other his asis[tants] in October 1576.

Wee present that the Erle of Desmound the ixth of June in the xviiith yere of the Queens Ma^{tys} Raigne that nowe is, haith sett nyne scorre men and certaine horses uppon cony and lyvery uppon the freeholders and inhabitaunce of Imokylly wthin this county of Corke, and so contynued for the space of foure weeks.

Wee present that the Lo. or Vicu'nt Barrymoorr and his sonnes do sinnce the pelamaĉōn use cony and liverie wthin his L^{ps} countrey.

Wee present that Sr Cormock McTegg used connye and lyverie wthn his country senne the pelamaĉōn made to the contrary, and also haith boenny beggy^a and keyerhintye^b wthin his countrey.

Wee present that the Earle of Clancartie in Donogh, and the Lo. Roches sonnes, do senne the pelamaĉōn use conny and liverie wthin their countries.

We present that the Vicount Roiche doth not suffer eny of his mannors nor the lands thereunto bellonginge nor any other landes that he haith or that he houldith frome eny of his freeholders ether by purchase or otherwise, nor eny of the lands apperteyng to his sonnes to be chardged nor contributarie to eny the Queens [cesse] or otherwise that is sett upon his cuntrye.

We present that the vicount Barry doth not suffer any his mannors nor the lands of the same to be chardged nor contributarie to eny the Quens cesse or otherwise that is sett uppon his cuntrye.

Wee present that Willm Barry, alias Barry Rowe^c doth not suffer

---

^a Bonnach-beg, i. e. small tribute for hired men.

^b Ceitherne-tighe, i. e. kerne of the chief's house.

^c Barry-*Roe*, or the Red Barry, the title of a chief of a sept of the Barrys. According to Lodge, The Barryroe at this time was named James fitz Richard Barry, who in 1557 had succeeded his cousin as Visct. Buttevant. (See vol. 1., p. 292.) But in this presentment The Barryroe and Visct. Barry are treated as different persons.

any of his thre mannors nor the lands thereto belonginge to be chardged in contributary to eny the Queens Ma^{ts} cesse that is sett uppon Barry Rowes countrey.

We present that as oft as any Lord or gent'man, of what degree so evere he be, that comith w^t a traine of horsemen or foottmen, or both, to the Vicunt Barrye, Vicount Roch, S^r McTeigg,[a] or to eny others the lords of this countie, and requireth mans meat and horsmeat for his said Traine, the same lord, of whome the same is asked, doth cesse all the same traine uppon the freholders and Inhabitannts of his cuntry, and so continue duringe the same Lords pleasure to the great suppresing of the said Inhabitance, &c.

Wee present that all the lords of this country useth this extorc̃on, that is to say to tak upp for thire rents, and other duties whatsoever, halffaced money,[b] whereof right they shuld have but currant money of the Realme.

We present that John Offynnygan, vicar of Lyslye, and steward to the Vicunt Barry, in Barry Rowes countrye, the vi^th of May or thereabouts in the xviii^th yere of the raigne of o^r soveraine lady that now is, haith taken for cony and livery at Tymolaggy w^thin this countie twoo mylch kynne of the good and cattells of Willam Omeirran of the same clercke.

We present that James bwy McThomas M^cE[nny] alias dict', Bashy Riough of Rossegrelly in the countie of Watterford, Kernagh, and McEnny Bo[gh] sonne to David Fitz John of Killhaily in the countie aforsaid, Kirnagh, the xxiiii^th of Sept. in the xviii^th yere of the Raigne of o^r sov̊aign ladie Quene Elizabeth, have felonyusly stollen from Castell Oliaghan and Bally Anisherry in the countie of Corke. four caples of sond[re] coullers, vallwed every caple xl^s st^rling, of the goods 't cattells of John Moell of Castell Oliaghan aforesaid and his sonne James Fitz John.

We present that Fynyne Ganegaht of Emeastic of Glanewoller, Kirnaghe, and Tegg Nabully of Gallane, both in this countie, horsmen, of the followers of McCartic Roigh, about the xv^th of Maye in

---

[a] Sir Cormac mac Teige Mac Carthy.

[b] Half-faced money were the silver groats and shillings of Elizabeth, coined in 1561, which, as appears by a statement at p. 366, supra, were one third more value than the current coin.

the xviii[th] yere of the raigne of o[r] soʋagne Laidye Queen Elizabeth, have slain at Gort Crosse w[th]in this countie, Dermond Odonovane of Carrybrighe gentellmane.

We present that Owen M[c]Carttye and Donyll M[c]Cartye, britherne to M[c]Cartie Roughe, and Fynyne M[c]Cartie,[a] sonne to the said M[c]Cartie Roughe, Do dayly at thire plasure tak meat and drinck, w[th] force and extorcon, for themselves and their traine of horsemen, galloglashe and kerne, of the frehoulders and Inhabitaunce of Carrybrighe, and bysides they tak of the same freholders and Inhabitaunce a some of money called cowe, to the number of fyve marks half face money yerly, in every people w[th]in Carrybrygh, against the will of the freholders and inhabitaunc, and also of the cessor of the cuntrye.

We p[r]sent that when the lord Deputie, the lord President, or any the commissioners, or any other Englishe mane cometh to the house of the said Vicunt Barrye, Vicount Roch, or any other lords of the cuntrye, the same lo. to whose house the same cometh, takith and rereth upp of the freholders and inhabitance of the cuntry as much Beoffes, money and corne as pleasith him, in recompence of such chardges and expences as he haith then bestowed, and will not be content to tak as much as he bestowed himself, but will tak thre or foure tymes so much then of the said frehoulders and inhabitaunce.

We p[r]sent that Will[a]m Barry, alias Barry Rowe, useth most comonly every night to take meat t drinck for him and his traine otherwishe called cosshirrie[b] by way of Earryth[c] s͠rvice of the frehoulders and inhabitants of his country, against their wills, and useth cony and livery within his country synce the pelamacōn and also haith Kerrentye, &c.

Wee p[r]sent that vicount Barray and vicount Roche, when the mary eny of their doughters, They tak all thee maraidg goods of kyne and caples of the frehoulders and the inhabitants of their

---

[a] This Fynyne was the famous Florence M'Carthy. (See his "Life and Letters," lately published by Daniel M'Carthy, Glasgow.)

[b] Cosshirrie, *Ciosa-rie*, i. e. cess for the king.

[c] "Earryth service," probably *eirreacht*. An "eriot" is defined in the glossary to the printed State Paper at a meeting where brehons gave judgment.

severall countryes, and if any of the frehoulders will refuse to paie the same, they will send their s^rvants to distraine for it as though it weare of very right due unto them, and if every of them had Twentie daughters they will never part of there owne kyne and caples to their maraidges but will make their severall frehoulders to pay the same.

Wee present that all the other lords of the countrey useth the lick extorc̃on, some by waye of peticõn, wch the frehoulders dare not denye, and some by compulsion as aforsaid expressed.

We p^rsent that the Vicount Barry useth this extorc̃on, that is to saye, To tak upp to his owne use, in lewe of cony and liverie and other exaccõns, the third parte of every frehoulders lande w^thin this country, and, when it pleasith his lord, he selleth the same thre parts to whom he listith as thoughe it weare his oune pper lande, and the other fourth p'te, wch he suffriet the frehoulder to have as fredome, shal be chardged wth all ceasses and other burdens that is sect uppon the country.

Wee present that the Vicount Roch useth the lick extorcion, and also when eny freholder w^thin his country doth not manne and occupie his oune lande, whereby to beare the exaccons of the country, his lord taketh that freholders land to his honors use, and will not suffer the frehoulder to receive any p'te of the frute of his owne land, nor will not suffer eny other to occupy the same for the poor frehoulder.

We present that we cane fynde no due proof for the Transport-inge any staple warre for [frō?] this cittie, how be it we perceve it is done by reson the said wares waxeth dearer then they weare wont to be afore the statute for the same provided.

We p^rsent that when any lo. or gent'mã of the Irishry w^thin this countie is made lord or captaine of his name or kindritie, taketh of ev̄y inhabitant, freholder and ten^ant under him a cowe, to be paid for receving a rodd in that name.^a

---

^a This levy was called "Rod money," and its object, to provide the new chief-tain with a stock of cattle, instead of following the old custom of *Sluaigheadh ceadnais raidhne*, or the excursion on receiving the headship, described by Martin in his "Western Isles," and which, besides giving proof of the capacity of the new chief in plundering, supplied him with cattle. The rod was handed to the chief or king during the inaugural ceremony, at the same time naming him, as "McCarthy-more," &c.

We p{r}sent that all the lords of this country usethmaner of extorc̃ons viz: That when anye frehoulder or inhabitant w{th}in their severall countries is maried, the rumor[a] of that lord caulled Olaff Danie[b] will take the best apparaill of the womane so maried or the juste value thereof.

We p{r}sent that the vicount Roch takith custome of everye thing that is bought by a m̃chant mane w{th}in his country, viz. out of ev̂y xx{d} a peny.

We p{r}sent that all the lords of this country, to coloure and mantaine there owne extorcions, have wrought such a pollicie to entertaine all the lawiers of this province, whereby no freholder nor poore mane cane have a lawier to speek in his cause be it never so just.

Of a great many of the extorcioũs in this book contained we might mak more certaine and speciall presentments then is done But that wee assuredly knowe if we should name the frehoulders or inhabitantes uppon [whom] the extorcions weare made, his lord woulde thinck that it should be that frehoulder or inhabitante that should enforme the court thereof, And that therefore the lord would seke all the waies that he could for the utter banyshment of the freholder, and his posterictie.

We present that all those whose names ensueth are notorius and open malefactorus, theefes, receptors of theefte, and commone disturbers of the common quiet of the countrye.

Malefactors—
    S{r} John of Desmonds men :
Remond M{c}Garrald of Broell[c] in the countie of [blank] gentellmane.

Kynagher Kiegh O Connyll, kernaghe, of the mē and retaine or the said Readmonde.

---

[a] Rhymer.
[b] Olamh Daun, i. e. Professor of Poetry.
[c] The Fitzgeralds of Broghill were of an older branch than the later Earls of Desmond; for the 6th Earl, having made an inferior marriage, was deprived of the Earldom by his uncle, who had the transfer conferred by Parliament. The deposed Earl had two sons, from the youngest descended the Fitzgeralds (here called M{c}Garrald), of Broghill, in the county of Cork. (See Lodge's "Irish Peerage.")

Moryshe O Comane of Kilmore, kernaghe.
Shane McKnogher McDonoghe Yeonnyll of the same, kernaghe.
Redmande Bwye londry, kirnaghe, of the said Redmond McGaroldes men.

Theobald Roches men:

Davie Offlvyn alias McErragh tirry, kernaghe, Owen O Morrowchowe, als Bodelier, of Cosorydy, kernaght.
Mahowne Occollaine of Conner Ellanes mē.
Tegg Olleighe, kernaghe.
Dermod Murrier Occollaine, Kernaghe, als boodde conwtiesse.
Teigg Duffe McDonogh Yeollane, kernaghe.

Carybrye:

Fynyne McDonyll vic Fynyne of Killyne in Carribrie.
Donell McFynyne father to the said fynyne McDonnell.

The said Fynyne McDonells men:

Donell Keigh, kernaghe.
Teigg Ballyf his brother, kernagh.
Thomas Ballagh, kernaghe.
Teigg Oteremon his brother, kernaghe.
Tegg Nestolly, kernagh.
Skufweary, kernaghe.

Notoriuse malefactors viz.:

Donogh McDonell McCormock, of Ballygonyeshy in Musery, his men.
Knoghoure buy Mc a Wockane, kernaghe.
Denys O Heallychic, kernaghe.
Davie Duffe, kernaghe.

Of the Whitt Knights countrye viz.:

Knoghoure McThomas Nagearr.
Moriertagh Kane McThomas Nagearr, bothe britherine and kernaghes.

The presentment of John Miagh Fitz Robarts and his associates at the Sessions houlden at Cork before Sr Will'm Drewrye, knight L. President of Mounster and other his associates in October 1576.

We present that Teigg Ettarremon McOwen and Donyll Keigh McThomas McTeigg, of Poble Ycallyghan, not only to be notoriuse theeffes but also wrongfully cam in August, the xviith yere of the Queens Magisties raigne that now is, wth force and armes, viz. in the night tyme, to Bernchelly in the county of Corcke and thene and their thre caples price iiii^l st^r of the goodes and cattells of Morrice Mirre, husb, and others of Wiltm Grogaves tenants, there fownde, felloniously toke and lead awaye contrarie to her Maties peace.

We present that Owen McAwley sonne to McAwley, Diermod Douff McShane McMorighe, Donoche McShane McMahowne Yvorchowe,[a] Donylloghe Schigane, Dermonde Duff McShane McDermod McMorighe, in Januarye, in the Queens Ma^{ts} Raigne that now is vxith, wrongfully came w^t force and armes viz. betwixt Killvyne [and] Killetowhill in the countye of Cork and then and their feloniously and traiterously have murthered Rickard McMahowny I Conell contrarye, 'tc.

We present that [. . .]nogh Fitz Edmound McShihe, the twoo sonnes of Farre Doroghe Fitz Wiltm McBrien, named Manus and Edmond Mergaighe, Rery Fitz Morrighe McTyrrelaghe, w^t diverse otherese unknowne malefactors the xvth daye of Maie, in the yere of the raigine of o^r soūaigne Ladie Queene Elizabeth that nowe is the xvith 'tc. wrongfully came wth force and armes viz. 'tc. to Killnegorie in the countie of Cork and then and their fyve pound ster. of readie money, foure bredyne mantells, price every mantell fyve shellings str., twoo caddowes, price every cadowe fyve shellings str., towoo shoettes, price every sheet iii^s str., to milch kynne, price xx^s st$\tilde{}$ling, of the goodes and cattells of Fraunces Terrie, of Corke ñchant, and others the inhabitaunce of Kilnegloric aforsaid, there found, feloniously toke, and lead awaye feloniously, and also then 't

[a] i. e. Cmorchowe.

there have w^t force and violence traitoriuslily ravished xii womē, of the wch some weare married and some meaydes, 'tc.

We present that the Erle of Clancare through owte all his country doth use cony and liverye, sorehen, sraghe, bcoffes, w^t such Irish extorcōn, wth all his freholders and tenants that will not geve him so m'ch lande or pay him so m'ch rents accordinge to his ounc contentacōn, so that the poor freholders are in a worse case nowe then evere befor, wch for their eires they dare not complaine the countrary.

We prsent that the vicount Barry, and in the Earle of Desmonds countrye, the use, in lick'wies, cony and liverie, soroghen, sraghe and beoves w^t m'ch other Irishe extorcōns of eVy freholder and tenants wthin their severall countryes, so that the poor freholders 't tenants are in worse case then ever befor.

We do present that the vicōunt Roch and Sr Cormock McTeiggh in their severall country do use the lick extorcōn by cony and livery, sorohan, sraghe, bcoffes, and such other lick, uppon the freholders and tenants, they for their cares dare not complaine to the contrarie, 'tc.

We present that all kind of staple and phibited warres are dayly transported owt of the cittie of corkf, Yowgholl, Kinsale and other places of Mounster, yea more, now this lat yeres, since Philpott came to the office of serchershipp then any tyme afore, and that so privilee or rather so craftily used, betwixt the sercher and the transporter that no proof or sufficient knowledg may be had, But the excedinge woonted highe price of all such wares nowe doth beare sufficient wittnes ye the same is transported wth owt any lett, but onlye to agree w^t the sercher or his deputie, 'tc. contrarie, 'tc.

We p^{r}sent that stellers^a and regraters of the markett of Cork cannot be presented, and that by resone that we have no market daie nor howre appointed nor kept accordingly, but every one buying where he lieste, when he liste, or what time he listeth, and as m'ch as he listeith, so that where one haith to m'ch, twentie haith nothinge, to the utter undoing of many, wch weare very necessarye to be reformed 'tc.

---

^{a} i. e. Forestallers.

We p^rsent that one Dermond Odayly in the name and to the use of Odaly Fynyne^a came to Kile Weybowd in the countie of Cork in June last past, in the yere of the raigne of o^r soũaigne Laidy Queen Elizbeth that now is the xviiii^th, haith forceably taken of Margeret Ny Scally of the said Kile waiebowed all the rayment that shee did weare, that day being newly marcid, or else the valwe of the same, to his oune contentacõn, alleadginge the same to be due to the forsaid Odayley of everye womane that is maried throughowt all Desmond and McDonoghe countrye, because he is their cheef Rymor otherwise cauled Olowe dane, contrarie 'tc.

We present that the Earle of Clancare, McCartic Reoughe, Sr Cormock McTegg and McDonogh do wrongfully rere of their cane poble,^b as to say Omahowny, Odonovane, Odriescalle, O Kieffe, O Hierlighe, and many such lick under them 'tc., a number of kynne or some of money for deli?ing them a rodd when they come, to their name, or some, wch some of money or number of kyne everie of the said kane poble do also wrongfully rere and take upp of their poor ten^ants, and also do not onlye reare upp of their poore tenants cony, liverys, cudihe, kyndufe, sraghe, beof, w' all Irishe exactions in as ample manner as evere the have ben accostomed befor, but also maraidge good for their doughters, their cost, and chardges when they are called to every sessions or hostilitie, to the utter undoinge of their afforesaid poor tenants, 'tc., contrarie 'tc.

We p^rsent also that the most part of the lords or gent' of the countie of Corck, have cutt no paces in the highe waie, w^thin their countries, as they and everie of them were straightly chardged and comanded by the lat lord President and her Ma^ts Commissioners, to the exceeding great danger of all faithfull travillers going in the aforesaid paces, and further that no pointe, to speck of it, of that pclamacõn then made, was not accomplyshed by none of them all accordinglie, not as m'ch as to kepp the stocks in places apointed for to punyshe stowt beggers, Idell vacabounds, naked

---

^a O'Daly Fineen was the title given to the head of a sept of the bardic family of O'Daly. See p. 373, *supra*, and notes.

^b "Cane poble," i. e. people subject to the *cana*, or fines, of that chieftain.

hasards,[a] shamelesse flatringe slaves,[b] (as to saie) Bards, Owlers, and manye such lick, whereby the foresaid lordes maie be lawfully suspected that they will soner nourishe mantaine and defende such rather then to see them punyshed accordinge to their desarts, 'tc.

We present that theire is a kinde of extorc̃on used by the seneshall of Imokelly and John Fitz Edmond of the same, gent'mē, uppon the landes of the freholders of Imokelly in the countie of Corke comonly cauled Serehen fere, wch is not used in no other countrye but only there.

We p^rsent also that the forsaid Seneshall and John Fitz Edmound, being ceassors of the aforsaid Imokelly, do not chardge them selfes wth any kynde of cesse, not wth standinge that they are richer and better able to beare theire parte of the same then all the other freholders in Imokelly, and the lick complaint is uppon every other cessor wch weare vearie necessarie to be reformede 'tc.

We present that the weares^c in the ryver or haven of Cork is brought so nighe the mayne channell to the great anoyannce and danger of everie boate or vessell passinge or repassinge to or from the said cittie, and specially in the night tyme or in the tyme of tempest, and this beinge divers tyme presented, and straight comandiments given to the contrarie, is not yeat reformed, contrary 'tc.

We p^rsent also that many comonwaies otherwise caled bohiers[d] w^thin the libertie of Cork are shamefully cutt digged, and fully undone, that nether man or cattell cane scant passe or repasse through such waies contrarye 'tc.

---

[a] "Hazards" probably were *carraghs* or gamblers.

[b] "Slaves." This term seemingly implies that some of the bardic castes were of slavish extraction.

[c] These weirs were, doubtless, formed of wicker work, and being extended from the shore ont to the channel of the stream, impeded the navigation. They were the same sort of engine for taking salmon as the kidles interdicted by the Great Charter, and the kidle was the fish basket at the head of the weir; thence the phrase, "a pretty kettle of fish." The Le Kiteller family, of whom was the Kilkenny Witch, Lady Alice, probably derived their surname from the trade of taking salmon by this means.

[d] Bohiers, i. e. lanes or roads.

made in the year 1576.

We present also that Donyll McDermody McTeighe McShane, of Crosvehig in Bantry in the countie of Cork, the xiiith of October in the yere of the raigne of oure soveraigne Ladie Queen Elizabeth that now is, the xviith, wrongfully w^t force and violence, have taken then and there of Nicholas Fitz Sthephen gould, of Corke, marchant, a milch cowe for passinge through Her Ma^{ts} highe waie, alledginge that he maie lawfully reare of everye one wearinge an Englishe capp cominge or goinge that waie, xvi^d sterlinge &c.

We p^rsent that Davie McMoris, sergiant, and other sergiants to the Lord Roche, do yeat leavie reare and tak upp w^t force and violence, in the name of custme, to the use of the Lord Roche and his Seneshall, John Ballwe, on penye out of everye xx^d that everye of Her Ma^{ts} faithfull subiects do bestowe at Castell towne and glannor,[a] perhaps for Gla*x*orth, co. Cork, and specially the forsaid Davye Fitz Morishe have forciably taken of Waulter Gould of Corek ñchant, for the foresaid custume, in October in the yere of the raigne of o^r soveraigne Ladie Queen Elizbeth that now is the xviith, the some of iii^s vii^d starllinge notwthstanding the same so often founde owt, presented and condepned by Her Ma^{ts} Commissioners, and very streaght comandiments geven by them to the contrarye &c.

We p^rsent that Mr Iden of Rosse O Caribrye in the countie of Corcke being an Englishmane doth not only use cony and liverie. But also doth reare foure gallons in everye Tonne of wynne, and also twoo whitt harpps,[b] in every gallon that he drinks himselfe of that wynne, and owt of everye flackett of aqua vite a pinte for himselfe and a pinte for his prayser, and further he rearesth mylch kynes costome for everye hide that is sold or bought at Rosse, and of every beofes that shall be there soulde he must have the hide painge but xv^d for bothe &c.

We p^rsent that Owen McGillewlanne, of Drome Braic in Bantrye in the countie of Corke, doth levie and taks upp unlawfull cous-

---

[a] Perhaps for Glanworth, co. Cork.

[b] Either the groat of Henry VIII., which was the first to bear the harp on the reverse; or, more probably, Elizabeth's fine silver groats of 1561, bearing a shield with three harps on the reverse: the latter would be naturally termed "white," to distinguish them from the baser coin of former years. See note, p. 366, *supra*.

tumes wth owt any authoritie from Her Matie, and specially have forceably taken of Nicholas Fitz Stiven Gowle, of Cork, m̃chant, the xvi^th of Maie, in the yere of the raigne of o^r soṽaigne Ladie Elizbeth that nowe is, the xvii^th, in the name of the aforsaid custume the some of iii^s starlinge, contrarie 'tc.

We present that all the lords of Mounster in generall do not suffer any of their mannors nor the lands thereinto belonginge, nor any other lands that they or any of them, or that houldith frome eny them, freholders, etheir by purchase or otherwise, nor any the lands apperteinge to their sonnes, to be chardger or contributarie to eny the Queenes Ma^ts ceasse or otherwise, sett uppon their countrye, to the utter undoinge of their poor freholders and ten^ants.

We p^rsent that Donell Nebipie. and McCartie Rowghes Young sonne, named Fynynne, the xv^th of Maie last past, in the yere of the raigne of oure soũaigne Ladie Queene Elizbeth that now is the xviii^th, wrongfully came wth force of armes viz 'tc. to Erdyrie Lemerarie in Corriebrie in the countie of Cork and then and theire have forceably taken upp and rearied the some of viii^l xvii^s ix^d starlinge of the pper goods and cattells of Fenyne McDermonds, Te clynyne Crymyne and theire poore ten^ants in the name of the said extorcion called cowe, contrary &c.

APPENDIX.

Irish Correspondence, P. R. O., Edw. VI., Vol. ii., 25, I. Inclosed in 1549, *March* 14; *Walter Cowley to Deputy Bellyngham.*

Indorsed.—From Walt̃ Collcc¹, in Marche, 1549, cõcerniḡ the reformacõns of Stayne exacc̃ōns in Kayr McKartes cõtreth.

Directed.—To my lorde Deputies right noble lordshippe.

To my Lorde Deputies Right Noble Lordshipe.

Although I daily trouble yor hono^{r}able lordshipe wth my rude writings, yet my own goode lorde, I beseche the same in humble wise to acccpte it to pcede (as it dothe) of a faithfull harte, whiche myndethe moost of any thing thavauncement of the Kings Ma^{tics} s$̃$vice ꝛ affaires, ꝛ specially in yor daies, who hathe alredy opened the gape, whereat eche gou$̃$nor thies cc. yeres befor yo^u stayed, ꝛ like as hethirto yee haue from tyme to tyme wth words directid me to followe a c̃taine trade therin, where (I thinke) I haue in sũ thing answered yor expectacion to the best of my litle poll, so do I nowe assay this othir way, whiche most depende uppon the putting of thothir things in effecte, whiche I towched befor.

Furst ꝛ specially, afᵗ the circuite ended of the instructions to be cõmitted to Sr Willm Wise, me, M^r. Derby ꝛ sũ other during whiche meane tyme, as we shall passe, then we may devise the putting of thies things following in ordre, beyng corrected ꝛ placed by yor hono^{r}able prudent wisdome, ꝛ that done yo^u haue brought Irlande to a wounderfull refor-

---

[1] Ancestor of the Colley-Wesleys, and so of the Duke of Wellington. Walter Cowley, or Collee, was of Kilkenny—see "Journal," Vol. II., first series, p. 102, &c.

macion, whiche most be pmanent 't suer. Seying Cahir Mᶜ Arte¹ hathe made a veray honest offer², whiche in my mynde (undre yoʳ noble correction) is mete to be inbraced 't well accepted, begyn cwn next wᵗʰ the counties of Kilkeny 't Tippary, and where as at this p'sent all their unmeasurable imposicions turnethe to disordre, inobediencie 't wasting of the Countre, 't infeblishing of the kings streynthe 't poũ, I shall devise that way with Godds grace 't yoʳ helpe, as thos inconveniencies shalbe avoyded, whiche partly shall ensue.

In stid of koyn 't liũy 't all like extorcions, a cesse uppõ c̃ũy plowe undre his rule for the captaine, oots for the wynt̃, one busshell 't a half, wᵗʰ the busshell he hathe for his horsses at this p̃sent; for soĩ, one busshell wheat, one busshell malt, a hoope beanes, a beofe c̃ũy two plowes, a shepe c̃ũy plowe, 't then shalbe yelden to the captaine there yerly iiiiᵉ beoffs, double so many shepe, cc. tonn oots, c. tonn wheate, c. tonn malt, xxx. tonn beanes, whiche shalbe hable wᵗʰ a litle helpe of the captaine to keape such a company togyther as neũ was seyne in Irlande, and may haue suche a stable of horsses as neũ was seyne in Irlande yoʳ lordshipe may heruppon then marke, howe moche chardge the captaine in his housholde shalbe hable to beare. I thinke he may well keape four score chief horsses in his stable, 't four stables, to be devided in four seũall quarts of the countre, 't all the chief horsses that shalbe in all the contre to be in that stable, except it be wᵗʰ a gent. of xlˡⁱ· a yere or brought uppe wᵗʰ ℓ̃taine to be made 't solde. Then shall ye haue no horsmen robbers (as they haue bene wonnt to be), as for hay, the hides of the beoffs 't shepe fellis shall suffice to bye sufficient therof, the captaine shalbe hable thus to keape iiiiˣˣ in housholde, 't xx kerne to be attendant in his house (as housholde kerne to take at c̃omaundement offendo⁷ˢ), nowe shall rest no chardge on the countre but this. Saving that at any mayne hosting, when the lorde deputie shall c̃omaunde the same shalbe contributary to wittaill as shalbe pclamed in the rest of the lande, if this pporcion be to litle or to moche, yoʳ lordshipe may alt̃ the thing alt̃ the debating hereof, as yoʳ lordshipe shall se cause.

Seconde, like as yoᵘ haue placed galloglasse in Leyse, 't woll do in

---

[1] Caher Mac Arte Kavanagh, Chief of his Nation, then holding a great part of their ancient tribe land, consisting of the mountain range which separates Carlow from Wexford and tracts of the adjacent lowlands on both sides.

[2] Search has been made for this document in the Public Record Office, London, but it has not been preserved. Cahir was subsequently created Baron of Ballyan. See p. 35, *supra*.

Appendix.

Leynest, so most there be sñ galloglasses in thos pties t other quarts, whiche shall joyne at nedes by cōmaundment wth the captaines there.

Thirdly, aft that yo^u haue thus takin ordre for Leynest t the Erle of Ormonds rule, take even the like ordre wth the barrons of Cahir t Donboyne, who assuredly woll willingly assent therto: but seying therle of Ormonde haue used to haue a ctaine chardge of galloglasse t koyn t lifly on their countries, when he hathe resorted thethir at all tymes amongs theim, take ordre t devide the thing, as therle of Ormonde shall haue the vth parte or othir porcion (as yo^u shall thinke mete of the barrons porcions), wherin it shalbe good to heare thadvice of the gentlemen in that quart. The kings captaine in the late Abbay of Wony[1] to haue the Rians, Doyers, bothe the Ormonds, the Meaghers, Are, the Bourkes t Breanes in this side the Shennon, to bear a ctaine contribution to him yerly, leving by estimacion half suche ctaine contribucions to the captaynes of the countries there, t bynding theim for their rate, to haue ther stables t a ctaine standing housholde.

IIIIth. the captaine of the late Abbay of Wonyes rule to extende oñ the countries p'mised, t to place c. galloglasses c. kerne to inhabite about him, wth a convenyent nowmbre of horsmen, who may attende uppon him at neades.

V^th. bringing that to passe to take like ordre amongs the Kerrollis t inforce theim to do the like, having their stables t standing housholde.

VIth. That the barron of uppir Ossfie do the like.

VIIth. That a captaine of leyse[2] shalbe ordayned, to whom the countre shall obey, in assembling togyther t sfving the King, t a Seneseall to be at the chardges of the countre for the keaping of them in quyete, t a sherriff to be made yerly there to sfue the Kings peesse, t that O Doyn t the Dempsies be joyned to the captaine of leyse t althoughe for to inhabite it the inhabitors most haue a ctaine fredome, saving their rent for the second yere, yet from two yeres forthe, there may be a ctaine chardge for the captaine, on the countre, as shalbe for othir captaines in othir countries, and furdre that there be four houses appointed, t resfued for the King viz., the ptector[3], Adamston[4], Strædbally t Biellaroyne[5], t reserue for efly of thies houses xxiiii plowe lande at the least, t ctaine

---

[1] Now Abingdon, Co. Tipperary.
[2] Leix, the tribe land of the O'Mores.
[3] The fort built to overawe the O'Mores, and so named after the Protector Somerset. When Mary made the district shireground the town which gathered round it received the name of Maryborough.
[4] Now Ballyadams, where a fine Edwardian is still habitable.
[5] Now Ballyroan.

medowes ports 't tithes : two of thies houses shalbe wth the captaine, as the ptector 't Stradbally, thother twayne, whiche is Adamston 't Biellaroyne to be res?ued by keaps or counstables for the Kings deputie, when he shall haue occasion to reasorte thethir, 't the lande ports 't tithes to be honestly surveyed at honest prises 't allovaunce to be made therfor to the King, 't that porcions of the priors lande, O Kellies lande, 't O lallors lande be res?ued for the King, for thos are the best 't moost cōmodious in Leyse, the rest may be sett in all the marches.

VIIIthly. that a captaine be in Sliewmarge wth like contribucion of chardges to him, beyng bounde there to finde men 't horsses, al't the inhabityng of the furst two yeres.

IXthly. the captaine of Cathirlaghe to haue undyr his rule O drone, the Dlowghe,[1] Foert 't Shielleille 't the rest there abouts of the cōm of Cathirlaghe, gyving a 8taine fredome for two yeres to inhabite.

Xthly. the captaine of the Foert at Dengyn̄,[2] to haue undre his rule Offaily, Mc Morrishe, Irreis countre, O Mulmoy, Mc Cogheghan̄, McCoghlan 't O Melaghlin, 't thothir captaynes to haue 8taine of the victaill 't pficte undre their rules, in estimacion to be thone half therof, beyng bounde to keape a stable 't 8taine men 't horsses eu̅y of them seu̅ally, as shalbe limited theim.

XIthly. the Kings deputie to haue one house 't 8taine tithes 't porte in Offaily, the captaine to haue the rest there. I haue not viewed there yet any place to be so res?ved for I was not there yet.

XIIthly. like ordre for rules 't captaynes ou̅ all Irlande.

XIIIthly. That captaynes shalbe made by Ir̄es patents, 't thos words to be therin "quamdiu se bene gesserit" the whiche words shall make theim bewarr howe to ordre theim silves.

XIVthly. the King shall thus haue no small noūbre of captaynes 't officers 't God willing there shall thus be reddy to s?ue the King two thousande horsses 't fywe thousande men.

XVthly. all thies things established, to viewe the pficts of the captaines 't their chardges, 't allowe honest cōmoditie to theim, and to accompte to the King in their allovaunce for the rest 't surplisage.

XVIthly. then to se 't consid? the hole chardges 't proficts 't whate

---

[1] The Dullough, afterwards in dispute between Sir Peter Carew and Sir Edmond Butler, brother to the Earl of Ormonde. It was the country round Clogrennan, in the county of Carlow.

[2] The fort of Dangin, subsequently named Philipstown, when the districts now comprised in the King's County were made shire-ground, temp. Philip and Mary.

may be cōnūted or saved to the Kings p̄ficte, hauing consideracion alway chiefly, that suche baarnes [barenness], be not used therin, as may brede pillis or furdre inconveniencies.

XVIIthly. then to viewe 't make estimacion of the hole revewnees [sic] of the newe won p̄ficts 't the rest, wth custūmes, havons 't fysshings that shalbe won during yor tyme, and to establishe a ppetuall ordinary chardge 't what shall rest yerly to be imploied uppon making of buyldings 't townes for the King alway, and eū to considre that Irlande, beyng oppyn uppon Spayne 't Skotlande 't othir realmes, 't far from their souūaigne lorde, most haue many captaines 't rulers that neū shall clayme inheritance therin, but othir at will, or at the furdist for t̄me of liffe, so as all their travaill 't study shall conūte to the Kings p̄ficte 't augmentacion of his roiall iurisdiction streynthe 't p̄ficte, 't not to their awn posterities, and because the Kings of Englande shalbe well assured neū hereafr̄ to be disceived wth suggestion or untrue surmyses of grants to be peured from theim by any psuacions or circūstaunces, my lorde cause a booke of all the Kings possessions, manors lordships cōmodities 't p̄ficts in Irlande to be made, 't then derifie [sic] out of the same ētaine lande, places 't manors, so as ye shall hawe therin, in eūy shire oū all Irlande, sū ētaine places or possessions to the King 't his successors in ētaine, 't thereuppon to enacte by pliament, declaring notable considr̄acion, that thos ētaine manors lordships 't possessions shalbe united to the crowne of Englande as insepall, for the maynetenn˚ce of this realm, 't that any grant 't gift to be made therof (oū the life of the grauntee) shalbe voide: by this meane the King shalbe suer nū to be drivyn out cleir from his subiects in any shire, as he hathe bene hethirto.

Finally (if it please yor lordshipe, furst to will my booke of ordres for the counties of Kilkeny 't Tippary to be published 't put in execution out of hande, 't to will the lorde Marshiall, M^r. Wise 't me so to do, 't then to will M^r. Wise, me 't othirs to put o^r instructions that yor lordshipe will cōmitt unto us in effect, if yo^u shall thinke it mete, 't then to put in ure this litle treatise touched in groose, whiche nedethe the correction of yor Lordshipe, then I woll not doubte (wth Godds grace) therby to se moche frute followe of yor happy 't godly inr̄prises.

My lorde, if thies chardges nowe put in ētaintie (as befor is mencioned) shall seme great, yet I assure yor hono^r that at this p̄sent, at one nyght in the yere, a pore man shalbe oppssed wth the disordre nowe no lasse then this hole chardges cūmethe unto for the yere, 't assure yor lordshipe, that thonely S^riaunts, constables, harbingr̄s callid in Irishe lyorons, 't their s{er}u{er}nts, pullethe, by colo{r} of the disordre nowe, no lasse then nyghe this {cer}taine chardge c{u with tilde}methe unto, and by this meanes all they shalbe cleirly put backe, whiche shalbe a veray great reliefe to the pore people {the} this {cer}taine chardge (if it were thought greate) may be bett{er} daily abredged or al{ter}ed, then the unhappy un{cer}taine imposicions hethirto used, wherin e{u with tilde} great difficultie {the} argument is moved to make it holde, as will not be framed in thothir case.

THE END.